LOUISIANA, YESTERDAY AND TODAY

Louisiana
Yesterday and Today

A Historical Guide to the State

John Wilds/Charles L. Dufour/Walter G. Cowan

Louisiana State University Press   Baton Rouge and London

05 04 03 02 01 00 99 98 97 96   5 4 3 2 1

Designer: Glynnis Weston
Typeface: Goudy
Typesetter: Impressions Book and Journal Services, Inc.
Printer and binder: Thomson-Shore, Inc.

Library of Congress Cataloging-in-Publication Data

Wilds, John.
    Louisiana, yesterday and today : a historical guide to the state /
John Wilds, Charles L. Dufour, Walter G. Cowan.
        p.   cm.
    Includes index.
    ISBN 0-8071-1892-3 (cloth : alk. paper), — ISBN 0-8071-1893-1
(pbk. : alk. paper)
    1. Louisiana—History.   I. Dufour, Charles L.   II. Cowan, Walter G.
III. Title.
    F369.W55   1996
    976.3—dc20   95-47383
                                                                  CIP

The paper in this book meets the guidelines for permanence and durability of the
Committee on Production Guidelines for Book Longevity of the Council on Library
Resources. ⊚

Contents

Preface ix

Acknowledgments xi

1 The First Inhabitants 1

2 The French 6

3 The Spanish Years 12

4 Americanization 19

5 The People of Louisiana 23

6 The West Florida Rebellion 31

7 The Battle of New Orleans 35

8 The Civil War 41

9 Reconstruction 49

10 Race 61

11 Economy 70

12 Diseases and Deliverance 82

13 Rivers and Ports 91

14 Education 104

15 Religion 109

16 Politics 115

17 Hard Winds and High Water 135

18 Pirates, Privateers, and Filibusters 141

19 Sports 148

20 Mardi Gras 157

21 Literature 161

22 Music 167

23 Art 173

24 Food 178

25 From the Swamp to Storyville 183

26 The Mafia Lynching 186

27 Duels 190

28 The Notorious Louisiana Lottery 192

29 Marie Laveau 195

30 Parishes 199

31 The Northeast 203

32 The Northwest 215

33 Central Louisiana 227

34 The Florida Parishes 233

35 River Parishes 241

36 The Southwest 251

37 The Southeast 265

Appendix: Louisiana State Parks and Commemorative Areas 277

Index 281

Maps

Louisiana Parishes and Parish Seats 198

Northeast Louisiana 204

Northwest Louisiana 214

Central Louisiana 226

Florida Parishes 232

River Parishes 240

Southwest Louisiana 250

Southeast Louisiana 264

PREFACE

If this were a college course we would list it in the curriculum catalog as Louisiana 101: An Introduction. We are presenting an overview of this unique state, an adopted sister with a background and character traits that differ from those of the hereditary American family. The analogy with a classroom setting is apt, we think, because if a history professor were teaching such a course, he or she might well adopt the same approach we have chosen. We believe the subject is more logically and more succinctly covered in a series of topical essays than in a purely chronological account. We hope, and are confident, that Louisiana's economy, for example, is more easily understood if the topic is pursued from beginning to end instead of being segmented by historical periods.

Engrossed in the research, the authors found themselves playing a game that is irresistible to newsmen, which all three of us were before retirement. How would the events that highlighted Louisiana's history have been rated as news stories had they been reported, as they occurred, in the style of today's newspapers and news programs? Which would have generated the largest headlines, the most interruptions in regular programming? Which would have excited the most public interest? Which would have had the greatest affect on the course of history? Articles are common on the top ten stories of the year, of the decade, and even of the century. We are contemplating the happenings of three hundred years, a period marked by enjoyment and emancipation as well as strife and suffering.

Any ranking, naturally, is subjective. But certain criteria apply. The first is *impact:* How did the developments affect the lives of the people? Other factors that must be considered include *human interest, magnitude, surprise, personalities.* We ruled out inclusion of the establishment of the original colony that developed into the state of Louisiana for the same reason that we would not consider the Creation if we were judging the stories of the Bible. We are concerned with occurrences after Louisiana became a political entity.

Our ranking is the consensus of a trio of longtime residents, and everyone is free to take issue with us. A writer on historical subjects can claim the prerogative of assessing the importance of the developments that he reports. In fact, he may have an obligation to the reader to make his opinion known. Thus we present our list of the ten most vital developments in the Louisiana of the eighteenth, nineteenth, and twentieth centuries.

1.　The Louisiana Purchase. Who knows what kind of turn history would have taken if Thomas Jefferson's deal with Napoleon Bonaparte had not made Louisiana American territory? Who knows, really, what would have happened to the United States itself?

2.　The Battle of New Orleans. Andrew Jackson's repulse of the British on the plains of Chalmette ended the last invasion by a foreign power of the contiguous United States.

3.　The fall of New Orleans to Flag Officer David Farragut's Federal fleet. A terrible blow to the Confederacy.

4.　Reconstruction. Years of political and racial conflict. Rival governments tried to take control of the state. A deal partly engineered by Louisianians seated a president of the United States.

5.　The reign and assassination of Huey P. Long. The chaotic seven-year heyday of America's most successful demagogue.

6.　*Plessy v. Ferguson.* The case, originating in New Orleans, in which the United States Supreme Court enunciated the "separate-but-equal" doctrine that governed the nation's racial relations for longer than half a century.

7.　The revolt of the French colonists against a Spanish governor, and the vengeance of "Bloody" O'Reilly.

8.　Nicholas Roosevelt arrives on the *New Orleans*, opening the age of the steamboat on the Mississippi River.

9.　The changing economy. The rise and fall of cotton and sugarcane growing. The offshore oil boom. The development of the industrial corridor along the Mississippi from Baton Rouge to New Orleans.

10.　The building of the Louisiana Superdome and the emergence of New Orleans as a tourist and convention center.

A fairly complete history of Louisiana might be written by covering only the subjects in the top ten. But we believe a more logical approach is our series of essays, which will help the reader to be selective if he wishes. Of course, no occurrence of a magnitude to be included in the ten is left out of the book.

We three are among the five authors of *New Orleans, Yesterday and Today*, which was published in 1984. We mourn the death of John Chase, and regret that the press of other undertakings prevented O. K. LeBlanc from working with us on this volume.

John Wilds
Charles L. Dufour
Walter G. Cowan

ACKNOWLEDGMENTS

Writers of history quickly learn they cannot ferret out all the facts they need to build their stories without the help of professional researchers or experts in various fields. Many such persons have contributed to this volume.

For the stories on the state's sixty-four parishes, the authors are indebted in large part to the librarians of those parishes. There are many other individuals to whom we are indebted, including Collin B. Hamer, head of the Louisiana Division of the New Orleans Public Library, and members of his staff; Nancy Burrus, librarian of the New Orleans *Times-Picayune*, and her staff; Dr. Wilbur E. Meneray, assistant librarian of the Tulane University Howard-Tilton Memorial Library, and Dr. Joan Coleman, head of the Louisiana Department of the Tulane Library, and her staff; John E. Bullard, director of the New Orleans Museum of Art, and William A. Fagaly, assistant director of the museum; John T. Magill and Judith Bonner of the Historic New Orleans Collection; Jessie Poesch, professor emeritus of the Newcomb College Art Department; Peter Finney, Bob Roesler, George Sweeney, and Bob Marshall of the *Times-Picayune* Sports Department; Mel Lagarde of the Tulane Sports staff; Jack McGuire, businessman and historian; and Iris Kelso, political columnist of the *Times-Picayune*.

The authors acknowledge with much appreciation the contributions of Gerry Anders of LSU Press, who went well beyond the scope of merely editing in handling this manuscript. Also, a welcome source of facts and figures has been recent editions of the *Louisiana Almanac*, edited by Milburn Calhoun and produced by the Pelican Publishing Company.

Louisiana, Yesterday and Today

1

THE FIRST INHABITANTS

When European explorers arrived in what today is Louisiana, people had already been living there for at least ten thousand years. They were the descendants of hunters who, in a time of lower sea levels, crossed from Asia by way of a neck of land that now lies beneath the waters of the Bering Strait. A trail of projectile points and other evidence testifies to the spread of these people across North and South America. Bones show that the game they hunted included mammoths, giant ground sloths, and other animals now thousands of years extinct. Much later, the early wanderers' descendants began to make pottery, build large ceremonial mounds, and leave other permanent artifacts of their presence.

One of the most important archaeological sites in the United States is at Poverty Point, in West Carroll Parish, where a mound more than 70 feet high and 600 feet long looms above six concentric, semicircular terraces, the outermost of which is three quarters of a mile across. These massive earthworks testify to the life of a community—and a culture—that accommodated several thousand people long before Athens or Rome existed. It is estimated that the Poverty Point culture arose about 2000 b.c. and reached its peak around 1000 b.c., at which time the Poverty Point site was the nucleus of a pattern of life that extended to at least a hundred communities in Louisiana, Arkansas, and Mississippi, with its influence reaching well up the Mississippi Valley and eastward as far as Florida. This widespread culture appears to have weakened soon after its high point and to have collapsed sometime around 750 b.c. The reasons for its downfall are unknown.

Although none was as large or long-lived as the Poverty Point culture, several other mound-building cultures rose and fell in Louisiana over the centuries—for example, between about 200 b.c. and 600 a.d. near what is now Marksville. The Caddo of northwest Louisiana were still building mounds in historical times.

The first written record of Louisiana's Indians—as the Europeans persisted in calling these native peoples—comes from the meandering expedition of the Spanish explorer Hernando de Soto through the American Southeast. In 1542 de Soto's force of several hundred men apparently entered what is now northeast Louisiana. Members of the expedition later de-

A colonial Louisiana sketcher's impression of an Indian family on the move in winter.

Courtesy the Historic New Orleans Collection; Acc. No. 1980.205.37

scribed large Indian towns amid fertile lands on the west bank of the Mississippi River.

A more detailed picture did not emerge until serious colonization of Louisiana began in the early 1700s. At that time, the area that forms the state was populated by an estimated 13,000 to 15,000 Indians, in groups speaking at least twenty-two distinct languages. The towns on the west side of the Mississippi no longer existed, although there were some on the east bank. Some historians suggest that diseases such as smallpox and cholera, possibly introduced by de Soto's men, already had ravaged the Indians, as they would continue to do.

Partly because of diseases, but also because of war (both with whites and among Indians), competition for land and game, and other factors, the native population underwent a long, steep decline as European colonists and, later, American settlers encroached. In 1950, the United States Census Bureau reported, only 490 Indians remained in Louisiana. Then the number began to rise, to 3,587 in 1960 and 5,294 in 1970. In 1980 the census reported 12,841 Indians in the state, and in 1990 the count was 18,361. This remarkable statistical turnaround partly reflects the difficulty in determining just who is an Indian, since the tribes have often mixed with other peoples. Undoubtedly it also reflects a growing pride in being a Native American. Federal and state benefits available to members of officially recognized tribes may have had an effect as well. As of 1994 there were five such tribes in Louisiana: the Choctaw, located mainly in the central part of the state; the Tunica-Biloxi, of Avoyelles Parish; the Koasati (Coushatta), of Allen Parish; the Chitimacha, whose reservation is at Charenton in St. Mary Parish; and the Houma, spread across south central Louisiana and recognized by the state but not the federal government.

When the French, Spanish, and English began trickling into Louisiana in the early 1700s, the Indians had a standard of living that compared well with the average European's. Many tribes were competent farmers; all had access to abundant wild plant foods and rich sources of fish and game. The major cultivated crops were corn, beans, and squash. The forests supplied a great variety of nuts, berries, roots, and wild fruit. The favorite large game animal was the white-tailed deer; bear and buffalo were also prized— although buffalo were relatively few in Louisiana. Small game of many kinds abounded, as did birds, including wild turkeys and migratory water-fowl. As John Sibley of Natchitoches wrote in 1805 to General Henry Dearborn, the secretary of war: "It is not uncommon in winter for a single man to kill from 200 to 400 fowl in one evening." He added that fish were available in similar plenty. Coastal tribes could add to this cornucopia vast quantities of clams, mussels, and other shellfish.

Unlike the tepee-dwelling nomads of the western plains, most Louisiana Indians lived in permanent or semipermanent villages, ranging in size from a few families to several hundred people. Their houses varied from one area to another. In the northern woodlands, wattle-and-daub construction was common. The Caddo sometimes made round, grass-thatched houses that resembled beehives. In the south, groups such as the Chitimacha made their homes out of palmetto fronds layered over a pole framework. Only the Attakapas of the southwest had portable, tepeelike dwellings. Many families, especially in north Louisiana, had a tightly built house for winter and a more-open one for summer. Large villages contained numerous buildings other than homes: temples, granaries, dance houses, even mortuaries.

Louisiana's Indians had a largely Stone Age technology. They knapped flint into arrowheads and spearpoints. Their main tools, the ax and the adz, both fashioned from stone, enabled them to make canoes and many other wooden articles. They were also skilled potters, basket makers, and tanners. Despite all this, they were quick to adopt such European implements as iron and steel tools, and especially firearms.

Groups throughout the region often ringed their villages with palisades for defense. Intertribal fighting was common both before and after the arrival of the Europeans. War or the threat of it often forced tribes to relocate. The Houma provide a case in point. In the late 1600s they lived just east of the Mississippi River, near today's Louisiana-Mississippi line. Then the Tunica, fearful of other tribes in their Yazoo River area, moved among the Houma. A few years later the Tunica rose up against their hosts, killing perhaps half of them. The surviving Houmas migrated to the southern shore of Lake Pontchartrain, then to what is now Ascension Parish. Later, many of them moved west into Attakapas country or south to the Terrebonne Parish area, where the town of Houma is named for them.

There were also, of course, numerous clashes between Indians and European settlers. The one that had the most far-reaching effect on the Louisiana colony occurred at Fort Rosalie (now Natchez, Mississippi) on November 28, 1729. Angry that the local French military commander, a Captain Detchéparre, had appropriated Indian land for his own uses, the Natchez Indians began an uprising that created turmoil in Louisiana for more than two years.

According to survivors' accounts, the Natchez came into the settlement as if returning from hunting. They offered game to the soldiers and settlers, by whom they were generally trusted; some even managed to borrow settlers' guns. A prearranged signal ignited the attack. Surprise was complete; a massacre followed. Different sources give different numbers, but it appears that at least 200 French men were killed, along with some women and children. Most of the settlement's 80 white women, as well as 150 black slaves, were taken prisoner.

Two survivors reached New Orleans a few days later. Their report threw the entire colony into panic. Paranoid at the possibility of attack, Etienne Périer, the commandant general at New Orleans, sent armed slaves to annihilate a group of thirty Chawasha Indians living peacefully south of the city. The brutality had an unexpected result: other small tribes in the area immediately swore their allegiance to France.

The destruction of Fort Rosalie was a blow from which Louisiana would not recover for years. The death toll represented roughly a tenth of the white population. The Company of the Indies, which operated the colony under an official monopoly, begged to be allowed to return Louisiana to the French crown. In 1731, Louis XV agreed.

That same year, the end came for the Natchez Indians, who were defeated in a series of military operations in north Louisiana by the French and their Indian allies, including Choctaws and Tunicas. Many Natchez were killed. About 450 surrendered and were sold into slavery in Haiti. The remainder—perhaps 300 from a tribe that had once numbered in the thousands—scattered westward and eventually were lost to history.

The fate of most of Louisiana's native peoples was not as spectacular as that of the Natchez, but it was often as final. Many groups simply slipped into oblivion like the Avoyel, a small trading tribe in the Marksville area who by 1805 had dwindled to a mere handful; within a few more years, all that remained was their name, gracing Avoyelles Parish. Assimilation, whether into surrounding black and white populations or into other Indian groups, led to the extinction of numerous lesser tribes' culture and language.

Some large tribes survived by retreating westward, either under force or semivoluntarily. In 1830 the Choctaw gave up their ancestral lands by imposed treaty and most of the tribe was relocated to the Indian Territory of Oklahoma. In 1835 the Caddo reluctantly sold their northwest Louisiana lands to the United States and moved first to Texas, then to the Indian Territory.

Like the Avoyel, many of the vanquished and vanished tribes left their words behind. From Bogalusa in the east to Calcasieu Parish in the west, from the Ouachita River in the north to Atchafalaya Bay in the south, Louisiana echoes its Indian heritage in the names of hundreds of its bayous, rivers, towns, and parishes.

—W.G.C.

2

THE FRENCH

Louisiana made its appearance in history before it was Louisiana.

Alonso Alvarez de Piñeda, cruising in the Gulf of Mexico in 1519, saw the mouth of a great river—possibly the Mississippi, although it may have been Mobile Bay.

In 1528, Alvar Núñez Cabeza de Vaca and three other survivors of the ill-starred Pánfilo de Narváez' expedition also encountered a great river in their long and hazardous wandering in search of Mexico. This, too, was probably the Mississippi. It is likely that Cabeza de Vaca and his companions crossed part of present-day Louisiana.

The first European to come in certain contact with present-day Louisiana was Hernando de Soto's second-in-command, Luis de Moscoso de Alvarado. After de Soto's death in 1542, Moscoso built boats and the remnant of the expedition floated by the future site of the city of New Orleans en route to Mexico.

One hundred forty years later, another European explored the river to its mouth and gave to the vast area which it and its tributaries drained the name Louisiana. This man was a Frenchman, Robert Cavelier, sieur de La Salle, and he claimed the land for his king, Louis XIV.

La Salle, a native of Rouen, was born in 1643. He made initial vows in the Jesuit order in 1660 but in 1667 was released from them without having been ordained. He was not quite twenty-four, eager for adventure, and Canada offered many opportunities. His brother, Jean Cavelier, a priest in Montreal, obtained for him a large tract of land at nearby Lachine. The young La Salle established a name for himself on the frontier, and his affairs prospered. He dreamed of descending the river to its mouth, claiming lands for France—and, not coincidentally, fur-trapping monopolies for himself. Louis XIV granted permission for the mission in 1678, but not until four years later was La Salle ready to launch his great adventure. On February 13, 1682, his party began the descent of the Mississippi. It consisted of La Salle; his lieutenant, Henry de Tonti; Father Zenobius Membré; twenty other Frenchmen; and thirty-one Indian men, women, and children.

After fifty-three days, on April 6, the party reached the mouth of the river. La Salle found that the river discharged into the Gulf through three channels. He reconnoitered for three days and then moved upstream a few miles, where on April 9 he claimed the land for the Sun King: "In the name of the most high, mighty, invincible and victorious Prince, Louis the

An artist's imagined rendering of the ceremony in which La Salle claimed Louisiana
for King Louis XIV of France.

Courtesy the Historic New Orleans Collection; Acc. No. 1991.34.1

Great, by the Grace of God, King of France and Navarre, Fourteenth
of that name . . . I, in virtue of the commission of his Majesty, which I hold
in my hand . . . have taken, and do now take in the name of His Majesty
and his successors to the crown, possession of the country of Louisiana,
the seas, harbors, ports, bays, adjacent straits, and all nations, people,
provinces, cities, towns, villages, mines, minerals, fisheries, streams and
rivers comprised in the extent of said Louisiana."

Despite threats and alarms from Indians, La Salle's band returned to Canada without the loss of or injury to anyone. La Salle then went to France to petition the king to launch a colonizing expedition to the mouth of the Mississippi. In July, 1684, the expedition was mounted. It was doomed to failure by a bitter feud between La Salle and Captain Taneguy de Beaujeu, the naval commander. A two-month delay at Saint-Domingue (present-day Haiti) did not ease relations between the two commanders, and when the expedition finally got under way again, it sailed past the mouth of the Mississippi (some historians blame La Salle, others de Beaujeu, for the error). Finally, on January 19, 1685, de Beaujeu dropped anchor in what is now known as Matagorda Bay, in Texas. La Salle landed four hundred miles west of his intended destination. Then followed two futile years of searching for the Mississippi, culminating in the murder of La Salle by his own men on March 29, 1687. Only six members of the expedition survived.

For a dozen years, France did nothing further about exploiting La Salle's claim, but when rumors mounted that Spain and England were planning colonies on the Gulf of Mexico, Louis XIV decided that France must make a countermove. To lead the expedition, the Canadian hero Pierre Le Moyne, sieur d'Iberville, was chosen. Iberville was in France following a brilliant sea victory over the British on Hudson Bay. Louis de Phélypeaux, the comte de Pontchartrain, minister of marine, picked him to sail to the Gulf of Mexico, rediscover La Salle's river, and make recommendations for French colonization.

On October 24, 1698, the expedition sailed from Brest in four ships. With Iberville was his eighteen-year-old brother, Jean-Baptiste Le Moyne, sieur de Bienville. Iberville spent a month in Saint-Domingue before sailing for the Mississippi. The Spaniards had settled Pensacola, in what is now Florida, in November, 1698, thus beating Iberville to the Gulf. But the race to the Mississippi was still on. The English colonizers had eliminated themselves by sheltering their vessels for the winter at Charleston.

Iberville cruised past Mobile Bay and Dauphin Island seeking a sheltered port for his ships. He found a sufficiently deep channel between two islands about a dozen miles off the mainland and dropped anchor on February 9. He named one Ship Island; the other he called Cat Island because the French sailors thought the raccoons that infested it were wildcats.

On February 27, Iberville began the search for La Salle's river. Two coastal vessels, called *traversiers*, each towing a canoe, carried the party of fifty-one men with enough provisions for twenty days. The weather was miserable—rain, wind, rough seas. For three disagreeable days Iberville skirted the coast, traveling a southwest course. On March 2, he sought the shelter of what appeared to be some rocks. The "rocks" were mudbanks. "In approaching the rocks to put myself in their shelter, I saw at once that there was a river there," Iberville recorded in his journal. He was convinced he had found La Salle's Mississippi. The next day the expedition entered the mainstream of the river and moved upward. They camped that night on a little point of land on the banks of a small bayou. The day was Mardi Gras, the pre-Lenten Carnival celebration, so Iberville named the small stream Bayou Mardi Gras and the point of land Mardi Gras Point. These were the first European place names on the map of Louisiana.

Iberville was certain that he was on La Salle's river, but he needed proof. It came when he encountered an Indian chief wearing a blue serge coat cut in the Canadian style, and also a red cravat. By sign language, Iberville learned that a man with an iron hand had given it to him. This was Henry de Tonti, La Salle's lieutenant, who had an artificial hand. Later another Indian chief gave Bienville a letter Tonti had written to La Salle. The occasion for this was Tonti's desire to make liaison with La Salle on the latter's fatal second voyage.

Iberville established Fort Maurepas at what is today Ocean Springs, Mississippi, then sailed to France to report on his mission. He made two more voyages to Louisiana and was planning a third when war with England committed him to naval activity in the West Indies. He contracted yellow fever and died in Havana on July 9, 1706. The command of the French settlement in Louisiana had already been assumed by Bienville, when he was twenty-two years old. At the time of Iberville's death, the young Le Moyne was twenty-six and a seasoned frontiersman.

On September 14, 1712, the king granted a charter to Antoine Crozat, an immensely wealthy native of Toulouse, for a commercial monopoly in Louisiana, with the exclusive right to trade in the colony for fifteen years. Crozat, who was perhaps the richest man in France—he is said to have been worth the equivalent of $8 million—initially invested 700,000 livres ($140,000) in his Louisiana project, but as time went on his losses grew to 2 million livres. In the summer of 1717, when his monopoly had been exercised for only five of the allotted fifteen years, Crozat asked the king to take back Louisiana, to release him from all obligations related to the colony. In his petition, Crozat stated: "My three principal projects: discovery of mines of gold and silver, the establishment and maintenance of workers for plantations of tobacco, commerce with Spain, were dissipated. . . . I find myself obliged to return my colonization to the King, praying him to take count of the two million livres my monopoly, merchandise and effects . . . and advances . . . have cost me."

On August 23, 1717, the Crown accepted Crozat's resignation from colonization and turned Louisiana over to John Law's newly chartered Company of the West. Law, a Scots financial wizard and a crony of the duc d'Orléans, regent for the child king Louis XV, had organized a bank and created paper money, and was ready to take over Louisiana. His Company of the West, soon renamed the Company of the Indies, was given a twenty-five-year monopoly and was capitalized at 100 million livres—fifty times what Crozat had invested.

Except for the founding of Natchitoches in 1714, French activity in the Louisiana colony had actually been confined largely to Mobile and its nearby Dauphin Island. The center of gravity in the colony did not shift to New Orleans until 1718, when Law authorized the establishment of a city on the Mississippi thirty leagues from its mouth. Law's company wound up bankrupting France, but it at least succeeded in gaining a tenable foothold for the settlement of Louisiana.

Although Bienville founded New Orleans in 1718, it was not until 1721 that the engineer Adrien de Pauger laid out what today is known as the Vieux Carré or French Quarter.

During the decade 1718–1728, the arrival of German colonists and African slaves brought a measure of stability to the agricultural economy of Louisiana, which nevertheless remained marginal for decades. Education received a boost when six Ursuline nuns, having reached New Orleans on August 6, 1727, opened a school for girls the following year. The Ursuline establishment, New Orleans' oldest institution, has been there ever since.

The political history of early colonial Louisiana is to some extent inseparable from the history of Bienville, who devoted almost forty years of his life to the colony. He appears to have been a very difficult man to get along with, and his feuds were numerous. From 1702 to 1713, he was commandant of Louisiana. He resented Governor Antoine de La Mothe Cadillac, who relieved him in 1713. When Cadillac was named governor of Canada in 1717, Bienville found himself acting governor of Louisiana. In 1724, Bienville was recalled to Paris to answer charges stemming partly from his controversial personality and partly from his own greed and corrupt self-enrichment. His final appearance on the Louisiana stage was his ten-year tenure as governor from 1733 to 1743. It was the first time that he held the actual title of governor. These were frustrating years, however, during which he spent considerable time in the field against the Indians.

At sixty-two Bienville had lost the fire of youth, and he wrote Paris asking to be relieved: "If success had always responded to my application to the affairs of this government and my zeal for the King's service, I should gladly have devoted the rest of my days to it, but a sort of fatality bent for some time on frustrating the majority of my best-concerted plans has made me lose the fruits of my labors. . . . I have therefore thought I ought not re-

Jean-Baptiste Le Moyne, sieur de Bienville, who during
more than forty years was deeply involved in the exploration,
colonization, and governance of French Louisiana.

Courtesy the Historic New Orleans Collection; Acc. No. 1991.34.7

sist my bad fortune any longer. I hope that the officer who will be chosen to replace me will be more fortunate than I."

Named to succeed Bienville was Pierre Cavagnial de Rigaud de Vaudreuil, a marquis who introduced elegance to Louisiana. Vaudreuil's ten years were a sort of golden age for the colony, an era of goodwill. The marquis served until 1753 and later became governor of Canada. During his administration, sugarcane was introduced into Louisiana. His successor, a distinguished French naval officer, Louis Billouart de Kerlérec, governed Louisiana throughout the Seven Years' War, during which French Canada fell to the British. It was Kerlérec who made arrangements to settle the first of the war-displaced Acadians of Nova Scotia in Louisiana. And it was he who was in office when, on November 3, 1762, a stroke of the pen severed Louisiana from the Bourbon court of France and joined it to the Bourbon court of Spain. On that day, the Treaty of Fontainebleau ceded Louisiana to Spain.

—C.L.D.

3

The Spanish Years

France's transfer of Louisiana to Spain in the Treaty of Fontainebleau brought on an uproar in Louisiana. It presaged a revolt in which the first Spanish governor was expelled—the first revolt in the New World against a European monarch.

Although the pact was signed in 1762, its details were not made public in Paris until April 21, 1764, and the news did not reach the colony until six months later. When it did, it struck as though a bomb had been dropped on New Orleans. Outraged residents assembled in a mass meeting in October of 1764 and decided to send a delegation to Paris to try to persuade King Louis XV to change his mind. But all pleas, including one by Bienville himself—the founder of New Orleans was then eighty-six years old—fell on deaf ears. Actually, the fortunes of Louisiana had floated in the balance for several years while France was embroiled in the Seven Years' War and had found its colony a heavy burden. Louis XV offered Louisiana to Spain, which at first turned it down, but when the French king later approached the Spanish monarch, Charles III, he convinced him that Louisiana should belong to Spain because of its proximity to the Spanish colonies bordering the Gulf of Mexico.

Great disorder resulted from the failure of the Spanish government to take the reins of authority promptly and firmly. The Spanish governor, Antonio de Ulloa, who was named to the post in May of 1765, arrived in New Orleans on March 5, 1766, but did not assume full control until August of 1767. By that time, things had gotten out of hand.

When the Spanish took over, meager trade existed in the colony, supplies were scarce, and the currency was worthless. There was little leadership, and times were extremely tough. Such were the conditions confronting Ulloa as he set foot on Louisiana soil. He made matters worse by refusing to present his credentials to the Superior Council, the governing body, saying he would not submit to a civil authority.

A fifty-year-old bachelor, Ulloa was sent to New Orleans from Havana, where he had gone to await assignment after failing as superintendent of a mining operation of the Spanish government in Peru. A career naval officer, Ulloa was also an internationally noted scientist who had been elected to England's prestigious Royal Society, among other organizations.

Unfortunately for him, his austere living, his intellectualism, and his rather humorless personality were out of character with the tastes of his new subjects.

Ulloa made at least two tactical mistakes when he assumed command: first, in deciding to coordinate his government with that of the existing French regime, and second, in not raising the Spanish flag in the Place d'Armes (now Jackson Square) to replace the French standard and confirm the takeover. He arrived with only ninety soldiers and three civil officers, having hoped to enlist the aid of the French garrison in maintaining order. The French troops, however, vowing loyalty to France, refused to join him. So instead of taking direct charge, Ulloa decided to work through Captain Charles Philippe Aubry, who had become military governor. Thus, Ulloa lacked a strong hand and did not possess effective diplomatic persuasion. Further, with no funds to operate the government, he was forced to reduce the Spanish and French troops to half rations. He found that the British were stealing practically all the maritime business in the port, even though they had been granted only rights to navigate in the river.

On March 23, 1766, Ulloa decreed that the colony would no longer do business with French colonies, but only with nine Spanish peninsular ports, using only Spanish vessels. The order severed Louisiana from its traditional markets and spelled commercial disaster. Even worse in terms of Ulloa's personal popularity, he ruled that wine could be imported only from Spain, which meant the colonists would be deprived of their beloved Bordeaux and other French wines.

Merchants, planters, and shippers protested violently. The protesters petitioned the Superior Council for a hearing but got nowhere because Ulloa withdrew from the city to the Balize—the entry station at the mouth of the Mississippi—ostensibly to await his Peruvian bride, the marchioness d'Abrado, whom he had married by proxy. They underwent a second ceremony upon her arrival and took up residence in New Orleans.

During the time Ulloa operated his post at the Balize, delegating governmental functions through Aubry, forces protesting his rule gathered strength. When he returned to New Orleans, Ulloa found hostility. French Creoles led by Nicolas Chauvin de La Frénière, the colony's attorney general, and Nicolas Foucault, the commissary, kept up a campaign against the governor through the winter of 1767–1768 and on through the spring and summer. A handsome man with a gift of oratory, La Frénière worked crowds into frenzies. Close study of the self-interest of La Frénière and Foucault suggests that their love for France was tied to their pocketbooks, because each had built up considerable wealth.

Planters and merchants drew up documents of protest, which were signed by some six hundred of them. The protests resulted in twenty-one formal charges of maladministration by the Superior Council against Ulloa. The unrest peaked in the fall of 1768. The governor and Aubry heard of impending trouble on October 25, just two days before the rebels made a show of force at the Place d'Armes. On October 28, as the Superior Council debated the charges against Ulloa, some five hundred Creoles, Acadians, and Germans assembled in the square, brandishing muskets and other weapons. Shops closed as the insurgents roamed the streets voicing their protests. Aubry called upon the demonstrators to desist and told LaFrénière the uprising could only lead to disaster. The captain of the Spanish frigate *Volante* cast off from the levee and anchored in midstream, fearing violence. The council remained in session into the night. The next day, the crowd in the square and streets numbered approximately a thousand. They wildly proclaimed they would never submit to any government but that of France.

Despite a feeble attempt by Aubry to head off the Superior Council's action, the body put Ulloa on notice to leave. He could not believe what had taken place, especially the ingratitude of the Acadians, to whom he had given homesteads, and of the Germans, whom he had come to trust. When it appeared that all hope of saving the governor from banishment had failed, Aubry urged him to take refuge aboard the *Volante*. Ulloa did so with his pregnant wife and baby daughter. Spanish officials left on shore quickly barricaded themselves in Ulloa's house, where they remained for four days. Ulloa ordered an inspection to determine if the *Volante* was seaworthy. When it was found unsafe, he chartered the French frigate *César* and took his family, several close advisers, and some Capuchin monks aboard, hoping to set sail on October 31. Early on November 1, merrymakers returning from a wedding party spotted the ship still moored in the harbor and began yelling, "Long live the King, long live Louis, the well-beloved, long live the wine of Bordeaux, down with the fish of Spain." Someone aboard the *César* cut a mooring cable, and the vessel shoved off for Havana.

From Cuba, Ulloa dispatched a full report to the Spanish crown, naming the persons who conspired to oust him. La Frénière was accused of organizing the plot, in collaboration with Foucault. Charles III sent General Alexander O'Reilly to New Orleans to restore order and punish the insurgents. O'Reilly, an Irishman who had joined the Spanish army in his early teens and had won Charles III's favor by saving his life in a Madrid uprising, sailed from Spain on July 6, 1769, with some 2,600 troops—a force that approximated the size of New Orleans' population of 3,200. O'Reilly and his fleet of twenty-four vessels anchored at New Orleans on August 28, and the general—soon to be known as "Bloody" O'Reilly—moved swiftly to punish the conspirators.

O'Reilly had six men charged with treason and sedition. They were Pierre Caresse; Jean-Baptiste Noyan, a nephew of Bienville; Pierre Marquis, who commanded the militia that paraded through the streets; and Joseph Milhet, Joseph Villeré, and La Frénière. Foucault was granted immunity because of his official French status but upon his return to France was imprisoned in the Bastille.

The trials were without jury, which was Spanish custom. For the six charged with treason and sedition, O'Reilly decreed the death penalty. All except Villeré—who had died mysteriously while in custody—were executed at 3 P.M. on October 25, 1769. Five other men charged as accomplices were imprisoned in Havana at El Morro fortress. Their sentences were soon commuted.

Aubry was permitted to leave New Orleans for France in January of 1770, but he lost his life when his ship foundered at the mouth of the Garonne River. O'Reilly stayed in New Orleans for only six months, during which he abolished the Superior Council and established the Cabildo, a Spanish-style governing body. He also established a number of commercial markets for the port, especially a flourishing trade with Cuba, which he nullified after he left. New Orleans lapsed into a recession; the Cubans did not want Louisiana's products and could not satisfy the tastes of Louisianians for French and English goods. O'Reilly took his forces to Havana and later went to Spain, where Charles III honored him for putting down the Louisiana insurrection.

Some historians view the events in Louisiana between October of 1768 and October of 1769 as the opening chapter in the movement for American independence. There are similarities and differences. The Louisiana colonists did not seek to establish a separate and distinct government, as did the eastern colonies. They sought to return to the governance of France. Yet as John Preston Moore points out in his *Revolt in Louisiana*, the cause of each revolution was economic, and in each case the rebels harbored feelings of opposition and resentment to European sovereignty. It is dubious, though, he observes, whether the leaders in New Orleans were patriot-martyrs, as were those in New England, and the Superior Council was hardly the counterpart of the English colonial assembly. Nevertheless, Moore concludes, the Louisiana colony was "animated by the same spirit as the English colonists of 1776."

General Alexander O'Reilly, the second Spanish governor of Louisiana,
firmly established Spain's authority over the colony by suppressing the
rebellion that had ousted his predecessor.

Courtesy the Historic New Orleans Collection; Acc. No. 1991.34.14

Following the rebellion, Spain moved to solidify its rule. The crown dispatched a new governor to Louisiana, Don Luís Unzaga. The fortunes of the
colony improved rapidly. Shipping picked up sharply. Unzaga, like his prede-
cessors, ignored the clandestine English trade so long as it was advantageous.

Eight governors followed Unzaga, who served until 1776. They included Bernardo de Gálvez, 1776 to 1785; Colonel Esteban Miró, 1785 to 1791; Baron Francisco Luis Héctor de Carondelet, 1791 to 1797; General Manuel Luís Gayoso de Lemos, 1797 to 1799; Francisco Bouligny and Nicolás María Vidal, who shared a brief rule in 1799 following Gayoso's death by yellow fever that year; Sebastián de Caso Calvo, 1799 to 1801; and General Juan Manuel de Salcedo, 1801 to 1803.

Gálvez, Miró, and Carondelet gave Louisiana more than two decades of the best government the colony had experienced. Gálvez aided the American colonies in their fight against England by capturing the British posts at Bayou Manchac, Baton Rouge, and Natchez in 1779, Mobile in 1780, and Pensacola in 1781. He settled many Canary Islanders and other Spanish colonists in Louisiana, also. During Miró's term, nearly four hundred families of Acadians were transported from France to Louisiana, where they were given land grants. Indeed, the colony's population, which had risen only modestly during all the years of French rule, skyrocketed under the Spaniards. It was soon to climb even faster.

The American states were fast expanding after the War of Independence, and in this process Louisiana was destined to play a major role. A frontier conflict with the United States was inevitable. Spain tried to halt the expansion through diplomacy but failed, and then turned to closing the Mississippi River to American trade. The right of navigation and the right to deposit goods in the port for transshipment became paramount issues. A group of Kentucky frontiersmen threatened to lead a movement to secede from the United States. The principal instigator of the movement was James Wilkinson, a former brigadier general in the Continental army who became a paid Spanish agent in 1784. Wilkinson got Miró's ear in furtherance of the scheme, and the governor became involved. Wilkinson proposed that the Spanish grant him power to issue permits for use of the river, but they refused; instead, in 1788, they decided to let all frontiersmen use the river as far south as New Orleans. Spain thus welcomed all settlers in a move to head off American expansion. The 1788 decree, issued by Governor Miró, sought to mollify the West, obtain immigrants, and to encourage the Kentucky revolution if it did not involve Spain directly.

Realizing the importance of the issue, President George Washington in 1789 moved to placate the Kentuckians by naming Thomas Jefferson secretary of state, selecting him over John Jay, who, in representing the American government in talks with Spain, had advocated closure of the Mississippi for twenty years or more in order to obtain Spain's recognition of the 31st parallel (roughly the northern boundary of Florida) as the southern boundary of the United States. That proposal had enraged the Kentuckians. Jefferson, by contrast, had championed the Kentuckians' fight for free use of the river.

At times, Spain still closed the river to all but her own trade, especially after the War of Independence, in an effort to deny the United States benefits from its victory over the British. This policy also met failure. Meanwhile, the New Orleans economy flourished as the Upper Mississippi Valley became more productive in agriculture. Export trade boomed.

Spain's fortunes began to sink in 1792 when France declared war on her. This brought to a head, temporarily at least, the Mississippi River question, for Spain on October 27, 1795, in the Treaty of San Lorenzo, agreed to allow free use of the river and right of deposit at New Orleans for three years. The treaty heralded a favorable turn of events for New Orleans, generating new enthusiasm in the American states to conduct business through the port. It was the forerunner of another agreement, the Treaty of Ildefonso, by which Spain on October 1, 1800, retroceded Louisiana to France, again signaling a new destiny for Louisianians.

—W.G.C.

4

AMERICANIZATION

The Americanization of Louisiana began during the Spanish regime and accelerated greatly after the purchase of Louisiana by the United States in 1803. During this time the original French settlers intermingled with the Spanish and the people of the emerging American states, especially following the American War of Independence, which ended in 1783.

Under terms of the secret Treaty of Ildefonso of October 1, 1800, Louisiana was returned from Spain to France, although the colony would actually remain under Spanish rule until 1803. When word of the transfer leaked out, President Thomas Jefferson expressed his fear of a Napoleonic Louisiana neighboring the United States. As Jefferson wrote to Robert R. Livingston, United States minister to France: "There is on the globe one single spot the possessor of which is our natural and habitual enemy. It is New Orleans, through which the produce of three-eighths of our country must pass to market. . . . The day that France takes possession of New Orleans fixes the sentence which is to restrain her forever within her low water mark. . . . From that moment on, we must marry ourselves to the British Fleet and nation."

People in the Mississippi and Ohio Valleys had become enraged over not having the free and unrestricted use of the river. They clamored for the United States government to do something. Jefferson was determined to try to buy New Orleans. He sent James Monroe to Paris to join Livingston in the negotiations.

Livingston, meanwhile, tried in vain to get information from Napoleon's foreign minister, Charles Maurice de Talleyrand-Périgord, as to the status of Louisiana. His request that France set a price for New Orleans and West Florida was ignored. "The minister will give me no answer to any inquiries I make on the subject," reported Livingston. Then one day Talleyrand suddenly asked Livingston: "Would you wish to have the whole of Louisiana?" Livingston replied in the negative, whereupon Talleyrand explained. "If we give up New Orleans, the rest would be of little value. I would like to know what you would give for the whole." Livingston replied that he hadn't given it a thought, but that 20 million francs seemed reasonable. Talleyrand said that was too little. Livingston broke off the conversation by saying he could do nothing until Monroe reached France.

Livingston assumed from his conversation with Talleyrand that Napoleon was ready to sell Louisiana to the United States. In fact, at this point, Napoleon intended to occupy Louisiana. He began staging troops at Dutch and Belgian ports, and he sent Pierre Clément de Laussat to New Orleans to make preparations for the troops and for the transfer of Louisiana from Spain to France. Then, on Easter Sunday, April 10, 1803, Napoleon changed his mind. War with England was imminent, and he knew that he could not defend Louisiana against the British fleet. He instructed his minister of the treasury, François de Barbé-Marbois, to open negotiations with Livingston and Monroe. The latter had just arrived in France with authority to pay $2,000,000 for New Orleans.

On April 13, Livingston gave a dinner for his newly arrived colleague. During the evening, Barbé-Marbois asked Livingston to call on him the next day. Thus did the negotiations for the sale of Louisiana open. In a little more than two weeks the Louisiana Purchase was worked out under the most amicable circumstances. The negotiators jockeyed over price but finally agreed on $15,000,000, which included dropping $3,750,000 in claims by American shipowners for vessels confiscated by France in the undeclared war of 1798–1800.

Barbé-Marbois described the atmosphere in which the treaty was accomplished: "A sentiment even superior to glory seemed to animate the three ministers, and never perhaps did negotiators taste a purer joy." Livingston, who had been on the committee to draft the Declaration of Independence and had sworn in George Washington as president, said at the signing: "We have lived long, but this is the noblest work of our whole lives. The treaty which we have just signed has not been obtained by art or dictated by force; equally advantageous to the two contracting parties, it will change vast solitudes into flourishing districts. From this day, the United States takes its place among the powers of the first rank. . . . The instruments that we have just signed will cause no tears to be shed; they prepare ages of happiness for innumerable generations of human creatures."

The news of the treaty was slow in reaching Washington and even slower in reaching New Orleans, where de Laussat was preparing to receive French troops. Napoleon apparently had forgotten de Laussat, who, when word did come, denounced it as an "incredible and impudent falsehood."

Five months were needed to establish procedures for the transfer of Louisiana from Spain to France and then from France to the United States. On November 30, 1803, de Laussat, on behalf of France, received Louisiana from Spain in ceremonies at New Orleans in the Cabildo and the Place d'Armes. For twenty days, de Laussat governed the colony for

The raising of the American flag over New Orleans' Place d'Armes in 1803 marked
Louisiana's transformation from a European colony to a territory of the United States.

Courtesy the New Orleans Times-Picayune

France. Then, on December 20, 1803, he delivered it to William C. C.
Claiborne, governor of the Mississippi Territory, and General James
Wilkinson. De Laussat described the scene in his *Memoirs:* "The beautiful
women and fashionable men of the city adorned all the balconies of the
square. . . . At none of the preceding ceremonies was there an equal num-

ber of spectators. The eleven galleries of the city hall [present Cabildo] were filled with beauties." To cannon and musket salutes, the tricolor of Republican France came down the flagpole and the Stars and Stripes ascended. Louisiana was now American.

—C.L.D.

5

THE PEOPLE OF LOUISIANA

The first settlers that France sent to Louisiana were hardly ideal material for starting a colony. Most were either disciplineless Canadian woods-runners or wretchedly paid and poorly trained soldiers. Very few were farmers, carpenters, or others with the skills needed for building a self-sustaining community.

When the Company of the Indies was running the colony a few years later, a bad situation turned, for a time, even worse. Finding it hard to recruit voluntary settlers, the company began siphoning off the denizens of France's jails and correction houses for shipment to Louisiana. Bienville complained: "It is very disagreeable for an officer charged with the defense of a colony to have . . . only a band of deserters, smugglers and scoundrels, who are all ready not only to abandon you but to turn against you." In 1720 the king prohibited further deportations of this kind.

It is ironic that the first real stability in French Louisiana came with the arrival of two very divergent groups, neither of them French.

In June of 1719 two ships, the *Aurore* and the *Duc de Maine*, landed with a total of 451 captive Africans—the first large shipments of slaves to the colony. Over the next two years another 1,500 blacks stumbled off slave ships onto Louisiana soil. The colony might not have survived without them. Not only were they desperately needed for the backbreaking work of clearing the wilderness and building rudimentary levees, but many of them had special skills that the French colonists lacked. Slave-ship captains had orders to procure African rice and slaves who knew how to grow it, as well as slaves who could raise and process indigo. In the years to come, rice was often all that stood between Louisianians and famine, and indigo was the colony's main—and sometimes only—cash crop.

In the wake of the first slave ships came transports bearing a new breed of settlers: German farm families, their passage paid by the Company of the Indies, which had lured them with extravagant claims about the fertile soil, benevolent climate, and generally idyllic conditions they would find in the colony. Reality must have set in for these men and women almost as soon as they left the dock. Conditions aboard their ships were as bad as those in the vessels that carried French criminals or African slaves. Scurvy and other illnesses ran rampant. Hundreds of the voyagers never lived to reach Louisiana.

John Law, the Scottish financial adventurer whose schemes
led to ruin for many of his investors but also brought thousands of French and German settlers to Louisiana.

No one knows how many Germans—along with some Swiss—entered
the colony in this period. Estimates range from a few thousand to a rather
improbable ten thousand. One confusing factor is that although the immigrants arrived in New Orleans as Germans, they were thoroughly gallicized
in name when the French notaries finished registering them. Typical
changes were Hymel for Himmel, Zeringue for Zehringer, Oubre for Huber,
Clompetre for Kleinpeter, Triche for Trischl, Casbergue for Katzenberg,
Delmaire for Edelmeier. Occasionally there was a direct translation and a
Herr Zweig became a Messieur LaBranche. Very few of the Germans pre-
served their original names.

Many of the newcomers eventually settled along the Mississippi River, on
a stretch of both banks beginning about twenty-five miles above New Orleans. The area became known as the Côte des Allemandes—the German
Coast. By 1724, these industrious farmers were producing not only food for

themselves, but also a surplus that they marketed in New Orleans. The hungry populace of the town plundered the first such shipment without paying for the produce, but the trade soon settled into more regular channels.

The Germans' modest success notwithstanding, these were brutal times in Louisiana. Conditions were primitive, mortality horrendous. Historians estimate that at the end of 1722, after the peak period of immigration, the total population of settlers and slaves was about 6,000. The first full census of the colony, taken on January 1, 1726, recorded not quite half that number. Some settlers may have managed to return to Europe, but most of the missing undoubtedly had died. Naturally, there was no crush of new immigrants to replace them. Nor did the Natchez Indian uprising of 1729, in which approximately a tenth of the white population was wiped out, do anything to improve the colony's reputation.

Louisiana stagnated. Even the importation of slaves all but ceased, with only one shipload arriving between 1731 and the end of French rule. In 1740 the colony had barely 5,000 people altogether, and the white population of 1,200 was lower than it had been in 1726. In 1763, on the eve of the Spanish takeover, the total population of just over 8,000—roughly 4,600 blacks and 3,600 whites—was only marginally greater than it had been forty years earlier. During all this time, the colony had steadily drained the French treasury. It seems unlikely that Louis XV harbored many qualms about handing over Louisiana to his royal cousin Charles III of Spain.

The Spanish succeeded no better than the French at making the colony profitable, but they did prove adept at putting people in it. In 1788, only twenty years after Spain assumed full control, Louisiana's population had mushroomed to 39,410, which included 19,737 free persons and 20,673 slaves.

This remarkable growth was achieved by two means. One was simple and tragic: under Spanish rule, the African slave trade to Louisiana reopened and flourished. But Spain also worked hard to attract free immigrants. For example, the crown subsidized the importation of about 2,000 Canary Islanders. The Isleños, as they came to be known—the only large group of Spanish-speakers to enter the colony—settled mainly in remote areas such as St. Bernard Parish, toward the toe of the Louisiana "boot." Many died in the early years, and the survivors developed a reputation for avoiding the outside world. Today their descendants remain a relatively small and isolated part of the population.

The same cannot be said of another group that came to the colony after the cession to Spain. The Acadians (*les Acadiens,* in French) were the unfortunate French-descended inhabitants of Nova Scotia who were expelled

A home in Cajun country, sketched by A. R. Waud. Born in England, Waud came to
Louisiana soon after the Civil War, during which he was a battlefield reporter/artist.
Over the next dozen years, he made more than five hundred drawings of the state, especially
its rural scenes.

Courtesy the Historic New Orleans Collection; Acc. No. 1974.25.31.73

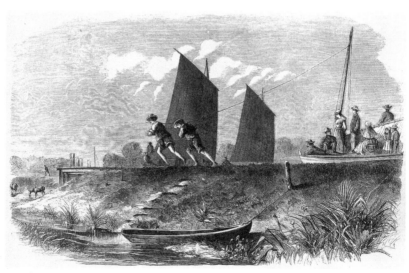

Acadians strain their backs to haul a boatload of their fellow colonists on Bayou Lafourche.
A sketch by A. R. Waud, probably from the 1870s.

Courtesy the Historic New Orleans Collection; Acc. No. 1974.25.31.4

from their homeland by the British beginning in 1755. They began drifting into Louisiana in 1763—although undocumented tradition holds that some arrived as early as 1760—and they settled along the Mississippi and Bayous Lafourche, Teche, and Vermilion in south Louisiana.

The greatest single movement of colonists from Europe to America in colonial history involved an enclave of Acadians who had returned to France. For thirty years they had eked out an existence there, and they were receptive to a proposal of the king of Spain to transport them at his expense to Louisiana. Over seven months, from May to December in 1785, seven ships delivered 1,600 Acadians at the port of New Orleans. The newcomers gravitated to the same areas where their compatriots had long been established. The Spanish authorities supplied them with land, seeds, livestock, and tools. Governor Esteban Miró was delighted with the newcomers. He reported: "The enthusiasm, industry, and loyalty of these new colonists will boost the prosperity of our province and increase its local and foreign trade."

The Acadians married among themselves, of course, but also with the Germans, the Creoles,* and others. They thrived far better than the Isleños. It has been estimated that more than 500,000 present-day Louisianians have Acadian blood in their veins. Today they are called "Cajuns," which is simply a corruption of *Acadiens*, and they make up one of the best-known ethnic groups in the nation.

At about the same time as the Acadians were arriving, rough, tough riverboatmen from the American frontier in the Ohio River Valley began drifting down to New Orleans with their goods. Called "Kaintocks" because so many of them were from Kentucky, this boisterous, bellicose contingent was augmented by enterprising fellow Americans from Virginia and New England who set up businesses in New Orleans. The clamor of both groups for navigation rights and port privileges eventually helped lead to the purchase of Louisiana from France. The Louisiana that these Americans invaded was described by a French merchant, James

---

*The term *Creole* is a slippery one. Over the centuries it has had many definitions, and to this day what it means depends at least partly on who is using it. For the purposes of this book, the word denotes the Louisiana-born descendants of the early French and Spanish colonists—more specifically, the white descendants, since those of mixed race occupied a very different social stratum. Admittedly this definition is narrow—for example, it excludes the offspring of the German settlers simply because those settlers were neither French nor Spanish—but it does serve to identify a relatively homogeneous group whose actions and attitudes have played an important role in the history of Louisiana. Note that Cajuns are not Creoles, both for cultural reasons and because (under our definition) the Acadians were not technically French, but French Canadian.

Pitot, who later, under the American flag, became mayor of New Orleans. Henry C. Pitot's English translation of *Observations on the Colony of Louisiana from 1796 to 1802*, which James Pitot prepared for French officials, provides the following: "The population of Louisiana, Spanish by its government, is still generally French in its tastes, customs, habits, religion, and language. . . . Some Frenchmen, Germans, and Canadians came at different times to settle here, and Spaniards in turn became part of the population through their government. Because they were so near, some Englishmen moved to Louisiana; and many citizens of the western settlements of the United States finally established their residence, resulting, particularly in New Orleans, in an assortment of manners, customs, languages, and interests."

Congress created the Territory of Orleans in 1804, with approximately the boundaries of the present state of Louisiana. William C. C. Claiborne, appointed governor by Thomas Jefferson, gave the president an appraisal of the new territory's inhabitants:

I believe the people of Louisiana are, generally speaking, honest, and that a decided majority of them are attached to the American Government. But they are uninformed, indolent, luxurious—in a word, illy fitted to be useful citizens of a Republic. Under the Spanish Government education was discouraged, and little respectability attached to science. Wealth alone gave respect and influence, and hence it has happened that ignorance and wealth so generally pervade this part of Louisiana. I have seen, Sir, in this city, many youths to whom nature has been apparently liberal, but from the injustice and inattention of their parents, have no other accomplishments to recommend them but dancing with elegance and ease. The same observation will apply to the young females, with the additional remark, that they are the most handsome women in America.

Thomas Ashe, an English traveler, visited New Orleans in 1808 and noted: "Virginians and Kentuckians reign over the brokerage and commission business; the Scotch and Irish absorb all the respectable commerce in exportation and importation; the French keep magazines [warehouses] and stores, and the Spaniards do all the small retail trade." There was also in New Orleans what the *Louisiana Gazette* called "a respectable party of Irishmen." In 1809, at the city's first St. Patrick's Day celebration, they and their guests, who included Governor Claiborne, drank the traditional seventeen toasts.

The Territory of Orleans grew impressively during the seven years that followed the Louisiana Purchase. The United States census of 1810 listed the territory's population at 76,556, of whom 34,660 were slaves and 7,585 were free blacks. The population of Orleans Parish was 24,552, with 17,252 in the city itself (the parish then extended all the way to Barataria Bay); the rest of the territory numbered 52,004. Seven years earlier, in 1803, the estimated figures had been 40,000 for the territory and 8,000 for New Orleans. The largest segment of the white population was of French origin, with Spaniards, Americans, English, Germans, and Irish well represented.

The *Western Gazetteer* described New Orleans' polyglot population in 1817: "Here in half an hour you can see and speak to Frenchmen, Spaniards, Danes, Swedes, Germans, Englishmen, Portuguese, Hollanders, Mexicans, Kentuckians, Tennesseans, Ohioans, Pennsylvanians, New Yorkers, New Englanders and a motley group of Indians, quadroons, Africans, etc."

About a century after the first Germans settled in Louisiana, a second wave arrived in the 1820s. These immigrants were known as "redemptioners" because they had to redeem their passage debt by becoming indentured servants for a specified period of time. Many redemptioners rose to positions of prominence in Louisiana.

The development of the steamboat trade on the Mississippi, the potato famine in Ireland, the rise of the plantation system, and the influx of Americans from other states in the Union combined to accelerate population growth in Louisiana. The following census figures tell the story:

1810	76,556
1820	153,407
1830	215,739
1840	352,411
1850	517,762
1860	708,002

In 1840, New Orleans became the third city in the nation, behind New York and Baltimore, to reach 100,000 in population. In 1860, out of a white population of 155,000, 41 percent were foreign born. Thirty-two nations were represented, the Irish leading with 23,000 and the Germans next with 19,000. The Germans had their own theater and German-language newspapers.

After the Louisiana Purchase, New Orleans was a port of entry for European immigrants. Some of these settled in Louisiana; many moved up the Mississippi. In the decade 1845–1854, more than 280,000 entered the

United States at New Orleans. It was during this time that a third wave of Germans, largely intellectuals and professionals, arrived in Louisiana. They were refugees from the European political disturbances of 1848. Among them were brewmasters who made New Orleans beer famous from the mid-nineteenth century on.

Italian immigrants began arriving in Louisiana in large numbers in the closing years of the nineteenth century and the opening years of the twentieth. A substantial colony of Yugoslavians, many of whom became Gulf of Mexico fishermen, was established before World War I. Two important influxes in the second half of the twentieth century contributed further to Louisiana's mixture of nationalities. The already substantial colony of Cuban expatriates in New Orleans expanded geometrically after Fidel Castro seized power in Cuba in 1959. Although the number of refugees who settled in the city never approached the volume that made Miami a sort of Havana-in-Exile, the Cubans nevertheless made their presence felt in business and cultural activities.

The last years and end of the war in Vietnam brought to the United States a flood of South Vietnamese who feared for their lives in the face of a North Vietnamese victory. Thousands of the newcomers settled in Louisiana, especially south Louisiana, which in many ways resembles parts of Vietnam. Today Vietnamese make up the largest single foreign-born group in the state, adding—with their American-born children and grandchildren—yet another ingredient to the rich cultural and ethnic gumbo that is Louisiana.

—C.L.D.

6

The West Florida Rebellion

For seventy-four days in 1810, there existed within a hundred miles of New Orleans the independent state of West Florida. Over its capital, Baton Rouge, flew the first Lone Star flag, more than a quarter of a century before the Republic of Texas unfurled its flag of independence and fifty years ahead of secessionist South Carolina's similar banner.

What later became known as the "Florida Parishes" was West Florida from 1763 to 1810. It extended from the Mississippi River east to the Pearl River, and from the Mississippi Territory line on the north to the shores of Lakes Pontchartrain and Maurepas on the south.

Briefly summed up, this corner of land was under four dominations before it finally came under the American flag in 1810. French rule prevailed from 1717 to 1763; Britain held control from 1763 to 1779; the Spanish flag flew over West Florida from 1779 to 1810; and from September 24 to December 7, in 1810, West Florida was independent—a "Tom Thumb Republic," as one historian called it.

The West Florida story begins with the end of the Seven Years' War—the conflict Americans call the French and Indian War. By the terms of the peace treaty, France was stripped of Canada and Louisiana east of the Mississippi, except for the so-called Island of Orleans. At the same time, France ceded Louisiana west of the river to Spain.

During the American Revolution, Spanish Louisiana rendered great assistance to the Americans by supplying them with gunpowder, ammunition, and other war materiel. In 1779 Spain too was at war with England, and the dashing young Spanish governor of Louisiana, Bernardo de Gálvez, decided to attack the British posts on Bayou Manchac (south of Baton Rouge), Baton Rouge, and Natchez. Gálvez's force totaled 1,450 and was composed of whites, blacks, and Indians. The Manchac outpost fell on December 7, and several days later Gálvez moved on the fort at Baton Rouge, which was defended by a moat, eighteen cannon, and 600 troops.

A frontal attack would be costly and likely to fail, so Gálvez resorted to a stratagem. As silently as possible, some of his troops dug artillery emplacements while the rest engaged in noisy activity in another area to attract the fort's fire. While the garrison wasted its shells on the diversionary position, Gálvez's artillery was getting ready for its own bombardment. The cannonade began at dawn and continued for three and a half hours. The fort capitulated. That is how West Florida became Spanish.

Spain was eager to colonize the newly acquired West Florida and was generous with land grants to American settlers. Many moved into the territory, joining fellow Anglo-Saxons who had remained in the Baton Rouge area after its capture by Gálvez. Villages sprang up at various places around Baton Rouge, such as Bayou Sara, St. Francisville, and Feliciana. With 90 percent of the white population Anglo-Saxon, it was inevitable that eventually the Americans would move to take over their own governance.

The inhabitants of West Florida believed the area was included in the Louisiana Purchase of 1803, and when they learned otherwise, they began to resent their Spanish administrators. This feeling led to an abortive uprising in 1804. The Spanish diplomatic position was that West Florida did not belong in the Louisiana Purchase because France could not sell what it did not own. Confusion existed even among American officials.

In the spring of 1810 disaffection for the administration of Don Carlos de Hault de Lassus had reached a dangerous pitch among the West Florida populace. Secret meetings culminated on June 23 in a gathering of more than five hundred men at Egypt Plantation, in the Feliciana district. Their stated object in meeting was "to secure themselves against foreign invasion and domestic disturbance." It was a flimsy pretext: "foreign invasion" referred to a vague, baseless rumor of a plot to seize West Florida for Napoleon, and the only "domestic disturbance" was of their own making. What took place at Egypt Plantation was the first step in the overthrow of Spanish rule in West Florida.

The meeting, following a prearranged plan, called for the appointment of representatives to a common council to be made up of four representatives each from the five districts of West Florida. This twenty-member congress would control the territory's destiny. In July a convention met and drew up a constitution—rather, it approved a constitution that had previously been drawn up. Essentially, the body was demanding equal authority with the Spanish colonial government.

On August 21, de Lassus held a council to consider the crisis. He seemed to favor conciliation, an attitude that drew criticism from some of his staff. In response, the governor contended that he was saving West Florida from civil war by appearing to accept the action of the convention. He even joined the convention delegates in signing a proclamation that called for "all the good people of this jurisdiction . . . to preserve good order and avoid every movement that may disturb the public tranquility." Meanwhile, he secretly sent for reinforcements.

An uneasy calm prevailed, with the governor and the convention delegates both lending lip-worship to concord. The convention was to appoint officials to govern West Florida under de Lassus. These officials included judges, a sheriff, and militia officers. Named brigadier general in command of the militia was an unlettered but natural leader, Philemon Thomas. W. H. Sparks, a contemporary of Thomas, wrote in his *Memory of Fifty Years:* "He was almost entirely without education, but was gifted with great good sense, a bold and honest soul, and a remarkable natural eloquence." Such was the man who would lead, shortly, the West Florida troops against the Spanish-held fort at Baton Rouge.

Governor de Lassus on August 25 rejected the appointment of Fulwar Skipwith as a judge and balked at Thomas' elevation to brigadier general, stating that Thomas' former rank of colonel was adequate. The convention delegates were becoming concerned about their relations with the governor, and when word leaked out in mid-September about de Lassus' call for reinforcements, a fight became inevitable.

The fort overlooked the Mississippi, standing on ground ten to fifteen feet higher than the surrounding area. It was guarded by a dry ditch nine feet deep and fifteen feet wide, and by high pickets slanting outward. Behind the pickets were mud embankments. Within the enclosure was a square stockade with a bastion at each corner. It was a formidable defensive ensemble supported by about twenty-four cannon. However, it was garrisoned by only about thirty soldiers, which meant that hardly any of the artillery was manned.

Considering his options, General Thomas—who had only seventy men himself—ruled out a direct attack. He received word that there was an opening in the palisade facing the river, through which the garrison's milk cows went to and from pasture. If cows could get in and out of the fort through the opening, Thomas reasoned, so could mounted men. A heavy fog hung over the river in the pre-dawn hours of September 23 as the horsemen in single file mounted the steep river bluff and entered the fort through the opening.

The surprised garrison fought bravely but hopelessly. Two Spaniards, including the fort's lieutenant, were killed while others were taken prisoner or fled. Governor de Lassus refused the demand to surrender his sword and was knocked down by a blow from a rifle butt. He was about to be bayonetted when General Thomas intervened. Not one of the attackers was killed or even wounded.

When daylight broke, one of the West Florida men pointed to the fort's flagpole. The flag of Spain was pulled down and the Lone Star flag was run up over Baton Rouge. The convention on September 26 issued a proclamation declaring West Florida to be a "free and independent state."

The *Louisiana Gazette* of October 3 stated that many foreigners in New Orleans, especially French and Spanish, believed "that the United States government are at the bottom of this revolution." The newspaper hastened to deny this. Nevertheless, Orleans Territory Governor William C. C. Claiborne, acting on orders of President James Madison, went to St. Francisville and on December 7 annexed West Florida to the Orleans Territory. Claiborne created a single county out of the combined districts of West Florida and named it Feliciana. The name is perpetuated to this day by the two Feliciana Parishes, East and West. Out of Claiborne's Feliciana, or the West Florida Republic, came eight parishes: the two Felicianas and East Baton Rouge, St. Tammany, Tangipahoa, Washington, Livingston, and St. Helena.

—C.L.D.

The Battle of New Orleans

What is generally known as the Battle of New Orleans—that is, the combat on the plains of Chalmette on January 8, 1815—was actually only one engagement, albeit the key one, in a month-long British campaign for control of the city and, with it, of the Mississippi Valley.

The British campaign began on December 14, 1814, on Lake Borgne, an arm of the Gulf of Mexico east of New Orleans, and ended on January 19 on the Mississippi River at Fort St. Philip, seventy-five miles downstream from the city. Ironically, most of the fighting was waged after a treaty of peace ending the War of 1812 had been signed on Christmas Eve, 1814, in faraway Ghent, Belgium. Ironically, too, the success at New Orleans was the only important victory the United States won in the war except for the naval exploits of Oliver Hazard Perry on Lake Erie.

The War of 1812 was not a popular one. President James Madison delivered his war message to Congress on June 1, 1812, and it was not until almost three weeks later—June 18—that the lawmakers acted. The vote for war was 19 to 13 in the Senate and 79 to 49 in the House of Representatives. All the New England states except Vermont opposed the war; New York and New Jersey joined in opposition to what was called "Mr. Madison's War."

Chief among the conflict's causes were British impressment of American seamen, British encouragement of Indian hostility on the American frontier, and American ideas of expansion in Canada.

The war did not go well for the United States. Detroit surrendered without a fight; two campaigns to Canada failed dismally; Washington, D.C., was captured and burned. The only bright spot was Lake Erie and Perry's thrilling words "We have met the enemy and they are ours!"

By mid-December, 1814, the New England states were talking secession. Such was the background against which the British campaign to take New Orleans occurred.

Before the campaign opened, the British sought the assistance of the notorious pirate Jean Lafitte and his Barataria Bay cohorts. They offered Lafitte a captaincy in the British navy and $30,000 in gold if he joined in the attack on New Orleans. Lafitte promptly turned the documents in the proposal over to the Louisiana legislature, thus alerting the authorities to the imminence of an attack. General Jackson, who once called Lafitte and his band "Hellish banditti," welcomed their assistance when the British arrived on Louisiana soil.

On December 14, an American flotilla of six small gunboats, with a total of twenty-three guns and 182 men, commanded by Lieutenant Thomas A. Catesby Jones, was attacked on Lake Borgne by a British force that included sloops-of-war and 45 oar-powered landing craft, each with a gun and together carrying more than 1,000 troops. Lack of wind denied Jones mobility, and the result of the unequal fight was inevitable. One by one the American gunboats were boarded and captured and their guns were turned on the other American craft. The battle opened at 10:50 A.M. The last American gunboat surrendered less than two hours later.

None of the Americans escaped to reach New Orleans with the news that the British were near at hand. Jackson was very much in the dark as to the whereabouts and size of the enemy. How big was the invading force? Present-day estimates vary from 7,500 to 10,000. The British commander was General Sir Edward Pakenham, brother-in-law of the duke of Wellington.

Nine days after the British cleared Lake Borgne, thus opening the way to New Orleans, advance elements of Pakenham's army reached the Mississippi at Villeré Plantation. This force, numbering about 1,600, surprised a token contingent of Americans under Major Gabriel Villeré. Villeré escaped by jumping from a window and brought the news to Jackson that the British were below the city.

"By the Eternal," exclaimed General Jackson, "they shall not sleep on our soil!" Jackson decided to attack the British camp that very night and called in all his detachments in the outskirts of New Orleans.

The night battle of December 23 at Villeré Plantation began at seven thirty with the gunboat *Carolina* lobbing shells among the British troops. This was the signal for the attack by Jackson's makeshift force. Confusion and chaos prevailed in the darkness, and the action was inconclusive, with both sides later claiming victory. At midnight, Jackson broke off and, leaving appropriate outposts, fell back with his main body to the Rodriguez Canal at Chalmette. Throughout the night breastworks were thrown up and the abandoned millrace was deepened.

Jackson's chief engineer, Major A. Lacarrière Latour, wrote that "the result of the affair of the 23rd was the saving of Louisiana." Latour explained: "It cannot be doubted but that the enemy, had he not been attacked with such impetuosity, when he had hardly effected his disembarkment, would, that very night, or early next morning, have marched against the city, which was not then covered by any fortifications and was defended by hardly five thousand men, mostly militia, who could not, in the open field have withstood disciplined troops, accustomed to the use of the bayonet, a weapon with which most of the militia were unprovided."

By December 27, Pakenham had landed all his troops and guns and had himself taken command in the field of his army. He decided to probe Jackson's entire front, and if a weakness was discovered, to exploit it with a full-scale attack. Such was the reconnaissance in force that Pakenham planned for December 28.

Jackson's line ran for about three-quarters of a mile from the river to the swamp. Oddly, he neglected to anchor his left flank well into the swamp, and this exposed flank almost brought disaster to the Americans. The British advance uncovered no readily exploitable spots in Jackson's line elsewhere, and in due time Pakenham called off the engagement. As the bugles sounded the recall, some British on the right had just discovered Jackson's exposed left flank and had begun a turning operation that would have made the American front untenable. But being seasoned, disciplined troops, they heeded the recall and retired. Jackson immediately rushed reinforcements to his left flank and bent his line deep into the swamp. It was a narrow escape.

The two forces settled into preparations for further battle, which was prefaced by an artillery duel on January 1. Among the gunners on the American side were two of Lafitte's men, Dominique You and René Beluche. These experienced cannoneers commanded Battery No. 3 in Jackson's light-battery defense and played an important role in the artillery clash.

For embrasures for the guns, Jackson authorized his troops to insert cotton bales in his defense line. The British used hogsheads of sugar, which they had appropriated, for the same purpose. Bales and barrels alike worked poorly as protection. British shells knocked the cotton bales about and set so many of them on fire that Jackson ordered them removed. Accordingly, tradition notwithstanding, there were no cotton bales in the American defense line when the British launched their grand assault on January 8. As for the sugar barrels, they were shattered by the American fire, and the sugar mingled with the mire around the guns, causing much discomfort.

At first the British fire was concentrated on the house where Jackson had installed his headquarters, and the general and his staff were forced to leave it. Throughout the duel, the British added Congreve rockets to their fire. Although creating a display, the rockets did little or no damage. Meanwhile, the American batteries matched shot for shot with the veteran British gunners.

Harassment by the *Carolina* and another American gunboat, the *Louisiana*, determined the British to eliminate this menace. They established batteries on the levee and concentrated their fire on the two vessels. The *Carolina* was blown up, and the *Louisiana* withdrew upstream.

Meanwhile, Fort St. Philip, seventy-five miles downriver from New Orleans, was besieged and in desperate need of supplies. In the port of New Orleans at the time was Captain Henry M. Shreve and his steamboat *Enterprise*. On January 3, Jackson called Shreve to his headquarters.

"Captain Shreve, I understand that you are a man who will always do what you have undertaken. Can you pass the British batteries on the bank of the river, nine miles below, and with your steamer bear supplies to Fort St. Philip?"

"Yes, if you will give me my own time," replied Shreve.

"What time do you require?"

"Twenty-four hours."

The *Enterprise* was loaded with supplies, its exposed port side was covered with cotton bales, and at midnight in a dense fog it slipped safely past the British batteries. Its mission accomplished, the *Enterprise* returned safely to New Orleans. There can be little question that this performance represents the first employment in war of a steam vessel.

His forces in place, Pakenham now had a plan for the major assault on the American line behind the Rodriguez Canal. He would send 1,600 troops across the Mississippi and launch a simultaneous attack on both banks of the river at sunrise. Once the American position on the West Bank had been taken, its guns would be relocated so as to deliver enfilading fire into Jackson's line at Chalmette. Raked by artillery fire both frontally and on the flank, and furiously attacked on the Rodriguez Canal, the Americans would be compelled to fall back toward the city.

Had the execution of Pakenham's plan been as good as its conception, the Americans would have faced a disaster. But nothing went right for the British. They dug a canal to get boats into the river with Colonel William Thornton's West Bank attack force, but the banks caved in. Instead of 1,600 troops crossing the river, barely 600 made it. Moreover, failure to consider the river's four-mile-per-hour current resulted in Thornton's landing his men far below the intended line of departure. Yet another misfortune for Pakenham was the designated regiment's failure to provide fascines and scaling ladders to cross the Rodriguez Canal.

Despite these circumstances, Pakenham threw his attack at Jackson's line at sunrise on January 8. He met a tremendous cannonade and withering rifle and musket fire. As he galloped past General John Lambert, Pakenham

General Andrew Jackson (astride white horse) receives a report from a lieutenant during the Battle of New Orleans, fought at Chalmette on January 8, 1815. The cotton-bale breast-works are part of the folklore about the battle but probably were not used on the crucial day.

Courtesy the Historic New Orleans Collection; Acc. No. 1958.43.1

called: "That's a terrific fire, Lambert." Shortly after, Pakenham's horse was shot from under him and a bullet shattered the general's knee. As he tried to mount another horse, he was mortally wounded when a ball struck his spine. General Samuel Gibbs also was struck down mortally, and General John Keane was seriously wounded. The British command now devolved on Lambert. Although some British troops penetrated a redoubt on Jackson's extreme right, they were quickly driven out. Lambert called off the attack and recalled Colonel Thornton from the West Bank.

Completely successful in his attack on Louisiana militia and Kentucky volunteers, Thornton occupied the position from which the Americans had fled. But this happened after the British defeat at the Rodriguez Canal, and Thornton responded to Lambert's recall.

In New Orleans, the Ursuline nuns and many citizens, keeping an all-night vigil in prayer in the convent chapel, were startled at morning mass when a messenger from Chalmette burst in crying out, "Victory is ours!"

Jackson's casualties were six killed and seven wounded; reports from Morgan's position raised the total of American casualties in the day's fighting to only seventy-one. The British losses were frightful. "The whole plain . . . was covered by the British soldiers who had fallen," wrote Major Latour.

The day after the defeat at Chalmette, a British flotilla of two warships, two bomb boats, and a tender began a futile ten-day attack on Fort St. Philip. Almost ceaselessly, the British fired at the fort, but more than 1,000 shells had hardly any effect. The ships raised anchor on January 19, the same day that General Lambert completed his withdrawal from Chalmette. The British campaign for New Orleans was over.

American losses from December 14 to January 19 totaled 333 killed, wounded and missing. British casualties totaled 2,429, including 393 killed, 1,514 wounded, and 522 missing.

The consequences of the Battle of New Orleans were most significant. Ultimately, the victory carried Andrew Jackson to the White House. Meanwhile, the troops who would have occupied New Orleans had the British captured the city sailed instead for Belgium, joining the duke of Wellington in time for the Battle of Waterloo. It is conceivable that Jackson's victory helped defeat Napoleon.

—C.L.D.

8

THE CIVIL WAR

The returns from the presidential election of 1860 clearly suggest that Louisiana was more pro-Union than pro-secession. True, Abraham Lincoln did not receive a single vote in the state—his name was not even on the ballot—but a majority of the 50,000 voters supported the pro-Union candidates, Stephen A. Douglas of Illinois and John Bell of Tennessee. Together, Douglas and Bell garnered 27,829 votes against pro-secession candidate John C. Breckinridge's 22,681.

From the November 6 election to the end of the year, however, sentiment in Louisiana changed. As 1861 dawned, the state was caught up in the secession movement that was sweeping the South. On January 26, in a convention in Baton Rouge, Louisiana adopted the Ordinance of Secession by 113 votes to 17. Ten days later in Montgomery, Alabama, Louisiana delegates joined in creating the Confederate States of America, with Mississippi's Jefferson Davis elected president.

Before Louisiana left the Union, Governor Thomas O. Moore had authorized the seizure of such federal properties as the arsenal in Baton Rouge; the mint and the marine hospital in New Orleans; and Forts Jackson and St. Philip, seventy-five miles downriver from the city. Thus, Louisiana was already committed to secession even before the secession convention opened.

Two of the Confederacy's eight full generals came from Louisiana. They were P. G. T. Beauregard and Braxton Bragg, both West Pointers with distinguished service in the Mexican War. Lieutenant General Richard Taylor, son of Zachary Taylor, was one of three civilians in the Confederacy to achieve that rank. Episcopal bishop Leonidas Polk, a West Pointer who left the pulpit for the field, reached the rank of lieutenant general before his battlefield death in 1864. Altogether, Louisiana provided the South with twenty-one generals and 56,000 troops. Two famous Louisiana units served in Virginia—the Washington Artillery, which fired one of the first shots at Manassas and one of the last at Appomattox, and Major Roberdeau Wheat's wild Louisiana Tigers.

Against this background of Confederate gray, it is easy to lose sight of the fact that a great many Louisianians wore blue in the Civil War. More than 24,000 Louisiana blacks—more than from any other state—served in the Union army. Nor were blacks the only residents of the state who chose

Pierre Gustave Toutant Beauregard, the Louisiana-born
Confederate general whose attack on Fort Sumter began the
Civil War.

Courtesy the Historic New Orleans Collection; Acc. No. 1972.28

the Union over the Confederacy. For example, several infantry regiments
and at least one cavalry troop were raised among the white citizens of occupied New Orleans, although it is true that the bulk of these enlistees
were German or Irish immigrants to the city and northerners living there,
rather than natives. Louisiana also made one notable indirect contribution
to the Union: William T. Sherman, a West Pointer and Mexican War veteran from Ohio, resigned as superintendent of the Louisiana State Seminary of Learning at Pineville when the state left the Union. Sherman was
commissioned a colonel in the United States Army and was soon promoted to brigadier general and then major general. In 1864 his capture of
Atlanta and march to the sea dealt a death blow to Confederate hopes.

Louisiana's last United States senators before secession, Judah P. Benjamin and John Slidell, played important civilian roles in the Confederacy.
Benjamin, called the "Brains of the Confederacy," held three successive

posts in President Davis' cabinet, first as attorney general, then as secretary of war, and finally as secretary of state. Slidell and James M. Mason were sent as diplomats to France and England, but they were seized by a Union warship that intercepted the British ship *Trent* after it left Havana. A diplomatic crisis between the United States and England blew over when President Lincoln ordered the release of Slidell and Mason and sent them off to Europe. Once established in France, Slidell spent the rest of the war trying in vain to persuade Napoleon III to recognize the Confederacy.

The Civil War began on April 12, 1861, when General Beauregard ordered the Charleston batteries to open fire on Fort Sumter. The realities of war were brought home to Louisiana on May 26 when the USS *Brooklyn* anchored at the mouth of the Mississippi River to begin the blockade of southern ports that would ultimately strangle the Confederacy. From that day until the fall of New Orleans, not a single ocean vessel reached the city.

The first land battle of the war was fought on July 21, 1861, at Manassas—or Bull Run—in Virginia. Louisianians played a significant part in routing the Union troops. Beauregard, second in command, directed the battle. The Washington Artillery and Louisiana Tigers performed valiantly. The Tiger's commander, Major Wheat, was carried from the field seriously wounded.

In the glow of victory at Manassas and with pride in the performance of Louisiana troops, few were inclined to heed the warning of the *Picayune:* "We must not suppose, in our exultations and our comfortings, that the winning of one great battle is the end of the war, or more than the beginning of an end which may be yet a long time off."

It has been estimated that approximately six hundred military engagements took place on Louisiana soil, but obviously the vast majority were trifling skirmishes. Only a handful of battles or events are sufficiently important to be noted or presented in some detail here. Heading such a list would be the fall of New Orleans to Flag Officer David G. Farragut in April, 1862.

Whereas the Union army's goal in the East was the capture of Richmond, the Confederate capital, the strategy for the West was to gain control of the Mississippi River. Accordingly, New Orleans was the primary Union target.

The city's defense had been assigned to General David E. Twiggs, who had joined the Confederacy after fifty years in the United States Army. But at the age of seventy-one and in declining health, Twiggs was not up to the task, and things were in chaotic condition when General Mansfield Lovell replaced him in October, 1861. Lovell worked feverishly to prepare New Orleans for attack. One of his accomplishments was to create a barrier across the Mississippi between the two downriver forts, Jackson and St. Philip. He gained encouragement from the fact that the *Manassas*, the Civil War's first ironclad, had recently driven a Union flotilla out of the river, and from the promise that the *Louisiana* and the *Mississippi*, powerful ironclads being built at New Orleans, would be ready for action by the end of January.

On the negative side, Lovell could not impress the Richmond government with the seriousness of the threat to New Orleans. Even after Farragut's fleet—seventeen warships and twenty mortar boats—entered the river and dropped anchor at Head of Passes, President Davis believed the greatest threat to New Orleans lay in a Union fleet more than four hundred miles upriver from the city.

The mortar boats, under Commander David Dixon Porter, fired away at the forts for five days and nights but could not silence them. Finally, Farragut decided to run past them under cover of darkness. An expedition cut a passage through the barrier, and at 2 A.M. on April 24, the Federal fleet made its move. Fourteen of Farragut's warships passed through the opening and steamed by the forts and out of their range. His flagship, *Hartford,* ran aground under the guns of Fort St. Philip and was set ablaze by a fire raft but, using full steam, finally tore free of the sandbar and ran to safety, the crew extinguishing the fire.

Meanwhile, only three Confederate ships fought valiantly, as a so-called River Defense Fleet fled ingloriously upstream when the action opened. The *Manassas, McRae,* and *Governor Moore* were heavily engaged with almost all of Farragut's vessels. The *Manassas,* disabled, ran ashore and was scuttled by its crew. The *McRae,* made helpless when its rudder cables were cut, somehow found shelter at Fort Jackson. The *Governor Moore* took on almost all the Union vessels and sank one, the *Varuna,* but was hopelessly outnumbered. Lieutenant Beverly Kennon threw his sword overboard and set fire to his vessel before surrendering. Fifty-seven men died aboard the *Governor Moore,* a greater total than in Farragut's entire fleet and the two forts combined.

Where were the two great ironclads, *Louisiana* and *Mississippi,* which were to have been in service by January 31? They were still unfinished. The *Louisiana,* unable to move by its own power, was towed to Fort St. Philip for use as a floating battery. The *Mississippi,* set afire to the waterline, floated down the river as Farragut arrived at New Orleans on April 25.

The levee was one huge fire as cotton, sugar, corn, and rice were put to the torch. The defending troops, largely militia, had left the city when General Lovell realized they would be useless against the heavy guns of the

With guns ablaze, the Federal fleet passes the Mississippi River forts en route
to New Orleans.

Courtesy the Historic New Orleans Collection; Acc. No. 1958.73.3

Union warships. Farragut took New Orleans without firing a shot. J. K.
Duncan, in command of the downriver forts, surrendered them upon learning the city's fate.

On May 1, Union general Benjamin Franklin Butler arrived with his
occupation troops. Farragut moved upriver and compelled the surrender of
Baton Rouge (Governor Moore had shifted the state capital to Opelousas).
Federal troops took over from the navy. On August 5, General John C.
Breckinridge, with about 5,000 troops, attacked the Federals at Baton
Rouge but, after initial success, was repelled.

During the battle at Baton Rouge, General Henry W. Allen received a leg
wound that left him crippled for life. Allen was elected governor of Confederate Louisiana in 1863 while still in service. He proved to be a tremendously
effective administrator of that part of the state not in Union hands. According to the historian Douglas Southall Freeman, "Allen was the single great
administrator produced by the Confederacy. His success in Louisiana indicates he might have changed history to some extent if his talents could have
been utilized by the Confederate government on a large scale."

Meanwhile, in Virginia, General Dick Taylor's Louisiana Brigade distinguished itself in Stonewall Jackson's Valley campaign in 1862. Taylor
was promoted to major general and named commander of the District of
Western Louisiana. When he took command at Opelousas, he found the

After the occupation of New Orleans by Federal forces, residents who refused to take an oath of loyalty to the United States were banished to Confederate territory. Here, exiles disembark at Madisonville after being ferried by steamboat across Lake Pontchartrain.

Courtesy the Historic New Orleans Collection; Acc. No. 1974.25.9.15

state virtually helpless. He had no troops, no arms, no supplies, no money. Somehow, between August and October of 1862, Taylor assembled an army of about 6,000 and captured large quantities of stores, guns, and ammunition, and even two Union gunboats. His most successful operation was at Brashear City (now Morgan City) on Berwick Bay. On June 3, 1863, he captured a dozen cannon, 5,000 rifles, a considerable amount of ammunition, and military stores, all worth in excess of a million dollars. Brashear City supplied Taylor with enough material not only for the remainder of 1863, but also for use in the spring of 1864, when the Union began its Red River campaign.

Union general Ulysses Grant's Vicksburg campaign in the spring of 1863 met with effective rebuffs until Grant hit on the plan of swinging down through northeast Louisiana, crossing the Mississippi River below Vicksburg, and attacking the city from the south. He first attempted to dig a canal by which to transport supplies beyond reach of the Vicksburg batteries. This project proving unfeasible, he marched down the river on the Louisiana side anyway, aiming to effect a crossing near Grand Gulf. Grant bombarded Grand Gulf's Confederate defenses but could not silence their batteries. He

Union general Benjamin F. Butler, who ruled New Orleans
after the Federal occupation. His repressive regime caused
residents to hate him.

Courtesy the Historic New Orleans Collection; Acc. No. 1991.59

then marched farther south and made a crossing on April 30. The successful
siege of Vicksburg followed, and on July 4, 1863, the city surrendered.

On July 9, 1863, the Confederacy suffered another irreparable loss when
Port Hudson, north of Baton Rouge, fell after a siege of forty-four days.
Coming less than a week after the fall of Vicksburg, Port Hudson's surrender opened the Mississippi along its whole length to the Union. The great
river now flowed "unvexed to the sea," as President Lincoln put it.

Governor Allen, inaugurated on January 26, 1864, set out at once to
make unoccupied Louisiana self-sufficient. He established state stores, labo-
ratories, foundries, and factories. He sold cotton to Mexico and got in return shoes, coffee, tobacco, flour, machinery, and other things not available
in Louisiana. Amazingly, he restored the value of Confederate paper money,
which elsewhere in the South was practically worthless.

Shortly after Allen took office, the capital—now at Shreveport—became the principal target of General Banks. The Red River campaign was part of a threefold Union plan: Grant would increase his pressure on Lee in Virginia, Sherman would drive southward to Atlanta, and Banks would advance up the Red River, capture Shreveport, and push into Texas.

Banks set out from New Orleans with 26,000 men, supported on the Red River by Admiral David Dixon Porter's fleet of nineteen warships. In addition, a Union force of 10,000 men would march on Shreveport from Arkansas, thus applying a pincer operation on Taylor's little army. With only about 5,000 troops when the campaign opened, Taylor at first could do no more than skirmish and fall back before a force five times the size of his, but at Mansfield, with reinforcements bringing his strength to 8,000, he decided to challenge Banks, whose long wagon train was beginning to tangle the advance.

Taylor placed his army across the road on which Banks was moving. He attacked at 4 P.M. on April 8, having outflanked Banks on both the right and left. General Alfred Mouton, a West Pointer and member of an old Acadian family, was killed, but his troops routed the Federals opposite them. Similar success along the line sent Banks into disorganized retreat. The Confederacy captured two thousand prisoners, two hundred wagons, twenty artillery pieces, and thousands of rifles.

Banks halted his retreat at Pleasant Hill, twenty-three miles below Mansfield. Taylor pursued and attacked on April 9. The failure of a subordinate to flank the Union left resulted in the repulse of Taylor's force. It was a tactical Union success, but it proved to be a strategic Confederate victory when Banks again retreated, this time all the way to Alexandria, where Porter's warships were stranded above the rapids by a drop in the level of the Red River.

Banks' Red River campaign was a disaster, but it would have been even more calamitous without the engineering genius of Lieutenant Colonel Joseph Bailey. Bailey constructed a dam that raised the water sufficiently for Porter's gunboats to slip free and escape. The episode has been called "one of the most imaginative engineering feats of military history."

The Red River campaign represented the last serious fighting in Louisiana. On May 26, 1865—nearly seven weeks after Appomattox—Generals Simon Buckner and Sterling Price surrendered the Trans-Mississippi Department to Union general E. R. S. Canby in New Orleans. It was the final important Confederate surrender of the war.

—C.L.D.

9

Reconstruction

Four years of war, and Louisiana's troubles were only beginning. A land trampled by contending armies now had to grope its way into a new existence for which its people were not prepared. Nearly 350,000 blacks had been emancipated, and most of them had no place to go except back to the cotton and sugarcane fields where they had worked as slaves. The federal government in effect dumped them upon the landowners who had been their masters. In order to produce the crops that were the economic lifeblood of Louisiana, the planters had no choice but to depend on the work of the freedmen, and the landed whites had no experience in dealing with free labor. Besides, fields had largely gone to weed during the war. The deterioration of untended levees left many thousands of acres vulnerable to floods. Roads were impassable when it rained. Land prices had plummeted, severely curtailing the borrowing capacity of planters, and there was a shortage of capital to begin with. It is not surprising that during the twelve years of Reconstruction—1865 until 1877—many people at times went hungry in Louisiana, and there were a few instances of starvation.

The freed slaves, together with some 18,000 blacks who had been free before the war, slightly outnumbered the white population. They had seen their shackles removed by Abraham Lincoln, but the experience of full citizenship was new to them and full of pitfalls. For example, because fearful owners had seen to it that they were not taught to read, most of the former slaves were illiterate—a shortcoming that made it easy to cheat them in legal matters. The breaking of the master-bondsman link left resentments on both sides. Blacks had their first taste of liberty, the opportunity of walking away from a farm if they wished—and if they could afford it. But many had been misled into believing that every freedman would be given forty acres and a mule. Instead, they often ended up working for starvation wages on the same plantations from which they had been freed. The reality of the situation brought disillusionment.

On the other hand, defeat in the war had not diminished the determination of Louisiana whites—planters as well as the yeoman farmers of the northern parishes—to maintain white supremacy. A factor in this sentiment was fear. The blacks were numerous, and they had reason to feel unfriendly toward whites. The only security for whites seemed to lie in keeping them subjugated. In white eyes, it was a matter of self-preservation. In truth, incidents of black violence against whites were few—far fewer than those of white violence against blacks.

Thus, with the surrender of the last Louisiana Confederates in the late spring of 1865, began a period of conflict that only ended with white supremacy firmly established for nearly a century longer. Reconstruction meant a battle involving several thousand men on the streets of New Orleans, massacres of blacks, stolen elections, impeachment of two governors and the ousting of a third, corruption, lynchings, rival governments battling for control, lawlessness, and near-anarchy.

The Reconstruction years from the standpoint of the Bourbons—the traditional name for state's white ruling class—and of others with similar racial views can be summed up in the words of Henry J. Hearsey, editor of the New Orleans *Daily States*, who long afterward wrote:

We bulldozed the negroes; we killed the worst of them; we killed carpetbaggers; we patrolled the roads at midnight; we established in many localities a reign of terror. Why? Not to suppress or restrict the freedom of the ballot. The Republicans had the niggers, the Carpetbaggers, the federal army and navy united in an effort to crush the white people out of the state. We had only our undaunted hearts and fearless arms to defend our liberties, our property and our civilization, and we defeated our oppressors with such resources as God and nature had placed in our hands, and we redeemed our state. (*Daily States*, July 25, 1899)

For blacks, Reconstruction meant elections in which it was possible for them for the first time to vote—that is, those who were not cowed by night riders. It meant some black political officials, even including brief tenures as acting governors. It offered visions of integrated public schools and unlimited access to transportation accommodations. But within a few years the ballot was withdrawn and Jim Crow laws made separation of the races virtually complete.

It may be more accurate to date Reconstruction in Louisiana from 1862 than from the end of the war in 1865. President Lincoln was anxious to begin the process of readmitting seceded states to the Union. He was motivated partly by the realization that Radicals in Congress yearned to punish the rebels, and he feared that harshness would delay and even possibly derail the progress of reconciliation. In order to try to keep the reestablishment of the Republic in the hands of the executive department, he devised his Ten Percent Plan: once 10 percent of a state's 1860 electorate took an oath to support the Union and the legislature voted to abandon slavery, the state would be readmitted.

The efforts to restore Louisiana began under the direction of General Benjamin F. Butler, the first commander of the Federal occupying force, and continued under General Nathaniel P. Banks, Butler's successor. More than the required 10 percent of citizens took the prescribed oath, and in an election on March 28, 1864, Michael Hahn was elected governor and James Madison Wells lieutenant governor. A convention elected by white voters drew up the Constitution of 1864, which abolished slavery. The constitution was adopted by voters in the occupied areas of the state, the vote being 6,836 to 1,566. The first legislature of the new government named Hahn to the United States Senate, and Wells became governor. Wells was elected to a governor's term of his own in November, 1865.

When Andrew Johnson became president upon the assassination of Lincoln, he offered a forgiving hand to returning Confederate soldiers and the rest of the conservative white oligarchy that had ruled Louisiana before secession. Wells also was conciliatory, intent upon ingratiating himself with the white supremacists. The restoration of local government was slow in most of the state. Under the circumstances, the conservatives moved to take the upper hand over their former slaves. A Black Code was adopted that was intended to restrict the movement of blacks and to put them at a disadvantage in their business dealings with the planters who hired them as field hands. Before the war, slaves had some rudimentary protection against physical abuse because they were property with monetary value, which would vanish if they were killed or maimed by assault. Now there was no such deterrent, and the stories of slayings and cruelties circulated in the North, affecting public attitudes about leniency to the rebels.

The pressure built as the black population realized that emancipation had brought them little but more misery. They were influenced by the former free people of color—blacks who had been free before the war and who often were better educated—and by the carpetbaggers, the epithet for outsider whites who wanted to capitalize on the situation.

A movement to reconvene the convention that had framed the 1864 constitution gained strength on the prospect that it could enfranchise Negroes. On July 30, 1866, came the eruption. Governor Wells, who formerly opposed black suffrage, had changed his mind and given official sanction to reopening the 1864 convention. The reconvened body met in the Mechanics Institute in New Orleans. Armed whites outside attacked a body of blacks who came marching from across Canal Street. Many of the blacks sought safety in the institute, and the few who were armed fired from the windows. It was a one-sided confrontation in which 38 men were killed and 147 wounded, almost all of the casualties being blacks.

The Mechanics Institute slaughter may have been a tactical victory for the Conservatives, but it was a strategic disaster. Public outrage in the North helped Radicals in Congress prevail over the policies of President Johnson and, in the spring of 1867, enact the first of the Reconstruction Acts. The legislation decreed that no legal civil government existed in the seceded states and divided the South into military districts. Louisiana and Texas made up a district commanded by General Philip Sheridan, who was as bumbling in political matters as he was brave in battle.

Congress also decreed universal adult male suffrage, except for some Confederate veterans. A registration campaign by Sheridan in 1867 resulted in 78,230 qualified black voters in Louisiana, compared with 41,166 whites. Sheridan ousted the Democratic government of New Orleans and, in a dispute over a minor matter, deposed Wells. The New Orleans *Times*'s editorial response to the removal was a line that has endured: "All's well that ends Wells."

The seething political unrest in Louisiana was accompanied by economic misery. Floods in 1866 and 1867 knocked out thousands of acres of cotton production. From 1868 until 1873, good crops and relatively good prices for cotton and sugar brought a period of moderate prosperity. But the national depression in 1873 and a long downward spiral in cotton prices brought hard times that persisted into the twentieth century. It was during Reconstruction that the sharecropping and crop-lien systems took root, dooming landless blacks and many whites to virtual peonage and inescapable poverty.

A convention composed of whites and blacks drew up a constitution that was adopted in 1868. It provided for black suffrage but disqualified some former Confederates. It was a liberal document for the times, setting up a system of public education and offering full civil rights to all. It represented a period of ascendancy by Republicans and blacks, who had the federal bayonets on their side. One provision lowered the age qualifications for office, enabling twenty-six-year-old Henry Clay Warmoth to win the governorship in 1868. In the same election, General U. S. Grant won his first term as president.

Warmoth was an Illinois-born lawyer who despite his youth had risen to a lieutenant colonelcy in the Union army. Louisiana was not to see his equal in political adroitness until the rise of Huey Pierce Long in the second quarter of the twentieth century. At the same time, he was a racist who insisted he would resist the "Africanization" of Louisiana. Warmoth persuaded the legislature to create a "Returning Board" that destroyed whatever slim chance there may have been that honest elections could be held in the state with the population so divided. The board had the authority to throw out disputed votes as it pleased—in effect, the power to disregard election returns and proclaim whatever results it wanted.

Oscar J. Dunn attained the highest office yet held by a black in Louisiana when he was elected lieutenant governor in 1868. He was almost alone in being widely respected by both whites and blacks. When he died, his place was taken by another black, P. B. S. Pinchback.

Free men of color had established the Republican Party in Louisiana, but whites had taken most of the leadership roles even though the party's strength was in the vote of ex-slaves. As blacks became disenchanted with Warmoth, the so-called Custom House Ring became the influential element in the Radical wing, which opposed Warmoth's moderates. The Custom House in New Orleans was a source of patronage for the federal administration. Prominent members of the ring were Collector of Customs James F. Casey, the brother-in-law of Mrs. U. S. Grant; William Pitt Kellogg, who served as a tax collector immediately after the war; and Stephen B. Packard, United States marshal.

A masked white group that resembled the Ku Klux Klan in its methods and its objectives was organized in St. Mary Parish in 1867 and took the name Knights of the White Camellia. It acquired a statewide membership. There is a question as to whether the KKK, which was active in other southern states, existed in Louisiana during Reconstruction, but the Knights showed the effectiveness of terror in the election of 1868. The aim was to keep blacks from voting, either by threats, by floggings, or sometimes by killing. "Bulldozing," it was called. The Knights wanted to keep Grant out of the White House.

In Opelousas, an editor who favored the Radicals was horsewhipped and driven out of town. Blacks came to his aid, and four of them were killed in the exchange of gunfire. A dozen blacks were arrested. During the night they were taken from jail and shot to death. A "Negro hunt" began. Democrats admitted killing thirty freedmen; Radicals contended that more than two hundred actually were slain. In Bossier Parish a mob of whites reportedly from Arkansas killed several blacks. After two whites were slain, a gang of about one hundred whites began to shoot blacks indiscriminately. Democrats estimated that more than forty were killed; Republicans said it was more than a hundred. An Italian merchant was killed in St. Bernard Parish and his store burned by blacks. A body of Sicilian immigrants who called themselves "the Innocents" marched in from New Orleans and conducted another "Negro hunt." The toll is uncertain. In late September a clash on Canal Street in New Orleans between Democrats and Radicals resulted in several deaths. The supervisor of registration in St. Landry Parish said, "I am convinced that no man could have voted any other than the Democratic ticket and not been killed within twenty-four hours." The election returns show how well bulldozing worked. Democratic nominee Horatio Seymour received 80,225 votes in Louisiana against 33,225 for Grant. New Orleans had more than 20,000 registered Republicans, but Grant received only 300 votes.

Warmoth was a nineteenth-century Kingfish during the first years of his term. He could have his way with the legislature and run the state as he wished. White Democrats took it for granted that his administration was corrupt. He did leave office a rich man, yet the evidence indicates that he may have taken advantage of investment opportunities rather than plundering the treasury. As the 1872 election approached, however, he found himself losing almost all of his black support, coming under fire from his Custom House enemies, and lambasted by Conservative Democrats.

The Radical Republicans nominated Kellogg, of the Custom House Ring, for governor. Warmoth joined the Democrats in an uneasy alliance that supported John McEnery. Meanwhile, the Radicals were maneuvering in the legislature to impeach Warmoth.

Both sides claimed victory in the election, and in the confusion two rival return boards certified different results. The upshot was that on January 13, 1873, Kellogg and his administration took the oath of office in the Mechanics Institute while at the same hour McEnery was being sworn in before a mammoth crowd in Lafayette Square. For a little longer than four years, Louisiana would have dual governments—and almost uninterrupted violence. Meanwhile, Warmoth was impeached by the state house of representatives, but his term as governor ended before the senate could try him.

On March 5 McEnery had his militia attack Kellogg's police station in the Cabildo, facing on Jackson Square. Three men were killed and eight wounded before U.S. troops intervened. McEnery would not defy the federal government.

The Cabildo battle was only a skirmish compared with an outbreak that occurred at Colfax, in Grant Parish, on April 13, Easter Sunday. Colfax, although the parish seat, scarcely qualified as a town, being mainly a group of old plantation buildings high on the banks of the Red River. The plantation's brick stable served as the courthouse. White Republicans of the Kellogg faction took over this building in opposition to McEnery men, and the Kellogg sheriff, expecting trouble, deputized a number of local blacks. Bands of armed whites soon appeared in the parish, and some 150 black farmers from the outlying area gathered at Colfax, with their families, seeking safety in numbers. There the white force confronted them.

On Easter morning, the whites demanded that the blacks lay down their weapons, which were mostly shotguns. The blacks refused. The whites gave them half an hour to evacuate women and children, then attacked. The two sides were roughly equal in number, but the whites, armed with rifles and even a small artillery piece, had greatly superior firepower. After a few blasts from the cannon, the blacks broke. One large group ran for the river. Mounted whites gunned them down at the water's edge, killing all but one. Riders also chased down and shot those attempting to reach the woods, although a few managed to escape that way. About sixty blacks took shelter in the courthouse. The attackers torched the roof. When the blaze forced the men out, they were cut down by volleys of rifle fire.

During the fight some forty blacks—the exact number is in dispute— were taken prisoner. That night, their captors shot them all. Only one, an old man who feigned death after bullets struck his back and face, survived. According to the Seventh Cavalry officer who investigated the massacre, at least 105 blacks were killed. Three whites died, two apparently by the fire of their own companions.

On May 22 President Grant publicly recognized Kellogg as the governor and ordered "turbulent and disorderly persons to disperse and retire peaceably to their respective abodes." Nine white men were tried in New Orleans for murder, but in the long run the only successful prosecution resulted in the conviction of three for violating the civil rights of blacks. Even that verdict was overturned by the United States Supreme Court, which ruled that the Fourteenth Amendment did not give the federal government power to try citizens for crimes punishable under state law. The Colfax Massacre, by demonstrating the inability of Washington to enforce the Reconstruction Acts, was a turning point in the battle of Louisiana whites to control the state.

Early in 1874 the formation of White Leagues began throughout the state. There was little, if any, effort to conceal their militant supremacist nature. Members wanted the word to spread that a new force was in being. By the end of August, the state White Leagues had 14,000 armed members. There were not nearly that many occupying Union troops in Louisiana.

The White Leagues opened a campaign against Republicans who held parish offices as a result of the disputed 1872 election. Several hundred gun-bearing men would ride into a parish seat and surround the courthouse. Some would display ropes with nooses. The leaders would demand the resignations of Republican officials, and under the circumstances there were few refusals. The Leagues showed their force in Natchitoches, St. Martin, Iberia, Lincoln, Avoyelles, and Claiborne Parishes, but nowhere more flagrantly and viciously than in Red River Parish, where a young man named Marshall Twitchell headed a Republican government with the solid support of the parish's 70-percent black majority.

Twitchell, a Vermonter who fought for the Union throughout the war and was severely wounded at the Battle of the Wilderness, had arrived in northwest Louisiana in 1865 as an agent of the Freedmen's Bureau. The following year he met and married a local girl. He prospered as a planter and businessman. In 1870, he brought his mother and other relatives down from Vermont. The following year, Red River Parish was created. By 1874, the parish seat, Coushatta, which had been a two-house landing in 1865, had grown into a thriving little rivertown, thanks largely to the enterprise of Twitchell and his brother and brothers-in-law, all of whom became involved in local government. Unfortunately for them, they were still carpetbaggers, and thus targets.

In August of 1874, Twitchell left Coushatta to attend the state Republican convention in New Orleans. In his absence a band of whites attacked and killed two black men, one of whom fought back, killing one of the whites. That was sufficient provocation. Hundreds of White Leaguers from as far away as Texas swarmed into Coushatta. Six Republican officials, among them Twitchell's brother and two of his brothers-in-law, as well as the sheriff and the parish attorney, were taken prisoner and forced to resign their offices and swear to leave the state. The six were taken under armed escort toward Shreveport. In Caddo Parish a lynch mob overtook them. The escort made no resistance as three of the prisoners were shot dead on the spot. The other three were executed firing-squad-style a few hours later. No one was ever brought to justice for the murders. As in the aftermath of the Colfax Massacre, the impotence of the government to combat lynching and terrorism was obvious.

On September 14, 1874, just weeks after the Coushatta episode, the climactic event of Reconstruction in Louisiana occurred in New Orleans. Two days earlier, the steamer *Mississippi* had docked with a cargo of rifles and ammunition for the local White League. Governor Kellogg ordered the shipment seized. Answering a summons from the White League, five thousand New Orleanians gathered around the Clay Statue, at the intersection of Canal Street and St. Charles Avenue. The men were instructed to arm themselves and return that afternoon. Meanwhile, D. B. Penn, the Democratic lieutenant governor, in the prearranged absence of Governor McEnery, directed the preparation of a fortified line extending on Poydras Street from St. Charles to the river. Streetcars were overturned as part of a barricade intended as a fallback position in case a retreat from the expected scene of action on Canal Street became necessary.

The Battle of Liberty Place, as it came to be known, was fought that afternoon after Kellogg rejected a demand that he resign. About 8,400 White Leaguers and their allies faced 500 members of the Metropolitan Police, perhaps 100 other police officers, and some 3,000 blacks of Kellogg's militia, commanded by General James Longstreet, a former corps commander in the Confederate army who had made his peace with the federals and become Kellogg's adjutant general, and by General Algernon S. Badger. Kellogg took refuge in the Custom House, where a contingent of federal troops was stationed, and had a closeup view of the fighting, marked by artillery and rifle fire from both sides. The battle lasted only about fifteen minutes before the Metropolitan Police and their allies were routed. General Badger was badly wounded. Eleven Metropolitans were killed, sixty wounded. Twenty-one White Leaguers were killed, nineteen wounded.

The Battle of Liberty Place as drawn for a popular newspaper of the day, published in New York. The original caption, "The Metropolitan Police Attacking Citizens on the Levee near the Custom House," suggests that the writer was not altogether neutral in his view of the event.

Courtesy the Historic New Orleans Collection; Acc. No. 1974.25.9.315

As acting governor, Penn took charge of all state offices in New Orleans after the battle, while Kellogg remained out of sight. But the next day President Grant ordered "turbulent persons to disperse within five days and to submit to the laws and constituted authorities of the State." Upon demand of the commander of federal troops, the White Leaguers surrendered their weapons. Meanwhile, Grant had dispatched three warships and reinforcing troops to New Orleans. McEnery yielded, saying he had no intention of making war against the United States.

After Liberty Place, it was obvious that Kellogg could attempt to function as governor only as long as he had the protection of United States soldiers, but the Democrats still were stymied. Two legislatures continued to hold sessions, but remained ineffective. A congressional committee held that the Democrats had won a majority in the house of representatives and the Republicans in the senate. Congressman William A. Wheeler of New York, later vice-president, proposed a compromise under which a house dominated by Democrats would be recognized along with a senate having a Republican majority. Part of the deal was an understanding that the house would not impeach Kellogg. The compromise broke down when the house did bring out articles of impeachment, but the senate immediately voted to exonerate Kellogg.

As their candidate for governor in the election of 1876, the Democrats nominated Francis T. Nicholls, who had lost an arm and foot while fighting in the Confederate army. The leader of the Custom House Ring, Stephen B. Packard, carried the Republican banner. In the same election, Samuel J. Tilden was the Democratic nominee for president, opposing Republican Rutherford B. Hayes. Once more the bulldozers roamed through the countryside in the familiar campaign aimed at keeping Republican voters away from the polls. White Republicans were slain in Ouachita, Red River, Caddo, Natchitoches, and East Baton Rouge Parishes. Federal troops were on duty at voting precincts in some parishes, and election day, November 7, was peaceful. An example of the thoroughness of the bulldozers was provided by East Feliciana Parish, where there was a heavy Republican registration. Not a single vote was recorded there for Hayes.

Preliminary returns indicated that Tilden had received 84,000 votes and Hayes 76,000, with Nicholls the winner over Packard by a similar count. But the count of the Returning Board was the only one that mattered in Louisiana, or so state law said, and that fact was to have nationwide significance. In the national election, Tilden won 184 undisputed electoral college votes, and needed only 1 more to be elected. But there were challenges to 20 electoral votes—1 in Oregon and the rest in Louisiana, Florida, and South Carolina. Only the Oregon vote was a surety for Hayes, and he would have to capture all 19 of the other disputed votes in order to be president. The three southern states involved were the only ones in which the presence of federal troops meant that Reconstruction was continuing eleven years after the war ended. In all three, Democrats and Republicans disputed the outcome of the election. The Democratic nominees who claimed the governorships certified to Congress that Tilden was entitled to their electoral votes; the Republican claimants attested to a Hayes victory. For the only time in history, Congress was given the responsibility of deciding who had been elected president.

According to some historians, former governor Wells, a member of the Returning Board, asked bribes of $200,000 from Republicans in Washington on behalf of himself and fellow board member T. C. Anderson, in return for which they would certify Hayes as the Louisiana winner. Unable to make a deal with the Republicans, Wells then allegedly dickered on an arrangement to deliver the state's vote to Tilden. No agreement was reached. On December 5, the Returning Board threw out enough Tilden votes to make the state total favor Hayes.

On January 8, 1877, a by-now-familiar spectacle was reenacted in New Orleans. At the St. Louis Hotel—the statehouse at the time—Packard was inaugurated as governor and a legislature seated. In Lafayette Square, Nicholls took the oath, and a legislature convened in St. Patrick Hall. For three and a half months Packard holed up in the hotel under the guard of Metropolitan Police. A unit of federal soldiery was billeted in an adjacent hotel, but by now President Grant was unwilling to make a show of force except to prevent a riot.

Meanwhile, confronted by an unprecedented situation, Congress created an electoral commission to sort out the rival claims to the presidency. Behind the scenes, there were talks among politicians representing the Congress and the states having the disputed electoral votes. Governor Nicholls was willing for Hayes to be president if at the same time Nicholls would be recognized as the legal governor and the federal troops would be withdrawn from Louisiana. The Democratic claimants in Florida and South Carolina also were prepared to sacrifice Tilden's hopes on similar terms. The electoral commission by eight to seven votes awarded the prize to Hayes barely in time for him to take the oath of office on the scheduled day, March 4. The Democrats had a majority in the national House and could have upset the arrangements, but the negotiators had done their job expertly, and the deal stood up.

Having taken the presidency partly on the basis of disputed votes in Louisiana, Hayes found himself in the ticklish position of conceding the same votes to the Democrat Nicholls. But after some face-saving maneuvers, he ordered Reconstruction ended in Louisiana. On April 24, 1877, the contingent of federal troops in New Orleans withdrew to Jackson Barracks in the first step toward leaving the state. Without protection from outside, Packard's hopes collapsed, and he and his Radical office claimants decamped.

The Bourbons emerged from the ordeal with their political and economic mastery nailed down. It was only a question of time before they would take away all of the gains that blacks had realized from the war and from federal intervention—everything, that is, except emancipation from slavery. Not until the civil rights movement in the second half of the twentieth century would half of the population gain the right to vote, to integrated schools, to equal access to public facilities.

—J.W.

10

Race

Slaves dreaded to be sold "down the river" to toil in Louisiana cotton or cane fields. C. Duncan Rice, in *The Rise and Fall of Black Slavery*, writes that the state "gained a reputation which made it the most terrifying of all the various hells of the deep South to which blacks from the older slave economies of the tidewater states could be sold." Not all historians share this harsh judgment, but it was not by happenstance alone that Harriet Beecher Stowe, in *Uncle Tom's Cabin*, chose the country near Natchitoches as the site of the plantation where Simon Legree cracked his whip.

Later, for a turbulent century after emancipation, Louisiana continued to be a troubled land for African Americans, most of whom found that they had traded slavery for what amounted to peonage. The cotton and sugar economy would have collapsed without cheap black labor. White landowners, merchants, and financiers, even while fearing and scorning blacks, had somehow to keep the field hands at work. There was no escape at the time for blacks, no place to get away from economic, social, and political repression. As historian William Ivy Hair notes in *Carnival of Fury*, "Somehow, the commingling of English-speaking and Creole-Cajun cultures had resulted in a milieu of political instability and unusual insensitivity to human rights." Events of a hundred years bear him out.

The history of blacks in Louisiana begins in the early colonial period when a few slaves—they numbered 20 in 1712—were imported from the West Indies. Joe Gray Taylor states in *Negro Slavery in Louisiana* that from the start, the economic development of the French colony depended upon a supply of slaves. Antoine Crozat's 1712 patent allowed importation of one shipload of blacks each year, although while he was in control none was brought from Africa. John Law's Mississippi Company charter required the introduction of 3,000 slaves each year, but the company was unable to supply anything like that number despite continual demands from the colonists.

In 1724 Bienville, then acting governor, put into effect the *Code Noir*, or Black Code, which regulated the practice of slavery as long as the colony remained French. The code gave owners almost total power over their chattels but also contained some humanitarian provisions, such as prohibiting the separation of young children from their mothers.

The fear of a slave rebellion was ever-present among whites, even though actual uprisings were rare in Louisiana. One large conspiracy was discovered in 1795. It developed on and around the plantation of Julien Poydras at Pointe Coupée, 150 miles upriver from New Orleans. The slaves undoubtedly were stirred by two events: the revolt in Haiti in 1791 in which François Dominique Toussaint-L'Ouverture and his fellow black countrymen threw off French rule, and the French Revolution, which emboldened dissidents in the New World—indeed, the revolutionary government had abolished slavery in France's colonies, and recorded testimony suggests that the Point Coupée slaves believed the Spanish authorities were keeping them in bondage unlawfully. Fifty-seven slaves were arrested. Twenty-three were hanged, the rest sentenced to floggings and imprisonment at hard labor. Three white men were found guilty of taking part in the conspiracy. All were deported, two being further sentenced to prison terms in Cuba.

In 1811 one of the largest slave uprisings in United States history erupted at what now is Norco, between Baton Rouge and New Orleans. From about 180 to as many as 500 slaves—the accounts vary—armed mainly with pitchforks, hoes, and other farm implements, started a march to New Orleans, burning, pillaging, and killing as they went. United States troops from Baton Rouge, militia from New Orleans, and a hurriedly gathered force of landowners from the West Bank intercepted the rebels. Sixty-six slaves were killed in the ensuing battle. Sixteen alleged leaders were captured, tried, and executed by firing squad. Their heads were staked on poles along the riverbank as a grim warning to others. Rebellion for slaves was hopeless. The whites had the upper hand, and the guns.

If white planters were anxious about possible slave revolts, it did nothing to blunt their hunger for more slaves. Despite an embargo on the introduction of foreign slaves into the Territory of Orleans in 1804 and a complete ban on the importation of slaves into any part of the United States in 1808, the number of slaves in Louisiana continued to grow. The census figures:

1810 34,660
1820 69,064
1830 109,558
1840 168,452

The prime sources of this rising flood of human property were old-line slave states such as Virginia and South Carolina, where slaves had become so plentiful as to form a major export commodity. Although the importation of foreign slaves was banned, it was perfectly legal to sell slaves across

The original caption of this etching—"Sale of Estates, Pictures and Slaves"—underscores
the fact that slaves were regarded as a form of property to be bought and sold like any other.
The setting of this auction was the Rotunda in New Orleans.

Courtesy the Historic New Orleans Collection; Acc. No. 1953.149

state lines. Of course, there were also other, less legitimate channels of supply. An able-bodied male slave could fetch as much as $1,300 in the New
Orleans auction, the same man who might be obtained for $300 or less in
Havana. Such profits could not be resisted by pirates or privateers, including Jean Lafitte and Louis-Michel Aury, and slave smuggling became a
wholesale activity. The buccaneers halted ships bound for the West Indies,
seized the slaves huddled below deck, and took them to Louisiana. Lafitte
sold as many as four hundred in a day at his hangout on Grand Terre. Aury
sometimes landed his booty near the entrance to Bayou Lafourche and
marched the Africans to the market at Alexandria.

By the outbreak of the Civil War, the cotton and sugar produced by
more than 300,000 slaves had made Louisiana one of the most prosperous
states in the Union. Per capita wealth was the second-highest in the nation, and property in 1860 was valued at $602 million. The wartime Fed-
eral occupation of some sections of the state and the campaigning in other
areas disrupted farming. Thousands of slaves abandoned their plantations

when Northern troops moved in. A rapid decline in the state's fortunes began, and by 1880 the total value of Louisiana property had sunk to $422 million and the state's per capita wealth ranked only thirty-seventh. For the next six decades Louisianians learned the meaning of poverty.

The twelve years between the end of the war and the departure of the last occupying troops were marked by a struggle for political, economic, and social control. A new way of life, without slavery, had to be established, and it was the plantation owners, bankers, and merchants who prevailed. In an age before mechanization, the state's major cash crops could be planted and harvested only by an army of low-paid workers.

Obviously, the situation was explosive, with about half of the population made up of ex-slaves, who outnumbered the whites in some parishes, living hand-to-mouth and seeing little hope for improvement. Almost none could read, and few had been prepared to live in a free society. Whites were quick to move against suspected agitators. The accepted wisdom was that blacks had to be cowed in order to be controlled, and most whites were ready and willing to act accordingly. The environment was wholly racist. Among influential whites there was general agreement that blacks should not vote, should not attend mixed schools, and should be segregated in public facilities. By the end of the nineteenth century all of these goals had been attained in Louisiana.

Despite the travails of Reconstruction, the period was a memorable one for the blacks. Under federal dictate, enforced by the presence of soldiers, many were able to vote. Jim Crow laws were wiped off the books, and the state constitution called for unsegregated educational opportunities (although in truth there were few schools of any kind for black children). Then the occupying troops marched away. Very quickly, the Bourbons began turning Louisiana into a bastion of white supremacy.

The key to a white-dominated society was the ballot. In 1880 there were 88,024 blacks registered to vote and 85,451 whites. In 1888 black registration had climbed to 128,150 against 124,407 whites. The figures seem to suggest that blacks were holding their ground, but that is an illusion. Actually, the conservative Democrats did not want to provoke any action by northern Republicans such as might occur if there were an immediate wholesale purging of the voting rolls. Instead, the strategy was to use terrorism to keep blacks from the polls, or else to allow them to vote but to count them out in the official tally. For years the election results in the parishes most heavily populated by Negroes showed lopsided majorities for the Bourbon candidates.

After a few years, the prospect of northern interference had lessened and the time had come to keep blacks from the polls by denying them registration. The constitutional convention of 1898 provided for the payment of a poll tax, required a literacy test that gave a parish registrar of voters the license to reject any applicant that he chose, and added a property-owning qualification. Black registration plummeted to 1,342 in 1904 and to only 598 in 1922. Former slaves and their descendants no longer were a factor in Louisiana elections.

Planters who used bulldozing methods to prevent blacks from voting were likely to be no gentler in their efforts to keep the labor upon which they depended. In 1879 what was known as "Kansas fever" swept over the plantations, and a movement called the "exodus" developed. Excited by reports of opportunity and better treatment for blacks in Kansas, as many as 10,000 farmhands left the state, most of them on steamboats. Some 50,000 others tried to make their getaway but either failed to obtain passage or were detained, many by landowners to whom they owed money. Some black leaders argued against the departure. In his newspaper, P. B. S. Pinchback, the former lieutenant governor, called it a wild goose chase. Crowds gathered on the levees of the Mississippi and other rivers as the "exodusters" sought to board steamboats.

William Ivy Hair notes that the threat of leaving won concessions, such as the forgiveness of debts, for some blacks. There was no forgiveness, however, by cane planters in 1887 when black workers, organized by the Knights of Labor, struck in demand for a dollar a day wage. In November the threat of a freeze put the year's ungathered crop in peril and precipitated a crisis. Hundreds of the strikers and their families had gathered in Thibodaux. A skirmish developed between strikers and gunmen imported by the growers. It turned into a battle in which at least thirty blacks were killed and a hundred others wounded. The strike collapsed.

The determination of the ruling Bourbons to impose segregation in transportation accommodations in Louisiana led to one of the most momentous decisions ever rendered by the Supreme Court of the United States, the *Plessy* v. *Ferguson* ruling in 1896 that relegated the nation's blacks to second-rate citizenship throughout the first half of the twentieth century and well into the second half.

In 1890 the Louisiana legislature had adopted Act 111, which ordained that railroads must require black passengers to ride in cars separate from those reserved for whites. Ironically, there were eighteen black members of the legislature, since the complete exclusion of blacks from the political process had not yet begun. Railroads opposed the act because of the expense of adding segregated cars to trains.

In 1891 a group of New Orleans blacks, most of whom had been free men of color in the days of slavery, organized the Comité des Citoyens for the purpose of contesting Act 111. The first challenge came on February 24, 1892, when Daniel F. Desdunes, described as an "octoroon" (a person of one-eighth black and seven-eighths white lineage), courted arrest by entering a car reserved for whites on a train bound for Mobile, Alabama. The test misfired when Judge John H. Ferguson of the Louisiana criminal court, ruling that the law was a burden on interstate commerce, ordered Desdunes freed from custody.

The committee tried again on June 7. Homer Adolph Plessy boarded an East Louisiana Railroad train with a ticket for Covington. He informed the conductor that he was an octoroon and then took a seat in a white coach. By prearrangement, he was arrested and released under $500 bond pending a hearing before Judge Ferguson. This time Ferguson held Act 111 constitutionally applicable, since Covington is in Louisiana and no interstate travel was involved. The Louisiana State Supreme Court upheld Ferguson's ruling.

Albion Winegar Tourgée and James C. Walker, white lawyers retained by the Comité des Citoyens, took an appeal to the Supreme Court of the United States and in April, 1896, argued *Plessy* v. *Ferguson* before the justices at Washington. On May 18 the Court, by a seven-to-one vote, upheld the constitutionality of the act. The only dissent came from Justice John Marshall Harlan, a former slaveowner from Kentucky. One of the sentences in his opinion has lived on: "Our constitution is color blind, and neither knows nor tolerates classes among its citizens." Plessy eventually paid a $25 fine.

Plessy v. *Ferguson* became the legal basis upon which racial relations in the United States—or certainly the southern states—were governed for one day less than sixty years. By ruling that constitutional guarantees were satisfied if so-called separate-but-equal facilities were provided for blacks, the Court gave official blessing to the apparatus that would lead to all-out segregation. Finally, on May 17, 1954, the Court reversed itself in the case of *Brown* v. *Board of Education* and thus touched off the racial revolution of the 1960s and 1970s.

But *Brown* v. *Board of Education* was far in the future as the nineteenth century, a hundred years of racial tension, slid into the twentieth. And just on the cusp of those centuries a fierce racial flareup seared New Orleans— the Robert Charles riots. Robert Charles, Mississippi-born, was like many other young black men who left cotton or cane fields for the cities, where they competed for jobs with unskilled whites—a new source of resentment between the races. One night in July of 1900, Charles was sitting on a residential doorstep in New Orleans waiting to meet a black maid who worked in the neighborhood. A white policeman confronted him. There was a scuffle, then an exchange of gunfire. Both men were wounded. Charles fled to his rooming house. There he killed two officers sent to capture him, and fled again. He hid out in a frame house on Saratoga Street. For three days while police searched for him, marauding gangs of whites roamed the city shooting or beating every black they could find.

When Charles's refuge was discovered, he shot the first two policemen who tried to reach him. Hundreds of lawmen and armed civilians surrounded the house, pouring rifle and pistol fire into it—afterward, five thousand bullet holes were counted. Somehow Charles held out, sniping with deadly accuracy at anyone he saw. An attempt to smoke him out with a smoldering mattress ended in setting the wooden house ablaze. Driven out by the flames, Charles died in a rain of bullets. He had killed or wounded twenty-seven persons, including seven policemen. The rioters had killed a dozen blacks and injured fifty others.

The Robert Charles riots were uncommon in the magnitude of the violence, but violence itself was far from uncommon in matters of race. William Hair's observation about "unusual insensitivity to human rights" by Louisianians undoubtedly was prompted in part by the frequency with which mobs carried out lynchings. One count indicates that between 1882 and 1952, at least 391 persons were lynched in the state, 335 of them blacks. In 1923 a publication reported that three Louisiana parishes—Ouachita, with 19; Caddo, with 18; and Bossier, with 15—led all other counties in the United States in the number of lynchings.

Ku Klux Klan activity in the state arose, peaked, and subsided in the decade of the 1920s. The historian Kenneth Earl Harrell has investigated the affairs of the hooded order and estimates the top membership in the state at about 25,000. The stronghold was Shreveport, where about 4,500 men wore the robes. Although blacks were the primary victims of Klan killings and beatings, the organization also opposed the Roman Catholic Church and made little headway in south Louisiana, where members of the faith were numerous.

The impact of *Brown* began to be felt in Louisiana in the late 1950s and hit with full force in the 1960s as the federal government moved to implement the the Supreme Court ruling that blacks have the civil rights due to all citizens. New Orleanians had a sample of what was to come in 1958

From the end of Reconstruction well into the second half of the twentieth century, white Louisiana devoted incalculable effort to keeping blacks intimidated, submissive, and "in their place." Few relics of the period express its prevailing atmosphere as clearly as this statue, erected in Natchitoches in 1927 in "grateful recognition of the arduous and faithful service of the good darkies of Louisiana." The statue stood on the town's main street for some forty years, but during the civil rights revolution of the 1960s, it ended up in the nearby Cane River. It was later donated to Louisiana State University's Rural Life Museum.

Photo by Jim Zietz

when segregated seating on streetcars and buses was ended. The real show-down came in 1960 when the desegregation of public schools in New Orleans was ordered by federal district judge J. Skelly Wright. Governor Jimmie H. Davis and the legislature tried every ploy that diehard lawyers could devise to circumvent Wright's directive, but the judge struck down each as soon as it was enacted. Four little black girls were led through a crowd of snarling, threatening women into the William Frantz school.

Despite the turmoil, it was clear that some whites had changed their racial attitudes, or at least were ready to accept integration. Several score of professional, mercantile, and financial leaders published a public appeal for an end to the demonstrations and acceptance of changes that were inevitable. The signers, every one, had credentials that would have included them among the so-called Bourbons who in years past had subjugated blacks. By 1960, the fiercest partisans of white supremacy were White Citizens Councils and their sympathizers.

The decisive initiative in the national civil rights campaign was the drive to ensure voting privileges for blacks. Barriers to registration were broken down and federal observers assigned to polls to enforce laws allowing every adult citizen to exercise his or her right to cast a ballot. As the percentage of blacks in the electorate rapidly increased, politicians had no choice but to respond to the new reality.

An early beneficiary was Moon Landrieu, an avowed liberal who as a state representative had cast the lone vote in the state legislature in 1960 against the measures that would have blocked school integration in New Orleans. With the help of black votes, he was elected to two terms as mayor of New Orleans. John J. McKeithen, who worked to put out racial fires in his first term as governor, beginning in 1964, won black support for his second term. The first major candidate for state office to openly court black votes was Edwin W. Edwards, who by 1991 had won four terms as governor—incontrovertible evidence that a new era in Louisiana politics had dawned. Ernest N. Morial became the first black mayor of New Orleans, serving two terms before being succeeded by another black candidate, Sidney J. Barthelemy, who in turn was followed by Morial's son, Marc.

—J.W.

11

Economy

Feast or famine, boom or bust, rags or riches: The Louisiana economy seldom, if ever, has known a middle ground.

No state in the Union came better endowed with natural resources: rich soil and an equable climate, a Midas trove of oil and gas, the most favorable of geographic locations in a burgeoning era for the American republic, a river on which a big share of the nation's commerce flowed. Yet in nearly three centuries of history, periods of poverty have outnumbered the heady times when Louisianians enjoyed the fruits of their advantages.

The first of only two golden ages began in the 1830s when the cotton and sugar produced by a multitude of slaves brought riches to the planters and relative prosperity to many other Louisianians—excepting, of course, the slaves themselves. The epoch ended with the Civil War and emancipation, and succeeding generations knew deprivation and frustration as an economy based mostly on agriculture lagged behind in an America rushing to industrialize. The second era of prosperity began in World War II when torpedo boats and landing craft built in New Orleans helped win battles from Normandy to Iwo Jima and the state's workers were busier making things than they were growing things. In the postwar decades, jobs and profits soared as the floor of the Gulf of Mexico became the new frontier for the petroleum industry, rockets built in New Orleans started Americans on the way to the moon, and refineries and chemical plants proliferated along the banks of the Mississippi River.

The colonial century—1699 until 1803, to be precise—passed without Louisiana's ever coming close to economic self-sufficiency. Antoine Crozat and even John Law could not withstand the drain of a proprietary colony, and the French government was happy in 1762 to cede the expensive dependency to the Spanish. Under pressure from Americans in the Kentucky-Tennessee-Ohio area who wanted an outlet at New Orleans for shipment of their goods to Europe, the West Indies, and the Atlantic coastal states, the new owners grudgingly lowered the bars against trade. Flatboats, keelboats, and rafts came floating down the Mississippi bearing salt meat, hides, bear grease, and flour. In 1801 nearly six hundred riverboats landed at New Orleans. Opportunities opened up for Louisiana traders and shippers, but the colony still was producing only a trickle of goods for sale in world markets. One cash crop, indigo, exported in modest quantities for decades, was in steep decline at century's end, its Louisiana planters losing out to competition from the East Indies and, eventually, to chemical dyes. Other exports included tobacco, meat, tar, pitch, rope, and tafia—the last a rough-edged rum made from cane juice. Near the end of the Spanish period, Etienne Boré developed his method of processing Louisiana cane into sugar, and shipments of this commodity began. Nevertheless, despite new opportunities, Louisiana continued to be a burden on the Spanish royal treasury, and Napoleon Bonaparte's decision to reclaim the colony for France was not unwelcome.

A new era dawned with the Louisiana Purchase, followed by statehood and sealed with victory in the Battle of New Orleans, removing the last threat of takeover by a foreign power. In these same years, the spread of a technological advance paved the way to the antebellum boom: Eli Whitney's gin facilitated the separation of cotton lint from the seed, allowing production on a boundless scale. American growers who had worn out the fields in the Atlantic seaboard states migrated by the thousands to the fertile lands of the Deep South, including Louisiana. Many of the newcomers settled in the northern part of the state, which soon became one of the nation's most productive cotton areas. Meanwhile, Boré's sugar-granulating process was setting off a phenomenal development in cane growing in the southern part of the state, rivaling and even eclipsing the expansion of cotton in the northern parishes.

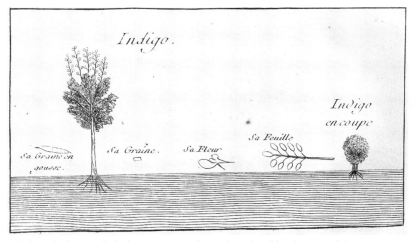

Indigo, the leaves of which were processed to make a deep blue dye, served the Louisiana colony as its first moderately successful cash crop.

Courtesy the Historic New Orleans Collection; Acc. No. 1980.205.40

Cotton and cane: they were the dynamite in the veritable explosion in Louisiana's population and economy that followed statehood. From just under 50,000 at the time of the Purchase, the number of inhabitants multiplied to more than 700,000 in 1860. The brightest years, a peak of prosperity that would not be matched for nearly a century, lasted from the middle 1830s until the Civil War. It was a time when New Orleans, with a population of 102,193 in 1840, was the third largest American city, with exports that sometimes exceeded New York's. During the period, Louisiana's per capita income became the second-highest in the nation. The productivity of the state's fields was storied. In 1853 the output was 449,000 hogsheads of sugar, each weighing 1,000 pounds. In 1860 cotton production was nearly 800,000 bales at 400 pounds each. The palatial plantation mansions that now attract steady streams of sightseers remain as testimony to this era of wealth.

The busy scenes in the countryside had their counterpart in the port of New Orleans, which with the advent of the steamboat in 1812 had solidified its place as a world shipping center. A visitor in the middle 1830s, Colonel James Creecy, picked up his pen to record a paean:

> With what astonishment did I, for the first time, view the magnificent levee, from one point or horn of the beauteous crescent to the other, covered with active human beings of all nations and colors, and boxes, bales, bags, hogsheads, pipes, barrels, kegs of goods, wares and merchandise from all ends of the earth! Thousands of bales of cotton, tierces of sugar, molasses; quantities of flour, pork, lard, grain and other provisions; leads, furs, &c., from the rich and extensive rivers above; and the wharves lined for miles with ships, steamers, flatboats, arks, &c. four deep! The business appearance of this city is not surpassed by any other in the wide world: it might be likened to a huge beehive, where no drones could find a resting place. I stepped on shore, and my first exclamation was, "This is the place for a business man!"

No boom lasts forever, and Louisiana's antebellum splurge could not survive changes in the conditions that triggered it. For all its wealth, the state had failed to develop a substantial industrial base. In the decade of the 1850s, the number of Louisianians working in foundries, shipyards, and other manufacturing enterprises never exceeded nine thousand. Millions of bales of cotton passed over the New Orleans levee destined for textile mills in Europe and New England, but almost none was processed in the state. One problem was that the machinery of the era was largely steam-driven, and Louisiana was a long way from the coal mines that provided the best fuel for the boilers. Vast deposits of oil and gas lay underground, but years would pass before their potential was realized.

Another unmet challenge came from new shipping routes and a new means of transport. At the time of the Purchase, the only outlet for products of the Ohio Valley was down the Mississippi River and through New Orleans. But within a few years, a canal system in the East opened a short-cut to the Atlantic coast, and New Orleans lost its monopoly on water-borne commerce in the heart of the continent. Then, beginning in the 1830s and rapidly expanding, railroads offered a faster alternative for shippers who had previously used the steamboat.

By the 1850s a time bomb was ticking on the sugar and cotton plantations where most of the state's economic well-being originated. The planting and harvesting of the two cash crops depended upon slave labor. As planters profited from an increasing demand, they imported more and more slaves, until in 1860 the census showed more than 331,000 of them in Louisiana, approximately one-half of the population. The voices of abolitionists in the northern states were growing louder and more urgent, and as the nineteenth century passed the halfway point, it became obvious that a crisis was nearing, a showdown that would decide whether slavery was to endure. Since their fortunes were tied to slavery, the landowners cast their lots with the Confederacy and took Louisiana with them.

The Civil War was an economic debacle for the state, with effects that persisted into the middle of the twentieth century. Almost at the first shot, the halcyon years abruptly ended. With the Federal blockade in the Gulf of Mexico, the cotton and sugar already on hand could not be delivered to the market. By 1862 there was fighting in Louisiana, and for the rest of the war, agriculture was disrupted. Slaves deserted plantations upon the approach of Union forces. The levee systems largely collapsed because there were few laborers and almost no engineers to maintain them; as a result, postwar floods took thousands of acres out of production.

The economic effects of emancipation were no less drastic than the changes wrought in the state's social and political structure. In one stroke, freeing the slaves wiped out hundreds of millions of dollars of the assets of their owners. No longer could workers be put up as collateral for loans needed for operating farms until crops were harvested and sold. At the same time, the state had emerged from the war with the value of land so far depreciated that bankers and factors would not make loans with a plantation offered as security. The only way that most planters could borrow operating funds was to offer a lien against the forthcoming crop. This was a high-risk transaction for the lender, reflected in exorbitant interest rates. Weather, floods, or pests could harm or ruin a crop, and market prices were subject to fluctuations.

If the master of a 10,000-acre plantation had financial problems, the plight of the former slaves and the white yeoman farmers—who owned small tracts—could only be worse. Many freedmen had no choice but to become sharecroppers. They and their families were assigned plots on the lands of planters, often their former masters. On these few acres they grew and harvested their own cotton crops and shared the proceeds with the landlords. They bought necessities on credit, usually at commissaries operated by the landowners, where prices were generally sky high. As a result, a sharecropper often could not realize enough from the sale of his crop to cover his debt. State law prohibited a sharecropper from moving if he owed money to the landlord, and in effect he became a peon. White small farmers also existed on credit obtained on the security of liens against their crops. A poor crop or low prices meant ending up in debt.

Sharecropping was not economical on sugarcane plantations, and most of the workers in the south Louisiana fields were paid wages, usually less than a dollar a day. But much of the wage was withheld until the crop was harvested, and field hands also lived on credit, having to pay premium prices at plantation commissaries. Louisiana sugar production became a marginal operation, dependent upon the protection of high tariffs or government subsidies because of competition from foreign cane growers.

Cotton and cane. They served Louisiana well when there were slaves to work the fields. After the Civil War they remained the mainstays of the state's economy until the beginning of the World War II. The years between those wars, however, were different from the 1830–1860 era. The per capita income fell far below the national average; Louisianians were poor until, at last, they were rescued by their state's natural resources.

At the end of the Civil War, about three-fourths of Louisiana's land area was still forested. By 1880 northern lumber companies were moving in to exploit this resource. Forty-one outside firms bought nearly a million and a half acres of the timberlands. At first they concentrated on yellow pine. Then they turned to swamps where great stands of cypress and hardwood trees had been developing for centuries. Sawmills sprang up over the state to drone away until the nearby forests were cut over. Then the mills were moved to new sites. Sawmills provided more than half of the industrial jobs in the state—until the forests were used up. By 1910 Louisiana was second only to Washington in board feet of lumber produced. In 1904 Henry Hardtner, a Pineville-born businessman and conservationist, set an example for the cut-and-move-on despoilers by beginning reforestation of exhausted lands. Hardtner's ideas were eventually encoded into Louisiana law. Today, even though 24,000 persons still work in the forest industry, new growth is being created at twice the rate of depletion. The state has become the nation's third-largest producer of plywood.

In the 1880s Seaman A. Knapp, president of the Iowa Agricultural College, was employed to study the potential of thousands of acres in southwest Louisiana that had been acquired by a group of British companies. He reported that the area between Lafayette and Lake Charles was ideal for growing rice. The companies arranged for hundreds of farmers from the Midwest to visit the holdings. Many of the visitors bought land, creating a major influx of immigrants and a new cash crop for the state. By 1900 more than half of the rice grown in the United States was produced in the flat prairie land of which Crowley is the center. By 1986 the state's crop was worth 200 million dollars.

Nothing testifies more clearly to the end of the old order in Louisiana agriculture than the rise of the unglamorous but versatile soybean. Introduced to the state around 1920, soybeans made steady gains as farmers came to appreciate the crop's relatively low-risk cultivation and as researchers developed new uses for soy products—especially for soy oil, today a key ingredient in margarine, mayonnaise, and countless other processed foods, as well as in nonfood products as diverse as linoleum, cosmetics, and insecticides. In the late twentieth century, soybeans surpassed first sugarcane and then cotton to become Louisiana's highest-earning field crop.

While Louisiana farmers reaped profits from their rice, cane, cotton, and soybean fields, Louisiana fishermen netted earnings from the Gulf of Mexico and the state's inland waters and coastal marshes. In 1990 the catch of fresh- and saltwater fish brought in 275 million dollars. Nearly three-quarters of that amount was accounted for by shellfish—especially shrimp, of which Louisiana is the nation's leading producer.

For all the wealth produced from the state's farmlands and waters, greater riches lie beneath them. Long before the Europeans came, Indians knew that there was oil under Louisiana's soil. They had found seeps where a strange liquid bubbled to the surface; some believed it had medicinal qualities. In the early 1540s the survivors of de Soto's ill-fated expedition came across such a spring and used the thick exudate to seal the hulls of the boats they were building to take them to Mexico. In 1860, with the Civil War approaching, a study concluded that Louisiana could furnish enough oil from Calcasieu Parish alone to meet the needs of the Confederacy; however, no effort was made to begin production. In 1866 the state's first well, also in Calcasieu Parish, turned out to be a dry hole. In 1870, a watchman's lantern set fire to gas escaping from a newly drilled water well near Shreveport; the gas was used later for illumination in nearby residences and business places.

In 1893, Anthony Lucas began prospecting for oil in southwest Louisiana. After several failures, he moved his equipment over the state line into Texas. In January, 1901, he discovered the legendary Spindletop field. The Spindletop bonanza spurred a renewed exploration in Louisiana. The Heywood Company, owned by five brothers who lived in Beaumont, Texas, began drilling in Jules Clement's rice field some five miles northeast of Jennings. On September 21, 1901, oil gushed forth, a flow of seven thousand barrels a day. It was Louisiana's first producing oil well, and it had economic implications for the state that were not fully realized for half a century. King Cotton's crown already was tottering at the time, and the overall importance of agriculture was in decline. Yet it would be a long time before the jobs created by the petroleum and related industries would outnumber those provided by cotton, cane, rice, and soybeans. Only in the 1980s did the number of Louisianians on farms fall below 5 percent of the overall population.

The discovery of oil generated the kind of excitement that marked the gold rushes in California and Alaska and the frantic searches for oil and gas in Texas and Oklahoma. Strike-it-rich stories titillated the imagination. There was the storekeeper at Mooringsport who received $30,000 a month in bonuses and royalties from land that he had purchased for seventy-five cents an acre. The flow from early wells near Jennings was so great that storage tanks could not be provided, and huge pits were dug to hold the output. Migrating ducks mistook the pits for ponds and alighted, only to find that they could not fly away once they settled into the syrupy liquid. Their bodies clogged outflow pipes until the problem was solved by the use of floodlights to scare the birds away.

Widespread exploration in north Louisiana began in 1902 and confirmed the existence of rich fields, but production was stymied at first by the eruption of gas from almost every new well. The value of natural gas as a fuel was not appreciated in the early days, and billions of cubic feet were wasted as it was allowed to escape into the air. One well spewed gas for three years before it could be controlled. Meanwhile, successful oil strikes brought on epidemics of prospecting fever and overnight booms in such places as Oil City, Vivian, and Mooringsport, which for a time resembled Wild West mining towns, complete with saloons, brothels, gambling halls, and the inevitable violence. The first successful well in Caddo Parish was completed in 1905. In 1916 the Monroe gas field, the nation's most productive, was tapped. The area was dotted with wild wells. Eventually, drillers gained control, but even then much of the Monroe gas was used uneconomically in the production of carbon black.

In the 1920s and 1930s, five-sixths of the oil taken from Louisiana came from the northern area. The Rodessa field, developed in the late 1930s, stretched from Caddo Parish into Texas and Arkansas.

South Louisiana's turn was coming, but first the oil companies had to develop drilling rigs and production platforms that could be used in the spongy coastal marshes and offshore in the Gulf of Mexico. An "offshore" well was drilled in Caddo Lake in 1911. The water was shallow enough to allow the construction of a platform set on pilings. Much more elaborate structures were needed for venturing into the Gulf. In the early 1930s the Texas Company acquired the rights to a submersible drilling barge developed by Louis Giliasso, a retired sea captain. The craft could be towed to a location, filled with water, and sunk to the bottom to provide a stable platform for drilling.

In 1937 a drilling structure was placed in the open Gulf, and in 1938 a well in fourteen feet of water on the coast brought forth crude. By this time seismic tests made it evident that vast deposits lay beneath the outer continental shelf in the Gulf, and after the Second World War the price of oil and the demand justified offshore exploration, which is far more expensive than drilling on solid land. In 1946 the Kerr-McGee company leased 20,000 acres of Gulf bottoms stretching ten or eleven miles off the Terrebonne Parish coast. On November 4, 1947, oil was hit by the first true offshore well.

As operations extended into ever-deeper waters in the 1950s and 1960s, the submersible barges were no longer adequate, and companies invested many millions of dollars in colossal structures with legs that rest on the seabottom and support platforms high above the waves. By the 1960s and 1970s many scores of the structures stood in the Gulf off Louisiana. The platforms brought a boom in deep-sea fishing because many large species schooled around the underwater legs. The servicing of the platforms became big business, with great fleets of helicopters and crewboats needed to ferry crews to and from land—and to evacuate them from the rigs whenever a hurricane threatened.

Oil brought unprecedented prosperity along the coast. Lafayette became one of the fastest-developing metropolitan areas in the country, an office and financial center for offshore operations. Morgan City and Houma began to resemble the steel towns of Pennsylvania, Ohio, and In-

Islands of concrete and steel, offshore oil-drilling rigs in the Gulf helped Louisiana to
prosper in the 1970s.

Courtesy the Historic New Orleans Collection; Acc. No. 1974.25.13.95

diana. They were the blue-collar communities where rigs were fabricated,
pipe stored.

New Orleans was the major beneficiary of activity that began picking up
during the Second World War, got a boost from the birth of the space age,
and reached new heights with the emergence of Louisiana as the kingpin of
offshore oil and gas production in the Gulf of Mexico. The name of Andrew J. Higgins heads all others in the wartime era. He built the storied PT
boats that battled the Japanese navy in the Pacific Ocean.

When President John F. Kennedy committed the United States to landing an astronaut on the moon within a decade, New Orleans won a key
role in the space age. The Michoud factory where Andrew Higgins, in another of his wartime enterprises, had made wooden airplanes was expanded
until it became one of the nation's largest manufacturing facilities under
one roof. There, the Chrysler Corporation produced rockets that launched
some of the earlier manned space flights, and there the Boeing Company
fabricated the behemoth first-stage Saturn 5 rockets that started every one
of America's moon-landing expeditions on its way. More recently, the

giant exterior fuel tanks of the space shuttle have been constructed at Michoud.

If Colonel Creecy could be moved to a rhapsodic description by the activity on the New Orleans waterfront in the 1830s, he would need an expanded vocabulary now to record his impressions of what he would see if he traveled on the Mississippi River from New Orleans to Baton Rouge today. On a journey of approximately 110 miles, he would never be out of sight of a major industrial plant—oil refinery, shipyard, grain elevator, aluminum-processing plant, or chemical facility. In the riverside fields where slaves once hand-harvested sugarcane, one of America's great industrial complexes has grown up. As long ago as 1909, the Standard Oil Company built the country's largest refinery on the riverbank at Baton Rouge. It was the first of the many facilities that now line the river. Although development along the Mississippi lagged for years, after World War II industrialists moved to avail themselves of the corridor's advantages: easy access to unlimited amounts of crude oil and natural gas, plant sites where ocean-going tankers and cargo vessels can tie up to load or unload, and strategic location on the nation's inland waterway system.

Louisiana is a Sun Belt state, of course, and would have been expected to share in the growth that accompanied the shift of the nation's population southward and westward after the war. However, it was oil and gas, and especially the offshore exploration and production, that finally enabled the state to break the shackles of poverty. By 1985, seven billion barrels of crude oil and condensate had been extracted from the outer continental shelf, and 93 percent had come from the area off Louisiana. Production of natural gas totaled 84 trillion cubic feet, of which 92 percent was from waters off the state. Louisiana was fourth to Texas, Alaska, and California in the pumping of oil products, and second to Texas in gas. In 1985 the total employment in all industries in the state was 1,543,381. Of these workers, 79,097 were employed in oil and gas exploration and production, 12,595 in oil refining, 28,538 in chemical operations having a basis in petroleum, and 1,141 in operating oil pipelines.

As impressive as these statistics may seem, they in fact tell a sad tale, for in 1985 Louisiana was in the throes of a devastating "oil bust" from which it has never fully recovered. Triggered by falling oil prices, the collapse gutted the state's economy and threw thousands out of work. At one point, people were leaving the once-booming Lafayette area in such numbers that a do-it-yourself moving company was sending in its rental trailers by the train-car load to meet the demand. Louisiana's oil production, which peaked at 907 million barrels in 1970, was barely half that in 1985 and declined to only

148 million barrels in 1990. The drilling of new wells was minimal. Gas production also fell, although not so dramatically. Revenues from oil and gas taxes and royalties—which in the lush years had covered a large portion of the state's budget—plummeted, leading to a long series of fiscal crises.

Nor was the outlook for the future overly encouraging. According to some geologists' estimates, by the year 2000, oil reserves in Louisiana will be depleted by 89 to 97 percent, gas by 81 to 90 percent. Yet only the most pessimistic economist would proclaim that petroleum is no longer a dependable resource. Market prices have always been cyclical, and a rise of only a few dollars would stimulate renewed exploration and production. And although known reserves are being depleted, no one knows what new fields are waiting to be discovered, especially offshore in depths that can be reached with modern equipment.

It was natural resources that brought prosperity after the World War II. But it was the people themselves—their joy in living, their pride of heritage—who provided an invaluable fallback that took up at least some of the economic slack when the petroleum industry faltered. Through good times and bad, Louisianians managed to lift themselves out of a humdrum existence and have fun, an accomplishment that was not unrecognized in a workaday outside world. Mardi Gras in New Orleans became known as America's foremost civic spree, and who knows how many millions yearned to share in a period of abandon and make-believe? Generations brought up on roast beef and potatoes learned about gumbo, crawfish bisque, and trout amandine, and planned to sample for themselves the spicy cuisine in its native habitat.

A highly developed sense of history impelled Louisianians to be preservationists, with the result that the past has not been forgotten. A visit to the state can be an excursion into nostalgia. As long ago as the 1920s, citizens voted laws that guarantee the architectural integrity of the French Quarter in New Orleans. One of the country's top half-dozen tourist attractions, it continues to look much as it did in the Spanish colonial period. Jackson Square, faced by the St. Louis Cathedral, the Cabildo, and the Presbytère, and flanked by the Pontalba Buildings, has hardly changed since the Civil War. Paddlewheel excursion boats, replicas of Mark Twain's packets, still chug up and down the Mississippi River. Stately plantation mansions dot the Louisiana countryside. The ageless Acadian country has lost none of its charm.

The attractions that could bring visitors to Louisiana had been known for years, but the full realization that the tourist and convention business could do wonders for the state's economy came late. Once it did, the result was a major facelift for the New Orleans skyline and the creation of thousands of jobs. The construction of office buildings, largely for oil companies, was accompanied by the erection of new hotels. By the time the boom was over, the metropolitan area could offer some 25,000 hotel rooms.

A catalyst was the Louisiana Superdome in the New Orleans business district, completed in 1974. The $163-million facility, the largest and most costly of the nation's indoor sports arenas, has hosted the Super Bowl, college basketball's Final Four tournaments, the Sugar Bowl, record-setting boxing championship bouts, rock concerts, and in 1988, the Republican National Convention.

Completed in 1984 in time for the Louisiana World Exhibition, New Orleans' second world fair, was the New Orleans Convention and Exhibition Center. Work began in 1989 on an addition that makes the hall large enough to accommodate almost any one of the trade exhibitions for which big cities compete. New Orleans has become a major contender for tourist and conventioneer dollars.

The Mississippi River waterfront has been transformed from a ship-loading area to a series of facilities that include retail stores, restaurants, fast-food outlets, parks, and other attractions designed to bring out tourists and residents alike A public bond issue financed a huge aquarium on the riverfront site.

A unique feature of New Orleans as a tourist and convention center is the proximity of the facilities. The French Quarter, the Superdome, the Exhibition Center, the riverfront, the largest hotels, some of the noted restaurants, two major retail shopping malls, some of the city's department stores, all literally are within walking distance of one another; although the air-conditioned shuttle bus is recommended on a New Orleans August noontime.

—J.W.

12

Diseases and Deliverance

The curse began in 1796, and for 109 years Louisianians, and particularly New Orleanians, lived for long seasons in the shadow of death. Intermittent attacks of yellow fever over that period claimed more than 100,000 lives in New Orleans, another 75,000 in the nearby countryside, and nobody knows how many in the rest of the state. When Yellow Jack appeared, the well-to-do fled, leaving the poor along with newcomers to tend the sick and bury the dead. War, civil disorder, the inhumanity of slavery, and natural disasters all brought misery to succeeding generations, but none could evoke the terror of an epidemic of the fever. There was no known defense other than to board the first train to safer scenes. For those without ticket money, unless they enjoyed the immunity provided by surviving a bout with the scourge, there was nothing to do but hope they would be spared until the cool weather of autumn reduced the daily list of victims to the vanishing point.

Eventually, there would be a happy ending to the tragedy of yellow fever, but not before a half-dozen major outbreaks left nightmarish memories of a helpless people who could make only futile gestures in defiance of a cruel and insidious enemy. As distressing as they were, however, none of the worst epidemics of the fever outmatched the suffering caused by a single wave of Asiatic cholera that in 1832 killed nearly one-third of the New Orleanians who could not run away from the menace, and forced overburdened gravediggers finally to bury as many as three hundred persons in a single trench, filling the spaces between adult bodies with the corpses of children.

The death rate in the 1800s would seem to imply a lack of medical care, but actually Louisiana had been served since colonial times by physicians and surgeons fully as competent as any in the United States; the profession as a whole simply had not yet learned to deal with yellow fever and cholera, or smallpox or malaria. In the early period, doctors who practiced in the state even had an advantage over those in other areas because many had been trained in France, which then led the world in medical advances. After the Louisiana Purchase, ambitious American practitioners moved into an area that offered opportunity because of a multiplying population as well as a plethora of illnesses.

A unique situation developed. The French-speaking Creole physicians dispensed a gentle type of treatment intended to help the body mobilize its own defenses against disease. Medicines were prescribed sparingly, with attentive nursing care emphasized. On the other hand, most of the Americans had served their apprenticeships in states where medical procedures had a rough-and-ready pioneer aspect, and these physicians tended to practice what is known as heroic medicine. They believed in bombarding a disease with all of the ammunition they could muster. They prescribed massive doses of calomel, a salt of mercury, and routinely bled patients to the fainting point. Each group scorned the methods of the other, and the competition for patients accented the antagonisms that resulted from differing backgrounds. Seventy-five years passed after the Louisiana Purchase before a lasting medical society could be formed that included both French- and English-speaking doctors. Nevertheless, New Orleans won recognition as a medical center.

Although there is some evidence of yellow fever in the state before 1796, historian John Duffy, the foremost authority on the matter, accepts that year as the beginning of the almost annual visitation by Yellow Jack. There were 638 deaths in New Orleans out of a population of 8,756 in 1796, and Duffy writes that at least 300 were caused by the fever. That summer, a cloud of black smoke shrouded the city, a scene that would be repeated numerous times. Nobody had any idea what caused the disease or how it spread, but one theory held that it resulted from a "miasma" that blanketed the populated area, and desperate residents burned barrels of tar, animal skins, hooves, and horns in the hope that the smoke would neutralize whatever it was that infested the air. In later years cannons were fired on the supposition that the concussion would disperse the miasma, and barrels of carbolic acid were dumped into gutters with the thought that the fumes might be effective. A cloud of smoke, the roar of artillery, and the stench of carbolic acid always confirmed that yellow fever again was present—these signs in addition to the rumble of carts bearing the dead to cemeteries where coffins piled up while gravediggers fell hopelessly behind.

By the first years of the nineteenth century, Louisianians had learned to expect almost annual outbreaks, which invariably began when hot weather settled in and continued until fall brought frost, or at least lower temperatures. Sometimes there were only isolated cases; in other years hundreds and even thousands of residents and visitors were stricken. Generally, nearly one-fourth of the victims died. In the first part of the century, yellow fever invaded the Atlantic seaboard states as well as Louisiana, but other areas were spared long before epidemics ceased in the state in which the port of New Orleans was the metropolis. Before doctors could identify the carrier, they knew that at least some of the outbreaks followed the arrival at New Orleans of ships from Havana and Central American ports where yellow fever was endemic.

In 1804 Governor William C. C. Claiborne lost his wife and a daughter in an epidemic. His second wife died when the disease hit again in 1809. Benjamin Latrobe, the architect who designed the national Capitol and the White House, was a victim in 1820.

As the population of New Orleans grew, the toll became higher. A popular, and in a way logical, explanation for the recurrence was the utter filth of the city. Visitors called it the most unsanitary urban area in the country. Few streets were paved, and drainage was far from adequate in a town that lay largely below sea level and had an annual rainfall of nearly sixty inches. An adequate sewerage system would be a development of the twentieth century. Nightsoil was collected from outhouses and simply dumped into the river. The current also would have flushed away the accumulated filth from a densely populated city, but careless residents either dumped garbage into gutters or deposited it on the batture, the area between the levee and the water's edge. They would not walk the few extra steps needed to throw the matter into the water, where it would be washed away.

The yellow fever epidemic of 1853 in New Orleans stands as one of the worst medical catastrophes ever to befall an American city. About half of the population of 150,000 rushed away when the enormity of the outbreak became evident, but as many as 9,000 of the stay-behinds—who were mainly the poor, of course—had fatal attacks. Duffy writes that the outbreak turned New Orleans into a ghost town, the streets almost deserted and most businesses closed. Whole families, along with their servants, were wiped out. In the cemeteries the scenes were hellish. Bodies were delivered by the hundreds, some in caskets, others only wrapped in sheets. Overwhelmed gravediggers did their best to get the dead into the ground with a thin covering of soil. But they fell far behind and putrefying bodies piled up, their stench adding to the horror. The shallow graves quickly filled with water, causing coffins to float. Duffy tells of the scene at night, when by the light of crude torches half-drunk laborers stood in water up to their waists as they tried to provide burial places. Estimates of the number of New Orleanians who were stricken run as high as 40,000. The survivors, of course, became immune, with the result that in 1854 and 1855 the death toll was only about 2,500 persons in each year, since the fever had fewer potential victims. By 1858, however, the number of nonimmune residents had risen, and in that year, according to one count, 4,856 died.

Carried in large part by refugees fleeing New Orleans, the 1853 epidemic spread over the state from corner to corner, attacking some areas that previously had been spared. In Thibodaux, for instance, 224 persons, about 15 percent of the population, died. Tiny Washington recorded 100 deaths, causing panic in nearby Opelousas, from which as many as three-fourths of the residents fled. The tragedy of yellow fever could be felt in a village as well as in a big city.

Many New Orleanians predicted—and hoped—that Yellow Jack would decimate the "unacclimated" Union troops who in 1862 occupied the city and some other parts of the state. It did not happen. The area was almost fever-free for the duration of the Civil War. Most authorities at the time credited the massive cleanup of New Orleans engineered by General Benjamin F. Butler, but now it is known that the falloff in the arrival of ships from fever ports was responsible.

In 1873 the fever struck north Louisiana with unaccustomed ferocity. At Shreveport, about half of the town's estimated 9,000 residents evacuated. Of those who stayed on, some 3,000 contracted the illness and at least 759 died. Travelers in the northern parishes reported going for fifty miles and seeing hardly a white person—all had fled to the pine hills, only the blacks remaining. (It had long been observed that blacks were far less susceptible to yellow fever than were whites. The reason, unknown until well into the twentieth century, was that the disease originated in Africa, where many generations of exposure had given blacks a measure of resistance to it. In especially virulent epidemics, however, blacks too died in

In this sketch of Shreveport's waterfront during the 1873 yellow fever epidemic, the only wagons on Commerce Street were hearses.

Courtesy the Historic New Orleans Collection; Acc. No. 1974.25.11.1791

large numbers.) The disaster was economic as well as physical. Surrounding communities quarantined Shreveport, and except for twice-a-week Texas and Pacific Railroad relief trains bearing food and medicine, rail service ceased. An artist's rendering of the town during the epidemic shows the normally bustling Red River waterfront as virtually deserted, the only traffic a small funeral procession.

New Orleans suffered only moderately in the 1873 outbreak, but Yellow Jack returned with a vengeance in 1878, when the toll of 4,050 lives was the third-highest in the city's history. Baton Rouge had 193 deaths, and smaller towns such as Donaldsonville, Morgan City, Plaquemine, and Thibodaux were also hard hit. The epidemic that year ravaged the entire Lower Mississippi Valley. Memphis, Tennessee, was literally decimated, suffering 5,000 fatalities in a population of 50,000.

After the great epidemic of 1878, eighteen summers in a row passed with extremely low incidences of yellow fever in Louisiana, and hopes rose that the fever was playing itself out, as it had done elsewhere in the United States. But in 1897 the optimists had a blow. Nearly 2,000 persons were stricken in New Orleans, and 298 died. A move to convert the Beauregard public school on Canal Street into an emergency hospital brought on a riot by neighbors, who set fire to an auxiliary building.

The economic costs of the fever had long influenced the handling of an outbreak. At the first report of a case in New Orleans, cities in Mississippi, Texas, Alabama, and elsewhere, as well as other towns in Louisiana, clamped an embargo on shipments from the port, with costly results to business interests. If fever did exist, the pressure was on the medical community to conceal it. Interests outside of Louisiana did not trust health authorities of the state to give honest reports. Once it became known that Yellow Jack was back in New Orleans, trains leaving the city were met at stations along the line by armed citizens who threatened to shoot anybody leaving the cars. The near-hysteria is understandable in light of the dreadful experience in Louisiana.

In retrospect, it is difficult to see how medical investigators could labor throughout the nineteenth century and fail to produce proof that a mosquito—specifically, the female of the species *Aëdes aegypti*—was the carrier of the disease. As early as 1794, a Dr. Drysdale reported that an invasion of mosquitoes accompanied a yellow fever epidemic in Baltimore, and in 1797 and 1805 Dr. Benjamin Rush, a signer of the Declaration of Independence, noted the prevalence of mosquitoes during outbreaks in Philadelphia. Indeed, by 1881 Dr. Carlos Finlay of Havana pointed a finger at *A. aegypti*. His theory was presented in the *New Orleans Medical and Surgical*

Journal by Dr. Rudolph Matas, who as a medical student had served as secretary of a fever commission session in Havana and had become a friend of Finlay's. But Finlay did not offer the indisputable evidence demanded by the skeptical profession.

Nevertheless, his suspicions aroused the interest of others, and in 1900 a commission headed by Dr. Walter Reed went to work in Havana. Some members donned the unwashed bedclothing of fever victims and slept in the beds in which they had died. These investigators did not become ill. Others, including Jesse Lazear, Hideyo Noguchi, and Adrian Stokes, allowed themselves to be bitten by mosquitoes that previously had attacked yellow fever patients. The three men died. Now the evidence was overwhelming, and in 1901 Matas, by then the leading surgeon in New Orleans, prompted the Orleans Parish Medical Society to make a study that determined the prevalence of the fever mosquitoes in the city.

The result was that when cases of yellow fever turned up in 1905, authorities knew what to do. A widespread campaign led to the screening of the city's many cisterns. These fixtures provided the drinking water for most residences, but they were also a prime reservoir of the clear, still water in which *A. aegypti* laid its eggs. Additionally, when a case of fever was reported, a so-called screening wagon raced to the patient's home. The crew screened a room so that the patient remained beyond the reach of mosquitoes. For the first time, an epidemic was halted, brought to an abrupt end before the first frost of autumn disposed of the carrier mosquitoes. Although there were 3,402 cases of fever and 452 deaths, the 1905 outbreak proved to be the last to assault an American city. For New Orleans, as well as Louisiana as a whole, there was deliverance.

The outbreak of Asiatic cholera in 1832 was part of the pandemic that was sweeping the world. Although the absolute death toll of 4,340 in New Orleans was exceeded by three later yellow-fever epidemics, the percentage of victims was greater in 1832. Some 15,000 of the city's 50,000 people already had evacuated because of a yellow-fever scare, and when the presence of the cholera became known, other thousands took flight. The first cases were brought in by the steamer *Constitution*, and almost all of the deaths occurred in a period of four weeks. The disease spread over south Louisiana, with a toll that was especially heavy among slaves on the plantations (unlike yellow fever, cholera tended to be even more dangerous among blacks than among whites). After a brief lull, the outbreak of 1833 began. About 1,000 persons died in New Orleans, hundreds more in the smaller towns and countryside. The second worldwide wave of the century reached Louisiana in 1848 and over the next two years caused more than 5,000 deaths in New Orleans alone. A last major outbreak, claiming about half that many victims, occurred in the years 1866–1867.

Cholera and yellow fever were the most terrifying health threats that Louisianians faced, but hardly the only ones. Not unexpectedly in a subtropical climate, malaria was endemic until its link to the Anopheles mosquito was identified and control programs established. Typhoid and dysentery were continual problems, especially in urban areas, until effective public-sanitation procedures took hold. Over the long run, smallpox probably killed more Louisianians than either yellow fever or cholera, but it seems never to have caused the mass panic that those two diseases engendered. Perhaps one reason was that a countermeasure existed: by the early 1800s, vaccination was recognized as an effective preventative. From 1825 to 1860, no major episodes of smallpox occurred in the state. After the Civil War, however, an influx of unvaccinated and nonimmune foreign immigrants and former slaves to the cities brought renewed severe outbreaks. Smallpox remained a perennial scourge well into the twentieth century, when vaccination was adopted all but universally.

One disease, although quite rare, stirred deep public concern and led to the creation of a unique Louisiana institution. The disease was leprosy. The very word triggered ancient fears, and after reports of scattered occurrences in the late 1800s, the legislature acted. In 1894 Dr. Isidore Dyer, later dean of the Tulane University Medical School, was granted state funds for the establishment of an isolation hospital for leprosy patients at what is now Carville, on the banks of the Mississippi in Iberville Parish. Prejudices were such that Dyer had to pretend he was buying land for an ostrich farm, and when the time came to move the first seven patients to the site from New Orleans, they had to be sent by barge because neither railroads nor steamships would carry them. The United States Public Health Service took over the hospital in 1920. The only facility of its kind in the nation, it has been responsible for great advances in the treatment of the malady now known as Hansen's disease.

It would be surprising if a busy world port such as New Orleans had avoided another anciently feared disease, bubonic plague, and in fact the city had a brush with the plague in 1914. In that year and the next, a total of twenty-eight cases were diagnosed. One immediate result was a citywide campaign against rats, from which the disease is transmitted to human beings by fleas. Buildings were ratproofed and 38,000 traps set, eventually catching 80,000 of the rodents.

Despite the fevers, filth, and fatalities, the story of human health in Louisiana is far from a gloomy litany of hopelessness and failure. New Orleans became a widely recognized medical center to which people from the southern United States and Latin America came for advanced treatment. As early as 1834 a group of young doctors founded the institution that has become the Tulane University School of Medicine. Later, Louisiana State University established medical schools in New Orleans and Shreveport. A 10,000-livre bequest in 1836 from seaman Jean Louis financed the establishment of what is now the Charity Hospital of Louisiana at New Orleans, where thousands of medical graduates have received their advanced training.

The second Caesarean section reported in the United States was performed by a French-born doctor, François Marie Prévost, on a plantation in Ascension Parish, near Donaldsonville, sometime between 1820 and 1825. His patient was a slave who could not be delivered naturally because rickets had caused a pelvic deformity. The mother and child survived, and Dr. Prévost later again performed the operation successfully on the same woman. Of the seventy-nine sections recorded in the United States between 1822 and 1877, nineteen were in Louisiana.

Dr. Andrew W. Smyth made medical news at Charity Hospital in 1864 when he took the bold move of treating an aneurysm in the upper arm of a patient by tying off the arteries leading to the lesion. The alternative was amputation of the arm because the patient would have bled to death had the weakened wall of the blood vessel given way.

An aneurysm also led to what was the most publicized operation ever performed in New Orleans. In 1888 Dr. Matas was confronted with a lesion in a patient's upper arm, the result of a gunshot wound. Dr. Smyth's solution of ligating the arteries did not work on this occasion, and in desperation Matas opened up the aneurysm itself. He found blood flowing from small vessels that had not been affected by the ligation of the principal arteries. Matas sewed up the small vessels and closed the incision in the aneurysm. In a few days the patient was able to return to work. The medical literature indicates that Matas was the first to attempt the procedure since it was done by the Greek surgeon Antyllus in about A.D. 300. Matas' fame was worldwide. He was the first American to experiment with spinal injection anesthesia, as early as 1888 tried saline infusion in the treatment of shock, invented a device for pumping air into the lungs in order to make surgery possible in that area, and devised a method of using catgut rings to keep intestines from crimping when they are sewed together end to end.

Matas was succeeded upon his retirement as chairman of surgery at the Tulane Medical School by another doctor of international stature, Alton Ochsner, who was the first practitioner to speak out with an authoritative voice in warning that cigarette smoking leads to lung cancer and other diseases. He was one of the founders and gave his name to the Ochsner Medical Institutions, the largest independent medical center in the South.

—J.W.

13

Rivers and Ports

The Mississippi is a river of many names. The first Spanish explorers called it "Río del Espíritu Santo"—River of the Holy Spirit. Later Spaniards referred to it as the "Río Palizado" because of mud formations that looked like palisades along its banks. Father Jacques Marquette, who with Louis Joliet explored the great stream as far south as the Arkansas River in 1673, called it "Conception." La Salle christened it "Colbert" in honor of Louis XIV's minister of finance, Jean-Baptiste Colbert. By the time New Orleans was founded, the French had given yet another appellation to the river, calling it "Fleuve St. Louis" for their sainted king Louis IX. Long before any of this, of course, the original inhabitants of the lands verging the river had their own names for it, and it is perhaps fitting that it is one of these that has endured: the Ojibway *Missi Sipi*, meaning simply "Great River."

The waterways of Louisiana—the rivers of the north, the bayous of the south—have played a profound role in the state's history, but none remotely rivals the Mississippi. From its trickling headwaters among several lakes in northern Minnesota, the river rolls and meanders 2,430 miles—the straight-line distance is about 1,500 miles—to the Gulf of Mexico. And the upper Mississippi is actually the least of the lower river's three great branches, the others being the Ohio River and Missouri River systems. Altogether, the Mississippi and its tributaries touch thirty-one states and two Canadian provinces.

The French understood the importance of the river, which is why, in 1718, they chose its banks as the site of the young colony's future capital. Bienville, directed by John Law to build a port, already knew the location he wanted. In 1699 an Indian guide leading him upriver had shown him a crescent bend from which there was easy access to nearby lakes. Nineteen years later, Bienville selected that very spot. It was a wise choice (although Bienville, looking out over vast flooded areas studded with forests of cypress trees, must have had his misgivings). The riverbank below that point, although closer to the Gulf, was not high or stable enough to support construction. As for the river itself, no records exist of its depth at that time, but today it is 192 feet at Algiers Point, varying to 103 feet elsewhere in the main harbor, with widths ranging from several hundred to 2,000 feet. Thus, a natural site for an inland port.

Building a port was one thing. Taming the river was another. From time out of mind, the Mississippi had known no bounds, and the low, rudimentary levees that the early colonists threw up did little to stem its floods. Moreover, the river was continually stopping its own mouth with blockading timbers that had to be removed and shifting bars of mud and sand that had to be scoured if sailing ships were to enter. Nevertheless, the little port of New Orleans survived, grew by fits and starts, and began to build a hinterland. The river became the colony's main highway and its lifeline. Down it also flowed Louisiana's exports to the Old World, although these—lumber, pelts, a smattering of agricultural products—were pitifully meager during the whole period of French dominion.

The colony's commercial stagnation began to lift in the aftermath of the Treaty of Fontainebleau, by which France in 1762 turned over to Spain New Orleans and all of Louisiana west of the Mississippi, and the Treaty of Paris of the following year, by which Great Britain, victorious in the Seven Years' War, gained Florida from Spain, and Canada and all other French territory east of the Mississippi from France. The Paris treaty also gave the British the right to navigate the river.

The Spanish did not gain full control of Louisiana until 1769, and when they did they incurred the wrath of shippers by restricting trade with traditional markets in French colonies. Nevertheless, port activity increased in New Orleans, and the Spanish quickly realized the importance of the port to world trade and to their efforts to colonize. In the 1770s, 1780s, and 1790s, Spain used the right to navigate the river as both a weapon of statecraft and a lure to colonists. However, frontiersmen of the then-western states were denied the right of deposit of goods for transshipment, a position to which the Spanish held steadfast until 1788, when they relented.

Pressure to settle the Mississippi River Question—unrestricted use of the river by Americans—increased on Spain when France declared war on her in 1792. When Spain signed the Treaty of San Lorenzo on October 27, 1795, guaranteeing those rights, a new era beckoned for Louisiana. The stakes went even higher when Spain retroceded Louisiana to France, which in turn sold the colony to the United States.

Commerce took an immediate upturn, and soon the colorful harbor at New Orleans was crowded with flatboats, keelboats, barges, and other vessels. Cotton exports, a leading business indicator, jumped from 18,000 bales in 1802 to 42,000 in 1810 and to 63,000 in 1815. In 1809 there were 1,100 flatboats and keelboats bringing goods to New Orleans; by 1817 the number had surpassed 2,000. The port suffered a temporary setback in 1807 when the United States declared a general cargo embargo and sent a gunboat fleet to the mouth of the river. These measures resulted from the *Chesapeake-Leopard* affair, in which the American frigate *Chesapeake* was attacked off the coast of Virginia by the *Leopard*, a British vessel. The embargo was modified in 1808 and lifted in 1810, but on June 12, 1812, Congress declared war on Great Britain, and it was not long before British warships appeared off the mouth of the river. Despite all this, commerce at the port increased because it had been freed of transshipment problems.

Throughout this same period there raged a legal battle involving the port and eventually entangling even the president of the United States. Known as the Batture Case—*batture* referring to alluvial land deposited by the river in front of the levee—the dispute began in 1803 when John Gravier fenced off his riverfront property in Faubourg Marigny, adjacent to New Orleans' central business district. Gravier's action aroused vigorous protest: for years people had regarded the batture as public property and had taken soil from it for their gardens and to build levees.

Responding to the outcry, the city council declared that the batture was indeed public property. But Edward Livingston, a lawyer and future United States senator, bought into Gravier's interests and in 1805 petitioned the Orleans Territory Superior Court to rule the batture private, which the court did. (In essence, the court held that title to the property dated to the time of Spanish law, under which the right of alluvium was incident to land formed by the river.) The ruling brought more protests, and the city council called upon Governor Claiborne for help. He put the issue before his friend President Thomas Jefferson, who had the United States marshal evict Gravier and Livingston from the batture in 1808. Jefferson, who saw the port as vital to national expansion, ignored Livingston's pleas for arbitration; Congress also rejected a plea to intercede.

In 1813, the newly established United States District Court at New Orleans ruled Jefferson's interference illegal. The matter dragged through the courts for another thirteen years before being decided largely in Gravier and Livingston's favor (in the interim, in return for the city's promise not to interfere with ships landing in front of their property, they had agreed to permit people to resume taking soil from the batture). One result of the litigation was that, for many years, docks and other port facilities on the riverbank in New Orleans remained private and largely unregulated.

None of this strife—not the warring of nations or the battles of lawyers—did much to impede the city's emergence as an increasingly important commercial center. Indeed, the main obstacle to still greater prosperity for New Orleans in these years was a technological one: the lack of a boat that could travel efficiently upstream. The hulking flatboats—anywhere from 50 to 150 feet long and 15 to 24 feet wide—that were floating down in ever-growing numbers from the Ohio Valley could not maneuver against the current at all and were broken up for lumber after their cargoes were unloaded. Keelboats, smaller and with pointed prows, could and did return upriver, but only through slow and laborious poling and towline dragging. Then, on January 10, 1812, a new and revolutionary craft appeared at the crescent bend in the Mississippi: the steamboat *New Orleans*, the first of its breed to arrive in its namesake city.

Conceived by Robert Fulton and Nicholas Roosevelt and constructed by them in partnership with Robert Livingston—the same man who had helped negotiate the Louisiana Purchase—the *New Orleans* stood in sharp contrast to the flatboats, keelboats, and sailing ships lining the levee in front of the Place d'Armes. Onlookers learned that the boat, piloted by Roosevelt, had come downriver all the way from Pittsburgh, where it was built. The *New Orleans* was not very large—116 feet long and 20 feet in the beam—and its relatively weak engine confined it to the wide, slow reaches of the lower Mississippi. Nonetheless, in a brief career of shuttling passengers and cargo between Natchez and New Orleans before hitting a snag and sinking in 1814, the craft earned for its owners $20,000 more than the $38,000 they had spent to build it.

Governor William C. C. Claiborne was impressed by the *New Orleans* and the potential of steamboating—and perhaps by the lavish hospitality he received from Fulton during a visit to New York. Claiborne recommended that the state legislature grant Fulton and Livingston an eighteen-year monopoly for steamboat operations in Louisiana. The move caused public cries of outrage and soon brought forth a challenger: the visionary riverman Henry Miller Shreve.

Shreve and his steamboat *Enterprise* arrived from Pittsburgh in 1814, just in time for the Battle of New Orleans, with a load of ammunition for Andrew Jackson's forces. After the American victory, Shreve remained in the port and put his boat to work in defiance of the monopoly. On one journey, he steamed all the way to Louisville, on the Ohio River. It was an eye-opening achievement—no steamboat had ever gone so far upcurrent. If his competitors were impressed, they were certainly not pleased. Livingston had the *Enterprise* seized and held under bond. Shreve in turn secured a federal court order against Livingston. The legal wrangle ended in 1817 with Fulton and Livingston abandoning their claim to a monopoly. By that time, Shreve and his second steamboat, the double-decked, 403-ton *Washington*—the first of the true Mississippi riverboats—were demonstrating once and for all the feasibility of steam navigation up and down the lower river and into the Ohio. The steamboat age had dawned.

By December of 1819, the New Orleans port register had logged the arrival of thirty-four new steamboats, with forty more by 1821. By the mid-1820s steamboats were no longer an unusual sight on the big river, and within a few more years they were commonplace. In 1845, some 1,200 of them were plying the waters of the Mississippi and its tributaries.

The first casualties of the new technology were the keelboats. There was never even a question of competition. It might take a keelboat's crew three long months to pole and row and haul their craft from New Orleans to St. Louis; by 1825, steamboats routinely made the trip in two weeks or less. The stalwart keelboats, once kings of the river, retreated farther and farther up the tributary streams, where they could still be of use, before vanishing altogether. Some of the last of them returned to New Orleans in the 1850s to end their days ingloriously as oyster scows.

By contrast, flatboating boomed throughout much of the steamboat era. For example, during the November-to-June shipping season of 1846–1847, three decades into the steamboat age, 2,792 flatboats tied up at New Orleans—more than double the total of 1,287 that had arrived in 1816, when Shreve was building his *Washington*. How did these primitive craft survive, and even flourish, for so long against the challenge of steam? For one thing, flatboats operated strictly downstream, so the upstream capabilities of the steamboats were irrelevant. For another, it was hard to beat the economy of the flats. Any enterprising Ohio Valley farmer with a load of grain or salt pork ready for market could knock together a big, boxy flatboat, enlist his sons and hired hands as crew, and float his produce to New Orleans himself. To top off the journey, they could all ride back home aboard a steamboat, whereas in the old days they would have had to hike the Natchez Trace. A typical flatboatman of the era was a rawboned farmboy named Abraham Lincoln, who in 1828 voyaged from Indiana to New Orleans as a nineteen-year-old deckhand. Three years later the future president repeated the trip on an 80-foot flatboat that he, a stepbrother, and a cousin built in Illinois.

Flatboating finally began to decline in the 1850s, done in partly by the increasing efficiency of steamboats and partly by competition from canals in the East, but most of all by the spread of railroads. After the Civil War, with its total disruption of shipping on the Mississippi, the flats never reappeared in their former numbers. By the late 1880s, they were little more than a memory.

If the 1850s were the beginning of the end for flatboats, they were only the end of the beginning for steamboats. The years immediately before and

New Orleans' riverfront piled high with bales of cotton and hogsheads of sugar in the days
when the smoke-belching steamboats were the monarchs of the Mississippi.

Courtesy the Historic New Orleans Collection; Acc. No. 1974.25.17.59

after the Civil War comprised the golden age of steamboating on the Mississippi. Not coincidentally, the prewar period was one of prosperity for
Louisiana as well—and especially for the port of New Orleans, which grew
into the world's greatest export center. In some years, the combined value of
river and oceangoing shipping through the port approached $500 million—
a sum several times greater than the annual federal budget in that era. In the
last full shipping season before the war, some 3,500 steamboats docked at
the city's riverfront. Cargo from upriver and down was piled high on the
wharves, with thousands of stevedores laboring to load and unload more.

When the war came, prosperity departed. Not until the 1880s did shipping through New Orleans return to antebellum levels. The steamboats,
however, did return—at least for a while—and they grew ever larger and
more palatial as their owners sought to lure passengers. Another area of
competition was in speed: rare was the captain who could bear to watch
another boat pass his. Thus arose one of the most celebrated events in the
history of the river, the race from New Orleans to St. Louis between the
Natchez and the *Robert E. Lee*.

On June 30, 1870, some 10,000 spectators jammed the levee above
Canal Street to witness the start. Captain J. W. Cannon steered the *Robert
E. Lee* across the line at 5:03 P.M. Captain T. P. Leathers and the *Natchez*

followed three minutes later. A carnival-like atmosphere prevailed as the boats churned upstream past bonfires and cheering onlookers on levees fronting plantations. The following morning at Natchez, a large crowd watched the *Robert E. Lee* dock briefly at 10:15. As the boat's crew hurriedly cast off to continue, the *Natchez* came into view. At Memphis, the *Lee* led by an hour and three minutes. At Cairo, Illinois, it had gained another seven minutes. When the *Natchez* then lost five hours because of fog, the race was as good as over. The *Lee* steamed into St. Louis late in the morning on the Fourth of July, having completed the trip in a record time of three days, eighteen hours, and fourteen minutes. The *Natchez* arrived at 6:00 p.m.

With hindsight, the race between the *Natchez* and the *Robert E. Lee* can be seen as a high-water mark of the steamboat age. Even though new boats, including some of the largest and most luxurious, would be built after 1870, and even though steamboats would operate—albeit in sharply declining numbers—well into the twentieth century, their fate was already being written in the gleaming steel rails extending inexorably across the continent. Trains were faster than boats, were not restricted to navigable streams, and were not affected by seasonally low or frozen water. Like the flatboats before them, the steamboats were bound to lose out in the end.

Louisiana was an early entrant in the national railroad-building spree. The state's first line, the Pontchartrain Railroad in New Orleans, was completed in 1831. Its little locomotive, semiaffectionately known by the line's passengers as "Smoky Mary," shuttled back and forth on 6 miles of track between the river and Lake Pontchartrain. By 1835, a handful of other short lines gave the state a total of 40 miles of rails. But rail construction soon began to lag, partly because Louisianians had come to rely on their abundant waterways. Not until the 1850s was New Orleans linked to such none-too-distant points as Jackson, Mississippi, and Brashear (now Morgan) City, Louisiana. In 1860, when the United States was crisscrossed by more than 30,000 miles of track, only 334 of them were in Louisiana—and much of this meager mileage was soon destroyed or damaged during the Civil War. Nor did the war's end bring a dramatic recovery: as late as 1880, the state still had only 650 miles of rails. Louisianians, it seems, were still wedded to their rivers and bayous.

At the same time, however, a problem arose on the greatest of these waterways. Following the war, shipping had taken on new dimensions. Much larger ships were being built, and their deep drafts made it difficult, if not impossible, for them to enter the Mississippi through the shallow channels of South and Southwest Passes. Unless a more navigable entrance to the river could be provided, New Orleans would be at an increasing disadvantage in competition with other ports (among other things, railroads were reluctant to build into the city, since only smaller ships could reach it). The problem that had dogged the founders of the port not only returned but became a national concern, since the prosperity of the Mississippi Valley depended upon access to oceangoing ships. Interested states appealed to Congress, which in 1872 enjoined the United States Army Corps of Engineers to study the matter. The plan that initially won the most support was to dig a canal from Fort St. Philip to Breton Sound, bypassing the mouths of the river altogether, but this idea eventually fell victim to controversy, red tape, and the genius of James B. Eads.

Eads, who had run away to work on steamboats at age thirteen and had been on the river for most of the forty years since, had trained himself as an engineer, had pioneered various salvage techniques, and had built armored gunboats for the Union navy. These achievements, however, paled beside his most recent accomplishment: bridging the Mississippi at St. Louis. Upon its completion in 1874, the bridge—considered an engineering miracle at the time—made Eads nationally famous.

Now Eads offered his solution to the problem of South and Southwest Passes: a system of jetties to increase the speed and direct the force of the current in the passes, causing the river itself to carve out a deeper channel. He personally guaranteed a depth of twenty-eight feet at average flood tide—enough for the largest ships of the day. Over fierce opposition from most of the army engineers, Congress gave Eads the project. Construction began at South Pass in 1875 and was completed in 1878. The Mississippi did the rest. In July of 1879, the minimum depth of the channel had reached thirty feet. In New Orleans, Eads was hailed as the savior of the port. Years later, the Corps of Engineers paid him the oblique compliment of adopting his methods when the Corps deepened Southwest Pass.

Its door to the Gulf cleared, New Orleans remained secure in its role of entrepôt between the Mississippi Valley and the rest of the world. As the nineteenth century gave way to the twentieth, the principal changes in the port were administrative and internal. In 1896, business interests persuaded the legislature that the state should manage the port, which had long been operated privately under lease. To this end, the lawmakers created the Board of Commissioners of the Port of New Orleans, soon known by all as simply the Dock Board. Because the commissioners were appointed by the governor, it was perhaps inevitable that the board would become a refuge for friends of whichever administration was in power. Yet the Dock Board also brought about major and much-needed improvements in the port.

When the board took full control after the private operator's lease expired in 1901, the New Orleans waterfront offered shippers only the crudest facilities. There were a few rickety wooden sheds, but most cargo sat exposed to the elements on the rotting wharves. Drayage was by mule-drawn wagon along potholed streets that became impassable quagmires in rain. Ships were loaded and unloaded almost entirely by the muscle power of sweating stevedores. Over the next two decades, the Dock Board directed projects that transformed this primitive scene. A line of modern warehouses went up, augmented by numerous large steel sheds. State-of-the-art grain elevators towered over a massive coal-storage facility and a cotton terminal that could hold 400,000 bales. Derricks, conveyors, and other mechanized equipment greatly sped the handling of cargo. The board also oversaw the construction of some sixty miles of publicly owned rail lines to service the port. Finally, in 1921, the commissioners could congratulate themselves on the dedication of the Inner Harbor Navigation Canal (Industrial Canal), which upon its opening two years later gave ships direct passage between the river and Lake Pontchartrain.

Many of the port's new facilities were added after 1914—the year the Panama Canal opened, cutting the sea distance from the Gulf to the West Coast and the Orient by thousands of miles. Almost overnight, New Orleans became a main terminus for the canal's traffic, and oceangoing shipping through the port climbed steeply. Indeed, seagoing shipping was now the port's stock in trade. River traffic had steadily declined as the railroads gained primacy; even such longtime staples as cotton and cane were now more likely to reach New Orleans by train than by riverboat. River commerce was about to reassert itself, however, and in a way that would have pleased the old-time flatboatmen and steamboaters; in fact, it had been their idea in the first place.

As early as the 1840s, a few flatboat owners were paying to have their craft towed back upriver by steamboats, enabling the flats to carry goods in both directions. A flatboat used in this way was called a barge. A natural next step was to have the flat towed downstream as well as up. After the Civil War, numerous flatboats became two-way barges as their owners attempted to compete with the railroads. In the end, both the flatboats and the steamboats lost out. But when the United States entered World War I, the mass of war materiel that required transport threatened to outstrip the railroads' capacity, and planners took a new look at the nation's inland waterways. In 1918 the government formed the Federal Barge Line to operate on the Mississippi and other rivers. When it became clear that large barges towed by modern tugs could move nonperishable goods as cheaply and

The sweep of the Mississippi River at New Orleans, looking across Algiers Point.

Courtesy the New Orleans Times-Picayune

efficiently as trains could, private operators entered the game. Today, powerful diesel boats propelling groups of thirty or forty barges—each with the capacity of fifteen or twenty rail cars—ply the Mississippi in an endless stream. If the ghosts of the old rivermen could witness the sight, they would recognize the barges instantly: the modern craft are larger, but their shape is identical to that of a typical nineteenth-century flatboat.

The return of the barges coincided with the rise of a new industry in Louisiana. In 1909, in a former cotton field beside the Mississippi at Baton Rouge, the Standard Oil Company had begun construction of a refinery that for decades would rank among the world's largest. Other oil and petrochemical operations followed, along with such facilities as Kaiser Aluminum's giant ore-processing plant, and the shipping associated with them made Baton Rouge a major port in its own right. Lake Charles, in southwestern Louisiana, also became an important petroleum port with its deepwater link to the Gulf via a forty-mile channel down the Calcasieu River and through Calcasieu Pass. After World War II, petroleum-related and other large plants sprang up in quick succession—

more than a hundred of them in the period 1945–1961 alone—on the Mississippi between Baton Rouge and New Orleans. Today a fifty-four-mile stretch of the river in this industrial corridor forms the Port of South Louisiana. The port features a high percentage of midstream loadings. Below New Orleans, St. Bernard and Plaquemines Parishes maintain similar but smaller operations.

In addition to the deepwater ports on the Mississippi and at Lake Charles, Louisiana has about thirty active shallow-draft ports. Notable for its history is the Port of Shreveport–Bossier City, on the Red River in the northwestern corner of the state—about as far from the Gulf as a boat can go in Louisiana. Shreveport came into being in the 1830s when Henry Shreve cleared a vast logjam blocking the Red. The jam kept reforming, however, until its final removal in the 1870s. Even then, the Red remained a difficult river, swift and dangerous in high water, shallow and choked with sandbars in the dry season, and shipping on it became sporadic and then virtually nonexistent. Finally, in 1995, a series of locks and dams opened the river to regular, year-round towboat-and-barge navigation, putting the "port" back in "Shreveport."

One Louisiana port stands in the Gulf itself: a private terminal known as LOOP (Louisiana Offshore Oil Port), which is used to transfer crude oil from supertankers to onshore refineries via pipeline.

Louisiana's rivers and bayous flow essentially north-to-south, but the state does have one major east-west water route, the Gulf Intracoastal Waterway, also known as the Intracoastal Canal. A combination of natural waters and artificial canals, the Intracoastal runs 1,109 miles from Florida to Texas and connects with some 14,500 more miles of navigable rivers. New Orleans was linked to it via the old Harvey Canal in 1934. Baton Rouge and Lake Charles also have direct access to the Intracoastal. Another artificial waterway, the Mississippi River–Gulf Outlet, completed in 1963, connects New Orleans with Breton Sound at a saving of forty miles compared with river passage.

Together, Louisiana's ports represent one of the state's most vital economic resources. Shipping to, from, and through them totals more than a third of the entire nation's tonnage of domestic waterborne commerce and a sixth of its foreign commerce. More than 4,500 oceangoing vessels and upwards of 100,000 barges operated by more than 100 steamship lines and towboat companies call at the state's ports annually. New Orleans, Baton Rouge, and the Port of South Louisiana consistently rank among the top five ports in the country in tonnage; the Port of Lake Charles is usually in the top twenty.

Lake Charles is the primary non–Mississippi River port of Louisiana.

Courtesy the Historic New Orleans Collection; Acc. No. 1974.25.4.52

As this chapter has shown, however, shipping by water is not a steady, straight-line enterprise, but one of ups and downs. Today it faces strong competition from railroads, the trucking industry, and (in the case of petroleum) pipelines. New Orleans and the Gulf ports suffered a marked decline in business in the 1980s, according to the United States Department of Commerce, because of changing shipping patterns and deregulation of the transportation. Under deregulation, combined ocean-rail rates now rival the all-water rates, making cross-country handling of shipments more attractive than before. Another factor is the increasing importance of supertankers and large container ships. The supertankers are too large to enter the Mississippi, and for the container ships, it is often more profitable to dock at such ports as Charleston, South Carolina, or Savannah, Georgia, and forward the cargoes by rail, than to voyage to Louisiana.

It seems likely that Louisiana ports will rise again, as they have done before. But for anyone concerned with truly long-term trends, there is the question of the Mississippi River itself. According to a study made more than a decade ago by Raphael G. Kazmann and David B. Johnson for the

Louisiana Water Resources Research Institute in Baton Rouge, the river is undergoing a powerful tendency to change its course. If it does, the Atchafalaya River would become the main distributary, with the current main stem remaining merely as an estuary of the Gulf of Mexico. The United States government took cognizance of this possibility at mid-century, when the Corps of Engineers began building the Old River Control Structure. Located forty-five miles north, northwest of Baton Rouge, this combination of revetments, dam, and spillway is designed to regulate the flow into the Atchafalaya and prevent a change of course from occurring. Still, Kazmann and Johnson's report warned, "The final outcome is only a matter of time."

Certainly only time will tell. Meanwhile, Old Man River keeps on rolling along.

—W.G.C.

14

Education

As early as 1725, Raphaël de Luxembourg, a Capuchin priest in New Orleans, opened an academy for boys. In 1728 the nuns of the Ursuline order, who had arrived in the colony the preceding year, established an academy for girls. The settlers had no option other than to look to the Church for the education of their offspring. The teaching of the catechism was basic, and the girls also were instructed in music, needlework, and the elements of refined conduct. Boys were taught Latin and mathematics.

A sizable portion of succeeding generations in south Louisiana, especially in New Orleans and the Cajun country, attended Catholic schools from kindergarten through college. For a period after the racial integration of public schools proceeded in the 1960s and 1970s, white parents enrolled their children in parochial institutions because the mixing of classes took place at a slower pace. Because of an economic slump, financing educational facilities became a problem for the church, which closed some high schools and many elementary schools.

Luis de Unzaga, the Spanish governor from 1770 to 1776, attempted to establish the first publicly supported state schools. He used Spanish priests as teachers, a choice that doomed his effort because French residents refused to send their children to what they called "Spanish schools."

When Louisiana was an American territory, from 1803 until 1812, Governor William C. C. Claiborne and Julien Poydras, president of the Territorial Council, called for the creation of a college in New Orleans and a system of academies and libraries in the rest of the territory, to be financed by the profits from lotteries. In 1811 the council discontinued the lotteries and appropriated $15,000 for the college in New Orleans and $24,000 for the libraries and academies. The last were called "beneficiary schools," and several were opened. When statehood was achieved in 1812, Louisiana's constitution made no provision for public education. The 1845 constitution finally authorized a system of free public schools.

By 1848, there were 646 schools operating in the state, open for terms averaging six months. Of a reported 43,000 potential students in Louisiana, 23,000 were enrolled in classes, many of them in religious schools in New Orleans.

The Civil War brought disaster to education, although in 1862 one of the first acts of Louisiana's Confederate legislature was the appropriation of nearly half a million dollars for public schools. In New Orleans, General Benjamin F. Butler, the first military governor after the occupation by the Federals, appointed a school board made up of Union sympathizers and supplied funds for classes available both to white and to black children. Almost no white children, however, enrolled. The carpetbagger legislature of 1867 authorized the city of Baton Rouge to maintain a school for whites in each ward, and designated a school district in New Orleans for whites. Throughout Reconstruction, most white children either attended nonintegrated nonpublic schools or did not go at all. By 1877, when Reconstruction ended, the economy was at a low point and public education continued to suffer. Catholic schools continued to offer instruction throughout the war and Reconstruction.

The Constitution of 1879 provided for public schools for children between the ages of six and eighteen years. In 1877 the legislature passed a compulsory-attendance law, but enforcement was delayed for years. The Public School Act of 1888 required police juries to appropriate funds for public schools in their parishes, and the Constitution of 1898 required the levying of taxes to support public education.

In 1898 there were 2,221 schools in the state for white children, with a total of 2,856 teachers, whose salaries averaged $240.43 a term. There were 982 schools for blacks, with 1,039 teachers, at an average salary of $139.55. Some schools conducted split terms, which freed pupils to help their parents with farm work. By the 1904–1905 term there were 43 authorized public high schools, and three years later the number had grown to 55. In the 1908–1909 term 4,088 students were enrolled in public secondary schools. In the 1923–1924 school year only 4 public high schools for blacks were operating in the state, but by 1947–1948 the number had grown to 87; there were 98 approved high schools for whites.

Opening of the Delgado School in New Orleans in 1921 was the beginning of an extensive trade-school system. Delgado itself has developed into a college-level institution.

In 1902 a storm destroyed a one-room schoolhouse in Lafayette Parish near Scott. Rather than have the students remain idle until a new facility could be built, two members of the school board—Dr. N. P. Moss and Alcide Judice—at their own expense arranged for a horse-drawn wagonette to deliver the children of the area to existing schools. Prophetically, the wagonette was called a "school bus," and it was the forerunner of today's system of transporting children to central schools.

In 1928 Governor Huey P. Long promised free textbooks as a vote-getting inducement; ever since, the state has provided the learning materials to all students. Governor Earl K. Long in 1948 pushed through the legislature a full, state-supported free-lunch plan, which had been instituted on a partial basis in 1938–1939.

Louisiana shared with other southern states the unrest and dislocations resulting from the federally enforced desegregation of schools in the 1960s and 1970s. Since then, although white resistance remains a factor, disruptive outbreaks have become rare and an uneasy peace has prevailed.

Higher education in Louisiana has been built largely through the state university and its subdivisions, developing in helter-skelter fashion. It had a meager beginning, prospered once a governor got the idea to use a severance tax on natural resources to fund it, and has rocked along through crises brought on by war, depression, and pure political pressure. Until the latter part of the twentieth century, there was no long-range, well-conceived plan for the orderly development of a statewide system.

Louisiana State University, along with its predecessor institutions, has been the heart of the public higher-education system, its various subdivisions the arteries that permitted the flow of education to all sections of the state.

Louisiana lived through the eighteenth century without higher public education. The first publicly aided college, the University of Orleans, was established in 1803 by the legislative council of the Territory of Orleans. It was abolished in 1812, the year of statehood, in favor of the College of Orleans, which lasted only until 1826. Following that, three state-assisted institutions were authorized—the College of Louisiana at Jackson, the College of Jefferson at Convent, and the College of Franklin in Opelousas. They functioned until 1843. Between 1826 and 1844, the state subsidized a number of institutions, the best known being the College of Rapides, the College of Baton Rouge, Mt. Lebanon University, and the Mansfield Female Seminary. In 1834 a group of doctors in New Orleans, concerned about education, began the Medical College of Louisiana, a forerunner of Tulane University.

The second era of public education was initiated by the 1845 constitution, which established the University of New Orleans, also a Tulane predecessor, and the Seminary of Learning and Military Academy in Pineville. The University of Louisiana came into being in 1847 as the University of Louisiana and the Medical College of Louisiana. When Paul Tulane endowed Tulane in 1884, the state turned over its property to Tulane. (Newcomb College, an adjunct, was founded in 1886.)

In August of 1859, General William Tecumseh Sherman was appointed superintendent and professor of engineering of the Seminary. Classes began on January 2, 1860, with a faculty of five and nineteen students. When Louisiana seceded from the Union, Sherman left; the school struggled on until April of 1863, when it closed. After the war, David French

Boyd became acting superintendent. The building housing the college burned on October 15, 1869, and the school was moved to Baton Rouge, where it occupied part of the quarters of the Institute for the Deaf, Dumb, and Blind. On March 16, 1870, the name was changed to Louisiana State University, and again in 1877 to Louisiana State University and Agricultural and Mechanical College, after being merged with the A & M college of New Orleans. Boyd was succeeded by William Preston Johnston, who resigned in 1883 to become president of Tulane.

Boyd and his brother, Thomas D. Boyd, were destined to play a leading role in Louisiana education. James W. Nicholson took over the presidency of LSU from David Boyd, who returned after two years and moved the campus in 1886 to the vacated federal barracks of the Baton Rouge Arsenal. Then Thomas Boyd succeeded David for a short period. Nicholson returned and Thomas Boyd became president of the newly established Louisiana State Normal School at Natchitoches.

It was this step that started Louisiana on a serious turn toward realization of the need and value of higher education, for the Boyd brothers and Nicholson won recognition by the political leaders of the state and aroused the citizenry in the cause.

Between 1900 and 1920, the legislature devoted more attention and funds to education, bringing a third period of change. Education became a political issue after the leadership of Thomas Boyd at Normal and Nicholson at LSU brought greater recognition to higher education.

The election of John M. Parker as governor on a reform ticket initiated a fourth era of educational advancement. He teamed with Thomas Boyd to expand educational facilities. The state university was moved from the barracks to a plantation site three miles from Baton Rouge, and Governor Parker led a move to enact a 2-percent severance tax that eventually supplied millions of dollars to fund education. Support for all colleges increased threefold, with enrollment at LSU jumping from some 6,000 to approximately 18,000.

Huey Long's election in 1928 brought further educational expansion, especially at LSU. Long urged President James Monroe Smith of LSU to enlarge the school's physical plant and arrange sale of some of its acreage to pay for it. He had the state build a medical school in New Orleans, as part of LSU, to satisfy a grudge against Tulane, which had refused to issue him an honorary degree.

One of the major developments in higher education during the current century has been the establishment of the University of New Orleans, which began in 1958 as Louisiana State University in New Orleans, a creature of the legislature in 1956. Governor Earl K. Long used his clout to take over property then being vacated by the U. S. Naval Air Station, a 178-acre tract dotted with hangars and other buildings. General Troy H. Middleton, president of LSU, chose Dr. Homer L. Hitt as the founding chancellor. Hitt, despite opposition from established New Orleans educational institutions that saw the new creature as competition, went to work with enthusiasm, and in a short time built a university that won academic respect throughout the state and region. By 1991, it was registering some 16,000 students per semester.

In 1968, the electorate voted to create the Louisiana Coordinating Council for Higher Education "in order that unnecessary duplication might be avoided and the resources of the state devoted to higher education might be better utilized." The council adopted a master plan in 1972, and the Board of Regents, a statewide planning and coordinating agency, was formed to work with the four-board system of supervision governing the various universities and colleges. The boards include the Board of Supervisors of LSU, the Board of Supervisors of Southern University, the Board of Trustees for State Colleges and Universities, and the Regents. There are twenty-seven units involved.

The LSU Board governs the main university at Baton Rouge and branches at Alexandria, Eunice, and Shreveport, plus the Hebert Law Center in Baton Rouge, the Medical Center in New Orleans (which includes the School of Dentistry), the University of New Orleans, and the Center for Agricultural Sciences and Rural Development.

The Southern Board governs Southern University in Baton Rouge, its branch in New Orleans, and Southern of Shreveport–Bossier City.

The Trustees for State Colleges and Universities manage Delgado Community College in New Orleans, Louisiana Tech University in Ruston, the University of Southwestern Louisiana at Lafayette, Southeastern University at Hammond, Nicholls State at Thibodaux, Northwestern State at Natchitoches (an outgrowth of the old Normal School), Grambling State at Grambling, and McNeese State at Lake Charles.

The Board of Regents is also charged with responsibility to coordinate the curriculums of seven independent regionally accredited institutions. These are Centenary College at Shreveport, Dillard University in New Orleans, Louisiana College in Pineville, Loyola University in New Orleans, Our Lady of Holy Cross College in New Orleans, Tulane University in New Orleans, and Xavier University in New Orleans.

—W.G.C.

15

RELIGION

Catholicism came down the Mississippi with La Salle in 1682.

Near the mouth of the river, La Salle raised a cross on April 9, claimed all the land drained by the Mississippi and its tributaries for France, and named it Louisiana in honor of the king, Louis XIV.

La Salle's little company, led by Father Zenobius Membré, sang the *Te Deum, Exaudiat,* and *Domine salvum.*

In 1724, when the colony of Louisiana was struggling to survive, the French court drew up the *Code Noir* (Black Code) to regulate the institution of slavery in the colony. But the code also regulated the practice of religion.

Article 1 of the *Code Noir* decreed the expulsion of Jews from the colony. Article 2 compelled masters to provide religious instruction for their slaves. Article 3 prohibited any form of religion other than the Roman Catholic creed. Article 4 provided for the confiscation of slaves supervised by anyone but a Catholic. Article 5 called for the strict observance of Sundays and holy days and provided for the confiscation of slaves found working these days.

In his *Church and State in French Colonial Louisiana,* Charles E. O'Neill summed up the state of religion in eighteenth-century Louisiana: "In matters purely spiritual, the Louisiana colony never attained the religious fervor of the Canadian; indeed, while there was a formal structure which paid deference to Catholicism, the society and its political organization were wanting in depth and inspiration. One might say in retrospect that religion for the Louisiana of Louis XIV and Louis XV was a pervading, tempering influence but not a dynamic, decisive force."

When what is today called the French Quarter in New Orleans was laid out in 1721, an area opposite the Place d'Armes was designated for a church. However, for years no church was built. Father François-Xavier Charlevoix complained that religious services were held in "half of a wretched warehouse that they had consented to assign to the Lord." In 1723, Father Raphaël de Luxembourg and a group of Capuchin priests arrived in New Orleans. It was under Father Raphaël's urging that the first permanent church was built. Completed in 1727, it was dedicated to Louis IX, the sainted king of France. However, it fell into such disrepair by

1763 that it was closed and religious services were held in a variety of places. The repaired church was destroyed in the great fire of 1788. The second church was completed in 1794 and became the cathedral of the newly designated diocese of New Orleans. The building, the gift of Don Andrés Almonester y Roxas, the wealthiest Louisianian of the time, survived to the mid-nineteenth century, when the present St. Louis Cathedral was built. It, the third church on the site, was dedicated on December 7, 1851.

From 1793 to 1835, New Orleans had six bishops. In 1835, Bishop Antoine Blanc was consecrated. Fifteen years later, when New Orleans was designated an archdiocese, he was named archbishop. From 1850 to 1991, New Orleans had twelve archbishops. The longest occupation of the see was by German-born Joseph Francis Rummel, whose twenty-nine-year span ran from 1935 to 1964. An epochal event for Roman Catholics came in 1987, when Pope John Paul II visited New Orleans on his American tour. Highlights of the visit were a youth rally that attracted an audience of 60,000 to the Superdome, and an outdoor Mass attended by 200,000 despite rain, at the University of New Orleans.

In 1991, a religious census showed that there were 1,404,411 Roman Catholics in Louisiana, the great majority of them being in south and southwest Louisiana.

Throughout the French and Spanish rules in Louisiana, very few citizens were not at least nominally Catholic. Following the Louisiana Purchase, Protestant Americans flocked into the Territory. They found no Protestant church, no Protestant congregation. It was then that a committee called a meeting to form the state's first non-Catholic congregation. The group met on June 2, 1805, in New Orleans at the Bourbon Street boarding house of Madame Elizabeth Fourage. The following week another meeting was held to decide on what denomination the church would follow. A vote was taken with the following result: Episcopalian, 45; Presbyterian, 7; Methodist 1. At this meeting it was decided to call the congregation Christ Church.

In November, 1805, the Reverend Philander Chase arrived in New Orleans to become pastor of Christ Church. He preached his first sermon in the Cabildo on November 17. Such was the beginning of Protestantism in Louisiana. In 1827, an Episcopal church was established at St. Francisville bearing the name Grace Church.

The Methodist church in Louisiana had its roots in the 1799 session of the South Carolina Conference when Tobias Gibson was named missionary to Natchez. Seven years later, and just three years after the Louisiana

Purchase, the first Methodist congregation in Louisiana was organized in Opelousas. It wasn't until 1820, however, that the congregation had its first church. Methodist ministers made the circuit of the Opelousas area, covering as much as five hundred miles on horseback to preach in the isolated areas.

The first Protestant church built in Louisiana was erected in 1808. It was a log structure, built in the Catahoula district by the Methodist preacher James Oxley. It was called Oxley Chapel.

By 1811, Methodism had spread to the Florida Parishes. The noted Lorenzo Dow, whose evangelical zeal took him from Maine to Louisiana, preached in the Florida Parishes in 1815.

Methodism in New Orleans gained impetus in the 1820s with the coming of the Rev. Benjamin A. Drake. During his service in New Orleans, the first Methodist church in the city was constructed in 1825. In 1993, the total number of Louisianians associated with the Methodist church was 128,803, served by 571 churches (these numbers do not include branches other than the United Methodist Church).

Before the Louisiana Purchase there were already a few Baptists scattered in Louisiana. They either went "underground" or were tolerated by the Spanish authorities. Despite difficulties, these isolated Baptists were often visited by ministers.

Ezra Courtney, a thirty-three-year-old Pennsylvanian, reached Louisiana at the time of the transfer of the colony to the United States. This Baptist missionary began preaching in 1804. In 1814 Courtney settled in East Feliciana Parish and thus became the first resident Baptist minister in the state. He found that two years earlier, the first Baptist church in Louisiana had been established in Washington Parish, near Franklinton. Situated near the Bogue Chitto River, the church was known as the Half Moon Bluff Church. It was organized on October 12, 1812.

That same year, but a month later, the first Baptist church west of the Mississippi, and the oldest existing Baptist church in Louisiana, was organized as the Calvary Baptist Church at Bayou Chicot in St. Landry Parish.

Baptist growth in Louisiana in the past century has been remarkable. From small beginnings the denomination expanded steadily throughout the twentieth century. Today it is the leading Protestant church in the state. Membership in 1993 stood at 589,771, and there were 1,365 Baptist churches (these numbers include only main branches of the church).

Although other Christian denominations have been historically important in Louisiana, they today comprise a relatively small proportion of the state's church members. For example, Episcopalians, Presbyterians, and

Lutherans each make up less than 1 percent of Louisiana Christians. Jews make up about two-tenths of a percent of the state's religiously affiliated citizens.

"It is a little remarkable that the first successful effort to plant Presbyterianism in the city of New Orleans should have originated with the Congregationists of New England."

So wrote Dr. Benjamin Morgan Palmer, noted Presbyterian minister, who served as pastor of the First Presbyterian Church in New Orleans for forty-six years.

The Connecticut Missionary Society, early in 1817, sent the Reverend Elias Cornelius on a missionary tour of the Southwestern states via New Orleans. En route, he met at Princeton, New Jersey, the twenty-one-year-old Sylvester Larned, who was finishing his studies for the Presbyterian ministry. Cornelius persuaded Larned to seek his first ministry in New Orleans. Cornelius reached New Orleans on December 30, 1817, and Larned followed him into the city on January 23, 1818. "The greatest service rendered by Dr. Cornelius was that of introducing Rev. Sylvester Larned," wrote Dr. Palmer. Larned was an instant success in New Orleans, which was charmed by the young man's personality as well as by his power and eloquence in the pulpit.

There were Presbyterians in Louisiana before Larned arrived but only in handfuls outside New Orleans, mainly at Alexandria, Thibodaux, and Covington. But it was not until Larned came that efforts were directed to the building of a church. The cornerstone was laid on January 8, 1819, on St. Charles Avenue between Gravier and Union Streets. Larned's ministry was essentially evangelistic; it was terminated by his death by yellow fever on August 31, 1820. Larned's successor was the Reverend Theodore Clapp, but not until 1822. In 1823—five years after the church was built—it was organized for the first time into an ecclesiastical body.

Meanwhile, Presbyterianism had made steady progress outside New Orleans. In 1823, the Reverend Richard Lanier preached in St. Francisville and its environs fourteen times in twenty-seven days. This indicates that Presbyterians were fairly numerous in the Florida Parishes. The same is also true for Alexandria, where the well-known preacher Timothy Flint organized a Presbyterian seminary.

Theodore Clapp, known universally as "Parson Clapp," was an eloquent speaker, and visitors to New Orleans frequented his church so often that it was known as the "Strangers' Church." During his pastorate, which began in 1822, the number of Presbyterians in New Orleans increased as the population grew in the 1820s and 1830s. But as time went on, Dr. Clapp found himself moving toward Unitarianism. He was tried by the Mississippi Synod for heresy and expelled from the Presbyterian church. So popular was Dr. Clapp that most of his congregation remained loyal to him. He thus became the founder of the Unitarian church in New Orleans. Dr. Clapp's church was destroyed in the great fire of the St. Charles Hotel in 1851.

Establishment of the Lutheran church in Louisiana came gradually, with German immigrants. The first German groups to come through New Orleans were en route to Arkansas, where John Law had promised them a prosperous life. Disappointed, they decided to return to their homeland, but stopped in New Orleans on the way back and were talked into trying life upriver from New Orleans. Some stayed in the New Orleans area, where they became associated with Protestant congregations, including Reformed, Evangelical, and Lutheran groups. While the first Protestant Lutheran group was founded in 1805, the first true Lutheran church was not established until 1856 under the pastorate of Christian Gottlieb Moedinger. Churches that practiced true Lutheran doctrine came to Louisiana from the Lutherans of Perry County, Missouri. By 1890, there were seven established congregations, six affiliated with the Missouri Synod and one with the Ohio Synod.

It was noted earlier in this chapter that the Black Code promulgated in Louisiana in 1724 called for the expulsion of Jews from the colony. Historians believe there were very few Jews to be expelled. As late as 1826, when Louisiana had been American for almost a quarter of a century, there were only about 100 Jews in the state.

In 1824, an attempt to organize a synagogue in New Orleans failed. Four years later, however, the Gates of Mercy Synagogue was established, mainly through the efforts of a New York merchant, Jacob de Silva Solis. Solis was in New Orleans during Passover and this prompted his efforts to form a congregation. Those interested met in a room on St. Louis Street. Judah Touro, merchant-philanthropist of New Orleans, gave financial assistance. Most of the members were of French and German extraction, with a few Spanish Jews. It has been estimated that in the early 1840s, when New Orleans' population had passed 100,000, there were about 2,000 Jews in the city. Jews of Spanish and Portuguese extraction settled in New Orleans at this time and set up a synagogue of their own. Judah Touro purchased from the Episcopalians their church on Canal and Bourbon Streets and gave it to the newcomers. By 1989, there were more than a dozen synagogues in Louisiana, with about 9,000 Jews following the rites of Reform Judaism. Orthodox Judaism has a small following both in New Orleans and the state.

In closing, it should be stated that there are in Louisiana as many as seventy splinter organizations that have devolved from the major churches.

—C.L.D.

16

Politics

Huey Pierce Long served as governor and United States senator for only a little longer than seven years but changed the political realities of Louisiana for most of the twentieth century. In building a power structure that made him a virtual dictator, he created turbulence in the state and even the national government. Clearly, he was the star of the century in Louisiana's political theater. His rule was so effective, and his following so faithful, that several members of his family, especially brother Earl K. Long and son Russell B. Long, rose to prominence after an assassin's bullet ended Huey's life in September of 1935.

A look into the conditions that brought Huey to the forefront is a study in the socioeconomics of Louisiana and the South, and his rise to power offers a strong contrast to other politicians of the day. As Louisiana moved from an agricultural economy to prosperity from the production of oil and gas, Long championed not the new bonanza, but the fortunes of those who did not share in it. In fact, he challenged big oil, principally the Standard Oil Company, the behemoth of the industry. He made the challenge the thrust of his campaign for the votes of the poor and underprivileged, the centerpiece of his populist appeal.

The social forces that produced Huey Long began gathering strength in the early 1890s but were not strong enough then to prevail. Louisiana was sharply divided between the old-line conservative Democrat (Bourbon) faction and the agrarian reformers. The Bourbons were the clique of wealthy planters, timberland owners, merchants, and professionals who had ruled the state since the end of Reconstruction. Often—although not always—their candidates also had the backing of the powerful New Orleans political machine known as the "Old Regulars" or the "Ring." The reformers included numerous small farmers and other working people. Many supported the Populist, or People's, Party, organized locally in 1891 and nationally the following year. The state's Republican Party, reeling from the scandals of Reconstruction days and the Democrats' increasingly successful bulldozing of black voters, was still a force, but in decline.

The gubernatorial campaign of 1892 saw the first direct electoral clash between the Bourbons and the Populists, but that confrontation was a sidelight in a race in which the dominant issue was the fate of the Louisiana

Lottery. The lottery's charter would expire during the new governor's term. Should it be renewed? The question evoked strong opinions in Louisiana. The Democrats and the Republicans both split bitterly on the matter, so that a prolottery and an antilottery candidate emerged from each party. The election boiled down to a battle between the antilottery Democrat, Murphy J. Foster, and the prolottery Democrat, incumbent governor Samuel D. McEnery. Foster won handily. That the balloting was rife with fraud shocked no one: Louisiana had not seen an honest vote in decades.

The Populist candidate in 1892, Robert L. Tannehill of Winn Parish—where Huey Long would be born the next year—ran last in the five-way race. Yet that result was deceptive. Tannehill carried four parishes (including Winn with an astonishing 76.7 percent of the vote), and several Populists won legislative seats. More important, the fledgling party was on the rise. Between 1892 and 1896 it gained supporters by the tens of thousands, especially among the poor white farmers who once had been a mainstay of the conservative Democratic cause. Then, in the race of 1896, something almost unthinkable in Louisiana happened: the largely white People's Party and the heavily black Republican Party joined forces. The new alliance, the so-called Fusion Party, chose as its candidate for governor a wealthy Democrat turned Republican named John N. Pharr.

Murphy Foster, meanwhile, had not idled away his four years in the governor's chair. While successfully demolishing the Louisiana Lottery—which was probably doomed anyway by new federal laws—he grabbed control of the Democratic political machine and reunified the party. His economic and racial conservatism pleased the Bourbon power brokers. He easily captured the party's nomination for the governorship in 1896.

The campaign was brutal. A coalition of blacks and poor whites was a Bourbon nightmare sprung to life. No weapon that could be used against the Fusionists was to be shunned. Flagrantly racist appeals in oratory and in print became the rule, not the exception. Terror attacks escalated. And then came the election itself.

It is generally conceded that more Louisianians marked legitimate ballots for John Pharr than for Murphy Foster in 1896. After the official count, however, Foster was named the winner by nearly thirty thousand votes. The fraud was massive even by Louisiana standards. Angry Populists and Republicans took to the streets. Foster called up the militia to quell the protests.

The election of 1896 stands as a turning point in Louisiana's political history. It broke the backs of the Populists and Republicans, both of whom not only saw the governorship slip away but also lost influence in the legislature. In 1898 the Democrats rammed through a new state constitution with voter-registration provisions that quickly resulted in 99 percent of the black electorate's being disqualified. Some of these same rules could be and were used against whites. In the end nearly one-quarter of the state's white voters were disenfranchised—and they were overwhelmingly the poor and often illiterate citizens who tended to vote Populist.

Having crushed their chief rivals, the conservative Democrats ruled Louisiana almost unchallenged for the next quarter century. A string of single-term governors—the Constitution of 1898 had prohibited successive terms in the office—included only Bourbons or men who carried the Bourbon stamp of approval. A modest threat arose in 1916 when John M. Parker ran plausibly for governor as a Progressive, but that situation was unique. The Progressive Party had been formed in 1912 as a vehicle for Teddy Roosevelt when the Republicans failed to nominate him for the presidency despite his two earlier terms in the White House. Roosevelt ran second to Democrat Woodrow Wilson that year. By 1916 the Progressive Party was moribund nationally—even Roosevelt declined its nomination—but in Louisiana it attracted sugarcane planters who were disgruntled by the tariff policies of Wilson and the Democrat-controlled Congress but could not bring themselves to vote Republican. Even with the cane-parishes vote, Parker lost to the Bourbon candidate, Ruffin G. Pleasant. But Parker was a Bourbon himself, a patrician planter who had added to his cotton wealth through New Orleans business dealings and was deeply conservative despite certain Progressive-influenced ideas. In 1920 he was nominated for governor again—by the Democrats. He won easily.

Two decades and more of Bourbon domination did not mean that populism had disappeared from Louisiana. The state was still heavily rural and poor. The black vote no longer mattered—indeed, it hardly existed—but in 1920 more than three out of five white voters lived in rural villages or in the countryside itself. Farmers, sharecroppers, laborers, trappers, fishermen, these people had long-ignored interests that differed greatly from those of the ruling elite. It was this vast, untapped constituency that Huey Long would ride to unprecedented power.

Huey started young. He was only twenty-four, a little-known lawyer practicing in his hometown of Winnfield, when he announced in 1918 for the north Louisiana seat on the three-member Railroad Commission (later renamed the Public Service Commission). He campaigned from farmhouse to farmhouse along the dirt roads, won in an upset, and immediately began making headlines by assailing two of the biggest targets in the state, Standard Oil and its "stooge"—Huey's word—Governor

Huey Long at the beginning of his meteoric political career.

Courtesy the Historic New Orleans Collection; Acc. No. 1978.3

Pleasant. Huey backed John Parker in 1920 but soon after Parker's election was blasting him as just another tool of big oil, and a millionaire to boot. It was talk the old-time Populists would have liked. It also made Huey and Parker enemies for life.

Parker's administration, like the man himself, mixed reformist tendencies with adherence to the status quo. Parker showed courage in taking on the Ku Klux Klan, which in the 1920s was running rampant throughout the South. He fiercely opposed the New Orleans Ring, although his efforts against the corrupt machine scarcely dented it. Many of his social programs, ironically, resembled those that Huey himself would later propound. Like Huey, he was an ardent booster of Louisiana State University and did much to lift it into the upper echelon of southern universities. Parker also pressed for more and better schools, roads, and flood-control measures, but his fiscal conservatism—he disdained new taxes and even bond issues—made funding these improvements difficult. He did succeed in imposing a 2-percent severance tax on natural resources, but the modest size of this tax allowed Huey to paint him as a minion of the oil and mining companies.

Huey Long turned thirty, the minimum age for the governorship, on August 30, 1923, and announced his candidacy that same day. He ran third in the 1924 election, polling 73,985 votes while the front runners, Lieutenant Governor Hewitt Bouanchaud and Henry L. Fuqua, received 84,162 and 81,382, respectively. It was an impressive showing for so young and untried a candidate, establishing Huey as a major threat to Louisiana's power structure. Fuqua, capturing most of Huey's voters, swamped Bouanchaud in the runoff.

From the moment the polls closed in 1924, Huey was campaigning for 1928. Using his Public Service Commission post as a pulpit, he spoke out regularly and loudly on controversial issues. When the state contracted with a Ring-connected company for the construction of a toll bridge across Lake Pontchartrain, Huey not only denounced the deal as crooked but also promised to build a free bridge "when I'm governor." When the telephone company steeply boosted its rates, he forced a cutback. Always he positioned himself as the common man's guardian—and made sure that the common man knew about it.

Governor Fuqua died in office in 1926, and Lieutenant Governor Oramel H. Simpson succeeded him. Simpson and Congressman Riley Joe Wilson emerged as Huey Long's main competition in the 1928 governor's race. Simpson, although a bit of a nonentity, had considerable conservative backing. Wilson also had strong conservative support, as well as the Ring's endorsement. Huey barnstormed the state and filled the radio waves with promises of paved roads, free school lunches and schoolbooks, better hospitals, homestead exemptions, and other lures. He worked especially hard in south Louisiana, where he had run poorly in 1924. Simpson and Wilson, along with business interests and a large portion of the press, devoted much of their campaign energies to labeling Huey a Communist.

On the night of the Democratic first primary, the early New Orleans returns gave Wilson a huge lead. Simpson ran well in Shreveport and Baton Rouge. Huey looked to be badly beaten. Then, hours later, results began to trickle in from the country districts. Huey was piling up majorities not only in north Louisiana as expected, but also in the rural parishes of south Louisiana. When it was over, he had polled 126,842 votes to Wilson's 81,747 and Simpson's 80,236. Long's plurality shocked Wilson into abandoning the race. Huey was in.

If there were any doubts that a new order prevailed in Louisiana under Governor Long, Huey dispelled them in the next session of the legislature, which he quickly whipped into submission. He choked off opposition by developing a patronage system that rewarded his supporters and penalized his enemies, and resorted to tactics that created a wall between the pro- and anti-Long forces, a political cleavage that would endure for more than a generation. First, he reorganized the highway and tax commissions, then took out after other agencies. With his men in place, he steered through the legislature laws that gave him control of taxing powers traditionally held by independent parish and state agencies. Then he consolidated the state's bonding authority so that he could control all spending. Meanwhile, he had the legislature double severance and gasoline taxes and place a tax on carbon black, an ingredient widely used by industry. The added taxes were sufficient to finance a $30-million bond issue, enough for Huey to deliver on his campaign promises.

Huey's ingenuity shone in his scheme to assure passage of his highway program. He placed in the bill authorizing the new roads a map showing which roads he planned to pave. If a senator or representative opposed the bill, he would have that legislator's parish stricken from the list. Louisiana at the time had roads comparable to the worst in any state, and his device worked despite cries of foul play.

Huey's tactics enraged the conservatives, who in 1929 decided to force a showdown. Huey had called a special session of the legislature to consider a five-cents-per-barrel tax on oil refined in the state. It soon became clear that the votes needed to pass the tax bill were lacking, and Long's forces planned to adjourn the session. But the anti-Longites wanted more: smelling blood, they had assembled a list of charges against Huey that they hoped would lead to his impeachment. At a night meeting of the house of representatives on Monday, March 25, matters came to a head. A young lawmaker from Caddo Parish, Cecil Morgan, sought to be recognized by Speaker John B. Fournet. Morgan meant to air a claim by a former bodyguard of Huey's that Huey had once told him to murder an anti-Long legislator. Fournet, a Long partisan, knew Morgan's purpose, ignored him, and entertained a motion to adjourn. The automatic voting machine flashed a vote of sixty-seven for and thirteen against. Long's opponents shouted that the machine had been rigged. Morgan, still unrecognized, spoke anyway, striding down the aisle amid a growing melee. As fist fights broke out all over the floor, Fournet temporarily left the Speaker's chair. It was a tactical mistake. The anti-Long forces reconvened the meeting and moved to reconsider the motion to adjourn. By a roll-call vote of seventy-one to nine, the legislators decided to remain in session.

The next day, the anti-Longites introduced nineteen specific charges of wrongdoing by the governor, ranging in seriousness from the alleged murder order, bribery, and misuse of public funds down to complaints that Huey had used abusive language against public officials and had behaved immorally in a New Orleans nightclub. A series of hearings pared the list to eight particulars (murder plotting and nightclub misbehavior not among them). On April 26 the house of representatives voted an impeachment indictment on these charges and handed it up to the senate, which under the Louisiana Constitution sits as a court in impeachment trials. The senate recessed until May 14 to give both sides time to prepare.

The antis should have moved faster. The lengthy hearings and the recess gave Huey time—time he put to good use. He mounted an all-out campaign against his detractors, taking to the radio, stumping the state, and using the state police to distribute circulars that castigated his opponents. He railed against "the underhanded cross of the manipulators who want to ruin any man they cannot control" and played heavily on his appeal to "help the sick, the lame and the blind." He lambasted the "lying newspapers" and raged that Standard Oil was out to get him. And somewhere along the way, he or one of his advisers came up with the idea that would become known as the Round Robin.

When May 14 dawned, Louisiana was ready to watch a political drama on which the eyes of the nation were also focused. It ended almost as soon as it began. After some technical fencing, state senator Philip Gilbert rose holding a document—the Round Robin. Signed by himself and fourteen other senators, it stated that because of the "unconstitutionality and invalidity" of the proceedings, the fifteen would not vote to impeach Long no matter what evidence was presented. A two-thirds majority was required for conviction, and the senate had thirty-nine members. Huey needed only fourteen votes to save him, but he had lagniappe, a little something extra. How he had obtained the fifteen signatures could be guessed at, but guesswork was beside the point. The impeachers knew they were beaten. They did not contest a motion to adjourn sine die.

Through his campaign for the governorship, and in blocking conviction on the impeachment charges, Huey had established himself as a masterful politician and a spellbinding speaker who frequently displayed a sense of humor. His adversaries branded him as reckless and ruthless. He got into a fight with Mayor T. Semmes Walmsley of New Orleans ("Turkey Head," Huey called him) and had the legislature strip the city of its taxing powers, rendering Walmsley powerless. Likewise, he crushed the city's leading political organization, the Old Regulars, luring many of them to his own organization. Despite this, however, Huey never carried the city in an election.

Huey's ambition soared above state lines; after some three years as governor, he decided to run for the United States Senate. But he had a problem. He and Lieutenant Governor Paul Cyr had become bitter enemies, and Huey had vowed never to turn over the governorship to Cyr. Huey decided to run against Senator Joseph E. Ransdell, whose term expired in 1931. But Huey's governorship ran until May of 1932. Thus, if he were elected senator, he would leave the governorship before the end of his term. The crafty Huey promptly noted that he would have to delay taking his Senate seat just four months, "leaving it just as vacant for that four months as it has been for the last 32 years," in his words. Huey beat Ransdell decisively, then supported O. K. Allen for the governorship. Still, he had to figure a way to keep Cyr out of the office, or delay taking his Senate seat.

Cyr became impatient after Huey was elected to the Senate and sued to have Long declared a senator. Then he had himself sworn in as governor, a move that spurred Huey to concoct one of the greatest finesses in politics. When Cyr took the oath as governor, Huey declared the office of lieutenant governor vacant and named Alvin O. King, president of the state senate, to the post. Hurriedly, he had the capitol surrounded by state troopers to keep Cyr from occupying the governor's office. Huey then hopped a train for Washington and arranged to take his oath as United States senator the minute King was sworn in as governor. King and Huey were in and Cyr out, although the issue was only resolved later, in the courts.

When Huey took the senatorial oath on January 25, 1932, someone asked him which title he preferred, governor or senator. "They call me Kingfish down in Louisiana," he responded, a reference to the nickname his cronies used, which they had appropriated from the popular "Amos 'n' Andy" radio show. Actually, Huey never ceased being governor. He was the de facto head of the state even while in Washington, and when he returned to Louisiana he took charge of the action in the governor's office and in the legislature. Governor Allen, a minion, would stamp his OK on any plan or bill Huey supported.

Striking back at the state's newspapers, which had criticized him from the outset of his gubernatorial term, Huey had the legislature impose a 2-percent tax on gross advertising income of newspapers with circulations of 20,000 or more. It happened that twelve of the thirteen newspapers affected had opposed Long. The state's press challenged the tax as violating the First Amendment to the United States Constitution. In 1936, the United States Supreme Court, by unanimous decision, found the tax unconstitutional.

Huey made himself heard in the Senate, filibustering legislation and grabbing the spotlight at every opportunity as he opposed President Franklin D. Roosevelt's New Deal, after initially supporting it, promoting instead his own Share Our Wealth program. He talked of running for president, and wrote a book, *My First Days in the White House,* in which he outlined what he would do.

It was never to be. Huey's vindictive tactics in firing his enemies from the state payroll and passing legislation against his opponents had polarized Louisiana and created an acrimonious atmosphere that led to his sudden death.

In Baton Rouge on the evening of Sunday, September 8, 1935, Huey visited the capitol to check on some of his legislation. As he emerged from the governor's office, a frail man in a white suit, holding a small black pistol, shot him. Huey screamed and ran down steps to the capitol basement. Within seconds, bodyguards and state police poured more than thirty bullets into the gunman. Pandemonium set in.

Louisiana Supreme Court justice John Fournet was within an arm's length of Huey when the gunman fired. In December of 1983 Fournet—the same man who had been Speaker of the House during Long's impeachment troubles—recounted to this writer that he saw the gunman approach and raised his arm to try to prevent the shot but could only deflect the man's aim by brushing his arm.

Bleeding internally, Huey was taken to the nearby Our Lady of the Lake hospital. Surgery obviously would be necessary. Two specialists were summoned from New Orleans, but they were delayed by an accident. Dr. Arthur Vidrine, superintendent of Charity Hospital in New Orleans, happened to be in Baton Rouge, and when the operation could be postponed no longer, he performed it. The bullet was found to have pierced the intestine and the right kidney. Vidrine repaired the damage and closed the incision. Soon, however, it was clear that something was wrong. Huey continued to weaken. He died early on Tuesday morning, September 10.

"Huey bled to death," said Fournet. "Vidrine botched the operation." Fournet blamed Vidrine for not probing for the bullet, which was never found, but in fact Huey appeared to have an exit wound as well as an entry wound. Other doctors who examined Huey suggested that Vidrine failed to detect damage to the kidney's renal duct, which then continued to bleed after the operation. And Dr. Edgar Hull, who was present in the operating room as a young intern, later said that Huey had fulminating peritonitis and probably could not have been saved anyway because at the time there were no drugs to control the infection.

By the time Huey died, the assassin had already been buried. He was Dr. Carl Austin Weiss of Baton Rouge. Weiss, twenty-nine, was the son-in-law of a state district judge who had been gerrymandered out of office by Huey's actions. Weiss's .32-caliber pistol was found by his body after the shooting but later disappeared. In 1991 it was discovered in the possession of the daughter of former state police superintendent Louis Guerre, who led the 1935 investigation. It was turned over to the state. In 1992 Weiss's body was exhumed and examined by forensics experts, but they found no conclusive evidence regarding the assassination.

Some writers over the years have tried to cloak the shooting in mystery, offering various theories about it, but Fournet's story, which he stood by until his death and which was corroborated by every other close eyewitness, disputes their claims.

One thing is certain: Huey's death produced a cataclysm in Louisiana politics. In less than three years, the dictatorship he had built came crashing down amid a multitude of scandals that reached from the bottom to the top of the state administration. Huey had once said of his followers: "If those fellows try to use the powers I've given them without me to hold them down, they'll all land in the penitentiary." Those words proved to be prophetic.

Ironically, the scandals had the effect of putting another Long in the governorship—Earl Kemp Long, Huey's younger brother. The story, like many involving Louisiana politics, is byzantine. Huey died with the 1936 Democratic primary barely four months away, and his machine had yet to choose its candidate for governor. Huey himself seems to have favored James A. "Jimmy" Noe, president pro tempore of the state senate. But the Kingfish's wishes died with him, and his chief aides—hotelman Seymour Weiss, businessman Abraham L. Shushan, and especially furniture dealer Robert S. Maestri (all from New Orleans, where Maestri would soon become mayor)—selected Richard W. Leche, an appeals court judge who resided in Metairie, to top the ticket, with Earl Long as his running mate (Earl, of course, thought that he should be the standard bearer, despite numerous public spats between him and Huey).

Leche and Earl campaigned on the martyr's memory, and Huey proved to be an even stronger vote-getter in death than in life: they won in a landslide, capturing 67.1 percent of the ballots cast; there would be no runoff. In an odd twist, the incumbent governor, O. K. Allen, died after the primary but before his term in office had expired. There was no lieutenant governor per se because Allen's former lieutenant governor—John Fournet—had vacated the post to take his supreme court seat. Louisiana's constitution specified that the president pro tempore of the senate came next in the line of succession. So Jimmy Noe became governor after all—for three and a half months.

Leche himself lasted three years. "When I took the oath of office," he once said, "I didn't take any vow of poverty." His actions as governor bore out the truth of that statement. Estimates of the amount skimmed by him and scores of other officials during his tenure range from $25 million to more than $100 million. The skein of corruption began to unravel after reporter F. Edward Hebert wrote a news story for the New Orleans *States* exposing the use of state-purchased materials on the new home of a Leche aide (Hebert, eventually a congressman, revealed years later that his source for the story was Jimmy Noe). Next, a nationally syndicated column detailed how federal WPA materials had been stolen and WPA workers forced to build homes owned by Leche and others in his administration.

Leche was teetering on the brink. The hand that pushed him over belonged to a fellow Long loyalist. Dr. James Monroe Smith, president of Louisiana State University, unhappy with his $18,000 annual salary, had embezzled a half million dollars of LSU funds to support his attempt to corner the wheat market. The scheme crashed when wheat prices fell. Before fleeing to Canada, Smith told Leche what he had done. That same day, June 21, 1939, Leche announced that he would resign. On June 26 he made it official, and Earl Long took the governor's oath.

By now allegations of official wrongdoing were cascading down by the hundreds, and the people of Louisiana were in a mood of near-revolt. When state criminal justice authorities, part of the corrupt system, would take no action against the alleged wrongdoers, citizen groups appealed to the federal government for action. The Justice Department dispatched a crusading young assistant attorney general, O. John Rogge, to New Orleans. Rogge found a morass of apparent misdeeds reaching from the governor's office to lesser offices and down through state agencies. He convened special grand juries and went to work.

First, Rogge prosecuted Dr. Smith, who upon returning from Canada said he had been "ill advised" to flee. Smith and four others, including Seymour Weiss, Huey's keeper of the "deducts" exacted from the pay of state employees to form a political campaign chest, were found guilty of mail fraud in the purchase and resale to the state of the old Bienville Hotel for use as a nurses' home. The defendants trapped themselves when, after selling the hotel and its furnishings, they sold the furnishings a second time.

Smith, Weiss, and three others were sent to federal prison, and Smith in addition wound up with convictions in state courts, in which local prosecutors brought actions after the federal government began its probe. Rogge next took up a case in which five persons, including Abraham Shushan, president of the Orleans Levee Board, were charged with defrauding the board in a $2-million bond-refunding scheme. The defendants, who divided a $500,000 fee for carrying out the refunding scheme, ostensibly to save the state money on interest charges, were sentenced to prison. With those two victories under his belt, Rogge went after Governor Leche and convicted him in the federal district court at Alexandria of defrauding the state in the purchase of trucks for the highway department. Leche went to prison. Rogge was tearing up the very fabric of state government. Looking deeper into reports of wrongdoing, he found that the state's former conservation commissioner, William G. Rankin, had conspired with Leche to buy with public funds a boat to be presented to Leche as a gift from his friends. Rankin, who had been forced to resign in the face of revelations of mismanagement, pleaded guilty to fraud in the boat scheme and was sentenced to a prison term.

The scandals and the prosecutions naturally dominated the 1940 gubernatorial campaign. The field included Earl Long, Jimmy Noe, and Sam Houston Jones, a Lake Charles lawyer who had been commander of the Louisiana American Legion. After twelve years of Longite rule, the conservative faction of the Democratic Party—mostly the anti-Long people— saw an opportunity to capture the governorship. Jones attracted the support of the state's press and the so-called "good government" forces. Earl led in the first primary, with Jones second. Noe, one of the three founders of the Win or Lose Oil Company, from which he and other Long followers benefited handsomely through purchase of state oil lands, finished a strong third in the race and became a key player in the runoff. Enter John Rogge. The Long forces expected Noe to support Earl, but Rogge had other ideas. Although his role as a federal prosecutor surely demanded neutrality, Rogge called a press conference on the progress of his prosecutions and told several reporters, including this one, that he had exacted a pledge from Noe to support Jones. He asked that the information be kept confidential and hinted that in return for Noe's swing to Jones, he would not press possible charges against Noe. With Noe's support, Jones won the runoff.

Jones's, election meant a swing to conservatism. He brought about numerous reforms, including establishment of a strong civil service system and the elimination of deadheads on the payroll and "deducts" from the pay of state employees. He purged voter registration rolls, stopped dual office holding, and enacted a public records act. He introduced voting machines to New Orleans and whacked 7,500 employees off the state payrolls. To satisfy the liberal wing of the party, he increased welfare benefits, promised to continue the road-building program, and reduced the price of automobile license tags from $15 to $3. It all was part of a move to break forever the hold of the Long group on state government. Jones's term coincided with World War II, a period when there was little unemployment.

In an effort to perpetuate Jones's style of government, his backers in 1944 chose Jimmie H. Davis, a former schoolteacher and public service commissioner who also was a noted country-music singer. Davis sang his way to an easy victory over Lewis Morgan of Covington, who was backed by the Old Regulars. The author of "You Are My Sunshine" and other popular songs, Davis turned out to be not only a warbler but a wobbler, finding it difficult to make up his mind on sensitive issues. During a protracted Tangipahoa Parish dairymen's strike when the governor's intervention was being sought, he left the state to make a movie in Hollywood. During his term, which ran through 1948, Davis was recorded as absent from the capital nearly half the time.

By 1948, as Davis' term wound down, Earl Long was girding for another try at the top prize. He worked up a platform that included old-age pensions, free hot lunches for schoolchildren, more charity hospitals, and better roads. Then he took to the stump and criss-crossed the state campaigning day and night. The conservative faction, sensing renewed strength in the Long camp, called upon Jones to run again. This time it was a mismatch, and Earl swept to an easy victory.

A $30-million treasury surplus left by Davis was just the thing to get Earl started on his stepped-up welfare program. He had the legislature place a five-cents-per-bottle tax on beer and increase the sales tax. Populism was back; Ole Earl was in a spending mood. But his return to power was viewed with alarm by the press and business. The New York *Times* noted on November 7, 1948, that "Earl is trying mighty hard to wear Huey's shoes, but he sort of rattles around in them. He hasn't got Huey's brains and he hasn't got Huey's finesse. Where Huey was fiery, this fellow is just loud. Where Huey outsmarted his opposition, Earl just slams into the center of the line." But the *Times* underrated Earl, judging by his later successes. He not only killed civil service and a number of the other Jones programs, but also took control of the legislature as had Huey and manipulated it at will, distributing patronage to his friends.

Shortly after Earl became governor, United States Senator John H. Overton died. Russell B. Long, Huey's son, who had campaigned for Earl, jumped in the race to succeed him. Russell was not yet thirty years old and if elected would have to wait several months to take his seat. Opposed by Judge Robert F. Kennon of Minden, Russell was elected by 10,475 votes in a race in which Kennon showed surprising strength. Only a heavy turnout in the rural parishes saved Russell from defeat, and the sheriffs friendly to the Longs were credited with putting him over.

When he took his seat, Russell said: "My main concern, just like my father's, will be for social legislation." As time went by, however, it was clear that Russell held some contrary views. Whereas Huey had made big oil his target, Russell took a kindly view toward the oil people in supporting increased depletion allowances and other measures. Business accepted him. He was, incidentally, the first man in history to follow his father *and* mother in the Senate: Rose Long, his mother, had served briefly by appointment following Huey's death.

Quarreling among the Longs was common, but they always seemed to coalesce at election time. Earl denounced Huey during a Senate hearing in 1933, and Julius, the eldest brother, often denounced Huey. In 1952, as Earl's term as governor was ending, he and Russell got into a public dispute. Earl sought to elect his successor, and picked Judge Carlos G. Spaht of Baton Rouge as his candidate. Russell backed Congressman Hale Boggs.

"Just two young squirts down from Washington," Earl railed. "He was Louisiana's leading deadhead," he added, referring to his nephew's service as an assistant secretary of state during the Leche administration. Russell replied, "Earl is getting as bitter toward me as he was toward my father. I have always earned my salary in every job." Neither won, however, as Kennon, an also-ran for governor in 1948, scored a stunning upset in the 1952 election. Kennon had never stopped running after that 1948 defeat, and although he had no formidable organizations behind him, ran a close second behind Spaht in the first primary and, with the support of Boggs and Mayor deLesseps S. Morrison of New Orleans, won easily in the runoff.

Kennon promptly restored civil service for state workers, cut income and gasoline taxes, and supported legislation that embedded the Welfare, Highway, Institutions, and Wildlife and Fisheries Departments in the constitution. Also, he returned home rule to the parishes, authorized the use of voting machines statewide, upgraded the prison and parole systems, and worked with Morrison to build the Greater New Orleans Mississippi River Bridge. He was praised as a reformer—a designation overshadowed, however, by his antigambling crusade, in which his state superintendent of police, Francis C. Grevemberg, rid the state of gambling operations, dumping thousands of slot machines into the Mississippi and raiding gambling houses continually.

Kennon opened a new dimension in state politics: while serving as a Democratic governor in 1952, he endorsed Republican Dwight Eisenhower for president. Eisenhower did not win the state in that election, but did poll 306,925 votes, compared with Democrat Adlai Stevenson's 345,027. Kennon again endorsed Eisenhower in 1956, when Ike won Louisiana in a vote of 329,047 to 243,977. The Kennon move gave impetus to Republicans to build their forces in a state dominated by the Democratic Party since Reconstruction.

Kennon's administration was strongly conservative, but it would not be long before the pendulum swung back to the more liberal Earl Long. Eligible to hold the governorship again because he had sat out a term, Earl in 1956 defeated deLesseps Morrison to reclaim the office. His campaign platform was pretty much the same as the one he had won with in 1948, and he said he "wanted to extend the olive branch to the metropolitan daily newspapers," which had opposed him. He didn't exactly mean it. On election night at the Fairmont Hotel, with *States* political reporter Iris Kelso and others in attendance, he received the press in his suite, where he had strewn on the floor copies of the newspaper. Pulling at his suspenders, and speaking in his familiar gravel-toned voice, he spat tobacco juice on the *States* to show his disdain.

In 1959 Long suffered a breakdown on the floor of the legislature. His wife, Blanche, and members of his staff decided he had suffered a mental collapse and flew him to John Sealy Hospital in Galveston, Texas, for treatment. In Earl Long style, he reacted violently, so his associates had him transferred to the East Louisiana State Hospital in Mandeville, where Blanche committed him for treatment. Earl, fighting and cursing, had to be dragged to a car. He may have been temporarily deranged, but he still was able to outsmart the people around him. In the mental ward at the hospital, he demanded a habeas corpus hearing and was taken before a district judge, who signed a writ to free him. On the loose, Earl began traveling around Louisiana and Texas, sending cantaloupes and other goodies to friends, and renewing his acquaintance with Blaze Starr, the Bourbon Street stripper with whom he had become infatuated.

Earl, who had run for governor twice and been elected, and for lieutenant governor three times, winning once, was now out of a job. "I am going to stay in politics until I am taken from this earth." he had said earlier in his life, and he meant it. After the end of his 1956 term and after he lost a bid for the lieutenant governorship, Earl ran for Congress in the Eighth District and was elected. Nine days after winning, he died without taking his seat. Drained of energy and still suffering from the exhaustion that had hospitalized him earlier, Earl had just run out of life.

Davis served his second term from 1960 to 1964, defeating Morrison in a bitter campaign in which the desegregation of public schools became the principal issue. Davis called five special sessions of the legislature in efforts to thwart desegregation. Fifty-one acts signed by Davis were thrown out by the federal courts. He became a member of the board of directors of the Baker Bank and Trust Company, to which $8.6 million in state funds found their way, bringing only 2 percent annual interest. Davis and his chief aide, Chris Faser, were widely criticized for investing idle funds at such a low return. Davis built a new governor's mansion, also amid much criticism.

Louisiana's constitutional prohibition against successive terms stymied many governors, who complained they could not complete their programs in four years. Earl Long made a try at calling a constitutional convention in 1950, but in the face of wide criticism withdrew the effort. It remained for John J. McKeithen, Earl's floor leader in the house of representatives, who won the governorship in 1964 by defeating Morrison, to bring about passage of an amendment permitting two successive terms. McKeithen rallied the press and voting groups to the cause, and then won a second term, defeating John Rarick in 1968.

In his first term, McKeithen was credited with shaping favorable attitudes toward business, obliterating much of the bitterness between rural Louisiana and the cities, working with Mayor Victor H. Schiro of New Orleans to arrange financing of the Louisiana Superdome, and removing tolls (later reinstated) from the Greater New Orleans Mississippi River Bridge. He said he became bored with his second term, and was widely criticized for letting his cronies gain special favors. One of McKeithen's opponents in the 1964 race was Gillis W. Long, a cousin of Huey's who represented the Eighth District in Congress. Gillis, of Alexandria, ran for governor twice, losing each time. Still another Long figured in state politics at this time—Speedy O. Long of Jena, who was a state senator.

In 1972, Edwin W. Edwards of Crowley, a Cajun who could speak French and who represented the Third Congressional District in Congress, won a close gubernatorial race over J. Bennett Johnston of Shreveport (Johnston later became a four-term United States senator). Edwards served consecutive terms. One of his first acts was to push through the legislature a call for a constitutional convention. The new constitution, adopted in 1973, provided for equalized property assessments, an increase in homestead exemptions to $75,000, and the creation of two education boards, one for elementary and secondary schools, and another for colleges.

Probably the most significant legislation in the Edwards years was adoption of the open-primary election law, which reduced the number of races for offices from three to two. Until this time, Democrats and Republicans held separate primaries, the winners of which faced each other in the general election. Democrats, who would build up high vote totals in the first and second primaries, would then face in the general election a Republican candidate who had won the nomination with relatively few votes because of the low Republican registration in the state. While crossover voting is possible in all general elections, the huge Democratic votes had the effect of overwhelming the GOP nominee. Under the open-primary law, all parties run at the same time, and then the two top vote getters meet in the general election. Thus, crossover voting became significant in the first, or open, primary. With crossover voting permitted in the open primary, the Republicans picked up many crossover votes at the outset.

David Treen, who had served as a member of Congress from the Third District, won the governorship in 1979, campaigning against corruption in government and for more aid to education. He made it possible for the New Orleans World's Fair to obtain state funds and supported numerous civic efforts over the state. The first Republican governor of Louisiana in the twentieth century, he served a single term, Edwards returning in 1983 to swamp him.

Between his second and third terms, Edwards, who had gained a reputation as a gambling governor because of frequent trips to casinos in Las Vegas, ran afoul of the federal government. He was charged with using his influence to obtain valuable state permits for hospital construction. The first trial, after fourteen weeks, ended in a hung jury, but Edwards' troubles weren't over. United States Attorney John Volz put him through a second, which lasted seven weeks. The jaunty Edwards put on a show of his own, denouncing the prosecutor and on one occasion arriving at the courthouse in a horse-drawn carriage, saying he chose a mode of transportation in step with the pace of the trial. Although testimony showed he profited by $2 million in his dealings, the jury decided no law had been violated and set him free.

Edwards in 1987 ran for a fourth term, facing Democrat Charles E. "Buddy" Roemer, congressman from the Eighth District. On the night of the open primary, in which he led the voting but saw Roemer running a strong second in a field of candidates, Edwards withdrew, leaving the way open for a possible future try. "For almost 16 years, in office and out," observed Allan Katz in a *Times-Picayune* column, "Edwards reigned as the most powerful and popular political figure Louisiana had seen since Huey P. Long."

Roemer, who campaigned on a platform to improve education and put the state's finances in order, faced a hostile legislature when he took office in 1988 and also found himself in the middle of a fight between anti- and proabortionists. He signed a bill outlawing abortions except in cases of rape and incest, but that did not satisfy the antis. His greatest contribution, perhaps, was the creation of the office of inspector general, to which he appointed Bill Lynch, a crusading New Orleans newspaper reporter who had gained much attention for exposing fraud and wrongdoing in government. Lynch began turning up incidents of illegality quickly, and almost as quickly became a controversial figure in the political arena.

Louisiana since its inception has been steeped in factional politics. During the Huey and Earl Long periods, and in the Edwards years, it was a political cauldron. Huey had a plan to try for the presidency, but did not live to perfect it. The state did, however, claim much national attention through the rise in seniority of its congressional delegation. All at the same time in the 1970s, Russell Long became chairman of the powerful Senate Finance Committee; Senator Allen J. Ellender, a Huey Long creature, headed the Senate Agriculture Committee; Congressman F. Edward Hebert chaired the House Armed Services Committee; and Congressman Hale Boggs, who would be lost in a plane accident in 1974 in Alaska, was majority leader of Congress. These men's exalted posts provided what many referred to as "Pelican Power," a reference to Louisiana's nickname and their standing.

The governor's race of 1991 brought more attention than any since Huey's era. Roemer, the newly converted Republican governor, was toppled from office in a Democratic sweep that resulted in a severe setback for GOP forces, who had turned Louisiana into a two-party state, and buried the gubernatorial aspirations of a former grand wizard of the Ku Klux Klan, David Duke, who had edged out Roemer to become the Republican standard bearer. It turned into a national embarrassment for the Republican Party, with the president of the United States (George Bush) and state GOP leaders finding it necessary to repudiate a Republican candidate. Also, it brought together a coalition of interests that catapulted former governor Edwards into an unprecedented fourth term as governor. The campaign was bitter and bizarre, creating new political alignments and voting patterns. Edwards carried with him into office the first woman lieutenant governor, Melinda Schwegmann.

David Duke became the center of a storm of controversy that enabled Edwards to forge a coalition of labor, business, industrial, and professional interests who feared what Duke's election might do to the economy and race relations. Duke found he could not outlive his past, which included parading for the Klan and expressions of sympathy for Adolf Hitler and the Nazis. He fired political passions, directing his campaign against welfare, affirmative action, and other social programs in an ultraconservative appeal.

Edwards warned of the possible effects of a Duke victory: an inability to attract new industry, loss of tourist and convention business, and diminished prospects of attracting black athletes to state colleges. Duke's rhetoric translated into an attack on the state's economy and threw fear into the ranks of white and black voters alike. The result was a polarized electorate; for the first time the black vote became decisive statewide. After the primary, in which Duke finished a close second to Edwards, knocking Roemer out of the race even though the governor had the endorsement of the president, Edwards benefited by receiving wide support from Democrats and Republicans. Although the pollsters declared that the election too close to call, Edwards himself predicted a 60–40 victory. In the official count, he ran up 1,086,820 votes, or 61 percent, to Duke's 701,024, or 39 percent. An analysis showed that Edwards got 75 percent of the Roemer vote and that Duke received 55 percent of the white vote.

The widely covered campaign propelled Duke to national recognition but left unanswered how far he might go. Undaunted by defeat, Duke laid plans to run for the presidency as a Republican but eventually withdrew.

Edwards would have been eligible to run for another term—his fifth—in 1995 but instead announced his retirement from politics. In the race to succeed him, Murphy J. "Mike" Foster—a grandson of the Murphy Foster who served two terms as governor in the 1890s—emerged from a field of twelve candidates in the primary and won the runoff handily, defeating Congressman Cleo Fields of Baton Rouge by 984,499 votes to 565,861. The campaign lacked the spice of the Long and Edwards runs, but it did produce some firsts. For the first time in the century, an African American—Fields—vied for the top spot after finishing second in the primary, and for the first time a woman, State Treasurer Mary Landrieu, became a major candidate, placing a close third in the primary. There was also a bombshell dropped into the legislative races. Edwards' last term covered a period during which legalized gambling and the influence that gaming interests exerted over elected officials became major issues, and before the election the FBI made public a series of affidavits alleging a conspiracy by the gambling industry to control votes by legislators. Of twenty-six lawmakers mentioned in the affidavits, six chose not to seek reelection and several others were defeated, including Senate President Sammy Nunez of Chalmette and Senator B. B. "Sixty" Rayburn, a veteran of forty years. Coupled with Edwards' departure, the results seemed to signal the end of an era.

As the dominant figures in twentieth-century Louisiana politics, Huey Long and Edwin Edwards had certain similarities, but also many differences. Huey's grip on the state's political system was so firm that no one could wrest it from him, but his career was short-lived compared with that of Edwards. Huey served less than one term as governor, leaving the office to win a seat in the United States Senate; he was only halfway into the

Senate term when he was assassinated. His impact was absolute during his governorship and remained in force while he was a senator. He built a dictatorship through social legislation that won him the support of the masses, and he was cunning enough to hold power in a manner never before experienced in an American state—power that permitted his heirs to maintain control long after his death. His opposition to Franklin Roosevelt and the New Deal in favor of his own Share Our Wealth program gained him national stature.

Edwards had no political impact outside Louisiana, but he handled the legislature with ease, putting over his programs, even daring to call a constitutional convention to change the state's basic law. The quick-witted, smooth-talking Edwards, who made no secret of his love of gambling and a flamboyant life, was a sharp contrast to Huey in handling his legislative agenda. Where Huey was ruthless in clearing out his enemies and pushing his programs, Edwards took a route of persuasion, building coalitions to accomplish his goals. Huey ramrodded his legislation, cajoling and threatening his way to success. He lashed out at opponents via radio and stump speeches in bitter, even personal, vituperation, although often injecting homespun humor. Edwards, on radio and television, was Huey's match in sarcasm and humor, but hardly his equal in vindictive eloquence. Each could deliver a spellbinding speech, and each mastered the art of winning crowd approval. Each brought a sense of drama to the political process that quickly moved him to center stage, and each pursued a liberal agenda. Also, each survived major attempts at ouster, Huey when he beat conviction in impeachment proceedings, Edwards when he won acquittal in federal court.

Huey built a new state capitol, main highways and farm-to-market roads, and boosted education in programs that benefited the populace long after his death. Edwards built bridges—most notably one crossing the Mississippi in midtown New Orleans—made possible millions of dollars' worth of public improvements across the state, and directed funds for building new sports facilities. He also gave the push that, for better or worse, brought the return of legalized gambling in various forms.

It is difficult to compare the impact of the Huey Long and Edwin Edwards' years, but the fact that Huey's came when the state had a barebones, mainly agricultural economy probably gave his reign greater force. What is certain is that both men left lasting imprints on Louisiana.

—W.G.C.

17

Hard Winds and High Water

Chita: A Memory of Last Island.

Where did the tragic facts leave off and Lafcadio Hearn's imagination take wing? The real events of that fateful August 10, 1856, have their place in Louisiana legend, and every reading of Hearn's novel, one of the state's literary triumphs of the nineteenth century, makes the memory more poignant.

Hearn spent a decade in New Orleans, writing for newspapers, before he emigrated to Japan, where he earned a literary reputation that peaked in the early 1900s. He delighted in vacations on Grand Isle, one of the barrier islands that stretch along the Gulf of Mexico coast west of the mouths of the Mississippi River, and wrote in his rhapsodic prose of the white beaches and glistening waves. His fancy was piqued by the story of Last Island. A watering place for the elite of the Creole and Acadian society, the island had been devastated by a hurricane that sent huge billows crashing over the narrow spit of land, where some four hundred men, women, and children were stranded.

"The sea tore it out in one night," Hearn wrote, "the same night when trees, fields, dwellings, all vanished into the Gulf, leaving no vestige of former human habitation except a few of those strong brick props and foundations upon which the frame houses and cisterns had been raised. Only one living creature was found there after the cataclysm—a cow!"

Hearn borrowed freely from the reality. Some of the visitors were boarding in a two-story frame hotel, and others were guests in the wooden cottages that lined the Gulf beach. And on the mainland, twenty miles away across Caillou Bay, Captain Abraham Smith did become alarmed about the safety of those on the island, and steered the small steamboat *Star* through the rising storm, only to have the vessel driven ashore and wrecked near the hotel.

The author uses dramatic license to describe a fancy dress ball at the hotel. Through the howling winds, Captain Smith discerns snatches of music. " 'Waltzing,' cried the captain. 'God help them! God help us all now! The Wind waltzes tonight, with the Sea for his partner.' " In the ballroom there is a shriek: a Creole belle has found her pretty slippers wet, the first warning of impending doom as the hurricane surge begins to tear at the hotel.

Hearn's plot continues. The next morning a fisherman on a nearby is-land sees bodies in the surf and then spots a movement. He swims out to find a living baby girl, clutched in the arms of her dead mother. The fisher-man and his wife rear the girl on their remote point of land. Meanwhile, a New Orleans doctor believes his wife and child perished in the storm. Years later he is summoned to the fisherman's outpost to treat a patient, is felled himself by yellow fever, and on his deathbed recognizes his daughter be-cause of her likeness to her mother.

Even without *Chita*, the disaster of Last Island would not be forgotten, although the 1856 hurricane was not as deadly as some others that have struck the Louisiana coastal area over the years. In fact, a dance was held at the Muggah Hotel, but it was on the Saturday night before the storm ripped the island during the daylight hours of Sunday. And it was good that Captain Smith risked crossing Caillou Bay because a number of the vaca-tioners lived through the fury by clambering aboard the hull of what was left of the *Star*. Actually, of the four hundred humans on the island, slightly more than half survived. Some managed to cling to the foundations of cot-tages while waves swept over them and flying objects driven by the furious wind threatened to decapitate them. The iron hoops of a cistern kept at least one family from being swept away. A few persons hugged timbers and were rescued from the bay into which they had been washed. Hearn's cow was a fact—fortunately for the survivors, who divided up the meat and lived on it until help arrived.

Louisianians have learned to accept as inevitable the warm-weather cy-clones that arise in the Atlantic Ocean and sweep through the Caribbean into the Gulf of Mexico before passing inland, or suddenly develop in the Gulf itself to smite the coast with devastating force and with little advance warning. New Orleans was barely four years old when, in 1722, the first recorded hurricane destroyed most of the flimsy early buildings. Storms in the next half century were comparatively minor, but in 1778 a blow played havoc with the establishment at the Balize, at the mouth of the Mississippi River. The following year a hurricane disrupted the plans of Governor Gálvez for a military expedition against the British in the Florida Parishes, and in 1780 another reportedly sank every ship in the river and the south Louisiana lakes. A storm in 1794 caused flooding of the lower river delta.

In August, 1812, three months after Louisiana became the eighteenth state of the Union, New Orleans was visited by a destructive disturbance, and in 1819 and 1821 other storms blew in. Hurricanes in 1831, 1837, and 1855 preceded the Last Island catastrophe. Severe storms struck in 1860, 1865, and 1886, the last destroying the town of Sabine and costing 89 lives.

The nineteenth-century storms, including even the Last Island blow, were only preludes to the disastrous hurricane that roared out of the Gulf on September 30 and October 1, 1893. The mighty cyclone struck first at Chenière Caminada, another of the Louisiana barrier islands that lay between Grand Isle and what was left of Last Island. The storm surge sent huge waves crashing all the way across the low-lying isle. Three hundred residents took refuge on the second floor of Julien Lefort's two-story combined residence and store. Otherwise, the loss of life would have been even more frightful. As it was, 822 persons perished out of a population of 1,471. The hurricane moved on across the southern part of Louisiana and into Mississippi and Alabama, claiming in all as many as 2,500 lives. The death toll, among storms that have affected the Gulf Coast, was exceeded only by that of the Galveston, Texas, hurricane of 1900.

In 1909 a hurricane that moved inland near Grand Isle caused 353 deaths. For years New Orleanians had vivid memories of the storm of September 29, 1915, which damaged some 25,000 buildings in the city and had a death toll in all of 275. For all its destructiveness, the 1915 hurricane held a silver lining in its clouds. The renowned meteorologist Isaac M. Cline,

The violence of the disastrous hurricane of 1893 is displayed in this depiction of the storm surge sweeping from the Gulf over the barrier island of Chenière Caminada.

Courtesy the Historic New Orleans Collection; Acc. No. 1989.91.30iii

district forecaster for the United States Weather Bureau in New Orleans, not only predicted the storm but also sent warnings to the coastal communities along its likely path—the first time that anyone distributed a hurricane warning so widely. As the twentieth century progressed, Cline and other government meteorologists greatly improved their ability to track tropical disturbances and predict their landfall. The resulting accurate warnings have saved countless lives.

Major storms were recorded in 1926 and 1947, and in 1957 Hurricane Audrey—the weather bureau by now assigned names to each season's hurricanes—struck in Cameron Parish, causing floods as far as twenty to twenty-five miles inland and resulting in at least 350 deaths. In 1964 a tornado spawned by Hurricane Hilda killed 21 persons at Larose. A year later, on the night of September 9–10, New Orleans felt the fury of Hurricane Betsy, the first hurricane in American history to do more than one billion dollars' worth of damage. By this time the great oil and gas boom in the Gulf of Mexico was approaching its height, and the offshore waters were dotted by drilling rigs and production platforms. The loss of facilities to the elements was heavy. Onshore, 58 lives were lost. On August 17, 1969, Hurricane Camille sideswiped Plaquemines and St. Bernard Parishes before crossing inland over Waveland, Mississippi. Even though there was extensive flooding and the death toll in Louisiana was 9, the state was fortunate. Camille was the most intense hurricane ever to hit the Gulf Coast. Mississippi bore the brunt. On August 26, 1992, Hurricane Andrew slammed into the Louisiana coast at Vermilion Bay. Besides homes, oil rigs, and other structures, the storm destroyed or damaged crops, timber, and fisheries along its curving path. The cost came to $2.4 billion in 43 parishes, and there were 10 deaths. Yet, again, Louisianians could perhaps count themselves lucky: Andrew had wrought far greater destruction in crossing heavily populated south Florida a few days earlier.

Louisianians accept the fact that hurricanes will come again and again, but there is sound reason to hope that Louisiana will have no repetition of the calamitous flood of 1927. It was the last occasion upon which the Mississippi River shook free of the straitjacket placed upon it by engineers, who finally prevailed after two hundred years of effort. The state's other rivers also went on a rampage, and parts of the northern tier of parishes were inundated by the overflow from the flooded Arkansas.

The statistics, while staggering in themselves, can only hint at the suffering and deprivation. In seven states, 16,570,627 acres were flooded, and more than one-third—6,200,343 acres—were in Louisiana. In this state,

The main street of Ferriday, in Concordia Parish, during the great 1927 Mississippi River flood. Scenes like this could be found all across vast stretches of Louisiana lowlands, even in places many miles from the river.

Courtesy the New Orleans Times-Picayune

277,781 persons were affected, either driven from their homes or forced to exist with water all around them, sometimes in the rooms where they slept. Many spent long weeks in overcrowded, unhealthy rescue centers. Much of the all-important cotton crop was lost, and thousands left destitute. Farm buildings and machinery were ruined. The actual loss of life was negligible in comparison with the toll of hurricanes, but except for that difference, the prolonged misery resulting from the flood affected more people and was harder to bear than the suffering in the aftermath of any of the storms. Herbert Hoover, then secretary of commerce, was in charge of the massive relief effort, in which 33,000 persons were involved in the seven states.

Originally, the meandering Mississippi, which with its tributaries drains two-fifths of the continental United States, overflowed its banks every year as snows melted and heavy spring rains fell. As the valley became populated and developed, the land was too valuable to lose to flooding, and a system of levees—earthen dikes—began to take form. By 1927 the levees on both banks stretched from Cairo, Illinois, to the Gulf of Mexico. That spring, heavy rains over the valley poured unprecedented volumes of water into the narrowed channel. The river could not handle the inflow, and water began backing up into the tributaries—for a brief period the Ohio River actually flowed upstream. Mainline levees began to crumble under the pressure in Tennessee, Mississippi, and Arkansas, and by May the breaks were occurring in Louisiana. The Red and Atchafalaya Rivers also broke through their levees, and as much as one-sixth of the Louisiana land area was inundated. New Orleans was saved from a ducking by the dynamiting of a levee at Caernarvon, just below the city, creating a crevasse through which water could flow to the Gulf.

The 1927 crisis made it clear that levees alone cannot keep the Mississippi within bounds. New Orleans now has the protection of the Atchafalaya basin floodway and the Bonnet Carré spillway. If the city is threatened, the structures can be opened to divert water from the river into the Atchafalaya or into the Bonnet Carré to turn the overflow into Lake Pontchartrain.

Only once since the levee system was upgraded after the 1927 flood has there been a break in a mainline Mississippi river levee. It was a minor crevasse just above Baton Rouge that was quickly closed.

—J.W.

18

PIRATES, PRIVATEERS, AND FILIBUSTERS

On May 25, 1820, Jean Desforges and Robert Johnson were hanged from the yardarm of a revenue cutter anchored in the Mississippi River off the Place d'Armes in New Orleans. It was one of the final scenes of an era when pirates and privateers sallied out of Louisiana to prey on vessels in the Gulf of Mexico and the old Spanish Main, the Caribbean Sea.

Desforges and Johnson fell into the hands of authorities of the United States while they were members of privateer crews operating in the Gulf. They were two of fourteen pirates sentenced to die under terms of an 1819 act of Congress making piracy a capital offense. It was the beginning of a crackdown by the federal government against the marauders in Western Hemisphere waters.

Piracy and privateering in the West Indian area had begun in the sixteenth century, when the targets were vessels transporting gold and silver from Spain's Central and South American possessions to the mother country. The British and French governments, among others, cut themselves into the action by issuing letters of marque during intermittent wars with Spain. Such a letter, in keeping with the customs of the time, made it legal to rob and seize an enemy ship. The borderline between privateering, as this activity was called, and plain piracy always was thin and hazy, and what skipper would be halted by niceties when a rich prize lay under his guns? In a fog, would it not be difficult to distinguish between a Spanish and a Dutch flag, for instance?

Early in the nineteenth century, most Spanish colonies in the New World were in revolt, seeking independence. The letter of marque offered a means of interrupting Spain's commerce. It was a ruse used most prolifically by Cartagena, a city-state on the northern coast of South America. And it was with letters of marque from Cartagena that most of the marine robbers fared forth from Louisiana during the time of the Baratarians.

Barataria Bay is an indentation on the Louisiana coast west of the mouths of the Mississippi River. Through the swamps, it is only about fifty miles from New Orleans. The bay provides an easily reached shelter from the open Gulf, a convenient hideaway two hundred years ago for pirates or anybody else carrying on nefarious operations. There the outlaws known as the Baratarians established a rude settlement that served as their headquarters. There they built storehouses where goods taken from ships could be kept until it was convenient to smuggle them into New Orleans for sale. The freebooters even conducted auctions for eager buyers who came down from New Orleans to seek bargains on which they paid no customs duties. Sometimes it was slaves who were offered for sale after the importation of blacks from Africa became illegal.

The leader of the Baratarians during their heyday was Jean Lafitte, often spelled Laffite, the most infamous of the plunderers who used Cartagenan letters of marque as their cover. Lafitte's antecedents and his eventual fate are subjects of controversy. But at one time he superintended as many as five hundred ruffians at the Barataria colony on the island known as Grande Terre, and he was the de facto admiral of a fleet of a dozen or more schooners that spread out over the Gulf and into the waters beyond in search of vessels with valuable cargoes. Lafitte worked with his brother Pierre and their colleague Dominique You (who, according to some sources, was in fact another Lafitte brother, Alexandre, operating under an alias). The three were well known and well received in New Orleans, where they made no secret of their roles as smugglers.

Even though many New Orleanians were willing to tolerate smuggling in view of the good buys they could pick up, the activities of the Baratarians became so flagrant that Governor Claiborne offered a $500 reward for the arrest of Jean Lafitte. Proof is lacking, but for many years the story has circulated that Lafitte responded by putting a $5,000 price on Claiborne's head.

On September 11, 1814, the American navy and army joined forces in an attack on Lafitte's lair. Lafitte and most of the Baratarians fled when the Americans approached. The invaders seized eight schooners—two flying the Cartagenan flag—destroyed forty houses, took eighty prisoners, and confiscated the loot piled in the warehouses.

The War of 1812 was in progress, and soon after the raid a British man-o'-war appeared outside Barataria Bay. The captain relayed to Lafitte an offer of $30,000 and a captain's commission in the Royal Navy if he would cooperate in the planned British attack on New Orleans. Despite his treatment by the Americans, Lafitte revealed the offer to Claiborne and volunteered to have the Baratarians join in defense of the city if charges against him and his brother were dropped. General Andrew Jackson, who had arrived to lead the Americans, accepted the proposal. During the Battle of New Orleans on January 8, 1815, the Baratarians, especially Dominique You, helped repulse the invaders. Piracy charges were abandoned, as promised.

Painting of Jean Lafitte (with uplifted noggin of rum), Pierre Lafitte (standing), and Dominique You, famous Gulf pirates.

Courtesy the Louisiana State Museum

Lafitte moved his headquarters to Galveston Bay, Texas, whence he mysteriously slipped from the public view sometime in the 1820s. Was he a pirate as well as a privateer? Some historians have said yes, others have raised doubts. In any event, generations of Americans have been intrigued by the stories about his activities.

French-born Louis-Michel Aury sailed into New Orleans in 1810 with at least $6,500 in his pockets as his share of the loot taken by a French privateer in the West Indies. He paid $4,500 for a small schooner, with which he planned to begin privateering on his own. But authorities confiscated the vessel, leaving Aury with a hatred for Anglo-Americans that lasted for the rest of his life. He acquired a half share in another privateer with the money he had left and reportedly with gifts from Madame Jack, who was notorious on the New Orleans riverfront. Aury went on to establish a tumultuous career in which, using the flag of Cartagena, he headed a privateering fleet of unprecedented size, competed with Simón Bolívar for leadership in revolutions in Cartagena, survived a bullet wound received in a mutiny, and finally succumbed in 1821 to injuries caused when he was thrown from a horse.

Aury sometimes worked with the New Orleans Associates, a shadowy group that had grandiose schemes and profited from privateering forays. Members were identified at the time only by numbers. The leaders were Edward Livingston and John R. Grymes, prominent lawyers, and Abner L. Duncan and Pierre Lafitte. On one occasion the Associates turned a profit of more than $100,000 on the sale of the cargo seized in a single privateering voyage. Some of the Associates had dreams of capturing Florida territory held by the Spanish and selling it to the American government. Another plot that never was carried out was to attack the city of Tampico and grab the output of the Mexican silver mines that was being shipped from that port.

One of the buccaneers bankrolled by the Associates was William Mitchell, an Englishman who left a wake of death and destruction behind his fifty-three-ton schooner, the *Cometa*. In 1816, using a letter of marque from Cartagena as his defense in case of capture, Mitchell and his crew raided the Spanish Royalist island of San Andrés. They burned the houses, robbed the residents, and killed the island's governor and the six soldiers of its tiny garrison. In New Orleans Mitchell ran afoul the determined collector of customs, Beverly Chew. Mitchell established an outlet for smuggled goods on the New Orleans lakefront but was wounded and arrested by a force that Chew sent after him. Acquitted in a trial, Mitchell plotted to gain revenge on Chew by preventing vessels from delivering imports to New Orleans (the collector's income was a percentage of duties levied in the port). Mitchell patrolled the waters off the mouth of the Mississippi and even ventured into the river to attack vessels bound for New Orleans. Once he captured a revenue cutter, but it was recovered.

One of the most active of the freebooters who slipped back and forth between the roles of privateer and pirate, Mitchell sometimes led his pack of seagoing robbers in rowboats when he had no larger vessel at his command. He was cruising in search of prey off Cuba in 1820 when Desforges and Johnson forfeited their lives to the new antipiracy act. "It may be assumed," writes Stanley Faye in his monograph *Pirates of the Gulf and Their Prizes*, "that Captain Mitchell valued his own neck. Discreetly he dropped out of the newspapers as completely as if the War to the Death had caught up with him at last." It is true that Mitchell's name is missing from later accounts in the New Orleans libraries, and there is no word as to whether he met a peaceful end or succumbed to lead, steel, or the noose.

Mitchell came along in the closing years of the age of piracy and privateering in the Gulf. By 1823, the *Louisiana Adventurer* was publishing a tribute to Chew: "He has protected the upright and driven the nefarious smugglers from their retreats. . . . So marked has been his course that we believe there is less smuggling now at this point than anywhere in the United States."

The pirates and privateers had not long been gone from Louisiana before the filibusters came. The filibusters have been called "Agents of Manifest Destiny" by Charles H. Brown in his 1980 book of that title. In the years before the Civil War, many citizens believed it was the "manifest destiny" of the United States to extend its borders to include most, if not all, of the Americas and to instill the ideals of democracy and republicanism throughout the hemisphere. There were men who were eager to organize and lead armed invasions to free other countries from governments that did not accord with their ideals. These men, and others who joined them, were called "filibusters"—the term has no connection with the ploy used in legislative halls of preventing votes on controversial bills by holding the floor with endless speeches.

The theme of Manifest Destiny was popular in Louisiana, and by the 1840s and 1850s there was another factor to help provide support for anybody with filibustering ambitions. As the national debate over slavery intensified, southerners could see an advantage in taking into the Union new states that would be friendly to slavery. The most likely acquisition would be Cuba, which of course was still a colony of Spain.

Just as the names of Jean Lafitte and Louis-Michel Aury stand out in accounts of the era of privateering, those of Narciso López and William Walker dominate the history of the filibusters. Both López and Walker made New Orleans their headquarters, and it was from the city that each sailed out to Latin America on his final, fatal expedition. Men of different backgrounds, they had in common only a desire to rise to glory in adventures in lands to the south.

The son of a wealthy Spanish landowner in Venezuela, López settled in Cuba. He became president of the Executive Military Commission that had the responsibility for thwarting movements for independence from Spain. Later he failed to prosper in business and became a revolutionary himself. He planned an uprising in Cuba but was dissuaded on learning that an invasion was being plotted in the United States. President Polk squelched the invasion—filibustering was contrary to the foreign policy of the United States. Government officials also tipped off López' plans to the Spanish minister in Washington. López managed to flee to Providence, Rhode Island. In the United States he raised money and volunteers for an expedition to Cuba, and by 1849 several hundred men were assembled on Round Island, off the Mississippi Gulf Coast, prepared to embark. However, the United States Navy, patrolling the area with orders to prevent any movement, seized three ships that had been chartered to transport the volunteers. In 1850 López moved to New Orleans. He found many southerners eager to enlist for the invasion, among them Louisiana lawyer Chatham Roberdeau Wheat, later leader of the Louisiana Tigers in the Civil War. In early May three ships finally sailed. López was aboard the *Creole,* under the Cuban banner.

On May 19 some 750 invaders landed at Cárdenas. The first disappointment was the failure of Cubans to rise up in a revolt as López had expected. Nothing else went right. Wheat was wounded in the first clash with Spanish soldiers. López was lucky to get most of his men back aboard the *Creole* and flee to Key West. The planners of President Kennedy's ill-fated Bay of Pigs landing in 1961 could have taken a lesson from López about what happens to a poorly prepared military expedition.

López and several others were indicted upon their return to the United States for violating the Neutrality Act. But getting a conviction was another thing in New Orleans, where the filibusters were regarded as heroes. After several mistrials, the charges against all of the defendants were dropped. Despite the failure of the invasion, efforts to launch another expedition continued, given impetus by reports of an impending uprising of Cubans. López sailed again from New Orleans. The invaders went ashore at Morrillo, a fishing village about sixty miles west of Havana. López, clad in a white jacket and pantaloons with a red sash tied around the waist, knelt to kiss the soil of the island he had come to free. The theatrics aside, the operation was an utter failure from the start. Again, the anticipated revolution of Cubans did not materialize. López was one of the last men captured by Spanish army units that had harassed the hopeful liberators. He was led into San Cristóbal, a rope around his neck and his arms tied behind him. The captured Americans were taken to Havana and killed by firing squads while a huge crowd of Cubans roared its approval. López' turn came on September 1, 1851. He mounted a platform near Morro Castle and made a short talk, saying: "I die for my beloved Cuba." Then he was killed by garrote.

There was rioting in New Orleans when newspapers reported the first of the executions. A Spanish-language journal was wrecked, as were Spanish restaurants and coffeehouses. The Spanish consul went into hiding.

William Walker, born in Nashville, Tennessee, earned a doctor of medicine degree at the University of Pennsylvania before turning to law. He was admitted to the bar in New Orleans, then became one of the editors of the New Orleans *Crescent*. He moved to San Francisco when the newspaper was sold. In California he began the activities that made him the most widely known and most successful of the filibusters, and for a time a hero to many Americans.

After an abortive attempt in 1853 to take over the Mexican state of Baja California as an independent republic, in 1855 Walker moved into Nicaragua at the invitation of one of the factions vying for control of the government. He emerged in 1856 as the president of the republic but was unseated by a coalition financed by his rival, the American tycoon Cornelius Vanderbilt. Walker, banished, nevertheless was received as a conqueror when he landed at New Orleans, where he immediately began planning for a return to Nicaragua. An 1857 expedition failed, and Walker was again sent back to the United States. In 1860 he mounted an invasion of Honduras, from where he could reenter Nicaragua. The filibusters captured the Honduran town of Trujillo, but there was a complication. Honduras and Great Britain were in the process of settling a dispute over territory. A British warship arrived at the scene, and the commander sent a note to Walker claiming British ownership of funds that the filibusters had seized at the customhouse in Trujillo. Commander Norvell Salmon demanded that Walker lay down his arms, return the money, and depart. He added that if his demand were met, the safety of the filibusters would be guaranteed by the British flag. The Americans abandoned the Trujillo fort and were then attacked by Honduran troops. Walker surrendered to Salmon, who promptly turned him over to Honduran authorities. On September 12, 1860, Walker was executed by a Honduran firing squad.

By then, Walker's popularity in the United States had been tarnished by his lack of success, and the news of his death caused less of a stir than it might have a few years earlier. Filibustering was in its last stages, and within a few months would be largely forgotten in the excitement of the Civil War.

—J.W.

19

SPORTS

"Sportsman's Paradise," a distinguishing title provided by legislative act, appears on many Louisiana automobile license plates, advertising perhaps the state's greatest attribute. The slogan might just as well be "Sports Paradise," for Louisiana has been agog over sports and the intense rivalries they foster since pre–Civil War days.

Today football—high school, college, and professional—claims the spotlight, with collegiate basketball gaining popularity, but horse racing was the first sport to win favor in Louisiana, in the early part of the nineteenth century. The first horse-racing course was built in 1814 or 1815 on the plantation of General Wade Hampton, and the second on the plantation of François de Livaudais. The *Spirit of the Times*, a New York sporting journal, reported that New Orleans had become the national center of thoroughbred racing in the 1850s, and reached its pinnacle in 1854 and 1855 when two of the leading horses of the time, Lecompte and Lexington, were matched in a series of heats. Lexington won the showdown after Lecompte won the initial races, one of which was attended by former president Millard Fillmore.

The Civil War interrupted the horse-racing boom, but the sport made a comeback after the war. The only surviving track in the latter part of the twentieth century is the Fair Grounds, established in 1872 after the Metairie course, which for a time was a Confederate camp, was sold as a cemetery site. Black Gold, one of the famous horses to race there, winning both the Louisiana and Kentucky Derbies in 1924, is buried in the infield. The Fair Grounds is the third-oldest track in the nation, behind Saratoga and Churchill Downs.

Other tracks in Louisiana are Jefferson Downs, at Kenner; Evangeline Downs, at Lafayette; Louisiana Downs, at Bossier City; and Delta Downs at Vinton. The tracks represent a multimillion dollar business, with betting at the parimutuel windows and in off-track locations as well.

Prizefighting, which occurred irregularly in New Orleans prior to 1850, was banned by the city in 1856; nevertheless, New Orleans played a key role in the sport. In 1837, Sam O'Rourke, who billed himself as the champion of Ireland and America, fought the English champion, James "Deaf" Burke, twice, winning each time. Dan Callahan of New York fought John

McLaughlin of New Orleans at the Metairie racetrack in February of 1857 in a 116-round, three-hour bout.

In 1869, Jim "Gypsy" Mace, generally recognized as the world champion, came to New Orleans for two fights. On May 10, 1870, he "shot off the headlights," as one writer put it, of Tom Allen, who claimed the American title, in a ten-round fight in Kenner. Then, on November 30, 1871, he battled Joe Coburn, another American title claimant, for eleven rounds during which neither inflicted damage, and then in the twelfth stood looking at each other until the referee declared a draw. Local fight interest dwindled after that, but picked up again after Paddy Ryan, of Troy, New York, established a clear claim to the title. Another easterner, John L. Sullivan of Boston, was knocking out opponents right and left, and inviting all comers. A fight arranged for New Orleans had to be held at Mississippi City on the Gulf Coast because of the ban. On February 7, 1882, Sullivan, in a bare-knuckle fight, knocked out Ryan in the eighth round. Then, on July 8, 1889, Sullivan kayoed Jake Kilrain in a classic bare-knuckle bout of seventy-four rounds at Richburg, Mississippi. Ironically, Mississippi also banned prizefighting at the time, but promoters found ways to skirt the law.

The first title fight in New Orleans was held in 1891, when the original Jack Dempsey, known as the "Nonpareil," lost his middleweight crown to Australian Bob Fitzsimmons. Then, on three successive nights in September, 1892, the Olympic Club at Royal and Montegut Streets staged a prizefighting "Carnival of Champions." There were several notable bouts, but the one that has endured in fame was the classic battle in which "Gentleman Jim" Corbett knocked out John L. Sullivan to win the heavyweight championship. Some 10,000 people paid up to $100 for seats. Corbett won $25,000. Louisiana has become accustomed to world champions, and championship fights. During the 1900s, Pete Herman won the bantamweight title, Tony Canzoneri and Joe Brown took lightweight crowns, and Willie Pastrano captured the light heavyweight championship. Building of the Louisiana Superdome in the late 1960s made it possible to hold super events such as the Muhammad Ali–Leon Spinks heavyweight title fight in 1978, a battle that drew 63,000 persons and was billed as the biggest indoor boxing event of the century.

Raquette, an Indian game similar to lacrosse and contested on fields at least 200 yards in length, was the only ball game played by organized teams prior to 1859, but baseball became popular soon after that, and flourished following the Civil War. For a score of years after the war, white and black baseball teams competed freely against each other. With the passage of Jim Crow laws, interracial games vanished.

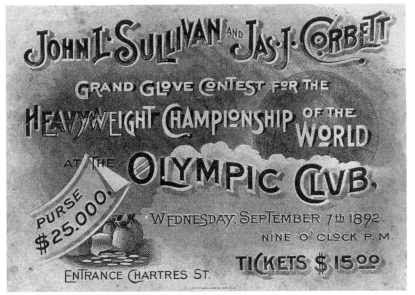

Poster advertising the heavyweight championship boxing bout between John L. Sullivan and
James J. Corbett, a highlight of the history of sports in Louisiana.

Courtesy the Historic New Orleans Collection; Acc. No. 1986.195.1.1

In December of 1886, Toby Hart obtained a Southern League franchise
and assembled fourteen players under the managership of Abner Powell.
Powell, incidentally, owned four franchises in the league. He is credited
with originating ladies' day and the rain check. The Southern League gave
way to the Southern Association in 1901. New Orleans, playing as the Pel-
icans, won ten pennants under the tutelage of a string of noted managers,
who included, besides Powell, Charley Frank, Johnny Dobbs, Larry
Gilbert, Jake Atz, Roger Peckinpaugh, and Danny Murtaugh. New Orleans
quit the league in 1961, but as of this writing has a new AAA franchise,
the Zephyrs.

Baseball has been popular over the state. Shreveport fielded a team as
early as 1895, and the Shreveport Sports played in the Texas League through
1975, except for interruptions brought on by financial problems, a fire which
destroyed their stadium, and shutdown of the league during wartimes. The
Sports won pennants in 1919, 1942, 1954, and 1955. Shreveport currently
has another franchise, the Captains, in the Texas League.

Several Louisiana cities had entries in the Cotton States League, organized in 1902, among them Baton Rouge, Monroe, and Monroe–West

Monroe. Baton Rouge won pennants in 1903, 1932 and 1933, while Monroe won in 1939, 1940, 1941, and Monroe–West Monroe in 1955. The Evangeline League, which existed from 1934 through 1957, had franchises at Lafayette, Jeanerette, Alexandria, Lake Charles, New Iberia, Houma, Thibodaux, and Crowley at various times during that span. Eventually, the Cotton States became the Dixie League.

Louisiana has contributed heavily to major league baseball. Two pitchers, Ron Guidry of Lafayette and Vida Blue of Mansfield, won the Cy Young Award. Mel Ott of Gretna, who joined the New York Giants at the age of sixteen, was the youngest player in the majors at the time. He hit 511 home runs during his major league career.

Gretna's Mel Ott, a star slugger for the New York
Giants in the golden age of baseball.

Courtesy the New Orleans Times-Picayune

Interest in college baseball picked up in Louisiana in 1991 when LSU won the College World Series. The Tigers won the national championship again in 1993.

Football quickly became the paramount intercollegiate sport in Louisiana after LSU and Tulane began playing the game in 1893. The universities met at Sportsman's Park in New Orleans on November 25, 1893, and that began a fierce rivalry which has continued through the twentieth century, although it lost much of its intensity when Tulane began to deemphasize athletics in the latter part of the century.

Football also is the major sport at other Louisiana colleges and universities, including Southeastern, Southwestern, Southern, Grambling State, McNeese State, Northwestern State, Louisiana Tech, and Nicholls State. These schools have formidable basketball and baseball programs, also. In addition, the University of New Orleans, which does not compete on the gridiron, has solid basketball and baseball programs that have gained wide recognition. Many of the schools have women's teams that compete in basketball and other sports. Louisiana Tech's women's basketball team is perennially a power and has won several national crowns.

The Sugar Bowl, which hosted its first game on January 1, 1935, has helped build football into a major attraction. It expanded Tulane Stadium to a seating capacity of more than 80,000 (the game is now played in the Superdome and the old stadium has been demolished). Fanatical interest in football at LSU, spurred on by the Tigers' many successes—especially a national championship in 1958—brought expansion of Tiger Stadium to 80,140 seats. At the opposite corner of the state, Shreveport has no college team but does host the annual Independence Bowl.

The quality of Louisiana players is reflected in the large number who are drafted into professional football. Nor do the stars come only from the large schools. Louisiana Tech's Terry Bradshaw quarterbacked the Pittsburgh Steelers for fourteen years, during which they won four Super Bowls, and Doug Williams of Southern led the Washington Redskins to a Super Bowl title. For its size, Grambling State has probably produced more NFL players over the years than any other school in the nation.

One of the greatest college stars developed in Louisiana was Christian Keener "Red" Cagle, who first gained fame as a quarterback on the Southwestern Louisiana Industrial Institute (later the University of Southwestern Louisiana) team in the mid-1920s, then went on to Army. Knute Rockne called him the greatest player of the time. Numerous LSU fans would assess their own legendary back, Billy Cannon, even more glowingly. Every fall in Baton Rouge, Cannon's electrifying eighty-nine-yard punt return that beat Ole Miss is replayed countless times on local radio

Shreveport's Terry Bradshaw, a Louisiana Tech all-American
and Pittsburgh Steelers Hall of Fame quarterback.

Courtesy the Associated Press

stations—even though the game took place in 1959. Cannon also won the
Heisman Trophy that year.

A football-crazy state was bound to have its own NFL team eventually,
and in 1967 the New Orleans Saints arrived. Despite being perennially disappointed in their hopes for a Super Bowl victory, Saints fans generally
have remained loyal; during one particularly bad spell, they wore paper
bags over their heads when attending games, but attend they did. As of this
writing, Louisiana has a second professional football team, in Shreveport,
which obtained a franchise in the Canadian—correct, Canadian—Football League in 1994.

Although basketball has not claimed the attention shown to football in
Louisiana, the state has produced some all-Americans and several top pros,
and LSU has held high national rankings many times through the years,
with Tulane and the University of New Orleans also producing strong
teams in recent years.

All-American center Shaquille O'Neal, who left LSU to become a dominating force in the NBA.

Courtesy the Associated Press

Outstanding individual players with Louisiana connections include a
trio of LSU Tigers. In the 1950s and 1960s, former LSU all-American Bob
Pettit averaged 26.4 points per game during his NBA career. At LSU from
1968 to 1970, Pete Maravich scored an incredible 44.2 points per game,
setting an NCAA record that still stands. And in 1992, Shaquille O'Neal
left LSU to become an instant star in the professional ranks.

O'Neal joins a cohort of great NBA centers linked to Louisiana. Willis
Reed led Grambling to an NAIA title. Bill Russell was born in Monroe.
Elvin Hayes was a native of Rayville. Robert Parish played his college ball
at Centenary in his hometown of Shreveport.

In recent years, LSU has established itself as a power in track and field.
The men's track team has won several national indoor and outdoor championships, and the women's team has developed into a dynasty: as of 1995,
the Lady Tigers had won nine consecutive NCAA outdoor titles.

Louisiana's climate, especially in the southern parishes, lends itself to year-round golf and tennis—although in the steamy days of July and August sensible players schedule their games for the mornings. Louisiana has had a major professional golf tournament since 1963, the Greater New Orleans Open (later known as the USF&G, then the Freeport-McMoRan). The New Orleans Lawn Tennis Club, founded in 1890, was the first in the nation. A somewhat more rarified outdoor sport, yachting, was popular even before the founding in 1849 of the Southern Yacht Club, the nation's second oldest, on the shores of Lake Pontchartrain.

As popular as other sports may be in Louisiana, perhaps none attracts as many participants as the two that inspired the "Sportsman's Paradise" label—fishing and hunting. For these pursuits, the state's swamps, forests, lakes, rivers, and warm Gulf waters form a perfect setting.

"Nature and man have combined to provide the most dynamic offering of angling anywhere," claims Bob Marshall, veteran outdoors writer of the New Orleans *Times-Picayune*. He extends the "paradise" theme by calling Venice, the little village near the mouth of the Mississippi River, "the doorway to a fisherman's heaven." The salt waters along Louisiana's labyrinthine coastline have always been rich fishing grounds, and today, scores of oil platforms in the Gulf make what has been described as the world's largest artificial reef. The catch includes amberjack, bonito, cobia, grouper, sheepshead, red snapper, spadefish, speckled and white trout, spotted drum (better known as redfish), tuna, and the king of the gamefish, tarpon. Heavily fished freshwater species include bass, bream, crappie, sac-a-lait (white perch), and catfish—the latter occasionally weighing upwards of sixty pounds.

No wonder that in many Louisiana neighborhoods, even in the suburbs of large cities, virtually every driveway seems to hold, along with the family sedan, a boat of one kind or another waiting atop its trailer.

From the beginning, hunting has been a popular pastime in Louisiana, and the state's abundance of game continues to attract not only natives but also thousands of visiting hunters every year. The main draws each hunting season are deer, field gamebirds, and waterfowl (literally millions of ducks either winter in Louisiana or use the state's vast wetlands as a waystation on their annual migrations to Mexico and points south). Rabbit, squirrel, raccoon, and other small animals are hunted more by locals than by out-of-staters.

In a state unusually devoted to outdoor sports, the premier sports venue is, ironically, indoors. The Louisiana Superdome, the brainchild of businessman and sportsman David F. Dixon, was built as a permanent home

The Louisiana Superdome in New Orleans.

Courtesy the New Orleans Times-Picayune

field for the New Orleans Saints, who began play in the National Football League in 1967. Besides providing the battlefield for the annual Sugar Bowl gridiron clash, the Superdome is on a rotating schedule of sites for Super Bowl games, hosts NCAA basketball playoffs (including occasionally the Final Four), and showcases the state high-school football and basketball championships, as well as many other sporting events. Seating 76,000 for football, the Superdome is a source of pride for Louisianians, who have been known to remind Texans that Houston's Astrodome would fit *inside* the New Orleans structure.

—W.G.C.

20

MARDI GRAS

They call it "the greatest free show on earth."

It is Mardi Gras, "Fat Tuesday," the climax of the Carnival season in New Orleans and in other communities in Louisiana.

Mardi Gras, dating from medieval times, is the day before Ash Wednesday, itself the first day of the penitential season of Lent. In ancient days, Mardi Gras was the final fling, the last hurrah before the imposition of the austerities of Lent.

In New Orleans, Mardi Gras is the culmination of the Carnival season, which begins on Twelfth Night, the Feast of the Epiphany, the sixth of January. Mardi Gras is a movable date, which may come as early as February 3 or as late as March 9. Why? Because Mardi Gras is geared to Ash Wednesday and Ash Wednesday is geared to Easter—which is geared to the phases of the moon. Here is the formula: Easter is the Sunday that follows the full moon that follows the spring equinox, which is March 21. Forty-seven days before Easter is Mardi Gras.

In New Orleans, from Twelfth Night through Mardi Gras, scarcely a night passes without a ball or a supper dance or perhaps two or more. Some sixty independent private organizations fill the Carnival calendar with their activities. Thirty-five of the more elaborate balls for years were held at the Municipal Auditorium. Many now are held in hotels.

Twelve days before Mardi Gras, the parade season starts. More than sixty parades take to the streets in New Orleans and adjacent parishes. Hundreds of thousands of men, women, children, and babes in arms turn out to see the colorful floats rumble past with masked riders tossing to the crowd beads, aluminum medallions called doubloons, plastic cups, and other trifles to a ceaseless chorus that screams: "Hey, Mister, throw me something!" Arthur Hardy, editor of *The Mardi Gras Guide*, estimates that more than 25,000 float riders each throw an average of $300 worth of trinkets to the crowds. "As for doubloons, they are not as popular as they once were," he adds. "Yet, I estimate that 25,000,000 are thrown annually."

Because Mardi Gras has been observed for centuries, it seems logical to assume that the holiday was celebrated with fetes and balls throughout the French and Spanish regimes in Louisiana, but no documentation has been found to establish such a fact. Indeed, the earliest documented Mardi Gras parade in New Orleans was in 1837. It was an informal affair, a sort of "follow the leader" with costumed participants in carriages, on horseback, or on foot. Such was also the nature of subsequent parades which, in the course of time, fell victim to rowdyism. The deterioration began when the parading maskers provided themselves with little bags of flour, with which they pelted the viewers. It wasn't long before the spectators brought their own bags of flour and fired back. The next step was recurring incidents of violence as the 1840s merged into the 1850s. The press, the public, the political leaders all clamored for the abolition of the barbarous observation of Mardi Gras.

Then it was that the Mistick Krewe of Comus emerged, on February 24, 1857, to save the celebration. The catalysts were six Mobilians who had moved to New Orleans. They wanted to stage a parade such as they were familiar with in Mobile. They formed themselves into a club, chose Comus as their ruling deity, created a pseudo–Old English "krewe" for "crew," and dubbed themselves Mistick. The house in which the Mistick Krewe was organized still stands at Jackson Avenue and Prytania Street.

Thirteen years, including the Civil War, went by before a second organization came into being. The Twelfth Night Revelers chose January 6 for their parade and ball. After several years, however, the krewe gave up parading. In 1872, Rex, King of Carnival, made his initial appearance. The krewe's organization was prompted by the visit to the city by Grand Duke Alexis Romanov of Russia. No special event was organized for the grand duke's visit, so a group of young businessmen organized a parade. They called its leader Rex, Latin for king, and took to the street on Mardi Gras itself. Rex immediately took the title of "King of Carnival" and keeps it to this day.

On New Year's Eve, 1872, the Knights of Momus made their debut in Carnival—actually the Carnival of 1873. Momus was the god of ridicule and mockery. An interval of ten years ensued before the Krewe of Proteus joined Carnival in 1882. It rounded out the "Big Four" of the nineteenth century. Other krewes came into existence and disappeared after a brief stay, but Momus, Proteus, Rex, and Comus all survived to attain more than one hundred years each.

More than a quarter of a century went by before another organization still parading joined in Carnival—the black krewe of Zulu, which has been a favorite of parade watchers since 1909. Zulu enjoyed one of its finest hours in 1949, when it installed Louis "Satchmo" Armstrong as its king. Iris, the first women's krewe, held its first ball in 1917. Venus was the first parading women's crew, taking the street in 1941.

A parade "explosion" came between the end of World War II and the present, with krewes spilling over into almost every neighborhood in adjacent and nearby parishes. The most innovative of the krewes are Bacchus and Endymion, which introduced larger floats than standard and invited celebrities to head their parades. Among Bacchus kings have been Raymond Burr, Bob Hope, Jackie Gleason, Charlton Heston, Kirk Douglas, Danny Kaye, Jim Nabors, Phil Harris, and others from the entertainment world. Among Endymion's float-riding guests have been Doc Severinsen, Englebert Humperdinck, Dolly Parton, and Kenny Rogers.

Mardi Gras beggars description, for until one sees it it cannot be believed. Police estimate that a million people are on the parade route of Rex and the two truck parades that follow it, and part of Zulu's route. The police figure is probably high, but at least 500,000 are out on Mardi Gras parade routes. For Rex and the truck parades that follow it to pass a given place requires anywhere from four to six hours.

Marching clubs are a feature of Mardi Gras, and they usually parade before the Rex parade. The oldest of these is the Jefferson City Buzzards, who celebrated their 100th anniversary in 1990. Another important group is famed New Orleans clarinetist Pete Fountain's Half Fast Marching Club.

Reaching hopefully for tossed trinkets, a sea of revelers shouts the traditional refrain of "Throw me something, mister!" as a Mardi Gras parade rolls down Canal Street.

Photo by G. E. Arnold

In the early 1990s a dispute developed with the city government over the exclusionary membership policies of some krewes. Although a compromise was eventually reached, three of the oldest krewes—Momus, Proteus and Comus—ceased parading because of the controversy.

One of the most colorful aspects of Mardi Gras is the appearance off the beaten track in both uptown and downtown New Orleans of the Mardi Gras Indians. Their costumes are the most elaborate in Carnival. The Mardi Gras Indians are a black tradition going back to about 1880. Their handmade costumes of beaded material and headdresses of brilliantly colored feathers are handcrafted throughout the year. They are dazzling monuments to the patience and skill of the so-called Indians. They are said to cost several thousand dollars each. One has to go in search of the Indians, two "tribes" of which conduct their activities in the vicinity of Claiborne Avenue and Washington Avenue uptown and Claiborne Avenue and Orleans Avenue downtown.

In many Louisiana cities and towns, Mardi Gras follows the pattern of Carnival in New Orleans, but southwest Louisiana maintains a tradition quite different from the one of float parades and marching clubs. There the celebration is called "Courir de Mardi Gras"—"the running of Mardi Gras." It comprises a wild ride on horseback by costumed riders who go from farm to farm collecting chickens, rice, sausages, and other ingredients of gumbo. From morning until 3 P.M. the "courir" continues, and then the gumbo cooking starts. At 5 P.M. a Cajun dance begins, and later comes the feasting. Places where this picturesque celebration of Mardi Gras takes place include Eunice, Mamou, Church Point, and Grand Prairie. Ville Platte's celebration includes La Danse de Mardi Gras.

Millions of dollars of New Orleans money—how much can only be guessed at—are spent by the dues-paying members of the various krewes to stage Carnival. Tourists bring in "fresh" money, although Carnival never has been "tourist bait." The economic impact of Carnival on New Orleans has been estimated at more than $450,000,000.

Anyone caught up in the Carnival whirl, especially natives, welcomes the coming of Lent. The noted humorist Ring Lardner expressed it this way years ago: "On Ash Wednesday, the people of New Orleans wake up Rex in a state of Comus."

—C.L.D.

21

LITERATURE

Literature in Louisiana was born in the wilderness, the product of the pens of the explorers themselves. La Salle's lieutenant Henry de Tonti and the notary Jacques de la Metairie were chroniclers of the explorer's first expedition. Henry de Joutel wrote a historical journal of La Salle's disastrous second voyage. Missionaries, such as Father François-Xavier Charlevoix and Father Paul du Ru, produced narratives of their travels. André Pénicaut, a carpenter, came to Louisiana with Iberville in 1699 and for the next twenty-two years recorded events in the colony. Pénicaut's *Narrative* is a prime source for the early history of Louisiana. Two Ursuline nuns who arrived in a group of eight in 1727 made valuable contributions to the source material of colonial Louisiana. Marie de Saint-Augustin Tranchepain, mother superior of the group, wrote an account of the voyage. Marie Madeleine Hachard, a novice, wrote letters from New Orleans to her father in Rouen that, full of charm and information, were published in France in 1728.

An early settler in Louisiana, who established himself on Bayou St. John before New Orleans was founded in 1718, was Antoine Simon Le Page du Pratz. He found the area too swampy for his taste and moved up the Mississippi to higher ground. Later he returned to France and wrote the first history of Louisiana, published in 1758.

The first actual literary figure in Louisiana was Julien Poydras, a wealthy plantation owner. He wrote in French three long poems, two of them in praise of Governor Bernardo de Gálvez. In 1777 Poydras published *Epître a Don Bernardo de Gálvez* and *Le Dieu et les Nayades du Fleuve St. Louis*. In 1779 he produced *La Prise du Morne du Baton Rouge* in celebration of Gálvez's capture of Baton Rouge from the British.

Until the Civil War, literary production in Louisiana was essentially French. The Rouquette brothers, Dominique and Adrien, were the chief poets among the Creoles, while Dr. Alfred Mercier and Charles Testut were the main Louisiana novelists of the era, all four men writing in French.

Many early Louisiana writers had gone to France for their education. Among these were the Rouquettes, who were greatly influenced by French romanticism as exemplified by Hugo, Lamartine, and Chateaubriand, into whose circle they were introduced. Dominique published *Meschacébéennes* in Paris in 1839 and *Fleurs d'Amérique* in New Orleans in 1857. Adrien published *Les Savanes* in 1841 and *L'Antoniade* in 1860. His masterpiece was an Indian idyl, *La Nouvelle Atala*, published in 1879. Ordained a priest in 1845, Adrien Rouquette was a missionary to the Choctaw Indians in St. Tammany Parish.

Among Mercier's novels, *L'Habitation Saint-Ybars*, based largely on his childhood experiences on an antebellum Louisiana plantation, ranks first.

One of the most important literary productions in the French language in Louisiana was an anthology of poems by free persons of color. Entitled *Les Cenelles*, it contained eighty-two poems by seventeen poets. It was published in 1845.

New Orleans-born Victor Séjour, a free person of color, forsook New Orleans for Paris, where he became a successful playwright in the mid-nineteenth century.

One of the last Louisianian authors to write strictly in French was Sidonie de la Houssaye. Born Hélène Perret in St. John the Baptist Parish in 1820, she raised eight grandchildren after her daughter's death and was never published until she was in her sixties. Her principal works were *Pouponne et Balthazar* (1888) and *Les Quarteronnes de la Nouvelle-Orleans* (1893).

George Washington Cable was the first Louisiana writer to gain national recognition in America. His stories of the Creoles established his reputation; at the same time, they ultimately made him an exile from his native New Orleans. The Creoles felt that Cable was holding them up to ridicule in his works, notable of which were his story collection *Old Creole Days* (1879) and his novel *The Grandissimes* (1880).

Grace King, like Cable an Anglo-American born in New Orleans, began her distinguished writing career essentially in order to answer Cable's perceived negative portrayals. Among her contributions to Louisiana literature are *Balcony Stories*, *Monsieur Motte*, *Tales of a Time and Place*, and *New Orleans: The Place and the People*.

Kate Chopin, not a Louisianian by birth, lived for a time in Natchitoches and New Orleans. She was one of the pioneers of realism in American literature. She wrote both short stories and novels, the most important of which was *The Awakening,* which when published in 1899 created an uproar for its daring theme, extramarital love.

Frances Parkinson Keyes, a prolific and popular novelist from the 1920s until her death in 1970, lived half the year in New Orleans in the Beauregard House, which she restored. Here she wrote many of her dozens of novels, including *Dinner at Antoine's, Once on Esplanade,* and *Madame Castel's Lodger.*

George Washington Cable, whose writings earned him fame
and the enmity of many New Orleanians in the late 1800s.
Creoles, especially, took offense at Cable's portrayal of what he
regarded as their racial hypocrisy.

Courtesy the Historic New Orleans Collection; Acc. No. 1974.25.27.56

King, Chopin, and Keyes are only three names in a long tradition of
successful women writers with Louisiana connections. A partial list of their
contemporaries and near-contemporaries would include Mollie Moore
Davis, Ruth McEnery Stuart, Alice Dunbar-Nelson, Fannie Heaslip Lea,
Gwen Bristow, Zora Neale Hurston, and Ada Jack Carver. One of the
state's best-known twentieth-century writers was New Orleans–born Lillian Hellman, who gained fame in the 1930s and 1940s as a dramatist (*The
Little Foxes; The Children's Hour; Watch on the Rhine*), then won a huge following in the 1970s as a memoirist (*An Unfinished Woman; Pentimento*).

Shirley Ann Grau, whose novel *The Keepers of the House* won a Pulitzer
Prize in 1965, was the forerunner of a veritable army of women fiction writers linked with Louisiana, especially with New Orleans. A mere sampling
of the most prominent would include Sheila Bosworth, Ellen Gilchrist,

Nancy Lemann, Valerie Martin, Christine Wiltz, and of course Anne Rice, who has attained best-sellerdom with her vampire series (*Interview with the Vampire, The Vampire Lestat, Memnoch the Devil,* and others).

Besides Grau, four other writers associated with Louisiana have won Pulitzer Prizes for works of fiction. The first was Oliver La Farge, a former Tulane ethnologist who received the award in 1930 for his novel *Laughing Boy.* The most recent was Robert Olen Butler, who won in 1994 for his story collection *A Good Scent from a Strange Mountain.* Between those two, Robert Penn Warren, who had taught at LSU in Baton Rouge, won in 1947 for *All the King's Men,* a novel at least partly inspired by the life of Huey P. Long, and John Kennedy Toole was awarded the prize post-humously for his novel *A Confederacy of Dunces,* set in his hometown of New Orleans. Ironically, Toole's book would never have appeared in print had not another Louisiana writer, the distinguished novelist Walker Percy, persuaded the Louisiana State University Press to publish it. In Toole's life-time, publishers had unanimously rejected the manuscript. (Percy, a native of Mississippi, lived for many years in Covington, Louisiana. His novels es-tablished him as a literary artist of the first rank. They include *Lancelot, The Last Gentleman, Love in the Ruins, The Moviegoer,* and *The Thanatos Syndrome.*)

Both the work and the life of the renowned playwright Tennessee Williams are linked with New Orleans, although he did most of his actual writing elsewhere. Williams was a two-time Pulitzer winner, first in 1948 for his quintessential French Quarter drama *A Streetcar Named Desire* and again in 1955 for *Cat on a Hot Tin Roof.*

As with its women writers, Louisiana currently boasts a large number of talented male authors who specialize in fiction, among them (and among many others) James Lee Burke, O'Neil De Noux, Andre Dubus, Richard Ford, Ernest Gaines, Virgil Suarez, and Lucian Truscott IV. Gaines, who grew up in a former slave quarters on a plantation in Pointe Coupee Parish, gained national recognition for *The Autobiography of Miss Jane Pittman* (1971), a fictional retelling of the life story of a 107-year-old black woman. Burke by the mid-1990s had become one of America's most popular writers with his novels featuring Cajun detective Dave Robichaux.

The current flowering of literary talent is in some ways reminiscent of the golden age of the 1920s, when New Orleans' French Quarter became the rendezvous of native, resident, and visiting writers who gathered around Sherwood Anderson. Among these were William Faulkner, Roark Bradford, Hamilton Basso, E. P. O'Donnell, Lyle Saxon, James Feibleman, Sam Gilmore, and John McClure. It was during this time that the *Double*

Ernest Gaines at River Lake Plantation, where he grew up in the black quarters. The setting appears in fictionalized form in several of his novels.

Photo by Marcia Gaudet

Dealer, one of the famed "little magazines" that sprang up in the 1920s, appeared. In it early works of Faulkner, Thornton Wilder, and Ernest Hemingway were published.

In a rather different vein of fiction writing, Louisiana has seen some extraordinarily fine children's authors, going back to the nineteenth century. Several generations of children grew up on the books of Cecilia V. Jamison, which had a setting in Louisiana. These included *Lady Jane*, *Toinette's Philip*, and *Thistledown*. Mrs. Jamison, born in Canada, lived for many years in New Orleans and Thibodaux. Ruth McEnery Stuart wrote many of her short stories for children. Later children's writers include Louise Reynes Jenkins, Mary Alice Fontenot, and Berthe Amoss. The latter, as gifted an artist as a storyteller, illustrates her own books.

In another subgenre, science fiction, Dan Galouye and George Effinger commanded not only a national, but an international, readership.

Since the time of *Les Cenelles*, Louisiana has turned out so many poets that this account can only brush the surface of the topic. They range from Mary Ashley Townsend, who wrote under the pen name "Xariffa" in the post–Civil War years, to the present state poet laureate, Pinkie Gordon Lane. Along the way, they have included poets as diverse as Alice Claudel,

John McClure, Andrei Codrescu, Elizabeth Brown-Guillory, and Brenda Marie Osbey.

Some of Louisiana's leading writers have devoted themselves to nonfiction, especially history. In the nineteenth century, François Xavier Martin's *History of Louisiana,* originally published in 1827, was the first to relate the story of the state in narrative order. Charles Gayarré's four-volume *History of Louisiana* appeared over the years 1854–1866. About the turn of the century, Alcée Fortier produced his four-volume history under the same title. In 1925 came Henry E. Chambers' *History of Louisiana, State and People.* E. A. Davis, of the LSU faculty, published *Louisiana: The Pelican State* in 1959. John Smith Kendall's three-volume *History of New Orleans* (1922) is still the standard work on the city after three quarters of a century. J. Fair Hardin's *Northwestern Louisiana* (1937), also in three volumes, remains an important resource for a full appreciation of the state.

T. Harry Williams, Boyd Professor of History at LSU, was an authority on Lincoln and the Civil War but is perhaps most remembered for his Pulitzer Prize–winning biography *Huey Long,* published in 1969. Stephen Ambrose, Boyd Professor of History at the University of New Orleans, in addition to his biographies of Dwight D. Eisenhower and Richard Nixon, has written on the Civil War, Custer, World War II, and other subjects. Another noted historian was Joe Gray Taylor, whose best-known works are *Negro Slavery in Louisiana* (1963) and *Louisiana Reconstructed* (1974).

It seems fitting to end by mentioning an utterly unique Louisiana-related autobiographical account, Solomon Northup's *Twelve Years a Slave.* Northup was a thirty-two-year-old black man living in Saratoga, New York, when, during a visit to Washington, D.C., in 1841, he was kidnapped, taken south, and sold into slavery on a plantation near Cheneyville, in Rapides Parish. When he was finally rescued in 1853, his written narrative of his experiences caused a sensation. It was inevitably compared to Harriet Beecher Stowe's *Uncle Tom's Cabin,* set in the same Louisiana countryside, and like that work of fiction it fueled abolitionist sentiment in the North, thus helping to bring about the war that ended slavery.

—C.L.D.

22

MUSIC

Few places can match Louisiana in the making of music, or in the variety of the music that is made—music that runs the gamut from grand opera to gospel, from country to jazz, from Cajun to the blues, and from rock to zydeco. The state even elected a popular singer/songwriter as governor.

If there were such a thing as an official starting date for the musical history of Louisiana, a likely choice for the honor would be May 22, 1796. On that date André Grétry's opera *Sylvain* was sung in a theater on St. Peter Street in New Orleans—the city's first known operatic performance. Although people the world over know New Orleans as the cradle of jazz, few even in Louisiana realize that the city was once the center of opera in America.

By the 1830s, when opera was still a sporadic entertainment in places such as New York and Boston, New Orleanians were recruiting singers and even entire troupes from France for what amounted to a regular season. Over the years, halls such as the Orleans Theater and the French Opera House saw the American debuts of works by Bellini, Donizetti, Halévy, Meyerbeer, and Verdi, among others. New Orleans remained an operatic capital—especially for French opera—until the outbreak of the Civil War. On the very eve of the conflict, in the winter of 1860–1861, the city interrupted its debate over secession to fall in love with eighteen-year-old Adelina Patti. The young Spanish-born soprano, who had first sung in New Orleans as a touring child prodigy in 1853, so enchanted audiences that her original engagement for a mere three or four performances was extended to forty.

A place so enamored of music was bound to produce accomplished musicians of its own. The first two Louisianians to gain international prominence in music were New Orleans born: Louis Moreau Gottschalk (1829–1869) and Ernest Guiraud (1837–1892). Both were prodigies sent to Paris in their early teens to hone their great talents. Guiraud returned briefly to New Orleans to attend the premiere of his opera *Le Roi David*; he was fifteen at the time. He went on to a long career as a teacher and composer, during which, among other things, he wrote music for the recitatives in Bizet's *Carmen* and completed Offenbach's unfinished *The Tales of Hoffman*. Gottschalk was a virtuoso pianist whose dazzling technique won him

The French Opera House in New Orleans, for decades a center of the city's musical culture, was in decline when this photograph was taken. Not long afterward, in 1919, it burned.

Courtesy the Historic New Orleans Collection; Acc. No. 1979.325.5859

the plaudits of Chopin, Berlioz, and many others. He also gained renown as a composer; fittingly, he often used Louisiana folk melodies for his themes.

With Gottschalk and Guiraud began a line of Louisiana opera singers and classical musicians that reaches to the present day. In the twentieth century, no fewer than eight New Orleans singers have performed with New York's Metropolitan Opera. Another New Orleanian, Norman Treigle, one of the superb bass-baritones of his day, never reached an agreement with the Met but had a stellar twenty-year career with the New York City Opera. Among instrumentalists, Shreveport-born Van Cliburn fell heir to Louis Gottschalk's piano virtuosity. Cliburn rocketed to fame in 1958 when at age twenty-four he won the International Tchaikovsky Competition in Moscow. He went on to a distinguished concert career.

As rich as it may be, Louisiana's classical tradition represents only a small fraction of the state's musical repertoire. Gottschalk had a plentiful source when he used local songs in his piano and orchestral compositions. Louisiana was a musical melting pot—not only in New Orleans, along whose waterfront a listener could hear music from almost any land on earth, but out in the countryside as well. It is not entirely fanciful to imagine a traveler stopping along a bayou or country road of a Saturday night to enjoy an old Spanish melody sung in Acadian-accented French to the waltz-time accompaniment of a German accordion, the lyrics perhaps translated from an Irish sea chantey or Kentucky hill ballad, while from a slave quarters across the fields come call-and-response echoes and intricate rhythms rooted in Africa.

Somehow, near the end of the nineteenth century, it all melded into a new kind of music that was Louisiana's gift to the world. Jazz was not born in Storyville—it existed well before that infamous New Orleans red-light district was defined—but it grew up there, as did its most renowned practitioner, Louis "Satchmo" Armstrong (1900–1971). Armstrong's trumpet virtuosity was unsurpassed, and his contributions to jazz place him in company with such seminal figures as King Oliver, Sidney Bechet, Buddy Bolden, Bunk Johnson, Tom Brown, Pop Foster, and Jelly Roll Morton. Like many other jazzmen, Armstrong migrated to Chicago in the 1920s, and there helped mold jazz into the uniquely American art form that it is today.

Traditional New Orleans jazz is still a lively presence in the city, heard in nightclubs, at jazz funerals, at the city's annual Jazz and Heritage Festival, and at Preservation Hall in the French Quarter, where veteran performers play it in a style that the young Satchmo would have recognized. Perhaps the best-known local jazz musicians today are Al Hirt (trumpet) and Pete Fountain (clarinet). Ironically, both first gained fame not in New Orleans, but in New York City, where they played on nationally televised music shows in the early 1960s.

If jazz is essentially city music, blues is its country cousin. Louisiana has produced its share of blues singers, greatest among them Huddie "Leadbelly" Ledbetter. Born in 1885 in Mooringsport, in the northwestern corner of the state, Leadbelly moved to Texas as a boy, learned blues singing from the legendary Blind Lemon Jefferson, and became an absolute master of the twelve-string guitar. He also developed a talent for trouble, spending prison time in Texas for murder and in Louisiana for attempted murder before being discovered in the 1930s by folk-music historian John Lomax, who helped to launch him on a belated but successful recording career. Leadbelly died in New York City in 1949.

Another Louisiana singer rising to fame at about the same time as Leadbelly was Mahalia Jackson (1911–1972). Beginning as a strong-voiced little girl in the choir of a New Orleans church where her father was the preacher, she went on to become the premiere gospel singer of her era, bringing this blues-oriented religious music to settings as venerable as Carnegie Hall.

New Orleans jazzmen (clockwise from top left): legendary trumpeter and vocalist Louis "Stachmo" Armstrong; Ferdinand "Jelly Roll" Morton, pianist and pioneering jazz composer; virtuoso Dixieland clarinetist Pete Fountain; trumpet great Al Hirt.

All courtesy the New Orleans Times-Picayune; *Fountain photo by Michael Lutch*

Perhaps the best and best-known Louisiana vocalist in the blues tradition today is Irma Thomas of New Orleans, who first gained recognition in the 1950s and is still going strong.

As radio and recordings became truly mass media in the 1930s, several Louisiana performers attained mainstream popularity. Dorothy Lamour of New Orleans began as a singer and went on to a movie career. The Boswell Sisters, also of New Orleans, were successful recording artists as a trio, and Connee Boswell later performed with singers such as Bing Crosby and Frank Sinatra. Gene Austin, raised in Minden, sold 80 million records in ten years—one of his hits was "My Blue Heaven"—and retired rich for life. In 1962 he ran unsuccessfully for governor of Nevada. Perhaps he was inspired by the example of Louisiana's "singing governor," Jimmie Davis, of rural Jackson Parish, in north Louisiana. In fact, Davis was elected governor twice—in 1944 and 1960—but outside the state he was better known as the singer/songwriter of "You Are My Sunshine," to this day a campfire-singalong standard.

It was only natural that Louisiana would contribute to that blend of black and white musical influences known as rock-and-roll when it swept the nation in the 1950s. Two first-rank stars among Louisiana's rockers were pianist-vocalists. One was Fats Domino, a New Orleanian who parlayed his idiosyncratic voice into a string of hits. The other was the legendary Jerry Lee Lewis, who came charging out of Ferriday to earn every bit of an international reputation for wild living and burn-the-house-down performances.

Rock-and-roll grew at least partly out of so-called country-and-western roots, and Louisiana—especially north Louisiana—provided fertile ground for that kind of music. From the late 1940s through the 1950s, Shreveport was a mecca for country singers and musicians because of the "Louisiana Hayride." Staged in the city's Municipal Auditorium and aired over the powerful local radio station KWKH, the show was second only to Nashville's "Grand Ole Opry" as a display case for talent. Dozens of country stars-to-be—including the great Hank Williams—gained their first fame on the Hayride. One audience favorite, a young Mississippi truck driver turned country singer, performed dozens of times on the Hayride before graduating to bigger things in the world of rock. His name was Elvis Presley.

Meanwhile, south Louisiana was harboring a musical secret—to be exact, two musical secrets: Cajun music and zydeco. Both forms were played mainly at little wood-frame bars and dance halls in towns like Lebeau and Plaisance and Breaux Bridge scattered across the south and southwest parts of the state. Few outsiders knew that such music existed.

Moreover, many Louisianians—including not a few Cajuns—considered the plaintive vocals, the pat-your-foot rhythms, and the clamor of fiddles and accordions to be "nothing but chanky-chank." All that changed in the 1970s. First, a highly successful Tribute to Cajun Music Festival, initiated in 1974 in Lafayette, gave the music new respectability on its home turf. Then a growing national fad for Cajun cooking helped to create a widespread appetite for south Louisiana music as well. Suddenly there were people from San Francisco to New York who recognized Dewey Balfa's Cajun fiddle or Clifton Chenier's zydeco accordion. (Although Cajun music and zydeco share certain similarities, there are also differences—beyond the fact that Cajun is played mainly by whites and zydeco mainly by blacks. For one, Cajun tends to be more lilting, zydeco more syncopated. Also, Cajun performers still prefer their lyrics to be in French; zydeco singers are more likely to use English, throwing in a French phrase now and then.)

Besides the ongoing popularity of Cajun music and zydeco, one of the most notable developments in Louisiana music toward the century's end was the emergence of several remarkably talented musical families in the New Orleans area. The Grammy-winning Neville Brothers achieved national fame, as did the Marsalis family, whose performers include father and music professor Ellis Marsalis and three of his six sons, trumpeter Wynton, saxophonist Branford, and trombonist Delfeayo. The Jordan family is virtually an orchestra: saxophonist Edward Jordan is head of the jazz program at Southern University of New Orleans; his wife, Edvige Jordan, is a pianist; their recording-artist children are flutist Kent, trumpeter Marion, violinist Rachel, and vocalist Stephanie.

Grammy-winning vocalist and pianist Harry Connick, Jr., would fit under the musical-family heading had not his father, a capable singer, gone into another line of work, becoming a longtime New Orleans district attorney. The combination of DA father and pop-star son might seem offbeat in some places—but not in music-loving Louisiana.

—C.L.D. / W.G.C.

23

ART

At the outset, artistic activity in Louisiana was concentrated almost entirely in New Orleans, which in the early-to-middle nineteenth century had no rival in size or wealth among cities of the South. The city's French, Spanish, and German heritage gave rise to a distinct character manifested even in the early paintings. The state's affluence following the Louisiana Purchase attracted artists in substantial numbers, creating an aesthetic climate that has endured. In turn, many of the artists responded to their natural surroundings by incorporating in their paintings the quiet bayous, the moss-draped oaks, the swamps alive with birds and animals, and the knotted cypress trees. The Mississippi River, with its paddlewheel, water-churning steamboats, lent an air of romance to works created in the late nineteenth century.

The earliest professional artist to work in New Orleans was José de Salazar, a native of Mérida, Mexico, whose paintings are the only ones of the Spanish period, 1769–1803. He painted Don Andrés Almonester y Roxas, New Orleans' great benefactor, in 1796, and Don Luis de Peñalver y Cárdenas, bishop of Louisiana, in 1801, among others. After the Louisiana Purchase came Ambrose Duval, of Gallic origin, who did a miniature of Governor William C. C. Claiborne. Louis-Antoine Collas, a Bordeaux-born miniaturist, arrived in 1822. Another artist of note, Jean-Baptiste Sel, of Santo Domingo, was active in New Orleans from 1810 until 1830.

Portrait artists began to find a ready market as New Orleans, and Louisiana, prospered from the 1820s until the Civil War. Perhaps the greatest portraitist active in New Orleans during that time was Jean-Joseph Vaudechamp, who arrived from France in 1831. One of his main contributions was a portrait of Antoine-Jacques Philippe de Marigny de Mandeville. Vandechamp brought to New Orleans the Dutch-born, French-trained Jacques Amans, in 1836. Among others who came from abroad were Alexandre-Charles Jaume and Adolph Rinck. Irish-born Trevor Thomas Fowler came in 1840 and wintered in New Orleans for twelve years.

One of the most widely known artists to visit in the 1820s was John James Audubon, who worked in New Orleans and St. Francisville, sketching eighty-two of his *Birds of America* series.

Most of the artists of this era were itinerants who fell into two classes—those who appeared at regular intervals in the winter to do commissions for local residents, and the resident itinerants who came to Louisiana and stayed for several years. Monumental church decoration came into vogue in antebellum New Orleans. French-born Leon Pomarede did three paintings for St. Patrick's Church in 1841. John Baptiste Rossi was the principal artist, in 1851, for the frescoes on the ceiling of St. Louis Cathedral. Frescoes in St. Alphonsus Church were painted by Dominique Canova in 1866.

At about midcentury, artists began painting the picturesque Louisiana landscapes and colorful steamboat scenes. The earliest landscape painter in Louisiana was Toussaint-François Bigot, active in New Orleans from 1816 to 1869. Pomarede did a panorama of the Mississippi River, and Hypolite Sebron, also French, made an impression with his *Giant Steamboats at the Levee in New Orleans* in the 1850s. John Antrobus worked in New Orleans in 1859 and did a series of paintings of plantation life.

One of the first native professionals was Julian Hudson, who also was the first black artist to work in New Orleans. French landscapists dominated the scene, among them Richard Clague, born in Paris in 1821, who came to Louisiana in 1850 and became the acknowledged founder of a Louisiana landscape school. Two of his pupils, William H. Buck and Marshall J. Smith, were active through the century. Everett B. D. Fabrino Julio also painted landscapes but is perhaps best known for his *The Last Meeting of Lee and Jackson*.

Gradually, a local colony developed in New Orleans and various organizations, such as the Artists' Association of New Orleans (1885–1903) were formed. William Aiken Walker, American-born and a classic example of the itinerant artist, visited Louisiana almost annually from 1878 to 1905. He produced numerous images of nineteenth-century blacks, depicting them in their humble post–Civil War settings. George David Coulon was active as a portrait and landscape painter, 1838–1904.

Though he did not participate in Louisiana's artistic life, Edgar Degas, the French impressionist, visited New Orleans during 1872 and 1873. He did a portrait of his cousin, Estelle Musson, which hangs in the New Orleans Museum of Art. His most famous Louisiana work, *The Cotton Office in New Orleans,* is in a museum in Pau, France.

The Woodward brothers from Massachusetts, William and Ellsworth, left their marks on Louisiana's art world. William came to the 1884 World's Industrial and Cotton Centennial Exposition (World's Fair) to teach drawing. His classes became popular, especially among women. He and his brother became associated with Newcomb College, where Ellsworth di-

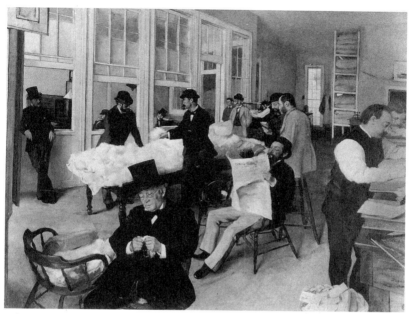

The Cotton Office in New Orleans, painted in 1873 by Edgar Degas while he visited brothers René, shown holding newspaper, and Achille, left background. Other relatives of the artist also appear in the painting.

Photo courtesy the New Orleans Times-Picayune

rected the art program, and Tulane University, where William helped to shape the architecture program. The Newcomb Pottery, a brainchild of the Woodwards, won a bronze medal at the Paris Exposition of 1900. The Woodwards were also instrumental in persuading Isaac Delgado, a sugar magnate, to donate funds in 1910 to build the Delgado Museum of Art, of which Ellsworth became the first director. The museum, completed in 1911 in City Park and known today as the New Orleans Museum of Art, changed the art scene dramatically by providing exposure for local, national, and international artists.

Much of the local art of the late nineteenth century and first half of the twentieth showed everyday life of the region. Cajun cabins, sharecroppers' shacks, black church scenes, and political rallies were standard subjects. Major contributors in this era included Knute Heldner, John McCrady, and E. Arthur Callender. Typical is Callender's painting of a black woman toting a loaded basket of vegetables on her head as she walks the levee, with the caption *New Orleans from Algiers*.

Prior to 1950, a number of artists established themselves in the fields of portraiture, landscape, and still life. Among this group were Clarence Millet, Will Henry Stevens, Josephine Crawford, Conrad Albrizio, Caroline Wogan Durieux, Paul Ninas, and Heldner. Durieux, who taught first at Newcomb and later at Louisiana State University, won acclaim in the 1930s and 1940s as a satirist in black/white lithography. The Vieux Carré with its Bohemian atmosphere was the magnet during the first half of the twentieth century.

Millet, a native of Hahnville, emerged as a recognized artist after World War II. He concentrated on plantation life, the marshes, and the Vieux Carré. Stevens was noted for his rich coloristic effects. Crawford, a modernist, evoked Creole images. Albrizio, a New Yorker who joined the faculty of LSU, painted murals at the outset but later turned to doing impressionist abstractions. Ninas' provocative works were influenced by cubism. Heldner produced a series of works depicting swamps and bayous, as well as impressionistic scenes of the French Quarter. A celebrated artist of southwest Louisiana was Weeks Hall, an example of the southern romantic painter.

The Isaac Delgado Museum of Art—now officially the New Orleans Museum of Art—was named for its great benefactor, a West Indies planter's son who arrived in New Orleans in the 1850s and made his fortune as a merchant and banker. Delgado, who died in 1912, returned much of his wealth to the city through philanthropy.

Among the most prominent artists in the latter part of the twentieth century are Ida Kohlmeyer, Robert Gordy, George Dureau, Robert Warrens, and Boyd Cruise. Sculptors Enrique Alferez, Angela Gregory, John Scott, Lin Emery, Rai Greiner Murray and Clyde Connell have won wide recognition. The late Frank Hayden, a leading African-American sculptor who taught at Southern University in Baton Rouge, is known for major works in Baton Rouge and New Orleans. The New Orleans Museum of Art gave him a special exhibition in 1989.

Clementine Hunter, a descendant of slaves, was born in 1885 at Hidden Hill Plantation near Melrose. As a teenager she moved to Melrose Plantation, where she picked cotton for years and worked in the plantation's kitchen. In the 1940s she took up painting almost by accident—she used paints left behind by a plantation guest. Within a few years she was a leading folk artist often referred to as "the black Grandma Moses." Her paintings hang in hundreds of homes in America and Europe, and her work has been the subject of special exhibits in New York and New Orleans museums. She died at age 101 on January 1, 1988.

George Rodrigue, a Cajun from New Iberia, has won international fame with paintings of scenes from his early life in southwest Louisiana. Although some critics dismiss his work as crude and untutored, he hit a popular vein and won huge commercial success with his series of "Blue Dog" paintings. Rodrigue himself describes his art as "naïve surrealism."

Walter Anderson, who was born in New Orleans but is most often associated with the Mississippi Gulf Coast, gained fame—mostly posthumously—for his drawings of the environment and wildlife on Horn Island, which lies off Ocean Springs, where Anderson lived for years.

Art has flourished in Louisiana in recent years largely because of the universities. Newcomb, Tulane, LSU, Xavier, Dillard, and the University of New Orleans have strong departments devoted to perpetuating the state's traditions in art. And, museums spread up and down and across the state have made significant contributions. The recognized leader is the New Orleans Museum of Art, which ranks with those of the principal cities of the South and Southwest.

—W.G.C.

24

Food

Forget for a little while the battles, elections, epidemics, riots, booms, hurricanes—these pages are about something of especial importance in Louisiana: food. Good eating not only is a fundamental part of Louisianians' way of life, but has also become a main attraction to free-spending visitors who keep the economic pot boiling.

The cuisines of New Orleans and Acadian Louisiana are unique, and how could it be otherwise? No other area in the hemisphere offers such a variety of ingredients—fish, shrimp, oysters, crabs from the Gulf of Mexico and the lakes and bayous; crawfish and turtles from the swamps; ducks, geese, and other fowl from the marshes; small game from the woods; year-round vegetables from truck farms; fruit from the groves and orchards. And nowhere else is there such a rich variety of influences on the cooking—French, Spanish, West Indian, African, German, Italian, Native American, Yugoslavian, British.

The development of the mouth-watering fare began, of course, when the French colonists brought their recipes from the old country and learned to experiment with the supplies at hand. The Indians used herbs unknown in Europe. Refugees from revolutions in the Caribbean islands brought in their know-how; so did the slaves from Africa. The Germans, Spanish, Italians, Yugoslavs, Anglo-Saxons, and others all made their contributions. No other group, however, had nearly so much impact as the Acadians, the "Cajuns," who started in France, spent years in Nova Scotia, and scattered over the Old World and the New before they settled down in Louisiana.

Most of the food served in Louisiana south of Alexandria is called either Creole or Cajun. *Creole* is the term for people born in Louisiana or the West Indies with European, usually French or Spanish, ancestors. It also is applied to products indigenous to the colonial region. The Acadians were the French people driven out of Canada when they refused to accept the English language, customs, and religion. The boundary between Creole and Cajun foods is blurred. Peter S. Feibleman, in *American Cooking: Creole and Acadian*, notes that most authorities say the difference is between city French cooking (Creole) and country French cooking (Acadian). He does not fully accept this distinction but writes that Acadian is a little spicier than Creole and includes a lot of rice. "Acadian cooks are likely to put all the ingredients for a course into one big pot," Feibleman relates. "Creoles like these ingredients separate." A good generalization that if you are eating in a New Orleans restaurant, the cuisine is Creole; if in south Louisiana outside New Orleans, it is Cajun.

A staple of both Creole and Acadian is gumbo. As long ago as 1885 William H. Coleman commented, "There is no dish which at the same time so tickles the palate, satisfies the appetite, furnishes the body with nutriment sufficient to carry on the physical requirements, and costs so little as a Creole gumbo. It is a dinner in itself, being soup, *pièce de résistance, entrément* and *vegetable* in one. Healthy, not heating to the stomach and easy of digestion, it should grace every table." Gumbo evolved as the Louisiana version of the French bouillabaise, an example of how imaginative cooks can improvise.

In *The New Orleans Restaurant Cookbook,* Deirdre Stanforth calls the city "the most food-conscious community in America; in fact, it may be the only city outside of France where eating is a major love affair of the population." It follows that the Paris of America is also a city of cooks because the prevailing preoccupation with dining puts the pressure on just about everyone to learn his or her way around a kitchen. The daily menus in a lot of New Orleans homes, from shotgun doubles to mansions, would earn a gourmet rating. Strangers generally get their introduction to the culinary delights, of course, in public eating places. The opportunities abound, from old-line establishments nationally known for four-star meals to storefront neighborhood places that please the discriminating locals upon whom they depend.

The tradition goes all the way back to 1791, when the Café des Emigrés opened to cater to newcomers who had fled a bloody revolt in Haiti or the equally bloody French Revolution. Rima and Richard Collin, in *The New Orleans Cookbook,* note that it was only one of the cafés and coffeehouses doing business in the French Quarter. The first memorable dining room was in the Tremoulet Hotel, which in 1820 faced on the Place d'Armes, now Jackson Square. The 1830s marked the beginning of a golden era with the launching of the St. Louis Hotel in the French Quarter and the St. Charles and Verandah Hotels across Canal Street in the American section. In their time they may have been the greatest hotels in America.

They were the haunts of plantation owners who took their families to New Orleans for annual visits and of the city's wealthy Creoles. Their years elapsed before svelte figures became fashionable and the difference between gourmet and gourmand was recognized. In the *Historical Sketch Book*

Coleman describes an antebellum hotel meal that might cost twenty dollars. The ten courses would include oysters, turtle soup, broiled pompano, beef or game with two vegetables, a second entree of duck or turkey, a souffle, pastry, dessert, and coffee—all accompanied by the appropriate wines. Coleman also offers advice for dining on a less epic scale: "A hungry man, dropping casually into a restaurant, should take a soup and some fish; then an entrée, say a sweetbread or a lamb chop; then say a spring chicken, or roast beef, or roast mutton or veal, with one or two dishes of vegetables. For dessert, some fruit or jelly, and cheese, and a cup of coffee. With a half bottle of claret, this would cost from $1.50 to $2.50."

The St. Louis Hotel, on the site now occupied by the Omni Royal Orleans Hotel, is reputed to have been the birthplace of the American innovation known as the free lunch. A customer who bellied up to the hotel's bar could, for the price of a cocktail, nibble away at a wide choice of dishes, enough for a full meal if he were hungry. The custom did not survive Prohibition.

The dining rooms of the St. Louis and St. Charles were still in business when the first of the modern generation of New Orleans restaurants made their debuts. Antoine Alciatore, from Marseilles, established a pension in the French Quarter in 1840. It was the forerunner of Antoine's Restaurant, which in 1874 moved to its present location on St. Louis Street. Presidents and kings have dined at Antoine's, the birthplace of oysters Rockefeller, pompano en papillote (in a paper bag), and potatoes soufflé (fries that swell up like balloons). Descendants of Alciatore still are connected with the restaurant.

Like Antoine's, some of the best-known New Orleans eating places, are known by their family connections: Galatoire's, Delmonico's, Commander's, Brennan's, Masson's, Arnaud's, and Manale's among them. The city by no means has a monopoly on restaurants with cooks who prepare Creole or Acadian food. Local inquiry all over Louisiana can lead a stranger to a memorable meal.

Almost every state has a motto, a flower, a song. If there were such a thing as a state dish, in Louisiana it would be gumbo, followed closely by jambalaya, a spicy concoction of rice, chicken, and sausage. Those are not, however, the only standards in the Creole-Cajun country. In recent years crawfish (elsewhere known as crayfish) offerings such as bisque, étouffé, and pie have been served with increasing frequency in homes and restaurants. This is partly because aquaculturalists have learned to propagate the mudbugs, which are therefore more plentiful than when they had to be hunted in the wetlands. In thousands of south Louisiana homes and cafés, red beans and rice are the Monday standby. Highly spiced kidney beans, cooked with ham, sausage, or pickled pork, are piled on top of mounds of rice. The rationale is that the plain food is antidote to the rich fare eaten over the weekend. It is also well known to bring good luck.

Another favorite is the poorboy (colloquially, po-boy) sandwich, the Louisiana version of the hero. Although the ingredients may vary tremendously, in one popular manifestation a loaf of French bread is split down the middle and filled with roast beef, ham, tomatoes, pickles, and other goodies. The secret to the unique goodness is the fact that the bread is first dipped into beef gravy. Messy, but marvelous.

The true Creole or Cajun excels at getting the most out of a shrimp, crab, or crawfish boil. The crustaceans are boiled in highly seasoned water and served, still in the shells, by heaping them on a table covered with wrapping paper or newspaper. The art lies in extracting the meat from the shell with one's fingers.

In 1857 Mrs. James Tyson Lane, a bride from the North, wrote about the menu of Sunday dinner at the plantation of her husband's family in East Feliciana Parish. She listed okra soup, boiled ham, beef steak, broiled chicken, fried chicken, chicken pie, peas, Irish potatoes, sweet potatoes, rice, hominy, peach jelly, muscadine jelly, apple jelly, sweet potato pie, pound cake, honey, milk, coffee. And that is one way of saying that the people in the rest of Louisiana have not gone hungry while the Creoles and Acadians were feasting on their exotic fare.

In an era of frozen foods, TV dinners, delicatessens, fast food, television cooks, newspaper recipes, and footloose life-styles, parochial diets hardly exist any more. But local influences and traditions still come into play, as does the availability of home-grown products. Don't be surprised to find trout amandine on the menu of a Shreveport restaurant or have a Monroe housewife serve you crepes suzette, but north Louisiana generally is the land of the barbecue pit and the deep fryer. Pork has been a staple in the region since the days of the earliest settlers, and a platter of ribs slow-smoked over hickory coals makes a treat not to be passed up. A classic north Louisiana feast consists of mounds of golden-fried catfish and hush puppies with a side order of cole slaw. North Louisianians also consider that they know more about the art of frying chicken than just about anybody.

As part of the old Cotton Belt, the northern parishes have a long acquaintance with "soul food." Often thought of as black cuisine, soul food actually reflects the traditional diet of poor southerners both white and black. Corn bread and collard greens, hog jowl and black-eyed peas, grits and gravy, sweet potato pie—many a sharecropper has dined happily on these down-home dishes, along with many an urban or suburban Louisianian who never touched a plow handle or harnessed a mule. Similar cooking, but with a spicy Cajun accent, can be found below Alexandria. Wherever you find it, as with food anywhere in Louisiana, good advice is to fill up a plate and enjoy.

—J.W.

25

From the Swamp to Storyville

Storyville came later; unbelievably, in view of its notoriety, a much-tamed-down aftermath to the Swamp and Gallatin Street. Beginning in late colonial times, the crews of flatboats and keelboats that drifted down the Mississippi River to New Orleans found their recreation in a center of depravity situated near where the Louisiana Superdome now stands. It was the Swamp, a primitive collection of plank hovels that served as saloons, bagnios, gambling dens, and flophouses for perhaps the crudest, most-untamed aggregation of bullies that America has known. Then, before and after the Civil War, Gallatin Street in the French Quarter was the dusk-to-dawn playground of the riffraff gathered in a combined seaport and river town. Not that Storyville lacked revelry in its two decades of existence at the very end of the nineteenth century and beginning of the twentieth. It was the country's most infamous red-light district, and only in comparison with the Swamp and Gallatin Street does its lurid history pale. Storyville is memorable more for its music in the nascent days of Dixieland jazz than for its abandon.

The brawling flatboatmen who ran the gantlet of pirates and other perils in their weeks-long journeys down the Ohio and Mississippi Rivers were paid off once they tied up on the levee alongside Tchoupitoulas Street. They headed down Girod Street to the Swamp for sex, drink, gambling, and rowdyism, and they found it all. Herbert Asbury reports that for as little as six cents each they could get a drink, a woman, and a bed for the night. In such dives as the House of Rest for Weary Boatmen or the Sure Enuf Hotel they also could be robbed, cheated in crooked gambling games, assaulted, or murdered. It is said that for twenty years slayings in the Swamp averaged as many as half a dozen a week. Authorities kept no statistics; in fact, in those two decades no policeman set foot in the area.

It was sin at its seediest. The unpainted shacks were utterly crude. A plank stretched between two casks served as a bar. A partition marked off a back room where prostitutes plied their trade in cubbyholes and the gambler sharpers fleeced the suckers. A sort of attic was the "hotel" part of the establishment, offering space for a man to sleep off a jag—a slumber from which he might not awaken if he had been foolish enough to display any money.

The Swamp reigned for decades as New Orleans' most notorious sink of debauchery, but in the late antebellum years another district rose to rival and then eclipse it. Gallatin Street, a French Quarter thoroughfare that no longer exists because of changes on the riverfront, extended roughly from the back of the United States Mint to the French Market. It was lined by barrel houses and dance halls, and was the hangout for prostitutes and the dregs of society. It did not take much cash to partake of the offerings of the joints—five cents could buy all the whiskey a man could drink, and the services of a prostitute did not cost much more—but the stranger who wandered onto the street with any bills in his pocket would be lucky to come out without a stab wound or a knot on the head. Once in a while the police, who knew better than to venture into the Swamp, would risk a trip onto Gallatin Street, but always in the daytime and in the safety of numbers. At night they stayed away.

Of all the whores who have made a living in New Orleans since colonial days, the ones who worked Gallatin Street were the most belligerent and the best-able to take care of themselves in a brawl. They had to be tough to survive. The champion was Mary Jane Jackson, known as Bricktop because of her flaming hair, who reportedly never lost a fight and who killed at least four men. The cocks of the walk were the Live Oak Gang, a collection of ruffians who terrorized the neighborhood, robbed, assaulted, and murdered. Sometimes the Live Oaks would descend upon a dance hall, wreck the premises with their oaken cudgels, and send the habitués leaping out of the windows.

In the dance halls, the women seldom had on anything more than a dress, and this often would be shed in the excitement of a fling. Sometimes the men patrons would get into the spirit and strip down to the skin. In the years after the Civil War the city's police gradually became more effective, and Gallatin Street went the way of the Swamp.

By 1897, however, prostitution was out of control in the most wide-open city in the United States. Families in respectable neighborhoods would find the houses next door turned into brothels, with the result that property values plummeted. Finally, City Councilman Sidney L. Story offered a solution. The council adopted an ordinance that banned prostitution except in an area bounded by Basin, Iberville, North Robertson, and St. Louis Streets. For once, police moved against establishments outside of the designated district, and a segregated area developed. To the consternation of Story, a highly respectable businessman, the district became known as Storyville. By 1899 there were 230 houses of prostitution, 30 places of assignation, and 2,000 whores in Storyville.

The establishments ranged from elegant houses on Basin Street, such as Josie Arlington's, to one-room cribs in the back of the district. This was no

*The Arlington Annex Saloon, a Storyville landmark. Its owner, Tom Anderson, was known as
"the mayor of Storyville."*
Courtesy the New Orleans *Times-Picayune*

Swamp, no Gallatin Street. A visitor was perfectly safe, except that he
might have his hat snatched by a woman trying to lure him into her quarters. Police quickly squelched any violence.

The larger houses provided music by small bands, mostly made up of
black players, and it was here that the bouncy two-beat sound known as
New Orleans jazz was given much of its early impetus.

City officials were generally pleased with the experience of segregating
prostitution, and the district might have continued for many years but for
interference by the federal government. After the outbreak of the First
World War, Secretary of War Newton D. Baker and Secretary of the Navy
Josephus Daniels forbade open prostitution within five miles of a military
installation. Mayor Martin Behrman tried to intervene because he believed that Storyville was the answer to a serious city problem. But Daniels
threatened to close the city to army and navy activities unless the district
were shut down. Local officials had to yield, and on November 12, 1917,
Storyville ceased to exist as a red-light district. The area now is a public
housing project.

—J.W.

26

The Mafia Lynching

It will be known forevermore as the "Mafia lynching," whether or not eleven men who were slaughtered in a mass assault on a New Orleans prison on March 14, 1891, in fact were connected with the Sicilian outlaw brotherhood. Whatever the background of the victims, the outbreak of civic fury caused the United States government to pay an indemnity of $24,330 to the Italian government, and for weeks some New Orleans residents feared that the Italian navy would come steaming up the Mississippi River and bombard the city.

There is no irrefutable evidence that elements of the Mafia were active in New Orleans in the last third of the nineteenth century, although by the middle of the twentieth one of the ruling gang families in the United States, headed by Carlos Marcello, was headquartered in the city. However, a wave of immigrants from Sicily in the 1870s and 1880s stirred prejudice among citizens who looked with dismay upon an influx of largely illiterate newcomers who had little choice but to take whatever jobs were offered, even at starvation wages. The Vieux Carré became a Sicilian enclave. For a period a stretch of Decatur Street was known as Vendetta Alley because of frequent knifings and shootings growing out of feuds among the immigrants. Early in the twentieth century numerous violent crimes were attributed by police to the Black Hand, a nebulous federation that preyed mostly upon the poor of Italian background.

A series of events that culminated in the so-called Mafia lynching of 1891 began the previous year with an ambush assault upon the Matranga family, who supplied laborers on the New Orleans riverfront. The shooting was attributed to the rival Provenzano clan, which competed for the jobs. David C. Hennessy, head of the police department, called leaders of the two factions together and demanded peace. "I mean business," he said. "This thing must stop. The Mafia cannot flourish while I am chief of police." Within months Hennessy was dead, waylaid and riddled with shotgun lead on the night of October 15, 1890, as he approached his home.

Newspapers reported that Hennessy gasped the word "dagoes" to those who came to his aid, but he died without answering questions about his attackers. Reflecting the prevailing prejudice, Mayor Joseph A. Shakspeare ordered police to arrest every Italian immigrant found in the vicin-

Police Superintendent David C. Hennessy, whose assassination
resulted in the storming of a New Orleans prison in 1891 and
the lynching of eleven suspects.
*Courtesy the Historic New Orleans Collection; Acc. No.
1974.25.25.233*

ity of the shooting. Eventually, nineteen Sicilians were indicted, including a sixteen-year-old boy who, a witness said, gave notice of Hennessy's
approach to the ambush site by sounding what became known in New Orleans as the Mafia whistle—two short notes, followed by two long notes
and then two more short notes, all in the same key and volume. For years,
until anti-Italian bias abated, New Orleans urchins used the whistle to
annoy Italian street vendors.

The trial became a spectacle. Each morning a crowd outside the building that housed the proceedings awaited the arrival of wagons bringing the
accused from the Orleans Parish Prison. "Who killa de chief?" came the

shout as the terrified prisoners were escorted through the doors. Newspaper accounts emphasized whatever damaging testimony prosecutors could present and downplayed points scored by the defense. As a consequence, the verdict was shocking. The jury reported it was unable to agree on charges against three of the men and acquitted the others. The defendants were taken back to the gloomy old prison, which stood behind Congo Square near the sites now occupied by the Municipal Auditorium and Theater of the Performing Arts. Meanwhile, vengeance-minded citizens were setting the stage for tragedy. They stashed weapons in a Vieux Carré hardware store and called a mass meeting to be held the next morning—March 14, 1891—at the Clay Statue, which then stood at the corner of Canal and St. Charles, the scene of the gathering that had preceded the battle of September 14, 1874.

Many hundreds of excited citizens crowded around the statue to hear speakers urge them to avenge Hennessy's death. Then they streamed through the streets leading to the prison, some stopping to pick up the waiting weapons. Jailers had barred the prison doors and turned the Sicilians out of their cells to find hiding places in the building if they could. The mob used a battering ram to break through a door, and swarmed through the prison in search of its victims. Nine men were shot to death as they cowered in the areas where they were cornered. Two were dragged outside and hanged to answer the roaring demand for blood. The sixteen-year-old boy was allowed to cringe under a bed until the massacre was over.

The lynching had international repercussions. The Italian government recalled its envoy to Washington, and relations between the two countries were strained until the payment of the indemnity moved the healing process along. Charges were dropped against the indicted Sicilians who survived the uprising.

Anti-Italian sentiment was not confined to New Orleans. In 1896 three Italian immigrants were lynched by fifty men at Hahnville, on the German Coast. One of the victims was Lorenzo Salardino, a store owner who was awaiting trial on a charge of killing a rival merchant. In 1899 five Sicilians were killed by a mob in Tallulah, in north Louisiana, as the result of the wounding of a physician.

The twentieth century would be well advanced before Italian immigrants and their descendants finally won general acceptance in Louisiana. For years they endured prejudices that approached the feeling of racists toward blacks, although of course they never were discriminated against by Jim Crow laws, nor were they barred from voting or from entering their children into white schools. The bias is puzzling, especially in south

Louisiana, with its mixture of nationalities. It is true that the Italian new-comers were penniless and ill-prepared for earning their way in a new land, but so were the Irish who were driven from home by the potato famines. Yet it is difficult to imagine a wholesale lynching had it been Irish who were accused of assassinating the police chief.

In 1936 Robert S. Maestri had become the first man of Italian heritage to serve as mayor of New Orleans, and in the 1960s two-term mayor Victor H. Schiro proved that a name no longer was a handicap.

—J.W.

27

DUELS

The Creoles were a proud, sensitive, inbred society with a rigid code of conduct that made a loss of face intolerable. Author Lyle Saxon wrote that "the word 'honor' hung in the air like the refrain of a popular song." The Americans who drifted down the Mississippi River were trigger-tempered brawlers. No wonder the imbecility known as dueling was commonplace in Louisiana, and particularly in New Orleans.

Herbert Asbury, in *The French Quarter*, notes: "Until the Civil War there was scarcely a man in public life in New Orleans or Louisiana who had not fought at least one duel; most of them had engaged in several." He reports that among the oak trees on the Louis Allard plantation, a spot that now is in the New Orleans City Park, the number of encounters ran into the thousands and the resulting fatalities into the hundreds. In 1837 on a Sunday, ten duels were fought there between dawn and noon, three participants being killed.

W. C. C. Claiborne, the first American governor, was wounded in 1807 in a duel with pistols with Daniel Clark, and the governor's brother-in-law, Micajah Lewis, was killed when he challenged a man who had criticized Claiborne. George A. Waggaman, United States senator, was fatally wounded in 1843 when he fought Denis Prieur, a former mayor of New Orleans. Their meeting, like many scores of other duels, was caused by a quarrel growing out of politics.

Before the coming of the Americans, the Creoles usually faced each other with the colichemarde, the rapier, or the sabre—these pointed weapons often allowing for satisfaction to be obtained when one of the contestants received a slight wound that brought blood. The Americans chose pistols, rifles, or even shotguns, increasing considerably the chances that the outcome would be fatal.

The romantic scene of blades flashing in the moonlight was repeated many times in the garden behind the St. Louis Cathedral to which Creole youths repaired to avenge real or fancied slights. Charles Gayarré, the premier Louisiana historian, related the story of six young Creoles who were promenading the empty streets after a ball. "Oh, what a beautiful night," one exclaimed. "What a splendid level ground for a joust! Suppose we pair off, draw our swords, and make this night memorable by a spontaneous display of bravery and skill!" Out came the blades, and shortly two of the contestants were dead.

Rules that governed the deadly business were handed down by word of mouth. In 1873, José Quintero, a local newspaper editor, wrote down and published the provisions that were customary in New Orleans. The person who was challenged had the right to select the weapons. Each contestant had seconds, who arranged the time and place and supervised the proceedings. The appearance of a drop of blood fulfilled all requirements for satisfaction, and a joust ended when this occurred. In pistol duels, if neither participant was wounded in the first exchange of shots, the challenger could decide whether he wanted to end the matter then or preferred to square off again. A cardinal point of the code was that a duel was an affair between gentlemen. If the challenged man did not regard the aggrieved person as a gentleman, he could say so and refuse to fight him. This, of course, was an ultimate insult that might force the other person to take action outside the strictures of the code. It was considered unseemly to shoot a man without warning, but if the foe was given an opportunity of drawing his weapon—and few men ventured out without one—then the aggressor was unlikely to go to jail.

In New Orleans, fencing masters were local celebrities, much admired by Creoles who wanted to learn to defend themselves in case they were challenged or to have an advantage over somebody against whom they had a grudge and wanted to face in a joust. Asbury estimated there were at least fifty of these masters, most of them operators of fencing academies facing on Exchange Alley. The most acclaimed of the group was Pépé Llulla (Yu-ya), who was as skilled with a pistol as with a sword and was a principal in at least twenty duels, a second in a multitude of others.

From the earliest years, dueling was forbidden by French, Spanish, and then American governors, and interdicted by the Catholic church. But hotheaded Louisianians learned to dodge police when they were headed for an encounter, and the frequency of the jousts make it plain that the prohibition was not effective. Good sense finally prevailed, but only in the closing years of the nineteenth century.

—J.W.

28

The Notorious Louisiana Lottery

The original Louisiana lottery was a twenty-five-year-long spree; the hangover lasted four times that long—actually, ninety-eight years. The last legal prize drawings of the Louisiana State Lottery Company were made in 1893. Not until the summer of 1991 did citizens allow Louisiana to join the list of states cashing in on the bonanza provided by public, government-operated lotteries. A referendum finally cleared the way, but only after a near-century during which the stench remaining from the controversial nineteenth-century company faded away. Few issues in the state's history were so divisive as a move to extend the lottery's charter. There were times, a contemporary wrote, when blood might have run in the streets.

Unlike today's state-operated lotteries, the company was a private enterprise given a charter by the carpetbag legislature of 1868. "Given" is the wrong word because one of the incorporators later swore that the company paid out $300,000 in bribes to public officials in seven years. For its time, the lottery was big business. Congress was told that it netted as much as $13 million a year, a stupendous profit in the years immediately after the Civil War. The capital prizes were pegged to ticket prices. A $40 ticket gave the buyer a chance at a grand prize of $600,000, awarded semiannually, and for as little as a nickel a citizen could buy a ticket on a daily drawing with prizes of only a few dollars. In New Orleans, it became easier to buy a lottery ticket than it was to purchase a loaf of bread. On almost every streetcorner there was a lottery outlet. Yet Louisianians bought only 7 percent of the chances; money flowed into the tills from every state in the Union.

The operation of the drawings was scrupulously honest. The respected former Confederate generals P. G. T. Beauregard and Jubal Early presided at the events, where the prize numbers were picked out by blindfolded boys. A winning ticket was the equivalent of cash. No matter the amount, the company paid off on the spot. There was no need to cheat. The odds against the players were a guarantee that the company would win.

The company paid the state only $40,000 a year for its exclusive charter but tried to assume the role of a public benefactor in courting the approbation of citizens. In 1890 it willingly donated $50,000 to the city of New Orleans to help finance a battle against a threatened flood. After the election of 1876, when two rival claimants were trying to govern the state at the same time, the company put up considerable sums to sustain the administration of Governor Francis T. Nicholls, the champion of the conservative Democrats against a carpetbagger regime. But all along there were people who opposed the lottery on moral grounds and others who feared a colossus that had its beginning through bribery and continued to exert unusual influence on government. The company spent $2 million annually on advertising and used its resources against unfriendly newspapers. By 1890 there were 173 prolottery newspapers in the state and only 28 opposed.

A final showdown between supporters and enemies took shape in 1890 when the company began a campaign to have its 1868 charter extended beyond its expiration date at the end of 1893. The lottery offered to pay the state $1,250,000 a year for a new charter. In one of its last victories, the company persuaded the legislature to adopt a proposed constitutional amendment giving it new life. Other problems arose. In 1890 President Benjamin Harrison succeeded in having Congress pass a law that effectively banned the use of the mails for selling and delivering lottery tickets. The company managed to overcome the problem for a period by using express companies instead of the postal service. Then came a ruling by the United States attorney general that caused the major express companies to refuse lottery shipments. Lottery company stock that had sold for $1,400 a share fell to $400, and nobody was buying. The coup de grace came in the election of 1892 when Louisianians voted 157,422 to 4,225 against extending the charter.

For all its freewheeling past, Louisiana spent most of the twentieth century under the constraints of puritan laws that forbade gambling, as well as prostitution. Periodically police would wink at lotteries and casinos that sprang up sporadically around the state, only to fade away whenever public tolerance wavered. The titillating aura created by the Swamp, Gallatin Street, and especially Storyville was only a memory, as was the legend of plantations lost and fortunes squandered in card games aboard the floating palaces that plied the Mississippi River.

It is true that it took years for Louisiana to lose its reputation as a good-time state with few inhibitions. In the early decades of the century, Storyville still went its bawdy way. During national prohibition the state was prized by drinkers for the easy availability of genuine, uncut foreign liquor provided by smugglers. After World War II, Bourbon Street was notorious for its show-it-all stripteasing. Meanwhile, however, other states let down the bars and lured away the high rollers who wanted to live it up. By the 1990s the primrose path no longer led to Louisiana.

A gambling crisis developed as Mike Foster was about to become governor, ending the two-decade Edwin Edwards era in Louisiana affairs. It was during Edwards' regime that public officials opened up the state to the gambling czars. Edwards made no secret of the fact that he himself was a high-stakes player, a frequent casino customer at Las Vegas—once he paid off a loss of thousands by sending to the casino a suitcase filled with stacks of greenbacks. Public officials arranged for the advent of gambling riverboats and a land-based casino without a public referendum on the question. Foster promised that he would give the electorate an opportunity to accept or reject local gambling. But there were legal questions about when existing licenses could be ended even if the vote rejected the games.

Meanwhile, Louisiana's gamble on gambling showed distinctly mixed early results. In some locations—such as Shreveport–Bossier City, where thousands of visiting Texans sweetened the pot—riverboat casinos prospered, pouring millions of dollars into the economy and local and state tax coffers. Elsewhere, however, some boats struggled and others failed, costing hundreds of employees their jobs and leaving state and local governments to deal with shortfalls in expected revenues. In Baton Rouge and New Orleans, most of the money risked at the tables was put up by residents, to the detriment of the local economies. And over it all hung the odor emanating from federal Justice Department allegations of widespread public bribery in the placement of video poker devices.

In 1995, Harrah's Jazz Company, which had won the license for the state's only land-based casino, opened a temporary facility in New Orleans and began construction of a permanent one—with a projected cost of $832 million—on the Mississippi riverfront. Harrah's issued $435 million in junk bonds to help finance its venture. Within weeks the company, without warning, filed for Chapter 11 bankruptcy, shut down the temporary casino, and halted work on the half-completed riverfront building. The skeletal steel beams and partly roofed domes and towers of the would-be showplace stood as a reminder that the future of legal gambling in Louisiana was chancy indeed.

—J.W.

29

Marie Laveau

Longer than a century after her death, the name of Marie Laveau still evokes memories of the practice of voodooism on Louisiana plantations and in New Orleans. No longer, however, does the burning of a black candle or the sticking of pins into a doll arouse superstitious fears of an enemy's spite. If, late in the twentieth century, magic powders, potions, or paraphernalia are sold over the counters of out-of-the-way drugstores, it most likely is for their novelty value and not for a belief in their effectiveness.

Few modern-day Louisianians, in fact, even know about one of the final myths, built around Marie, that developed during the years when belief in occult folkways was dying out. The priestess died in her sleep on June 16, 1881, and was buried in the St. Louis No. 1 Cemetery in New Orleans. To this day there exists a superstition that one will be granted a wish if he or she performs rituals including the drawing of a cross on Marie's tomb using a crumbly red brick. In reporting the death, the *Daily Picayune* had commented: "Marie Laveau's name will not be forgotten in New Orleans."

Voodooism, an amalgam of African religious beliefs involving, among other things, ancestor worship, was introduced into Louisiana by slaves. The practitioners were rebellious enough that Spanish governor Alexander O'Reilly was moved to forbid the importation of slaves from Martinique, Guadaloupe, and Saint-Domingue (Haiti), where voodoo was especially popular. But belief in the efficacy of the potions and incantations already had taken root.

Believers in voodoo were offered the opportunity of visiting a *gris gris* upon their enemies by performing certain prescribed actions that would bring the foes to grief. Measures included sticking pins into dolls and drawing ominous designs on doorsteps. Such signs dismayed the intended victims. Voodooism also offered defenses, such as wearing on one's person a little red-flannel bag containing the bones of a black cat.

The influence of the voodoo priests and priestesses waned on the plantations when a federal embargo slowed the importation of foreign-born slaves into Louisiana in the early 1800s, but received a boost in New Orleans when more than nine thousand Haitian refugees, including thousands of slaves and free blacks, were allowed entry in 1809 and settled mainly in and around the city. Throughout the nineteenth century

New Orleanians still visit the tomb of voodoo queen Marie Laveau in St. Louis Cemetery No. 1. A red X marked on the vault is reputed to secure the petitioner a granted wish.
New Orleans States-Item *photo by Charles F. Bennett*

voodooism flourished in New Orleans, most spectacularly in the form of orgiastic rites. These were scheduled and presided over by Marie Laveau or the high priestesses who preceded or succeeded her. Sanité Dédé was the ruler before Marie, who held sway for some forty years and was followed by Malvina Latour. There also were men practitioners, such as Doctor John, Doctor Yah Yah, and Doctor Jack, who, for a price, could prescribe remedies to offset a *gris gris* hex. On June 25, 1873, the *Picayune* reported that there were three hundred voodoos in the city, including eight or ten white women who took part in what the newspaper called "hellish orgies."

Marie Laveau annually staged a voodoo ceremony on St. John's Eve, June 23, in a hut in what then was a swamp where Bayou St. John empties into Lake Pontchartrain, and also summoned the faithful to celebrations in the yard of her St. Ann Street cottage. Frequently, curious citizens or newspaper reporters watched the proceedings.

The routine included the handling of a huge snake by the reigning high priestess and dancing to the throb of drums by a circle of scantily clad, even nude, men and women who abandoned themselves to the excitement. They took copious swigs from jugs of rum as they danced, and late in the evening paired off in the shadows. The participation of white women scandalized many in the community.

Marie reportedly was born in New Orleans in 1804. She married a carpenter, Jacques Paris, in 1819 and upon his death entered a common-law relationship with Captain Christophe Duminy Glapion, bringing him fifteen children. She seems to have named several of her daughters Marie, and at least one of these girls practiced voodoo as Marie Laveau, engendering further confusion in the already jumbled legend of the high priestess.

A professed Roman Catholic as well as a sorceress, Marie devoted much of her time to visiting and comforting prisoners who were awaiting execution.

—J.W.

CADDO • Shreveport
Benton •
WEBSTER • Minden
CLAIBORNE • Homer
BOSSIER
Arcadia •
UNION • Farmerville
MOREHOUSE • Bastrop
Oak Grove •
WEST CARROLL
Lake Providence
EAST CARROLL
LINCOLN • Ruston
Monroe •
OUACHITA
Rayville •
RICHLAND
Tallulah •
BIENVILLE
JACKSON • Jonesboro
Columbia •
CALDWELL
Winnsboro •
FRANKLIN
MADISON
DE SOTO • Mansfield
RED RIVER • Coushatta
WINN • Winnfield
Harrisonburg •
CATAHOULA
TENSAS
St. Joseph •
NATCHITOCHES • Natchitoches
GRANT • Colfax
Jena •
LA SALLE
Vidalia •
CONCORDIA
Many •
SABINE
Leesville •
VERNON
Alexandria •
RAPIDES
Marksville •
AVOYELLES
De Ridder •
BEAUREGARD
Oakdale •
ALLEN
EVANGELINE
Ville Platte •
WEST FELICIANA
St. Francisville •
EAST FELICIANA
Jackson •
ST. HELENA
Greensburg •
WASHINGTON
Franklinton •
ST. LANDRY
Opelousas •
POINTE COUPEE
New Roads •
EAST BATON ROUGE
WEST BATON ROUGE
Port Allen •
Baton Rouge •
LIVINGSTON • Livingston
TANGIPAHOA • Amite
Covington •
ST. TAMMANY
CALCASIEU • Lake Charles
JEFFERSON DAVIS • Jennings
ACADIA • Crowley
Lafayette •
LAFAYETTE
ST. MARTIN • St. Martinville
IBERVILLE • Plaquemine
Donaldsonville •
ASCENSION
Convent •
ST. JAMES
ST. JOHN THE BAPTIST • Edgard
Lake Pontchartrain
ORLEANS • New Orleans
CAMERON • Cameron
VERMILION • Abbeville
IBERIA • New Iberia
ST. MARTIN
Napoleonville •
ASSUMPTION
Hahnville •
ST. CHARLES
Gretna •
Chalmette •
ST. BERNARD
Franklin •
ST. MARY
Thibodaux •
LAFOURCHE
JEFFERSON
TERREBONNE • Houma
Pointe à la Hache •
PLAQUEMINES

N

20   0   20   40 miles

Louisiana Parishes and Parish Seats

30

PARISHES

Everywhere else in the continental United States they are called counties, but in Louisiana they are parishes, those political subdivisions that have the responsibility for much of local government. The very name reflects the influence exerted by the Roman Catholic church in the colonial years. The areas of some of the original parishes coincide roughly with the territories served by early churches, and indeed several took their names from these churches.

Actually, the first division of the Orleans Territory after the Louisiana Purchase was into counties. There were twelve of them created on April 10, 1805: Orleans, German Coast, Acadia, Lafourche, Iberville, Pointe Coupée, Attakapas, Opelousas, Natchitoches, Rapides, Ouachita, and Concordia. Two years later the territorial legislature supplanted the counties with nineteen parishes, named Orleans, St. Bernard, Plaquemines, St. Charles, St. John the Baptist, St. James, Ascension, Assumption, Interior Lafourche, Iberville, Baton Rouge, Pointe Coupée, Concordia, Ouachita, Rapides, Avoyelles, Natchitoches, St. Landry, and Attakapas.

Gradually the original parishes were added to, subdivided, and realigned until today there are sixty-four, most of which date from the nineteenth century. Sometimes the impetus for the creation of a new parish came from residents of remote areas who found it difficult to travel to the existing parish seats in order to do business with public officials. They wanted the government within reach, ideally situated at a central point to which they could make a round trip by horseback, buggy, or pirogue between dawn and dusk.

At times the pressure did not come from residents of the area of the new parish. An example is Cameron, which came into being in 1870 at the instigation of the carpetbagger governor Henry Clay Warmoth as a political favor for a friend, Colonel George W. Carter. Carter wanted to have a seat in the legislature but was not selected by his home parish, Calcasieu. He had no difficulty in the new parish, and even became speaker of the house of representatives. Six other parishes were created during the years of Reconstruction. Radical Republican politicians engineered the formation of two or three in order to generate public jobs for their friends. Lincoln, named for the president, and Grant, for the Union general, come to mind.

Almost all Louisiana parish governments include police juries, which correspond to the traditional American county commissions, having both executive and legislative functions. Other officials include sheriffs, coroners, judges, tax assessors, and school board members. In most parishes there are municipalities with their own separate governments responsible for the urban neighborhoods. Notable exceptions are the state's two largest cities, New Orleans and Baton Rouge. The City of New Orleans and the Parish of Orleans form a single political subdivision, as do the City of Baton Rouge and the Parish of East Baton Rouge.

Each of the sixty-four parishes has made contributions to the history of Louisiana, but the heritage of those situated within certain geographical areas is so similar that a detailed account of the past of each would be repetitious. An alternative approach is to treat the parishes of each section together. The groupings in some cases may appear arbitrary, but they can be explained logically on the basis of a similarity in population, economic activity, or historical heritage, or a combination of these criteria.

Northeast Louisiana, the eleven-parish section of which Monroe is the principal city, was settled mostly by Americans of Anglo-Saxon descent who migrated after the Louisiana Purchase from the older states east of the Mississippi River. The country alongside the river was ravaged during the Civil War by Union forces in the campaign that resulted in the capture of Vicksburg, a turning point in the conflict. The parishes of the northeast are Caldwell, Catahoula, East Carroll, Franklin, Madison, Morehouse, Ouachita, Richland, Tensas, Union, and West Carroll.

Northwest Louisiana, an eleven-parish section of which Shreveport is the metropolis, also is Anglo-Saxon country. Through it flows the Red River. The oldest European settlement in Louisiana was at the site of present-day Natchitoches, and at nearby Robeline are the remains of the Los Adaes presidio that for years was the capital of the Spanish domain in Louisiana and Texas. The so-called Neutral Strip that separated the United States from Spanish territory after the Louisiana Purchase stretched up into the northwest. Shreveport was the capital of Confederate Louisiana in the last months of the Civil War and held out against the Federals until nearly seven weeks after Robert E. Lee surrendered at Appomattox. Parishes of the northwest are Bienville, Bossier, Caddo, Claiborne, De Soto, Jackson, Lincoln, Natchitoches, Red River, Sabine, and Webster.

Central Louisiana, the five-parish section of which Alexandria is the largest city, has kinship with northern Louisiana but also shares some of the culture of the Creole-Acadian south. Avoyelles and Rapides Parishes are a meeting place of the cotton-growing north and the sugarcane-growing south, producing both crops. Alexandria was set afire by Union forces in the Red River campaign during the Civil War, and it was on that river, just above the city, that Major Joseph Bailey devised a plan that saved a Federal fleet that was about to be stranded and probably destroyed. Winn Parish was the birthplace of Huey P. and Earl K. Long, the most controversial and in some ways the most successful Louisiana politicians of the twentieth century. The central parishes are Avoyelles, Grant, La Salle, Rapides, and Winn.

Southwest Louisiana, a fourteen-parish stretch of prairie, forests, wetlands, and rice fields, with Lake Charles and Lafayette being the biggest cities, remains the bastion of the Acadian heritage, one reason why Louisiana is different. But migrating Americans also did their part in developing an environment where the fishing and hunting are good, the food enticing, and life fun. The present Beauregard, Vernon, and Calcasieu parishes were the heart of the so-called Neutral Strip, the lawless no-man's-land that separated the United States from the Spanish Southwest until the boundary finally was established at the Sabine River. Farmers from the Middle West made southwest Louisiana the most productive rice-growing area in the United States, and it was here that the first producing oil well in the state spouted forth in 1901. This is *Evangeline* country. The parishes are Acadia, Allen, Beauregard, Calcasieu, Cameron, Evangeline, Iberia, Jefferson Davis, Lafayette, St. Landry, St. Martin, St. Mary, Vermilion, and Vernon.

The eight River Parishes stretch from the suburbs of New Orleans all the way up the Mississippi River past Baton Rouge to the northern boundary of Concordia Parish. The Germans settled here in the Louisiana colony's infancy, only to be outnumbered and eventually assimilated by the Acadians. Here lay vast cane fields and plantation mansions representing wealth that allowed the owners to live like royalty. In the upper reaches, cotton fields stretched to the horizon. And between New Orleans and Baton Rouge in the twentieth century developed a Louisiana phenomenon, a string of refineries, petrochemical plants, and other production facilities along the Mississippi, forming one of the nation's great industrial corridors. The parishes are Ascension, Concordia, Iberville, Pointe Coupée, St. Charles, St. James, St. John the Baptist, and West Baton Rouge.

The Florida Parishes, an eight-parish country of tall trees, east of the Mississippi River and partly abutting the state of Mississippi, was once an independent nation-state, the Republic of West Florida. The only part of Louisiana ever to be in the British Empire, the area has a population that devolves largely from Anglo-Saxon settlers, although there were some

French, Acadian, and German early comers. The scene of warfare between England and Spain, the Florida Parishes also played a part in the
Civil War. The capture of Port Hudson by Union forces after a long siege
gave them final control of the Mississippi River. The parishes are East
Baton Rouge, East Feliciana, Livingston, St. Helena, St. Tammany, Tangipahoa, Washington, and West Feliciana.

Seven parishes lie within Southeast Louisiana. New Orleans, the area's
metropolis, was created as the capital of French Louisiana in 1718, and it
was from the Crescent City that the expanding colony was governed. The
section retains the largest concentration of Creoles in the United States,
a Creole being defined as a native-born descendant of the Europeans who
established the French and later Spanish colony. Assumption, Lafourche,
and Terrebonne Parishes lie within the fringes of the Acadian country,
and their population makeup reflects that fact (Cajuns are not Creoles,
since their ancestors were not original settlers). The Southeast Parishes
are Assumption, Jefferson, Lafourche, Orleans, Plaquemines, St. Bernard,
and Terrebonne. Plaquemines is river's end, the soggy delta where the
Mississippi flows into the Gulf of Mexico.

Note: As a guide for visitors, the discussion of each parish includes a listing of sightseeing attractions and of fetes and fairs. Since events are subject
to cancellation, and dates may change from year to year, readers are advised to seek up-to-date information before making their plans for visits.
Most of the data included here were provided by the Louisiana Office of
Tourism, Department of Culture, Recreation and Tourism (P.O. Box 94291,
Baton Rouge, Louisiana, 70804-9291).

In the Sightseeing sections, the names of plantation mansions and
other historic houses are printed in italics. Their locations are indicated by
the listing of the nearest town, although of course many are in rural areas.
Directions for reaching them can be obtained by local inquiry.

—J.W.

31

THE NORTHEAST

It was into a densely wooded land that French hunters and trappers pushed their way in the eighteenth and early nineteenth centuries to stalk bear, buffalo, and deer in what is now northeast Louisiana. They descended to New Orleans in canoes on the Mississippi to sell tallow, pelts, bear oil, and buffalo meat. Wrote John Sibley in 1805: "Bear oil is much esteemed for its wholesomeness in cooking, being preferred to butter or hog's lard. It is found to keep longer than any other animal oil without becoming rancid, and boiling it, from time to time, upon sweet bay leaves, restores its sweetness, or facilitates its conservation." Bear oil brought a dollar a gallon, and the yield from an adult bear was eight to twelve gallons. A bearskin sold for a dollar. An idea of the near-impenetrability of the forest wilderness is provided by an incident that occurred as late as 1840 in the terrain that now is Richland Parish. Three engineers, all experienced woodsmen, went out to survey a route for the first road. They became lost in the area between the Boeuf River and Bayou Macon and wandered for ten days, subsisting on alligator meat and wildcat steaks, before finding their way home.

In 1829 Henry Bry came upon the fossilized skeletal remains of a leviathan in a collapsed riverbank near present-day Columbia, in Caldwell Parish. Could it possibly have been 400 feet long, a figure advanced by a few incredulous observers who saw the line of bones stretched out? Of course not, but the discovery nevertheless created a stir. Dr. Richard Harlan of Philadelphia, an authority, said the skeleton represented a huge reptile, for which he proposed the name *Basilosaurus*. A London paleontologist, Richard Owen, more accurately suggested that the bones were those of a whalelike mammal. Another expert, T. A. Conrad, reported it to be the first time that material from the Eocene period had been found west of the Mississippi River. When the word got out, it developed that the massive vertebrae already were being used by settlers as doorstops, flowerpot stands, and andirons.

Indians were living in the country as long as 3,700 years ago. At Poverty Point, in West Carroll parish, they left a complex of earthen mounds in what is one of the most important archaeological sites in the United States. Their culture group is the earliest yet uncovered in the Mississippi Valley. (Details on the Poverty Point site appear in chapter 1.)

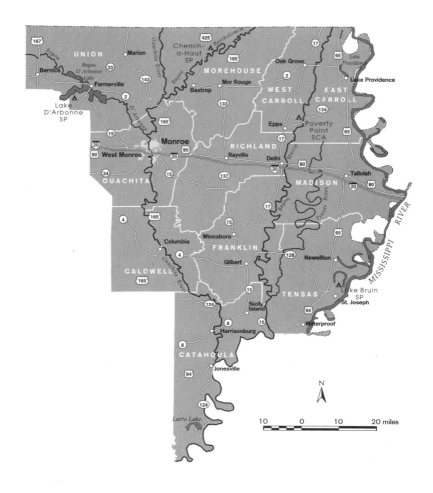

Northeast Louisiana

The first European outpost in the northeast was Fort Miró, established in 1786 by Don Juan Filhiol on the Ouachita River nearly seventy years after French *coureurs de bois* began hunting and trapping in the region's forests. The people living around Fort Miró renamed their settlement Monroe in 1819 upon the arrival of the steamboat *James Monroe,* the first powered craft to travel on the Ouachita. During the Spanish period the governors wanted to encourage settlement but feared encroachment by the aggressive and sometimes lawless Americans. Thus, when Governor Francisco de Carondelet in 1796 gave a tremendous land grant—twelve leagues square—to an alleged Dutch nobleman, Baron de Bastrop, the contract required Bastrop to settle 500 families on the land but "not to admit or establish any Americans." In any event, Bastrop was able to lure only 99 persons altogether—not 99 families—and his funding was suspended. He wandered off to Kentucky, where in 1799 he met Abraham Morehouse (or Morhouse). The two made a deal by which Morehouse bought an interest in the grant and contracted to bring in settlers. Morehouse eventually sold about 100 parcels of land. By that time the Louisiana Purchase had gone through, and he ignored the grant's no-Americans clause. One result was a cloud of confusion and litigation that hung over local land titles until 1851, when the United States Supreme Court voided Carondelet's stipulation.

For Morehouse's efforts in populating the area, the legislature in 1844 named a newly created parish after him. The parish seat adopted the name of the land grant's first holder, Bastrop. There is irony here, as Bastrop himself appears to have adopted the name. According to the *Dictionary of Louisiana Biography,* he was born Philip Hendrik Nering Bögel in Dutch Guiana, served briefly in the Dutch cavalry as a young man, then became collector general of taxes in the Dutch province of Friesland. Charged in 1793 with embezzlement, he fled the country to avoid arrest. In 1795 he arrived in Louisiana with his new identity, claiming to be a refugee from the French Revolution. In his later years the "baron" migrated to Texas, where he helped gain permission from the Spanish government for Moses and Stephen F. Austin to bring in American settlers. The Texas county of Bastrop is named in his honor.

Morehouse is one of nine parishes that once were part of the vast County of Ouachita, which when created soon after the Louisiana Purchase constituted nearly all of the northeastern Territory of Orleans. Two of the split-off parishes, East Carroll and West Carroll, bear the name of Charles Carroll of Carrollton, a signer of the American Declaration of Independence, although he never saw the country at the extreme northeastern corner of Louisiana. The name was bestowed by Honoré Morancy, who with his brother, Emile, settled in the Milliken's Bend vicinity in the 1820s. The brothers were among the members of the noble Montmorency family who fled to Saint-Domingue during the French Revolution. In the insurrection of 1791 in Saint-Domingue, their father was killed by a mob. A servant concealed the young brothers and their sister in a hogshead that was taken aboard a ship bound for Philadelphia. There they were befriended by Carroll. Honoré Morancy remembered the benefactor when, as a state senator from Ouachita Parish, he helped create Carroll Parish, which in 1877 was divided into East and West. East Carroll holds the oldest settlement in Louisiana north of Natchitoches, Lake Providence, which began as a trading post in the 1700s and was incorporated in 1812.

The stretch of the Mississippi River alongside East Carroll was a hangout for pirates who preyed on flatboats and keelboats. Stack Island was one hiding place for the marauders. There are many legends but few solid facts about the Stack Island pirates. One tale is that the tide turned when Kentuckians concealed themselves below decks on a boat and swarmed out to overwhelm and kill a band of robbers who had boarded the craft. Legend also has it that Stack Island largely disappeared beneath the river waters during the great New Madrid Earthquake of December 11, 1811.

Settlement of the northeast began with the influx of Americans from the older states after the Louisiana Purchase. At one time, as many as fifty covered wagons a day crossed by ferry from Rodney, Mississippi, into what was then Concordia Parish but now is Tensas.

Northeast Louisiana played a part in one of the pivotal campaigns of the Civil War. Across the river from Madison Parish was Vicksburg, a city that the Confederates had made a bastion because its loss to the Federals would give them control of the Mississippi and split the Confederacy. The Union commander, Ulysses S. Grant, having failed in an attempt to approach the city from the north on the east bank of the river, decided upon an end run: he would move his army down the Louisiana side, recross the river, and attack Vicksburg from the south. Grant landed a force in what is now East Carroll Parish, and for months that part of Louisiana—especially the parishes of East Carroll, Madison, and Tensas—knew the terrors of war.

Grant hoped to find a water route by which to shift his troops and supplies. He could not use the Mississippi itself because Vicksburg's heavy batteries, secure on high bluffs, commanded it. Grant tried to bypass the city with a canal, but the project proved unfeasible. Plans aimed at connecting natural waterways for the same purpose also came to nothing. Grant gave up and set his engineers to building roads and bridges through the swampy terrain. Finally they opened a route along a series of bayous, and the army marched south. A Union fleet, having run past Vicksburg's guns, ferried the land force back across the river at Bruinsburg, Mississippi, where began the campaign that ended with the surrender of Vicksburg on July 4, 1863.

The parishes along the Mississippi suffered most in the passage of the invading army. For example, on March 29, 1863, the Federals burned Richmond, at that time the seat of Madison Parish. In Tensas Parish, few substantial houses were left untorched by the northerners. One was Dr. Haller Nutt's plantation home on Lake St. Joseph, near Newellton. The rambling old house may have been spared because several Union generals, probably including Grant, employed it as a headquarters. (Contrary to wide belief, however, the plantation's name—Winter Quarters—does not come from the Yankee stopover. Job Routh, the wealthy Natchez planter who built the first house on the place in 1803, named it thus because he used it mainly as a winter hunting camp.) The fate of Pleasant View Plantation was more typical. Its owner, Albert Bondurant, left it in his wife's charge while he was serving as a captain in the Tensas Rifles. When Grant approached, Mrs. Bondurant ordered her slaves to burn 100 bales of cotton—worth $600 each—rather than yield them to the enemy. In retaliation, the invaders shelled the plantation mansion.

As the war progressed, more-interior sections of northeastern Louisiana felt the sting. In one of many incidents, on April 15, 1864, Federal gunboats on the Ouachita River blasted Monroe, destroying many public and private buildings and the railroad bridge.

Inevitably, many people took steps to protect their valuables, just as inevitably giving rise to postwar legends of buried treasure. In at least one case, fact bore out the legends. At the war's outset, Captain A. C. Watson withdrew $80,000 in gold from a bank. He used part of the money to help equip a Confederate regiment and buried the rest at Lakewood Plantation, on Lake Bruin. Many years afterward, the sister-in-law of a later owner found $5,000 in a jar buried in a flower garden. There exists a far older tale of hidden treasure in Tensas Parish. Bayou L'Argent is allegedly named in memory of a Spanish sloop that in colonial days was sent upriver from New Orleans bearing money to pay soldiers who were fighting Indians. According to legend, the crew mutinied, killed the officers, took the money, and scuttled the vessel. The crime was recalled when a worker on James Miller's plantation near Waterproof plowed up an ironclad keg that contained Spanish coins minted in the eighteenth century.

After the fall of Vicksburg, northern speculators moved into the eastern part of Carroll Parish (now East Carroll) and took over some of the rebels' plantations. Federal army contingents were kept busy trying to protect the plantations from raids by guerrilla gangs made up largely of outlaws hiding out in what is now West Carroll Parish. A retaliatory foray by the Union troops was organized. The adjutant, Peter Karberg, wrote a biased, unflattering report that nevertheless gives some insight into what the area was like:

> We left the large cotton-plantations and were now traveling through a poorer and less valuable region of farming country, divided into small farms and occupied by an ignorant, I might say, depraved class of inhabitants: snuff-dipping women, and rough, boasting men, mostly too poor to own slaves themselves, yet the bitter enemies of this unfortunate race. It was this class which, to·some extent, deserved to be called "poor white trash," accepting the word "trash" as merited, although their poverty had, I believe, given birth to the name among their wealthy neighbors. Uneducated and ignorant they became the ready tool of the aristocrats.

Of course, the officer was writing about enemies. But there were major differences between the east, where wealthy owners established large plantations on land enriched by almost annual flooding, and the less-fertile acres of the west, where yeoman farmers did the best they could with the small holdings they could afford.

In contrast to its effect on the rest of Louisiana and on the Confederate States as a whole, the Civil War brought improved economic conditions to Morehouse Parish, even though most of the able-bodied men were off fighting the Yankees. Before the shooting started, Morehouse planters had used most of their land for growing cotton, and residents had to import much of their food and other necessities. Captain C. T. Dunn, who wrote a pamphlet about the parish in 1885, reported that after the first year of the war, the agriculturists had made the parish self-sufficient by producing grain, pork, rice, molasses, and the like in abundance. "Never before or since in the history of the country," Dunn said, "have the people of Morehouse Parish lived so comfortably or been so independent as they were during these times." The Confederate government had insisted that cotton grown before the war be burned in order to ensure that it did not reach the mills of New England. But Morehouse farmers secreted thousands of bales for the duration and sold the hoard at wildly inflated prices when the South surrendered. Money flowed into the parish, and by 1866, Dunn related, all classes were seized by a mania to produce cotton. Then disaster struck. In 1866 the cotton crop, for the first time ever, was almost a total failure because of storms and caterpillars. It was even worse in 1867. "Everybody lost everything," Dunn commented.

In the second decade of the nineteenth century, steamboats provided a link with the outside world for the settlers in the northeast country. The Ouachita River, the boundary between Union and Morehouse parishes, flowed on down through Ouachita, Caldwell, and Catahoula and was the most-traveled waterway. Two ports in Union Parish, Alabama Landing and Ouachita City, not only were the starting points for cotton shipments to New Orleans, but also became flourishing gambling centers. Steamboats were busy in Richland Parish on the Boeuf River, regulars including the *Stella Black, Tom Parker, City of Alto, Parlor City,* and *Era No. 10.* Ion Landing, a loading point, once boasted a horseracing track along with its warehouses. In Franklin Parish the smoke-belching craft operated on Bayou Macon and the Boeuf River.

There was some stagecoach service in the area before the first railroad began operations just before the Civil War. One stage line through Richland Parish changed horses at Charles Carpenter's house near Dunn. The first railroad train, bound from Vicksburg to Monroe, moved through Richland in January, 1861. Newspaper correspondent J. W. Dorr visited Monroe in 1860, when the Monroe-Vicksburg line was nearing completion. His report supplies an insight to the times: "A great camp-meeting was held last week ten miles from Monroe, on the Bastrop road, and the enthusiasm was transferred to the town, where a protracted meeting has been going on day and night for several days. Some of the bar-rooms close when the church bells ring in the evening, that the bar-keepers may follow their customers to the place of meeting. There are a number of preachers here, and the excitement is very considerable." Ouachita Parish then had eight thousand inhabitants, half of them slaves.

One of the last of the old-time train robberies occurred in August of 1901 in Caldwell Parish. A St. Louis, Iron Mountain, and Southern Railroad train was speeding through the night when the engineer saw a fire on the tracks ahead and jammed on the brakes. As the train stopped, a young passenger, pistol in hand, made his way into the baggage car and handcuffed two federal marshals on duty there. The crew was ordered at gunpoint to uncouple the baggage car and move it a mile from the scene. The young man and four accomplices blew open the express-company boxes and rifled the mail sacks. The robbers must have been chagrined by their haul, reportedly only about $50. The robbery apparently had been planned on the basis of reports that the train would be carrying a shipment of cash from a St. Louis bank to New Orleans.

Franklin Parish is home to a historical oddity in the hamlet of Fort Ne-cessity. Named for George Washington's French and Indian War fort in Pennsylvania, the settlement had its beginnings, according to legend, when two keelboats simultaneously ran aground nearby. One boat suppos-edly carried a cotton gin, the other the iron hardware for a sawmill. Rather than unload the boats, free them, and reload the heavy cargo, the boatmen decided simply to unload the gear, assemble it, and settle where they stood. So the story goes, anyway.

The most exciting days, economically, in Ouachita Parish were saved for the twentieth century. In 1916, according to local legend, Louis Lock tossed a half dollar into the air and began drilling an oil well on the spot where it landed. The well, Spyker No. 1, was the first development of the Monroe gas field, which by 1924 was producing three-quarters of the world's supply of natural gas.

At Tallulah, in Madison Parish, the United States Department of Agri-culture pioneered the spraying of pesticides from airplanes onto cotton and other crops. In the mid-1920s in Monroe, a parish agricultural agent named Collett Everman Woolman helped establish one of the nation's first aerial cropdusting services. The little company began flying passengers in 1929 and developed into Delta Airlines, of which Woolman served as pres-ident and chairman. Monroe was also the retirement home of Louisianian Claire Lee Chennault, founder and commander of the Flying Tigers, heroes of countless aerial combats with the Japanese. The name came from the athletic teams at Louisiana State University, which Chennault attended.

It was a dark night in 1930 when attorney D. W. Gibson of Harrisonburg took it upon himself to move the seat of government of Catahoula Parish. And nobody knew the difference until he told about it himself a few years af-terward. The police jury had voted to replace the brick courthouse that had stood in courthouse square at Harrisonburg since 1842, and the building was demolished. A committee named by the jury had a stake driven to mark the spot where members wanted the new courthouse to stand. Gibson argued that the chosen location was too close to the street and would necessitate the sacrifice of a beautiful oak tree, but the committee overruled him.

Gibson brooded for the rest of the day and couldn't sleep when he went to bed. Finally, in the dead of night, he arose and hurried to the square without encountering anybody. He pulled up the stake and drove it into the ground about twenty feet closer to the middle of the square. Nobody noticed the change, and the new building was constructed where he had designated.

Catahoula and neighboring La Salle Parish have the distinction of being the original home of Louisiana's official state canine, the Catahoula Leopard Dog, also known as a Catahoula Cur, Catahoula Hound, Catahoula Hog Dog, and by several other appellations. The word *leopard* refers to the spots that sprinkle the dog's motley patchwork coat, which may contain any or all of a dozen colors. A Catahoula's eyes tend to be milky white, giving a Hound of the Baskervilles touch to an otherwise friendly canine face, but they may also be green, yellow, or brown, often in unmatched combinations. Webbed toes are another distinctive feature. Catahoula fanciers claim that the breed goes back to Hernando de Soto's expedition in the 1540s; the explorers brought along bloodhounds, which supposedly bred with Indian dogs and perhaps wolves. The American Kennel Club is more circumspect, calling the Catahoula a blend of several stockdog breeds. One thing everyone agrees on is that Catahoulas, Louisiana's gift to dogdom, are unique.

CALDWELL: Population 9,810. Parish created March 6, 1838. Believed to be named for Matthew Caldwell, a pioneer from North Carolina. Economy based on agriculture (cotton, soybeans), cattle, forestry.
>Sightseeing: Columbia, Art and Folk Museum.
>Fetes and Fairs: Columbia, Louisiana Art and Folk Festival, October.

CATAHOULA: Population 11,065. Parish created March 23, 1808. Name derived from Tensas Indian word meaning "big lake" (although Catahoula Lake is now in La Salle Parish). Economy based on agriculture (cotton, soybeans), forestry, cattle.
>Sightseeing: Jonesville, Larto Lake. Sicily Island, *Battleground* (1830), *Ferry* (late 1800s), *Pine Hill* (1820–23).
>Fetes and Fairs: Jonesville-Harrisonburg, Four Rivers Raft Race, summer. Jonesville, Louisiana Soybean Festival, September.

EAST CARROLL: Population 9,719. Parish created May 11, 1877. Named for Charles Carroll of Carrollton, a signer of the Declaration of Independence. Economy based on agriculture and forestry.
>Sightseeing: Lake Providence, the lake itself, a scenic oxbow.
>Fetes and Fairs: Lake Providence, Louisiana Soul Food and Heritage Festival, June; Lake Providence Triathlon, summer; Lake Fest, September; Lights Along the Lake, December.

FRANKLIN: Population 22,387. Parish created in 1843. Named for Benjamin Franklin. Economy based on agriculture (cotton, corn, soybeans, potatoes, peanuts), forestry, oil and gas production.
>Sightseeing: Gilbert, *Chennault House* (1910). Winnsboro, Jackson Street Historic District.

FETES AND FAIRS: Gilbert, Spring Folk Festival, June. Winnsboro, Catfish Festival, April.

MADISON: Population 12,463. Parish created in 1833. Named for President James Madison. Economy based on agriculture (cotton, soybeans, corn, rice), cattle, forestry, petroleum production.

SIGHTSEEING: Tallulah, Grant's March Marker.

FETES AND FAIRS: Tallulah, Delta Cotton Days, November; Bayou Spring Festival; Christmas Festival.

MOREHOUSE: Population 31,938. Parish created in 1844. Named for Abraham Morehouse (or Morhouse), large landowner. Economy based on agriculture (cotton, wheat, soybeans), forestry, industry (paper, clothing manufacture).

SIGHTSEEING: Bastrop, Chemin-a-Haut State Park.

FETES AND FAIRS: Bastrop, North Louisiana Cotton Fair and Festival, September; Fall Arts and Crafts Show, November. Mer Rouge, Louisiana Waterfowl Festival, October.

OUACHITA: Population 142,191. Created in 1804 as a county, became parish in 1807. Named for Ouachita Indians. Economy based on natural gas, diversified manufacturing, agriculture (cotton, soybeans).

SIGHTSEEING: Monroe, Louisiana Purchase Gardens and Zoo; Elsong Gardens; Masur Museum of Art.

FETES AND FAIRS: Monroe, Ouachita Riverfest, June; Ark-La-Miss Fair, September; Harvest Days, October. West Monroe, Old-Fashioned Folk Festival, July; Louisiana Legend Heritage Festival, July–August; Louisiana Passion Play, May–September.

RICHLAND: Population 20,629. Parish created in 1868. Named for its highly productive soil. Economy based on agriculture (cotton, soybeans, rice), forestry, light industry.

SIGHTSEEING: Delhi, alleged Jesse James hideout.

FETES AND FAIRS: Delhi, Poverty Point Fall Festival, October. Rayville, Southern Pickin' and Ginnin' Festival, August.

TENSAS: Population 7,103. Parish created in 1843. Named for Tensas Indians. Economy based on agriculture (cotton, soybeans, rice), forestry, grain elevator.

SIGHTSEEING: Newellton, *Winter Quarters* (1803); St. Joseph, *Tensas Library and Plantation Museum* (1858); Lake Bruin State Park.

FETES AND FAIRS: St. Joseph, Tensas River Road Tour, October.

UNION: Population 20,690. Parish created in 1839. Named for the union of American states. Economy based on forestry, agriculture (cotton, corn, oats, soybeans, watermelons, peanuts), oil and gas production.

SIGHTSEEING: Farmerville, Lake D'Arbonne State Park.

FETES AND FAIRS: Bernice, Corney Creek Festival, June. Farmerville, Louisiana Watermelon Festival, July.

WEST CARROLL: Population 12,093. Parish created in 1877. Named for Charles Carroll of Carrollton. Economy based on agriculture (cotton, soybeans).

SIGHTSEEING: Epps, Poverty Point State Commemorative Area.

FETES AND FAIRS: Oak Grove, Poke Salad Festival, April; Fall Arts and Crafts Festival, September; West Carroll Parish Fair, October.

—J.W.

Northwest Louisiana

32

THE NORTHWEST

Louis Juchereau de St. Denis wrote the first chapter alongside the Red River in 1714, and for the next century and a half much Louisiana history was recorded in the northwest portion of the state. St. Denis, one of Bienville's lieutenants, established the first outpost of European colonists in what is now Louisiana, Fort St. Jean-Baptiste. It became Natchitoches, Louisiana's oldest city, the seat of Natchitoches Parish.

Three years later the Spanish, thrusting their empire eastward from Mexico through Texas, planted an installation of their own, the fort later known as Los Adaes, near present-day Robeline. Only fifteen miles of disputed territory separated soldiers of France and Spain, and thus began a long era of confrontation in the eleven-parish corner of Louisiana that abuts Texas and Arkansas. In time there also would be face-offs that included settlers and Indians, Americans and Spanish, Americans and Mexicans, Yankees and Confederates, even the short-lived Lone Star Republic of Texas and the Caddo Indians. Sometimes there was shooting, sometimes only hot words. For more than half a century, Los Adaes was the capital of Spanish Texas.

Natchitoches was the pivotal point of the area in the French colonial period, not only a military bastion but also the principal nexus of trade with Indians and with the Spanish in Texas. It continued as an important commercial center until, in 1839, the Red River drastically changed its course, leaving the town figuratively high and dry, no longer a port. The former bed of the Red was taken over by Cane River Lake, which goes nowhere.

The standoff between the French and Spanish ended in 1762 when France ceded Louisiana to Spain. But the Louisiana Purchase in 1803 raised the threat of war between the United States and Spain over the ownership of the land between the Sabine River and the Rio Hondo, now the Calcasieu River. A truce arranged in 1806 created a no-man's-land in the disputed area.

In 1844, war with Mexico being imminent, the United States government established Camp Salubrity in Natchitoches Parish. One of the officers stationed there with a regiment that departed in 1845 for the fighting in Mexico was a young lieutenant, Ulysses S. Grant, not long out of West Point.

Union general Nathaniel P. Banks occupied Natchitoches in 1864 in the course of his ill-fated Red River campaign. Grand Ecore, the port on the Red, also was captured and was burned by the retreating Federals. Near Natchitoches, the Rebel State Commemorative Area holds the gravesite of the Unknown Confederate Soldier, whose body was never identified after he was killed in the 1864 fighting. A memorial service is held each year for the soldier, who appeared to have been about twenty years old.

The territory of the present Sabine Parish was part of the Neutral Strip and figured in both Texas' fight for independence from Mexico and, later, the American invasion of Mexico. In 1822 American troops began clearing the land for Fort Jesup. Some United States Army units attached to the fort marched into Texas and aided the Texans in their fight for freedom until the government at Washington, not seeking a showdown with Mexico, ordered them back to American soil. A later commander of the fort was Zachary Taylor, "Old Rough and Ready," who owned a plantation near Baton Rouge. Taylor commanded the first American army to go to the front in the Mexican War. Regiments from Jesup were the first to cross the border in the invasion.

Vestiges of Fort Jesup can still be seen, but all traces of notorious Shawneetown have disappeared. The settlement, a cluster of saloons, gambling halls, and probably bordellos two miles west of Fort Jesup, provided the fort's garrison with an early version of the army's rest-and-recreation program.

In 1831 the federal government made available thousands of acres for settlement in Sabine. The influx later led to crop gatherings, at which neighbors pitched in to help one another harvest their fields. The women spent the day quilting, and at night there would be a dinner and dancing. As late as 1847 wolves still prowled the woods, leading the police jury to offer a two-dollar bounty for every one that was killed.

By simply substituting another name, the early history of Bienville Parish could become the story of almost any of the parishes in the northern half of Louisiana. The circumstances of the settlement and development are usually the same, or markedly similar. Bienville's beginning is well described by Philip Charles Cook in his thesis "Ante-Bellum Bienville Parish."

By the 1830s the farms in the Atlantic coastal states were wearing out, and second-, third-, and fourth-generation Americans, most of family origin in the British Isles, were ready to seek new starts to the west, where vast tracts in the public domain had been opened up by the Louisiana Purchase. Congressional acts in 1796 and 1820 had provided for the purchase by settlers of virgin property for as little as $1.25 per acre. Free grants were available to soldiers of the Revolutionary War, the War of 1812, and the Indian wars, and to their heirs. Later there would be opportunities to acquire property by homesteading. Newcomers could be assured a warm welcome, except in areas occupied by Indians still resisting encroachment. The state of Louisiana needed taxpaying citizens far more than it needed undeveloped, uninhabited lands.

Those who chose to migrate were generally hardy, self-reliant, independent souls. Some made the trek in covered wagons drawn by oxen, horses, or mules. Some made part of the trip by boat. A few well-off migrants brought their slaves along. All crossed the Mississippi River at a few points where ferries operated, then forged on through the Louisiana terrain of dense forests or of near-impenetrable swamps in the lowlands, an area interlaced by rivers, creeks, and bayous. Some pushed on into Texas. Others either halted at sites in Louisiana for which they had made previous arrangements, or simply squatted on unoccupied property.

The most productive soil was in the lowlands, enriched by centuries of flooding by rivers and bayous. The waterways also provided the best means of shipping cotton to market from the almost roadless wilderness. But flooding continued to be an annual threat, and some newcomers chose less-fertile farms on higher ground. Of course, land had to be cleared before any crops could be grown, and the first task was the backbreaking process of cutting down trees and digging out the roots. It was a time for neighborliness, and the log-rolling became a social occasion. The host provided food and drink, and the other settlers spent a day or so helping him hew out his first cotton field. Of course, a family had to live on its savings or go into debt for a year or longer before the first cash crop could be marketed.

In Bienville Parish as elsewhere, the predominantly Anglo-Saxon settlers fell into three classes. The gentry consisted of a few affluent slave-owners who acquired large plantations and often built mansion homes, some of which still stand. More numerous were the independent farmers who owned few if any slaves and planted as much acreage as they could handle with the help of relatives and hired hands. And then there were the poor whites who could afford only small plots of their own or who worked as sharecroppers on farms owned by others and lived hand-to-mouth after paying off the landlord. Bienville had fewer slaves than did parishes abutting main rivers, where the big plantation owners held sway.

The Indians encountered by Bienville's early settlers were members of the Caddo federation, who boasted that they had never shed the blood of whites. Although the threat of being scalped was absent, the newcomers shared with others throughout north Louisiana a spartan existence in a primitive setting. They were Protestants (those in Bienville mostly from South Carolina and Georgia) who held the hard belief that man was put upon earth to labor and suffer. Few opportunities existed for amusement or artistic pursuit, and religion and politics became the main avenues to relief from a workaday world. Colonists believed that gambling was sinful and strictly observed Sunday as a day when all frivolity was to be eschewed. They did not see eye-to-eye with the eat, drink, and be merry Acadians and Creoles of Catholic south Louisiana—a fundamental philosophical difference reflected in state politics for generations.

The first permanent Baptist church in north Louisiana was established in 1837 in Bienville Parish, at Mount Lebanon, where the Baptist Convention of Louisiana also was organized (1848). George Washington Baines, great-grandfather of President Lyndon Baines Johnson, was the first signer of the convention charter. A revealing sidelight on antebellum Bienville was provided by J. W. Dorr, who in 1860 toured Louisiana and sent a series of dispatches to the New Orleans *Crescent*. From Bienville he reported attending a barbecue for slaves given by the brothers John and Thomas Dennard. "I never saw a nicer lot of darkies than those of the Messrs. Dennard," said Dorr. "The overseer boasted to me that not one of them had received a stroke of the lash during the year past."

It was slow going especially for the immigrants who slogged their way through the Jackson Parish area in covered wagons, on horseback, or afoot. Sometimes the low-lying bogs were almost impenetrable, as reflected in the fact that a family about to halt in the dusk could look back and still see the smoke from the fires at last night's camp.

Through local lore comes the story that Jesse Wyatt, born in Kentucky in 1777, traded a keg of gunpowder for a big parcel of land where Vernon is situated now. Vernon was the original parish seat. In 1878 the courthouse burned, resulting in the destruction of all governmental and property records. Years passed before the resulting legal problems could be solved. In 1911 Jonesboro became the parish seat, and on January 26, 1936, the courthouse there was wrecked by a natural-gas explosion. This time the records were spared. Before the building of a railroad, the stagecoach line between Monroe and Shreveport passed through Vienna, where passengers found refreshments and overnight lodging at a tavern. The fare for the three-day trip was $15. Jimmie Davis, country singer, movie actor, and two-term governor of Louisiana, was born in Jackson Parish.

Claiborne is one of the northwest parishes that were a happy hunting ground for early settlers. The area appeared to be an immense park, roamed by buffalo, deer, and turkeys, along with wolves, bears, and panthers. Fertile, well-drained soil provided good farming. The parish government began its functions at Russelville, then moved to Overton. Athens became the seat in 1846, but a fire destroyed the courthouse. Finally, Homer was chosen in 1849.

A museum at Germantown, near Minden in Webster Parish, recalls a colony established in 1835 as an early experiment in communal living. It was founded by disciples of the mysterious Count de Leon, supposedly an exiled German revolutionary. He was indeed German, born Maximilian Mueller near Kostheim in 1788. As an adult, he became a religious mystic who claimed to be the messiah. His marriage to Elizabeth Heuser was, as the *Dictionary of Louisiana Biography* delicately puts it, "never recorded." In 1831 he left Germany and sailed with a number of his followers to America. Evidence suggests that the ship's passenger list was doctored; in any event, Mueller landed as Count de Leon, with Elizabeth as "Elisa, Countess de Leon." The group sojourned in Pennsylvania until, apparently, questions about the past made another haven seem preferable. In early 1834 the "count" arrived with his flock at Grand Ecore, Louisiana, where a few months later he died of cholera. The next year the "countess," helped by a land grant from President Andrew Jackson, opened the Germantown site. Under her leadership and that of her sister's husband, Johann Goentgen, the colony operated on communitarian principles. All property was jointly owned, and the members shared equally in the labors and rewards of their farming and handicraft activities. The commune thrived for decades, until the Civil War sent it into decline. It failed financially in 1871. The members drifted away, although descendants still live in the area. The "countess" died in Hot Springs, Arkansas, in 1881, remembered in north Louisiana as a model of courtly European elegance.

The Civil War left the Lincoln Parish area physically unscarred, but Reconstruction was a different story. The very existence of the parish, as well as its name, is testimony to the ascendancy of the Radical Republicans. State Senator Allen Greene of Jackson Parish introduced a legislative measure to create jobs for his fellow party members by making a new political subdivision from territory carved from Jackson, Claiborne, Bienville, and Union Parishes. Disorders occurred in Vienna in advance of the disputed election of 1876. Squads of black Metropolitan Police paraded on horseback through Vienna, and authorities arrested Democrats and hustled them off to Monroe to keep them from voting. Many voters hid out in the woods until they could get to the polls on election day. During the strife, Greene, who had immigrated from Georgia, observed, "As long as ignorance, whiskey, and six-shooters rule, so will the country groan in poverty and trouble, and too, carpetbag rule." By 1877, a faction of Democrats known as the Redeemers had seized political control.

Lincoln Parish became the educational and cultural center of the northern part of the state in 1890 with the organization by the Louisiana Educational Association of the Louisiana Chautauqua Society. The society built near Ruston a tabernacle described by the *Times-Picayune* of New Orleans as the "largest and best in the South." It seated two thousand persons. The society also provided halls of music, science, and philosophy. Between 1891 and 1905 the facility trained many teachers and provided inspiration and entertainment for thousands. Among the speakers who appeared over the years were Henry Watterson, Thomas E. Watson, Fitzhugh Lee, and William Jennings Bryan.

As many as nine thousand or more civilian workers have been employed at the Barksdale Air Force Base in Bossier Parish, across the Red River from Shreveport. The base has been the home field for the B-52 long-range bombers that figured prominently as carriers of nuclear weapons in the strategy of the United States during the Cold War. The base is named for Lieutenant Eugene H. Barksdale, a World War I flying ace later killed while testing a plane. Bossier City also is the site of the Louisiana Downs horseracing track.

The Old Shed Road, said to be the first all-weather, year-round turnpike in the South, was completed in 1880. It was suggested by Judge John W. Watkins to facilitate the transportation of cotton to market when rains handicapped traffic on unprotected roads. The road was roofed over for nine miles, extending from the Red River to Red Chute.

The town of Rocky Mount jumped the gun on the Louisiana state government when a meeting of Bossier Parish citizens voted to secede from the Union on November 26, 1860, two months ahead of similar action at Baton Rouge.

For three northwestern parishes, the clearance in 1838 of a 165-mile-long logjam that for centuries had impeded navigation of the Red River was the biggest economic development of the age. Other parishes benefited, but not to the extent of Caddo and Bossier, separated along their lengths by the river, and Natchitoches, through which it flowed. The breaking up of the "Great Raft," as the jam was known, opened the Red to steamboat traffic all the way from its confluence with the Mississippi River up into the Texas-Arkansas country above Shreveport. No other event could have done as much to stimulate trade.

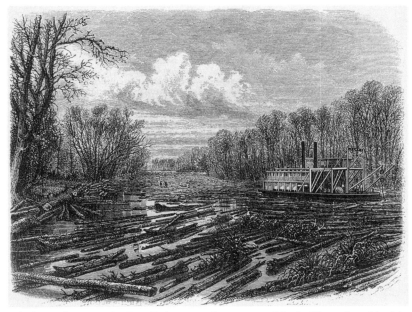

The logjam known as the Great Raft prevented navigation of the Red River above Natchitoches until the 1830s, when it was cleared by Captain Henry Shreve.

Courtesy the Historic New Orleans Collection; Acc. No. 1974.25.30.541

The sensational engineering accomplishment was the work of Henry Miller Shreve, who devised and directed the cutting up and removal of the tree trunks and limbs that had blocked the river from time immemorial. The raft was of a magnitude not equaled in any other American river. Shreveport, named for the captain, grew into what for a time was the second-most-populous city in Louisiana, and today is the third.

It also was in 1838 that Major General Theodore J. Rusk led a small army from the Republic of Texas in an invasion of Caddo Parish. He was not seeking to annex the northwest Louisiana area to the country that flew the Lone Star flag, although since then there have been movements led by those who believe Caddo is more spiritually akin to Texas than it is to Louisiana. The purpose of Rusk's expedition was to keep the Caddo Indians from supplying guns and ammunition to tribes that were fighting white settlers in northern Texas. The invaders confronted a party of Caddos near Caddo Lake. No shooting ensued because both sides wanted a peaceable settlement. Three years earlier the Caddos had sold to the United States all of their landholdings in northwest Louisiana and agreed to migrate to a reservation in Oklahoma. The price was $80,000, of which $40,000 was paid at the time, with the Indians to receive an additional $10,000 a year for four years.

What started the Texans on the march was the word that the Caddos were accepting part of their payments in arms, which were then sent to Indians in Texas. On November 29 a second treaty was signed through which the Indians gave up their arms and arranged to remain in Louisiana until the troubles on the Texas border were settled.

Shreveport became the capital of Confederate Louisiana in May, 1863, after Federal forces had driven the government out of Opelousas. The city also was the headquarters for the Confederacy's Trans-Mississippi Department. In 1864 Union general Nathaniel P. Banks conducted his Red River campaign aimed at Shreveport, and Union forces moved through Natchitoches and into De Soto Parish. But on April 8 Confederate general Richard Taylor turned back the invaders in the Battle of Mansfield, and Shreveport remained in southern hands until May 26, 1865, when the Rebel forces in Louisiana finally surrendered.

Reconstruction was a bitter time in the northwest, and nowhere more so than in Red River Parish. In 1874 the parish seat, Coushatta, was the focal point of one of the era's most notable episodes of lynch violence. Several hundred armed White Leaguers rode into the town and demanded that the members of the parish's Republican government resign. Although the officials acceded, six of them, all white, were killed as they were leaving the parish under a promise of safety. The event is covered in more detail in the chapter on Reconstruction.

BIENVILLE: Population 15,979. Parish created March 14, 1848. Named for Jean-Baptiste Le Moyne, sieur de Bienville, founder of New Orleans and governor of the French colony. Economy based on agriculture (sweet potatoes, watermelons) forestry, oil and gas production.

   SIGHTSEEING: Driskill Mountain (highest point in Louisiana, 535 feet). Mount Lebanon, Mount Lebanon Baptist Church (1857).

   FETES AND FAIRS: Arcadia, Possum Festival, June–July. Gibsland–Mount Lebanon, Stagecoach Trail Tour of Homes, May.

BOSSIER: Population 86,088. Parish created February 24, 1843. Named for Natchitoches-born militia general and congressman Pierre-Evariste Bossier. Economy based on oil and gas production, forestry, agriculture (cotton, soybeans, corn, grain, hay), large military installation.

SIGHTSEEING: Benton–Bossier City, Cypress–Black Bayou Recreation Area. Bossier City, Eighth Air Force Museum (Barksdale AFB). Rocky Mount, historical trail (unmarked; inquire locally).

FETES AND FAIRS: Bossier City, Barksdale AFB Open House, spring (during Holiday in Dixie); Louisiana Downs Super Derby Festival, September. Plain Dealing, Dogwood Festival, late March–early April.

CADDO: Population 248,253. Parish created January 18, 1838. Named for Caddo Indians. Economy based on manufacturing, petroleum industry, and agriculture (cotton, soybeans, hay).

SIGHTSEEING: Shreveport, American Rose Center; R. S. Barnwell Memorial Garden and Art Center; Walter B. Jacobs Memorial Nature Park; *Land's End* (1847); Louisiana State Exhibit Building; Meadows Museum; R. W. Norton Art Gallery; Pioneer Heritage Museum.

FETES AND FAIRS: Blanchard, Poke Salad Festival, May. Mooringsport, Fall Festival, October. Oil City, Gusher Days Festival, May. Shreveport, Mardi Gras in the Ark-La-Tex (dates vary); Holiday in Dixie, April; Mudbug Madness, spring; Red River Revel, fall; Louisiana State Fair, October; Independence Bowl (football game), December. Vivian, Louisiana Redbud Festival, March.

CLAIBORNE: Population 17,405. Parish created March 13, 1828. Named for William C. C. Claiborne, first American governor of Louisiana. Economy based on agriculture (cotton, corn, soybeans, peanuts, sweet potatoes), oil production, forestry.

SIGHTSEEING: Homer, Lake Claiborne State Park. Summerfield, *Alberry Wasson Homeplace* (ca. 1850).

FETES AND FAIRS: Athens, Home Place Acres Bluegrass Festival, June; Oil Patch Festival, September. Haynesville, Claiborne Parish Fair and Northwest Louisiana Dairy Festival, October.

DE SOTO: Population 25,346. Parish created April 1, 1843. Named for Spanish explorer Hernando de Soto. Economy based on forestry and light manufacturing.

SIGHTSEEING: Keatchie, Keatchie Plantation Store (ca. 1840). Mansfield State Commemorative Area (Civil War battle site).

FETES AND FAIRS: Logansport, Frontier Days, February; River City Fest,
May. Mansfield, Louisiana Blueberry Festival, June.

JACKSON: Population 15,705. Parish created in 1845. Named for Andrew Jackson. Economy based on forestry, manufacturing (paper products), cattle, truck farming.

SIGHTSEEING: Jackson-Bienville Wildlife Management Area.

FETES AND FAIRS: Jonesboro, Jackson Parish Junior Livestock Show, September.

LINCOLN: Population 41,745. Parish created in 1872. Named for Abraham Lincoln. Economy based on forestry and manufacturing (wood and glass products).

SIGHTSEEING: Ruston, Louisiana Tech Arboretum.

FETES AND FAIRS: Ruston, Louisiana Peach Festival, June; North Louisiana State Fair, October.

NATCHITOCHES: Population 36,689. Parish created in 1807. Name comes from Native American word for "chestnut eaters" or "chinquapin eaters." Economy based on agriculture (cotton, soybeans), cattle, light manufacturing.

SIGHTSEEING: Marthaville, Rebel State Commemorative Area (includes Louisiana Country Music Museum). Natchitoches, Fort St. Jean-Baptiste State Commemorative Area; Immaculate Conception Catholic Church (begun 1856); *Lemee House* (1830); *Prudhomme-Rouquer House* (*ante* 1800, remodeled *ca.* 1830); *Roque House* (early 1800s); Trinity Episcopal Church (begun 1857); entire downtown area is a National Historic District. Natchitoches-Cloutierville area, *Beaufort* (*ca.* 1790); *Melrose* (nine buildings, oldest 1796); *Oaklawn* (completed 1840). Readhimer, *Briarwood* (home and gardens of Louisiana naturalist Caroline Dormon). Robeline, Los Adaes State Commemorative Area.

FETES AND FAIRS: Cloutierville, Cloutierville Heritage Festival, September. Natchitoches, Melrose Arts and Crafts Festival, June; Natchitoches Folklife Festival, July; Fall Pilgrimage (tour of homes), October; Christmas Festival of Lights, December.

RED RIVER: Population 9,387. Parish created in 1871. Named for river. Economy based on agriculture (cotton, soybeans, corn), forestry, cattle, oil and gas production.

SIGHTSEEING: Coushatta, Red River Parish Courthouse.

Fetes and Fairs: Coushatta, Lignite Festival, May; Red River Parish Fair, September.

SABINE: Population 22,646. Parish created March 7, 1843. The most widely accepted explanation for the name is that it comes from the Sabine River. Economy based on cattle, poultry, manufacture of wood products.

Sightseeing: Many, Fort Jesup State Commemorative Area; Hodges Gardens; Zwolle, North Toledo Bend State Park.

Fetes and Fairs: Florien, Sabine Freestate Festival, November; Many, Hodges Gardens Easter Sunrise Service; Sabine Parish Fair, September; Pleasant Hill, Battle of Pleasant Hill Reenactment, April; Zwolle, Tamale Festival, October.

WEBSTER: Population 41,989. Parish created in 1871. Named for Daniel Webster. Economy based on agriculture (vegetables), dairy farming, diversified manufacturing.

Sightseeing: Doyline, Lake Bistineau State Park; Germantown, Germantown Colony and Museum.

Fetes and Fairs: Minden, Germanfest, May.

—J.W.

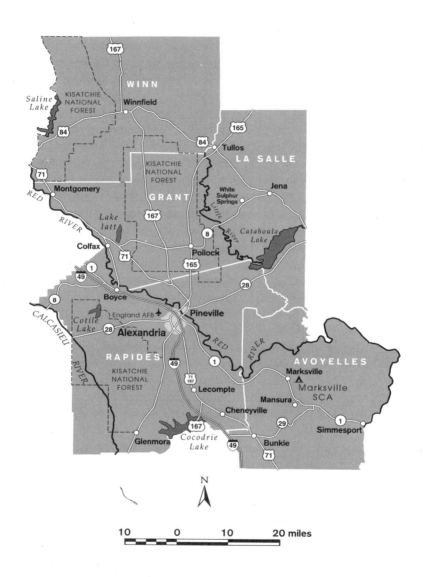

Central Louisiana

33

Central Louisiana

Rapides Parish is at the geographic center of Louisiana and is also caught in the middle culturally, religiously, agriculturally, and politically. It is the home of cotton growers and sugarcane planters, Protestants and Catholics, Bible Belt fundamentalists and fun-loving Cajuns. In no other population center are the state's diverse heritages so intermingled.

Alexandria and, just across the Red River to the east, Pineville, form the region's metropolitan center. In 1723 a small detachment of French troops established a post on the Pineville side, calling it Rapides because of the nearby Red River rapids. In 1769 a Spanish census counted thirty-three white persons and eighteen black slaves at "rapido on the Red River."

During the Spanish era, numerous Anglo-Saxons from the East Coast were attracted to the area, and before long the original French and Spanish settlers were outnumbered. The Alexandria side gradually became the greater focus of activity. In 1834 a visitor wrote that the settlement had become "a place of wealth," with a horse track where "extensive bets are made on the result."

The Louisiana State Seminary of Learning and Military Academy, the forerunner of Louisiana State University, opened at Pineville in 1860. Its first superintendent was William Tecumseh Sherman. Being busy elsewhere during the Civil War, Sherman did not apply his scorched-earth practices in Rapides, but other Union generals did. General Nathaniel P. Banks's forces put Alexandria to the torch during their retreat in 1864 after the failed Red River offensive. Almost every structure in the town was set ablaze that May 13.

At the rapids of the Red River just above Alexandria, Joseph Bailey rescued the Federal fleet of Captain David Porter from certain destruction as Banks's army departed. About thirty naval steamboats lay stranded above the rapids by a seasonal decline in the river's level. The riverboats' cannon were valuable weapons to an accompanying army, but without support from the riverbanks, the vessels were sitting ducks to enemy fire. Bailey superintended a herculean ten-day, around-the-clock effort by three thousand Union soldiers employing three hundred wagons in constructing a dam that concentrated the current into a narrow channel and enabled the trapped vessels to move downstream and out of danger.

During the First World War, 30,000 troops were trained at Camp Beauregard in Rapides Parish. In World War II the area became the greatest training center in the south as Camps Beauregard, Livingston, and Claiborne were activated. Rapides Parish was the scene of some of the maneuvers in the 1941 war games in which Dwight D. Eisenhower won recognition as a talented commander.

The early settlers of La Salle Parish did not take to farming; instead, they became hunters along with the Indians, existing on corn bread and game—bear, deer, turkey—plus some domestic meat. Following the Louisiana Purchase, the number of settlers rose sharply. They made once-a-year trips to Natchez or Alexandria in small parties for protection against outlaws.

Jena, the parish seat, is credited with having had the first woman mayor in Louisiana. She was Mrs. Lula V. Coleman, wife of Dr. J. A. Coleman. She was appointed by Governor John M. Parker in 1920.

The community of White Sulphur Springs became nationally famous as a spa. In 1833 Joseph P. Ward, of White Sulphur Springs in what is now West Virginia, was traveling through La Salle and became enchanted by the springs that bubbled from the hillsides. He pitched camp, and after drinking the water for a time decided it had health values. The idea to build a resort somewhat like his hometown came naturally. By 1850, there were two hotels and other businesses. The Civil War and Reconstruction dealt the spa a financial blow, but it was nothing compared with what the Louisiana Board of Health dealt in 1911, when it ordered an analysis of the water. The board found that the water had no curative value and was actually harmful to drink. Thus did the bubble burst.

Oil was discovered in the parish in 1925, and over the years it has been a big producer.

No surprise was occasioned among Louisianians when the most controversial politicians the state has produced—Huey Long and his brother Earl—came out of Winn Parish. With the Louisiana Purchase, adventurous settlers from the Atlantic seaboard and contiguous areas dreamed about the promised land of Louisiana and Texas and started trekking westward. An extension of the much-traveled Natchez Trace led through the country that now is Winn. Some found the heavily forested land inviting and settled there. Among these was John Murphy Long, the grandfather of Huey and Earl.

The settlers were mostly small farmers, few of whom owned slaves. Their ancestors were freethinkers who took the risks of migrating to America, and they themselves were eager to move on when opportunity lagged in the older states. They showed their independence with a coolness toward the secession movement when it swept the South. David Pierson, at twenty-one the youngest delegate to the Louisiana secession convention, voted against proposals to leave the Union and refused to sign the Ordinance of Secession. Once the Civil War began, Winn became a problem area for the Confederacy. So-called jayhawkers—robbers who preyed on the families left behind by those who joined the southern armies—roamed through the parish. In September, 1862, Confederate general Richard Taylor moved into Winn and Jackson Parishes with five companies to round up deserting Confederates, arrest men who had been conscripted but refused to report, and break up the jayhawking gangs. Later, a group of Winn farmers sent a letter to Union General U. S. Grant in which they said the Confederate states were designed to be aristocratic and oppressive, adding that "we hold no further allegiance to the Confederate States except when overpowered and compelled by the sword."

After the war Winn became the hotbed of populism in Louisiana. Such organizations as the Grange, the People's Party, and the Farmer's Alliance sounded the protest of small farmers against what they said were unbearable conditions imposed by the Conservative Democrats who held sway in Baton Rouge. When Huey Long sounded his "every man a king" philosophy in the 1920s and 1930s, he was doing as might have been expected from a politician born and reared in Winn. The parish's small farmers also tended to be less racist and more sympathetic to blacks than the average white Louisianian of the time, and both Huey and Earl Long reflected their attitude.

As early as 1805 a man named Postelwaite was producing six bushels of salt a day in Winn. In 1841 Ruben Drake dug a well to a depth of 1,011 feet by using oxen to turn the drill stem. He fashioned the drill casing out of hollow cypress logs. The briny water was evaporated to extract the salt. During the Civil War nearly a thousand men worked at the salt works in Winn, an important source of the commodity for the Confederate army. Winn produces the most diverse range of mineral products in Louisiana. In addition to salt, the output includes oil, gas, condensate, limestone, and gypsum. Beginning in about 1900 the parish attracted lumber companies that started cutting virgin pine. Reforestation programs began early. Winnfield calls itself the "Forest Capital of Louisiana."

The rich lands of the Red River plains in Avoyelles Parish attracted Joseph Rabalais, who had quit Pointe Coupée Parish because of flooding. Others followed him. The early settlers built along rivers and bayous in order to have access to New Orleans by boat. The first money crop was indigo, but by 1810 cotton had taken the lead. Avoyelles was one of the few parishes with soil suitable for both cotton and cane, and the latter became an important crop in the middle of the nineteenth century.

Marksville, the parish seat, incorporated in 1843, was founded in 1794 by Marc Eliche of Alsace-Lorraine. The town, first called Marc's Village, is on the site of a prehistoric Native American civilization, today known as the Marksville Culture. The first European settlement in the parish was Avoyelles Post in Tunica Indian country.

The parish's golden decade, economically, was from 1850 to 1860. During the Civil War, there was fighting at Fort De Russy, near Marksville, and skirmishing at Mansura.

Avoyelles was a bastion of the *fais do do,* a favorite pastime of the Acadians in which the young children were put to bed and the adults danced through the night to the music of fiddlers and banjo players. The first church was Our Lady of Mt. Carmel, built in 1796 at Hydropolis, near Mansura. By 1815 as many as nine steamboats a day were churning their way up the Red River to parish trading centers.

Grant is one of the so-called "Reconstruction parishes" created by Radical Republican politicians while they ran state and local governments during the postwar occupation of Louisiana. It was the scene of a climactic event of the postwar era, the Colfax Riot of Easter Sunday, 1873, in which white vigilantes assembled from the nearby area killed at least a hundred black citizens who had seized control of the parish seat. It was an important political development because, in its aftermath, judicial rulings limited the power of the federal government in local law enforcement, opening the way for white Democrats to restore home rule as they interpreted the term.

The area that was to become Grant had a big boost in 1838 when Captain Henry Miller Shreve with his snagboat, the *Archimedes,* broke up the great Red River logjam. Afterward, steamboats on the way to or from Shreveport could load or unload at stops on the Grant shore, facilitating trade and the shipment of cotton.

AVOYELLES: Population 39,159. Created on March 31, 1807. Named for Avoyel Indians. Economy based on agriculture (cotton, corn, soybeans, truck farming).

SIGHTSEEING: Mansura, *Defossé House* (ca. 1796). Marksville, *Hypolite Bordelon House* (1800–1820), Marksville State Commemorative Area (archaeological site, prehistoric Indian culture).

FETES AND FAIRS: Bunkie, Louisiana Corn Festival, June. Mansura, Allons aux Avoyelles Tour of Homes, October. Marksville, Cochon de Lait Festival, May.

GRANT: Population 17,526. Created in 1869. Named for Ulysses S. Grant. Economy based on agriculture and forestry.

SIGHTSEEING: Kisatchie National Forest (Catahoula District), including Little Falls (waterfalls) and Grant Parish Dogwood Trail. Lakes Iatt and Nantaches.

FETES AND FAIRS: Colfax, Louisiana Pecan Festival, November. Pollock, Grant Parish Dogwood Festival, April; Shady Dell Bluegrass Festival, May and September.

LA SALLE: Population 13,662. Created on January 1, 1910. Named for Robert Cavelier, sieur de La Salle, French explorer. Economy based on agriculture (cotton, peanuts, corn, sweet potatoes), cattle, forestry, and petroleum.

SIGHTSEEING: Catahoula Lake and Catahoula National Wildlife Refuge.

FETES AND FAIRS: Jena, Summerfest, June; La Salle Parish Fair, September.

RAPIDES: Population 131,556. Created in 1806. Named for Red River rapids just above Alexandria. Economy based on manufacturing and agriculture (sugarcane, cotton, corn, soybeans).

SIGHTSEEING: Alexandria, *Kent House* (1796); *Tyrone* (1846); Cheneyville, *The Cedars* (1830); *Loyd Hall* (1816); *Walnut Grove* (1835). Kisatchie National Forest (Evangeline District), including Cotile Lake and Wild Azalea Trail.

FETES AND FAIRS: Alexandria, Cenlabration, May. Lecompte, Louisiana Nursery Festival, March. Pineville, Catahoula Lake Festival, October.

WINN: Population 16,269. Name derivation unclear; perhaps for Alexandria attorney Walter O. Winn, Rapides Parish congressman Richard Winn, or even Mexican War general Winfield Scott. Economy based on forestry, mining, light industry.

SIGHTSEEING: Kisatchie National Forest (Winn District). Winnfield, Earl K. Long Commemorative Area.

FETES AND FAIRS: Winnfield, Louisiana Forest Festival, April; Winn Parish Fair, September–October.

—W.G.C.

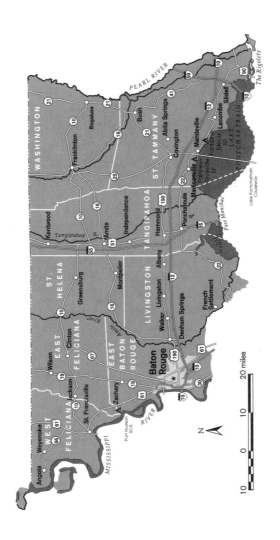

Florida Parishes

34

THE FLORIDA PARISHES

Once, for two and a half months, the area of Louisiana lying east of the Mississippi River and north of Lakes Pontchartrain and Maurepas was an independent nation-state, the Republic of West Florida. It still is known as the Florida Parishes. It is also a study in contrasts. The eight-parish region encompasses the most heavily industrialized corridor in Louisiana, some of the most sparsely populated woodlands, and a series of bedroom communities that New Orleans commuters call home. Here lies the so-called Ozone Belt, a healthy haven to which residents of the city fled to escape nineteenth-century epidemics of yellow fever and cholera. The towering pine trees still are locally reputed to produce a salubrious emanation. The biggest lumber-mill in the world once screeched away at Bogalusa, in Washington Parish.

The Florida Parishes make up the only part of present-day Louisiana ever to be controlled by the English. An earlier chapter of this volume records the story of how Spanish governor Bernardo de Gálvez defeated the British at the time of the American Revolution and won West Florida for the Spanish. The inhabitants later revolted against the Spaniards and set up a republic of their own that lasted for seventy-four days until Governor William C. C. Claiborne brought the area under the American flag. Some early colonists migrated during the era of English ownership, and Gálvez later welcomed settlers of Anglo-Saxon background, with the result that the Florida Parishes attracted colonists from Mississippi and other American states and made up a population resembling that of north Louisiana more than it did the French, Spanish, German, and Acadian peoples found in New Orleans and the rest of south Louisiana.

The newcomers moved into a gently rolling, heavily forested land drained by rivers that emptied into Lake Pontchartrain. The lake was part of the Gulf of Mexico until the delta of coastal Louisiana, built of the silt deposited by the Mississippi River, converted Pontchartrain into an enclosed body of water as large as some of the world's inland seas.

The lake figures prominently in any history of the Florida Parishes. It was the scene of a naval engagement in 1779 between an American vessel captained by William Pickles and a British sloop that had been preying on American shipping in the lake. Pickles and his crew managed to board and capture the Britisher. The Americans then landed on the coast of what is now St. Tammany Parish and required fifteen or twenty English or Scottish families that had been given land grants on the lakeshore to take oaths of allegiance to the Revolution.

During the Civil War, Rebel vessels that succeeded in penetrating the Federal blockade of the Gulf Coast sailed into Lake Pontchartrain and unloaded their cargoes of contraband goods in St. Tammany. Union troops made occasional raids from the lake into the parish, but the Florida Parishes remained largely Confederate for most of the war. On December 18, 1862, rebel residents of occupied New Orleans who refused to take an oath of allegiance to the United States were marched aboard a steamboat, transported across the lake, and landed in exile at Madisonville.

For years regular steamboat service operated between New Orleans and Mandeville. In 1957 a 23.87-mile causeway, the longest highway bridge in the world, was completed to link the New Orleans metropolitan area with St. Tammany. The causeway brought the conversion of Covington, Mandeville, and several real estate subdivisions into bedroom communities. Other commuters live in Slidell, in eastern St. Tammany, and get to their New Orleans jobs by way of Interstate 10.

By the time the West Florida area was absorbed by the Territory of Orleans in 1810, immigration was well under way, and settlements dotted the vast forest. In 1814, aiming to defend New Orleans against British invaders, General Andrew Jackson marched his small army that had been campaigning against the Indians in Florida into Louisiana through what is now Washington Parish. The new settlers responded to Jackson's call for help, and even twelve-year-old boys joined in the march that led to the victory at Chalmette on January 8, 1815.

During the Civil War, most of the action in the Florida Parishes occurred in East Baton Rouge Parish. The city of Baton Rouge was captured by David Farragut's sailors and a Union army, and Port Hudson, above Baton Rouge, was the scene of a siege that ended in July, 1863, with the surrender of the last Confederate stronghold on the Mississippi River.

The Florida Parishes established a reputation for healthfulness in the early years. In 1892 a Methodist cleric, Henry Skipwith, published *East Feliciana, Louisiana, Past and Present*. He wrote that in his opinion, no county in the United States could outdo East Feliciana's record for longevity. In a sixteen-year-long pastorate, he said, he had officiated at funeral services for twenty-nine persons ranging in age from seventy years to ninety. Counting three oldsters who died during his absence, the average age at death for thirty-two residents was above seventy-four years. "We do not believe this record can be beaten," he said.

Louisiana's State Capitol Building in Baton Rouge. In the background rise the smokestacks of dozens of petrochemical plants, which along with state government and universities provide the booming city's economic lifeblood.

Photo by G. E. Arnold

Its situation on the Mississippi River, accessible to oceangoing vessels as well as to barge tows, and its proximity to oil and gas production, all but ensured that Baton Rouge would develop into a busy port and industrial center. It did, becoming the state's most intense concentration of refineries and chemical plants. It is also the state capitol and the site of Louisiana State University. The city and East Baton Rouge Parish are a single political entity.

Elsewhere in the Florida Parishes, vast stands of pine and cypress, along with some hardwood trees, dictated the development of a lumber economy. Washington and Tangipahoa Parishes, especially, owed their livelihoods to that industry. In the early 1900s there were thirty sawmills in Washington Parish, including at Bogalusa the largest one in the world, which could turn out 700,000 board feet of lumber a day, compared with about 300,000 for each of the others. The cut-over lands were not allowed to remain denuded, and a big reforestation program by the lumber companies provided a renewable source of material for a pulp-and-paper-mill industry that largely supports Washington Parish today.

In Tangipahoa—land of many creeks and rivers—longleaf yellow pines reached up to eighty or a hundred feet. There also was a wealth of cypress and other varieties, bringing an influx of logging camps and sawmills in a wave of prosperity that marked the late nineteenth and early twentieth centuries. Following the Civil War, immigrants of Italian ancestry introduced the growing of strawberries. Hammond, the principal shipping point, bills itself as "Strawberry Capital of the World." Where Tangipahoa verges on Lakes Maurepas and Pontchartrain lies the foreboding Manchac Swamp, one of Louisiana's true wildernesses.

In 1821 John James Audubon spent four months at Oakley Plantation in West Feliciana Parish, tutoring the three daughters of Mrs. Robert Percy, the widow of an English naval officer. In West Feliciana, Audubon painted thirty-two pictures of his *Birds of America* series. Before the Civil War the parish boasted cotton plantations that brought great wealth to their owners and now are recalled by some of the most-visited of the mansions. Among the early ones are The Cottage, Greenwood, Oakley, Highland, and The Myrtles, all built between 1795 and 1830 in the neighborhood of the charming town of St. Francisville. A world away, although it is only a half hour's drive, the vast Louisiana State Penitentiary at Angola, one of the most isolated of American prisons, sprawls alongside the Mississippi River.

Five other Louisiana parishes have smaller populations, but St. Helena is perhaps the most rural. It has no community—not even Greensburg, the parish seat—with as many as a thousand residents. St. Helena was a prosperous antebellum parish. More than half of the households owned slaves, compared with not quite one-third in the South as a whole. It was one of the original Louisiana parishes but lost more than half its territory with the establishment of Livingston Parish in 1832.

It was after midnight on October 15, 1875, when the fire in the Livingston Parish Courthouse at Port Vincent was detected and it already was too late to save the building and avert destruction of all the parish records. Obviously arsonists were at work in the climax of a continuing dispute over the choice of a parish seat. Three years earlier the government had been moved from Springfield, where the police jury had been meeting since 1838, and residents there were angry, even though in a referendum the parish vote had been Port Vincent, 238; Springfield, 183; French Settlement, 65; and Cedar Ota, 46. Reflecting the suspicions of many citizens, the New Orleans *Republican* reported that "the old courthouse party determined that the records should do their antagonists no good, so they organized a surprise party and burned the records." Although he did not directly deny that his fellow citizens of Springfield might have made a surreptitious late-night jaunt to Port Vincent, Dr. George Colmer replied with a letter to the editor in which he pointed out that the burned records included indictments for serious crimes, even murder, and suggested the desperate felons might have wanted to destroy the charges against themselves. In the long run, the battling over the location of the seat did neither Springfield nor Port Vincent any good. The seat today is Livingston. The Livingston Parish town of Albany is said to be the oldest Hungarian settlement in the nation to have kept its cultural heritage alive.

EAST BATON ROUGE: Population 380,105. Baton Rouge is state capital as well as parish seat. Parish created in 1811. Named by French explorers for a red stick, or pole, on the Mississippi River bank marking a boundary of Indian tribal realms. Economy based on state government, education (Louisiana State and Southern Universities), petroleum and chemical plants, shipping.

SIGHTSEEING: Baton Rouge, Old and New State Capitol Buildings; Hilltop Arboretum; USS *Kidd;* Louisiana Arts and Science Center; *Magnolia Mound* (1796); *Mount Hope* (1817); Pentagon Barracks (1823–24); River Road; Rural Life Museum. Zachary, Port Hudson State Commemorative Area (Civil War siege site).

FETES AND FAIRS: Baton Rouge, Blues Festival, April; FestForAll, May; Greater Baton Rouge State Fair, October; Plantation Day at Magnolia Mound, October; Louisiana Folklife Festival, November.

EAST FELICIANA: Population 19,211. Parish created in 1824. *Feliciana* means "happy land" in Spanish, or it may have been bestowed in honor of Félicité de Saint-Maxent, wife of Spanish governor Bernardo de Gálvez. Economy based on agriculture (cotton, soybeans).

SIGHTSEEING: Clinton, *Lawyers' Row* (several buildings, 1840–60); St. Andrew's Church (1842). Jackson, *Asphodel* (1820); Centenary State Commemorative Area; *Milbank* (1836). Wilson, *Glencoe* (1870); *Oakland* (1827).

FETES AND FAIRS: Clinton, East Feliciana Pilgrimage, April; Feliciana Peach Festival, June. Jackson, Jackson Assembly Antique Show and Sale (includes driving tour), March.

LIVINGSTON: Population 70,526. Parish created in 1832. Named for one of the Livingston brothers, Edward or Robert, both prominent on national scene early in nineteenth century. Economy based on truck farming, poultry, cattle, dairy farming, forestry.

SIGHTSEEING: Amite River/Blind River area (scenic network of rivers, bayous, and canals leading to Lake Maurepas).

FETES AND FAIRS: Albany, Hungarian Harvest Festival, October. French Settlement, Creole Summer Festival, July. Livingston, Livingston Parish Fair, October. Walker, Pine Tree Festival, May.

ST. HELENA: Population 9,874. Parish created in 1810. Named for Saint Helen, mother of Constantine the Great. Economy based on forestry, dairy farming, truck farming.

SIGHTSEEING: Amite and Tickfaw Rivers (scenic streams suitable for canoeing). Greensburg, Land Office Building (1820) and St. Helena Parish Jail (1855).

FETES AND FAIRS: Greensburg, St. Helena Parish Forest Festival, August.

ST. TAMMANY: Population 144,508. Parish created in 1810. The name may honor a Delaware Indian chief, Tamanend, who befriended early European settlers on the Atlantic coast. Economy based on forestry and activity attendant to being a bedroom community for commuters to New Orleans.

SIGHTSEEING: Covington, Christ Episcopal Church (1846). Madisonville, Fairview-Riverside State Park. Mandeville, Fontainebleau State Park; Lake Pontchartrain Causeway. Pearl River area, Pearl River Wildlife Management Area/Honey Island Swamp.

FETES AND FAIRS: Abita Springs, Water Festival, September. Bush, Five Lakes Bluegrass Festival, May. Covington, Makin' Music, March; Civil War Reenactment, May; St. Tammany Parish Fair, October. Lacombe, Bayou Lacombe Crab Festival, June. Mandeville, Seafood Festival, August. Pearl River, Catfish Festival, June. Slidell, Bayou Liberty Pirogue Races, June.

TANGIPAHOA: Population 85,709. Parish created in 1869. Named for Tangipahoa Indians (*tangipahoa* being Choctaw word for "corn gatherers"). Economy based on agriculture (strawberries, truck farming), forestry, dairy farming.

SIGHTSEEING: Hammond, Zemurray Gardens. Manchac, Manchac Swamp (tours available).

FETES AND FAIRS: Amite, Oyster Festival, March; Tangipahoa Parish Fair, October. Hammond, Louisiana Balloon Festival and Air Show, May; Annual Alligator Day, August. Independence, Italian Festival, April. Kentwood, Southern Gospel Music Festival, fall. Ponchatoula, Strawberry Festival, April.

WASHINGTON: Population 43,185. Parish created in 1819. Named for George Washington. Economy based on forestry, cattle, dairy farming, truck farming.

SIGHTSEEING: Bogalusa, Louisiana Museum of Indian Culture; Bogue Lusa Pioneer Museum. Franklinton, Bogue Chitto River; Mile Branch Settlement (replica pioneer community).

FETES AND FAIRS: Bogalusa, Dogwood Festival and Tour of Homes, March; Louisiana Paper Festival, July. Franklinton, Washington Parish Watermelon Festival, July; Washington Parish Fair, October.

WEST FELICIANA: Population 12,915. Parish created in 1824. Name derivation same as for East Feliciana. Economy based on agriculture, tourism, service of large state penitentiary.

SIGHTSEEING: St. Francisville/Weyanoke area, Afton Villa Gardens; Audubon State Commemorative Area; *The Cottage* (1795); Grace Episcopal Church (1858); *Greenwood* (1830; reconstructed); *Highland* (*ca.* 1804); *Live Oak* (1808); Locust Grove State Commemorative Area; *The Myrtles* (1796); *Oakley* (1799); *Rosedown* (1835).

FETES AND FAIRS: Angola, Angola Rodeo (prison rodeo with admission to public), October. St. Francisville, Audubon Pilgrimage, March.

—J.W.

River Parishes

35

River Parishes

The German Coast: No doubt it is going too far to call its indomitable settlers the salvation of colonial Louisiana. There is no question, however, that the immigrants from the Palatinate, Alsace-Lorraine, Baden, Württemberg, Mainz, and Treves provided stability previously lacking in a colony partly made up of criminals and vagabonds deported from France. The French colonial authorities had ample reason to be thankful for the presence of the German peasants who had been hoodwinked by John Law's agents into seeking new lives in the New World, and then were abandoned when Law's Mississippi Bubble burst.

The German Coast is the stretch of country on the Mississippi River above New Orleans that now is part of St. Charles, St. James, and St. John the Baptist Parishes. In the first half of the eighteenth century, the Germans shared the land with the French. Over the years the French influence prevailed by weight of numbers. Even the names of the earliest German settlers have been gallicized. But if their customs and language have been lost, it was largely the pluck and energy of Law's recruits that converted swamps and woods into productive fields.

In 1720 Law's Company of the Indies sent representatives into war-weary German states to offer land, seeds, tools, and livestock to farmers who would move across the ocean to help develop French America. Law especially wanted workers for a tremendous concession he had been given near the confluence of the Arkansas and Mississippi Rivers. The recruits let themselves in for hideous experiences. Many died of disease on their way to French ports or in the coastal towns where they awaited the ships that would take them across the ocean. The disaster was only beginning. In 1721 there were 875 Germans and 66 Swiss on four ships that sailed from Lorient. Several hundred other émigrés followed. The vessels were ravaged by epidemics; only 200 passengers survived of 1,200 who had sailed.

The Germans who went to the Arkansas concession were still clearing land and working to provide shelter for themselves when Law's financial structure collapsed and he fled France. The colonists found themselves bereft of promised assistance. They built rafts, drifted down the Mississippi to New Orleans, and demanded passage to Europe. Governor Bienville persuaded them instead to join another contingent of Germans under the leadership of Karl Friedrich d'Arensbourg, a former Swedish army officer, in settling along the river. They all went to work.

It was a hard and dangerous time. In the early days, women climbed trees to keep watch and fired rifles to warn their husbands, clearing the forest or working in the fields, of the approach of Indians. For a period before enough horses and mules could be obtained, the men took the place of draft animals and pulled the plows themselves.

At first the basic crop was indigo, but long before Etienne Boré demonstrated that sugar could be produced on a large scale, some fields on the German Coast were being planted in sugarcane. After the Louisiana Purchase the banks of the Mississippi in the area became an almost unbroken succession of cane fields. The same banks now are part of the industrial corridor, the array of petrochemical plants stretching all the way from Baton Rouge to New Orleans.

The enterprising Germans soon were growing more food than they needed. Some would load pirogues with vegetables, paddle down to New Orleans on Saturday, and sell their produce at the Place d'Armes on Sunday. On several occasions food grown in the area kept New Orleanians from going hungry when supply ships from France failed to arrive on schedule.

Governor Antonio de Ulloa borrowed provisions from the Germans to feed several hundred Acadians who were sent by the Spanish government to establish a colony. He was slow to pay for the produce, and the farmers of the St. John the Baptist area were among the rebellious settlers who opposed the governor in 1768. In an effort to appease the Germans, Ulloa sent a messenger to St. John with 1,500 piastres to pay toward the debt. It was too late. Karl d'Arensbourg arrested the envoy, and four hundred Germans from the colony marched to New Orleans to take part in the revolt that sent Ulloa packing.

In 1770 Governor Alexander O'Reilly, who succeeded Ulloa, appropriated from Jacques DuBroc property at Edgard that became the site of the Church of St. John the Baptist. Records in the church date back to 1772.

Not all of the descendants of the founding Germans and Acadians prospered. In 1860 many residents on the Mississippi levee depended for a livelihood on catfishing and on chopping wood to fire the boilers of steamboats that pulled up to the bank in order to refuel.

Some 50,000 acres in St. James Parish are planted in sugarcane, but the most talked-about crop is produced on only seventy-five acres. It is perique tobacco, which is used to add a special fragrance to tobacco mixes. The soil in St. James is the most suitable in the world for the growing of perique.

One of the most admired antebellum buildings in Louisiana is the Manresa Retreat House at Convent. Operated by the Jesuit order, it once was the home of Jefferson College, founded in 1831. The college closed in 1835 and the property was bought by Valcour Aime, a wealthy planter, who donated it to priests of the Marist order. The Jesuits purchased it in 1931.

The German Coast was one of the twelve Territory of Orleans counties created in 1805. When the territory was redivided into nineteen parishes in 1807, St. Charles became a political entity, as did St. James and St. John the Baptist. St. Charles took its name from St. Charles Borromeo Church, the so-called Little Red Church (its color), on the Mississippi shore twenty-five miles above Canal Street in New Orleans. The church, built in 1806, stood as a landmark for rivermen—traditionally, it was the point at which they received their pay on a downriver voyage. The current church building, dating to 1921, incorporates some elements of the 1806 structure.

On January 3, 1787, Robert Antoine Robin de Logny hired a free black man, Charles Pacquet, to build a house on Robin de Logny's plantation eighteen miles above New Orleans. Pacquet finished the job in 1790. He built well: the house still stands, one of the oldest intact structures in the Mississippi Valley. Its name, Destrehan Manor, comes from Jean Nöel Destréhan de Tours, who married one of Robin de Logny's daughters and bought the property after his father-in-law's death in 1792.

Richard Taylor, son of President Zachary Taylor, was working 150 slaves on his Fashion Plantation at the start of the Civil War. He became one of the Confederacy's most successful generals. He never was able, however, to carry out his dream of recapturing New Orleans from the Federals. After the war Taylor had financial reverses. Some of his former slaves offered to lend him money.

St. Charles, St. James, and St. John are among eight parishes that stretch along the Mississippi upward from the outskirts of New Orleans. The six in the area between Baton Rouge and New Orleans are known as the River Parishes. Two others, Concordia and Pointe Coupée, are brought into this chapter because their background is similar.

"The mother parish of northeast Louisiana," Concordia originally extended all the way up to the Arkansas border, and over the years gave birth to East Carroll, Madison, and Tensas Parishes, and to Warren Parish, which existed only from 1811 until 1814. Now Concordia reaches a point only a few miles above Natchez, Mississippi, which is on the opposite bank of the river. An early, and perhaps the first, settler was Don José Vidal, who petitioned in 1789 for a land grant and who in 1801 became commandant of the Post of Concord, directly across from Natchez.

Rivers—the Mississippi, Black, Tensas, and Red—were alternately blessings and curses in the early years of Concordia. Almost-annual floods deposited some of the richest soil to be found in the country. At the same time, residents were periodically driven from their homes, their livestock imperiled. The people responded by laboriously shoveling up mounds of earth—overnight hills—to which cattle and hogs could be driven to remain high and dry until the water receded. Some of the mounds can still be seen. For themselves, Concordians built huge "choctaws," or rafts, moored them to trees, and lived on them for long periods. Not until the 1950s brought completion of a ring levee around the parish could residents be sure of dry feet.

On September 19, 1827, on a Mississippi sandbar near Vidalia, occurred one of the most notable of Louisiana duels. Dr. Thomas H. Maddox and Samuel L. Wells faced each other with rifles. Each missed with two shots, and their difficulty was pronounced settled. But there was bad blood between two of the seconds, Sheriff Norris Wright of Rapides Parish and Jim Bowie, a slave trader who was fated to die in the siege of the Alamo while fighting for the independence of Texas. A free-for-all broke out, and Bowie killed the sheriff with the knife that bears his name. Bowie's plantation home was burned by the Union invaders during the Civil War.

Antebellum Concordia was visited by the New Orleans *Crescent*'s roving correspondent J. W. Dorr, who wrote: "Many of the planters who own and cultivate these lands are among the largest agriculturists in the State, and exercise the authority of ownership over estates as broad as some German principalities, and yielding far greater revenues. But very few of these lords reside on their estates, but have their residences across the river, on the higher but scarcely more pleasant lands of Mississippi—in Natchez or elsewhere. The actual white population is mostly a population of employees, not of owners—a population of overseers." Dorr reported that the parish population in 1860 included 11,000 blacks and 1,400 whites. There was not an incorporated town in Concordia, and not more than three or four stores.

In 1699 Iberville and Bienville, making an exploratory trip up the Mississippi River, found that they could avoid having to paddle along a twenty-two-mile-long oxbow curve by portaging across the curve's narrow neck. Afterward the river changed its course to follow the shortcut. Whether the axes of the exploring party actually influenced the flow of the mighty Mississippi or the river simply went on one of its periodic meanderings is not known, but Iberville called the area "Pointe Coupée"—cut point. The oxbow now is False River, a principal geographic feature of Pointe Coupée Parish.

In 1717 John Law made large land grants in the area to friends, who sent in French settlers. After Law's bankruptcy, the Company of the Indies established in 1723 a settlement known as the Pointe Coupée Post. Later the parish became a stronghold of the Acadians.

In 1770 Julien Poydras first made his appearance as a pack-peddler, carrying his wares on his back as he visited the farms. He prospered, emerging as one of the richest men in Louisiana. Once he had as his guest on his plantation Louis-Philippe, the future king of France. After the Louisiana Purchase, Poydras became president of the Legislative Council of the Territory of Orleans. In 1809 he was elected the delegate to Congress from the territory, and it was he who sponsored the bill to admit Louisiana to statehood. He engaged in a bitter debate in the House with Congressman Josiah Quincy of Massachusetts, who said that Louisianians were "foreigners incapable of being citizens of the United States."

In 1824 Poydras bequeathed $30,000 each to Pointe Coupée and West Baton Rouge Parishes to finance dowries for brides who came from needy families. More than a century and a half afterward, the dowries still are being paid.

Pointe Coupée in 1808 established public schools, the first in Louisiana.

West Baton Rouge, one of the smallest of Louisiana's parishes, with an area of 194 square miles, was one of the original nineteen parishes established by the Orleans Territory government. From colonial times until recent years, when industry moved in, West Baton Rouge was primarily rural and agricultural. Sugarcane and cotton are the principal products. Corn and soybeans are also raised.

Before the coming of the French, the parish was inhabited by the Bayougoula Indians. The terrain was largely wilderness until the first Acadians arrived. The entire parish is level except for two Indian mounds at the upper end.

The largest antebellum plantation was Allendale, owned by the wealthy Henry Watkins Allen. When Louisiana seceded from the Union in 1861, the forty-one-year-old Allen enlisted as a private in the Delta Rifles. He was soon elected lieutenant colonel, then colonel, and subsequently was appointed brigadier general. He was wounded in both legs in the Battle of Baton Rouge. While still on active duty, General Allen was elected governor. With remarkable skill, he administered the part of Louisiana that was still unoccupied by Federal troops. The *Dictionary of American Biography* characterizes him as "the single great administrator developed by the Confederacy." When the Confederacy collapsed, Allen went to Mexico City, where he edited an English-language newspaper. He died in 1866, never returning to his West Baton Rouge plantation. Allen is buried on the grounds of the Old Capitol in Baton Rouge. A statue of him by the distinguished New Orleans sculptor Angela Gregory stands at the Port Allen Courthouse site.

A Jesuit priest, Paul du Ru, who accompanied Iberville on his historic journey up the Mississippi to the Bayougoula village, in what today is Iberville Parish, remained behind when Iberville returned to France. The first religious service in the region is credited to Father du Ru, who said Mass in a tent on March 28, 1700. In Iberville's absence, the Bayougoula Indians were almost wiped out in a surprise attack by the Houmas. Iberville County was formed in 1805, and two years later became a parish. In 1827, Bayou Grosse Tete and Bayou Maringouin were taken from West Baton Rouge Parish and placed in Iberville because the Iberville courthouse was more accessible than the West Baton Rouge courthouse. The following year, a provision was made to return them to West Baton Rouge on condition that the latter build a road from hard-to-reach settlements. The road was built, but the settlements remained in Iberville. A dispute continued until the legislature in 1859 settled the issue by leaving the settlements in Iberville.

Carville, a small town on the east bank of the river, has the only leprosy hospital in the United States. It was founded in 1894 but was not established at its present site until 1917. Known as the Gillis W. Long Hansen's Disease Center, it is in effect a national home devoted to the treatment of Hansen's disease (leprosy) and is situated on more than 350 acres. At one time leprosy was considered to be highly contagious, but great strides in its control have taken place at the Carville hospital.

Iberville was the location of the famous Belle Grove plantation house, which contained seventy-five rooms and sat on the 6,000-acre estate of John Andrews. Built in the 1850s, it was a beautifully columned Greek Revival structure. It burned in 1952.

On January 9, 1830, the Louisiana state senate convened in a tavern at Donaldsonville, while the house of representatives met in an Ascension Parish courtroom. Thus began a two-year period when Donaldsonville, with a population of 261 whites, 155 slaves, and 76 free persons of color, was the capital of Louisiana. Legislators complained that Antoine Peytavin had failed in his contract to build a statehouse in time. Surely Donaldsonville was one of the smallest, if not the smallest, village ever to serve as an American state capital, and it was only a question of time before the government moved back to New Orleans.

Désiré LeBlanc and other Acadian immigrants had moved into a heavily wooded area where hunting and fishing provided a ready supply of food. The names of early settlers read like those in a present-day tele-

L'Hermitage, near Darrow in Ascension Parish, in the late stages of a now-complete restoration to its antebellum grandeur. Built in 1812, the house belonged to Michel Bringier, who in 1815 fought beside Andrew Jackson in the Battle of New Orleans and then adopted the name of Jackson's Tennessee home for his own.

Photo by G. E. Arnold

phone directory in the Cajun country: Landry, Dugas, Hébert, Melancon, Boudreaux, Gautreaux, Gaudin. American financiers in New Orleans, including Wade Hampton, Evan Jones, and John Burnside, bought tracts and gave their support to the economic development of the area. By 1770 a small chapel was built near the present site of Donaldsonville. Two years later the parish of the Church of the Ascension was established; it has been in continuous existence ever since. In 1806 William Donaldson purchased a site from Mrs. Marguerite Allain, and there he established Donaldsonville.

By 1860 Donaldsonville had a population of about 1,500 persons. J. W. Dorr described the Planters' Hotel, "a roaring concern if there ever was one, with a popular 5 cent bar, a popular cock-pit in the yard and a popular rush of all sorts of populace playing 'kino' all day Sunday in the bar-room, a cock-fight coming off in the pit at stated intervals of one hour from morn till night."

In 1862 Federal gunboats operating on the Mississippi after the capture of New Orleans came under sniper fire from the shore near Donaldsonville. Flag Officer David Farragut, the Union commander, retaliated. He told the mayor to evacuate every woman and child from the town, and on August 9 the fleet bombarded and destroyed most of the buildings. Some of the responsibility for the action was claimed by General Benjamin F. Butler, the military governor, who wrote: "I burnt down the hotels and wharf buildings; also the dwelling house and other buildings of a Mr. Philip Sandy, who is said to be a captain of Guerrillas."

Originally, Bayou Lafourche reached a confluence with the Mississippi River at Donaldsonville, but the two no longer connect. However, the northern end of "the longest street in the world," as the bayou is called, stretches into Ascension Parish. The allusion to a street results from the fact that along both shores of the bayou, from Ascension and through Assumption and Lafourche Parishes almost to the Gulf of Mexico, run two nearly unbroken rows of residences and occasional stores.

ASCENSION: Population 58,214. Parish created in 1807. Named for Catholic church at Donaldsonville. Economy based on petrochemical industry and agriculture (sugarcane, soybeans, strawberries).

> SIGHTSEEING: Burnside, *Tezcuco* (1855); *Houmas House* (1790; reconstructed 1840). Darrow, *Ashland–Belle Helene* (1841); *The Hermitage* (1812).

> FETES AND FAIRS: Donaldsonville, Sunshine Festival, October. Gonzales, Jambalaya Festival, June. Prairieville, Ascension Parish Fair, October. Sorrento, Boucherie Festival, October.

CONCORDIA: Population 20,828. Parish created in 1807 out of county (1805). Origin of name uncertain. Economy based on agriculture (cotton), cattle, fish farms, chemical and petroleum plants.

> SIGHTSEEING: Frogmore, Haphazard Plantation Gardens. Vidalia, *Taconey*.

> FETES AND FAIRS: Vidalia, Chambre Festival, October; Jim Bowie Festival, fall.

IBERVILLE: Population 31,049. Created as county in 1805 and parish in 1807. Named for Pierre Le Moyne, sieur d'Iberville. Economy based on agriculture (sugarcane, corn, soybeans), forestry, cattle, oil and gas production.

> SIGHTSEEING: Plaquemine, City Hall (1849); *St. Louis* (1858). White Castle, *Nottoway* (1859).

> FETES AND FAIRS: Plaquemine, International Acadian Festival, October.

POINTE COUPEE: Population 22,540. Parish created in 1807 from 1805 county. Name means "cut point," as explained in text. Economy based on agriculture (sugarcane, cotton, soybeans), cattle, industry (sugar mill, grain elevator, garment factory).

SIGHTSEEING: New Roads, *Le Jeune House* (*ca.* 1820); *Parlange* (1750).

FETES AND FAIRS: New Roads, Blessing of the Boats, spring; Pointe Coupée Parish Fair, October.

ST. CHARLES: Population 42,437. Parish created in 1807. Named for St. Charles Borromeo Catholic Church. Economy based on petrochemical industry, agriculture (sugarcane).

SIGHTSEEING: St. Rose, *Destrehan Manor* (1787); *La Branche Plantation Dependency House* (1792).

FETES AND FAIRS: Des Allemands, Louisiana Catfish Festival, July. Destrehan Manor, Destrehan Plantation Fall Festival, November; Spring Festival of the Arts, May. Luling, Cochon de Lait Festival, November.

ST. JAMES: Population 20,879. Parish created in 1807. Named for St. James, disciple of Jesus. Economy based on petroleum industry, agriculture (sugar cane, tobacco).

SIGHTSEEING: Convent, *Judge Poche Plantation* (1837); Manresa Retreat House (1831). Vacherie, *Oak Alley*.

FETES AND FAIRS: Mississippi riverbank from Lutcher to Gramercy, Bonfires on the Levee, Christmas Eve.

ST. JOHN THE BAPTIST: Population 39,996. Parish created March 31, 1807. Named for St. John, baptizer of Jesus. Economy based on petrochemical industry, agriculture (sugarcane).

SIGHTSEEING: East Bank, *San Francisco* (1849). West Bank, *Evergreen* (*ca.* 1820).

FETES AND FAIRS: LaPlace, Andouille Festival, October.

WEST BATON ROUGE: Population 19,419. Parish created March 31, 1807. Named for red pole Indian boundary marker across the Mississippi River. Economy based on agriculture (sugarcane), port activity, diversified industry.

SIGHTSEEING: Brusly, Back Brusly Oak (historic tree more than 350 years old). Port Allen, cabins at *Poplar Grove* (plantation village, drive-by); West Baton Rouge Museum.

FETES AND FAIRS: Port Allen, Potpourri Festival, October.

—J.W.

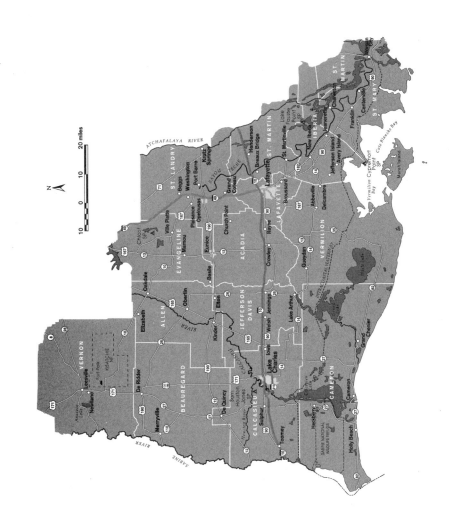

Southwest Louisiana

36

The Southwest

Think of southwest Louisiana and the image of Acadians pops into mind, people who have become popularly known as Cajuns, people who have added spice to Louisiana life through their particular culture. Also, a people who provided a spark to the colonization of a region of the state where they found a natural environment in which they could express joie de vivre in their inimitable style.

The area that became St. Martin and Lafayette Parishes became home for the Acadians, descendants of French Canadians of Nova Scotia who fled or were deported from their home beginning in 1755 for refusing to swear allegiance to the British crown. Some of the refugees migrated more-or-less directly to Louisiana. Others went to France or resettled temporarily in English colonies along the Atlantic seaboard or in the West Indies before wending their way to rejoin their compatriots. Once in Louisiana, they spread, over the years, across the southwestern prairies and bayous, and live today not only in St. Martin and Lafayette Parishes, but also in Iberia, Vermilion, St. Mary, Terrebonne, Acadia, Evangeline, and others. Their impact on Louisiana, politically as well as in the industries developed from their original pursuits in fishing, trapping, and farming, has been great. While they came to Louisiana from France and Nova Scotia, where they had gone seeking a better life, they developed the Cajun character or culture in their Louisiana environment—a folk mentality punctuated by dialects that vary from area to area, the various tongues resulting from intermarriage with other nationalities.

Although they settled in what at the time was a remote part of Louisiana, the Cajuns found themselves less isolated as colonization advanced. Despite increasing exposure to other cultures, they never abandoned their particular love of life, which they expressed in music, festivals, food, and humorous folklore made famous over America. Perhaps it was that love of a way of living that brought solidarity to their ranks after years of persecution, and that life-style which resulted in the modern Cajun's creed, which says, "When you work, work hard; when you play, play like hell." In other words, enjoy life.

The romance of the Acadians is embodied in Henry Wadsworth Longfellow's epic poem *Evangeline*, which ensures a never-ending chapter in the history of St. Martin Parish, where according to tradition the first group of Acadians settled in 1765 (most of them, however, arriving in three groups in 1785).

Longfellow's poem, written in 1847, told the story of a betrothed couple who had been put on separate ships in the expulsion from Acadia, never to find each other again. Longfellow, who never visited Louisiana, based his poem loosely on the life of one of the refugees, Emmeline Labiche, who became separated from her lover. Research has proved that Emmeline actually lived and that the name of her sweetheart (in the poem, Gabriel) was Louis Arceneaux. After being sidetracked on his trip to Louisiana, Arceneaux supposedly waited three years for Emmeline, then, concluding her lost, married, only to eventually meet her under the now-famous Evangeline Oak in St. Martinville. The story does not bear scrutiny, and there are differing versions.

St. Martin de Tours Catholic Church, St. Martinville. Although a bit older than most—it dates to 1832—the lovely little church is typical of those that were, and often still are, the focal points of towns all across Catholic south Louisiana. The statue in the foreground represents an Attakapas Indian.

Photo by G. E. Arnold

Not all of the French immigrants to St. Martin were Acadians. Ordinary French colonists had settled there as early as the 1740s, and later arrivals included aristocracy who had fled France because of the Revolution. Poste des Attakapas, which became St. Martinville, for a time was known as "Le Petit Paris." Whereas the exiled Acadians found livelihoods in farming, fishing, trapping, and raising cattle, the aristocratic group found this frontier life too hard. Some sank into poverty.

The fertile soil of Lafayette Parish prompted the Chicago *Tribune* in the middle years of the nineteenth century to write: "If by some supreme effort of nature Western Louisiana, with its soil, climate and productions, could be taken up and transported to the latitudes of Illinois and Indiana . . . it would create a commotion that would throw the discovery of gold in California in the shade at the time of the greatest excitement. . . . Every man would be intent on securing a few acres of these wonderfully productive sugar plains."

Lafayette also had a part of the thriving cattle trade that supported much of the Attakapas country prior to the Civil War. When a state of near-anarchy developed after rustlers disrupted law enforcement and aroused class resentment against the owners of herds, vigilantes took matters into their own hands. It was difficult to convict a cattle thief in court even if the evidence was overwhelming. On September 3, 1859, six hundred vigilantes from Lafayette and surrounding parishes, armed with rifles, pistols, and one cannon surprised a gathering of rustlers at a farmhouse and demanded that they forfeit their weapons. The show of force unnerved some of the thieves; dozens dashed into the woods. Many were captured. The only casualty was Geneus Guidry, who killed himself when he was about to be taken prisoner. Those who fell into the hands of the avengers were horsewhipped, after which the victors put on a barbecue.

Lafayette today is the center of a campaign to preserve the Acadian heritage. The city is particularly noted as a place to hear Cajun music.

Early settlers of Vermilion Parish had to be aware they were invading the country of the Attakapas Indians, reputed to be cannibals. The Attakapas country included also the parishes of St. Mary, Iberia, St. Martin, and Lafayette. The first European to enter the area appears to have been François Simars de Bellisle, a French officer shipwrecked on the Texas coast in 1719. Bellisle was trying to hike to New Orleans when the Attakapas caught him. They held him as a slave for eighteen months before he was rescued through the efforts of a group of Assinais Indians.

Besides vast coastal wetlands, Vermilion has prairies offering excellent natural pastures; as a result, pioneers concentrated on raising cattle and horses instead of farming. After World War II, Vermilion became a major beneficiary of the activity in oil and gas exploration and production. The parish excels in its hunting and fishing facilities.

Iberia Parish has a Spanish and Acadian heritage; in 1778, Spanish colonists joined Acadian settlers who had arrived in 1765. Iberia boasts that it is "the sweetest, saltiest, oiliest, and pepperiest parish in the state." Who can dispute it? The sugarcane fields are productive and so are the oil wells. Three of the world's principal salt mines are within its boundaries, and on Avery Island the fiery Tabasco sauce is produced.

Thomas Berwick settled on the shore of Berwick Bay in 1790 and ten or twelve white families followed in the St. Mary area in the next few years. By 1810 half of the settlers were of Anglo-American origin. They found the soil and climate ideal for growing cane, and by 1840 St. Mary was one of the state's major shippers of sugar. The first steamboat arrived in the area in 1835 on Bayou Teche, and the New Orleans, Opelousas and Great Western Railroad was completed to Brashear City, now Morgan City, in 1857.

St. Mary was the scene of fighting during the Civil War, the Battle of Franklin being the major engagement. In 1867, during Reconstruction, the Knights of the White Camellia was organized at Franklin. The white-supremacist group was a forerunner of the Ku Klux Klan.

Acadia Parish, sandwiched between Jefferson Davis and Lafayette Parishes, originally was part of St. Landry but in 1888 became a separate entity. Acadians were among the settlers who moved into the area beginning in the 1760s, attracted by treeless, fertile land ready-made for cultivation. Along with the Acadians came a colony of Germans.

After the Civil War and Reconstruction, residents of Crowley and Rayne petitioned for a new parish with a seat of government closer than Opelousas, where the St. Landry government was headquartered. Crowley was chosen parish seat by referendum. Acadia Parish's birth coincided with the recognition that the area held great promise for rice growing; the first mill was built at New Acadia in 1893. Crowley became the center of activity. Rayne became the principal shipping point for frogs' legs, considered a delicacy, after the Civil War.

On September 27, 1819, a gang of cutthroats with blackened faces stormed into the plantation home of John Lyon on Bayou Queue de Tortue, tying up members of the family, ransacking the house, and kidnapping ten slaves. They turned out to be members of buccaneer Jean Lafitte's gang, who had new headquarters at Galveston. A United States naval vessel patrolling the Gulf of Mexico headed for Galveston, where Lieutenant James M. McIntosh went ashore and demanded the surrender of the raiders. To McIntosh's surprise, Lafitte told him, "Tell your commander I found the principal of this gang so old an offender, and so very bad a man, that I saved the trouble of taking him to the United States. I hung him myself."

The romance of Evangeline and her lover inspired the naming of Evangeline Parish when it was created in 1910, even though the famous Acadian love story is set in St. Martin Parish. The original land grant in the area that became Evangeline Parish went on July 11, 1783, to the widow and other heirs of Le Bray de Gaynor. Early settlers were largely the French and Acadians, although people of Irish descent were also represented. A sizable portion of the citizens of Ville Platte still speak the Acadian version of eighteenth-century French. The city is the site of the annual "Tournoi," a carryover from medieval France. Horsemen race full speed and try to direct lances through small rings suspended at the edge of a track.

Evangeline was a favorite hunting area for the Attakapas Indians and remains a fruitful haunt for present-day hunters and fishermen. Chicot State Park, with 7,000 acres of camping facilities and picnic areas, attracts many visitors.

Hundreds of thousands of visitors like the marshes of Cameron Parish so much they return yearly—to the delight of hunters and lovers of wildlife, because these visitors are the estimated 1,500,000 ducks and 125,000 geese that follow the flyway from Canada and winter in Cameron, which supports one of the largest transient wildlife populations in America. The birds found their way to Cameron long before its early settlers, who got there by way of buying land grants given to veterans of the War of 1812.

Geologists say Cameron once was on the bed of the Gulf of Mexico, and at other times farther inland. Its seventy miles of beaches and 750,000 acres of marshland are exposed to hurricanes, which have hit with devastating fury in 1886, 1915, 1918, 1940, and 1957. The parish was formed as the result of a political favor; carpetbag governor Henry Clay Warmoth created it for his friend Colonel George W. Carter, letting him set up its government.

The legislature created Calcasieu Parish in 1840 out of the western section of St. Landry Parish. Its boundaries stretched sixty-five miles from east to west, and fifty-seven miles north to south. Then, in 1866, Cameron Parish, was carved from the south part of Calcasieu. In 1912 Calcasieu again was divided, this time to form Allen, Beauregard, and Jefferson Davis Parishes.

Timber was the drawing card at the outset, and petroleum brought prosperity after the forests were cut over. The port of Lake Charles was originally built to handle the timber and lumber shipments; by 1876, Calcasieu had twelve sawmills and the port held as many as fifteen big white-sailed windjammers at a time. Railroads doomed the schooner trade, but then vast deposits of sulphur were discovered, leading to the building of a chemical industry. Lake Charles became a deepwater port in 1926.

The area that became Beauregard Parish was part of the Neutral Strip, so named because the United States and Spanish Texas agreed not to occupy it until the boundary between the two could be determined. The United States and Spain almost went to war over the issue before it was settled by the Adams-Onís Treaty of 1819, ratified in 1821. While the issue was being debated, the strip was a no-man's-land, the lawless haven of bandits, smugglers, and fugitive slaves. In 1812, a Spanish party en route to Natchitoches was waylaid by American bandits, resulting in a shootout in which three bandits were killed and another wounded. The same year, thirty American robbers attacked seventeen Spaniards and took between $15,000 and $20,000, which was recovered. The United States Army sent Lieutenant Colonel Zebulon M. Pike, two other officers, and forty troops to seek out the marauders. They destroyed the houses and tents of the bandits and captured sixteen men, along with thirty-five horses and mules.

When the United States purchased Louisiana in 1803, just after the colony had been retroceded from Spain to France, none of the three nations knew where the Louisiana-Texas boundary lay. Before the treaty was negotiated, there was a showdown involving the American ministers in Madrid, Secretary of State James Madison, and Governor William C. C. Claiborne of Louisiana.

Spain threatened to establish jurisdiction to Arroyo Hondo, only seven miles from Natchitoches. General James Wilkinson, at the time governor of the Upper Louisiana Territory, with headquarters in St. Louis—the man who had been part of the "Spanish Conspiracy" by which the western territories were to have been separated from the United States and placed under the protection of Spain—drew up an elaborate plan to build a series of forts to protect Louisiana's interest, and he and the governor of Texas, Colonel Antonio de Cordero y Bustamente, exchanged threats. Neither, however, wanted a direct confrontation. The Americans pressed their claim to put the boundary at the Sabine River, which Beauregard Parish abuts, and Texas acquiesed in the 1819 treaty.

The early settlers of St. Landry Parish found that the prairie country would support cattle superbly, and St. Landry became a supplier of beef for the New Orleans market. The parish's culture is in some ways more Creole than Cajun, a fact that sets it apart from its neighbors. Cotton, not sugarcane, was the principal crop for many years. Today St. Landry is a major producer of feed grains and soybeans.

The St. Landry Parish seat, Opelousas, was founded as a trading post during the French regime but was never much more than that until the days of Spanish rule, when settlers, including many Acadians, began to arrive. At the time of the Civil War, Washington, just north of Opelousas, was a thriving steamboat port. After the fall of New Orleans to the Federals in 1862, Opelousas became the capital of Confederate Louisiana until a big Federal force moved into the area and the government fled to Shreveport.

St. Landry began to share in petroleum prosperity in 1932. Since 1939 it has grown paprika for the American market, the result of the efforts of an immigrant who found that the soil and climate in St. Landry could produce the peppers as a cash crop.

Lumbermen in the early part of the twentieth century cut the virgin forests of Vernon Parish so thoroughly that it was left as the most despoiled area in the state. In 1938, more than two-thirds of its 800,000 acres were listed as cutover land, and in a twenty-one-year period the assessed valuation of woodlands dropped from $40 million to $6 million. At one time, the parish had eleven sawmills, one of them the world's largest.

Reforestation efforts, begun in 1934 under the Civilian Conservation Corps, were joined later by private landholders. Prosperity returned to the area in 1941 when the United States Army built Fort Polk near Leesville. One of the major training camps during World War II, the fort remains in service but has been scaled back during peacetime. Leesville, the parish seat, jumped from 3,500 to 18,000 population when the base was established.

The Vernon Parish area, sitting as it does just above Beauregard Parish, was part of the Neutral Strip. A few French and Spanish settlers moved in before the Louisiana Purchase, but development was slow, principally because of the sovereignty dispute. In terms of land area, Vernon is the largest Louisiana parish, its 1328.5 square miles edging out Rapides' 1322.7.

Vernon was the location of two communal colonies that failed in the depression of the 1930s. Jon Harriman, a Los Angeles lawyer, founded the New Llano Cooperative Colony, which moved in 1917 to a 20,000-acre site below Leesville. The colony attracted the interest of economists and sociologists as an experiment in cooperative membership and sharing of labor. No money was circulated within the colony. It lasted twenty years. In 1931, the Christian Commonwealth Colony was opened by Dr. Samuel W. Irwin on a site purchased from the New Llano group. The colony lasted only four months.

Oil, gas, and agriculture are key elements in the story of Jefferson Davis Parish, and Jennings, the parish seat, claims to be the cradle of the Louisiana oil industry. In fact, although the town was the center of activities that led to the drilling of the first well—a gusher that came in on September 21, 1901—the actual site of the well is at Evangeline, in Acadia Parish, some five miles east of Jennings.

The Heywood brothers of Beaumont, Texas, operating out of Jennings, contracted with the Spencer Company, later the Jennings Oil Company, to drill two wells, each to 1,000 feet. The Heywoods—Alba, O. W., Dewey Clint, and Walter Scott—had been members of a touring musical group when they heard of the discovery of oil at the Spindletop field in Texas. They decided to try their luck. When the first well reached a depth of 1,000 feet, there was no sign of oil. In lieu of a second well, the Heywoods ordered the drillers to continue for another 1,000 feet. The crew was about to run out of pipe, using the final ten feet of a thirty-foot joint on hand, when black gold gushed from a depth of 1,832 feet.

Agriculture, however, has been the mainstay of the parish's economy. Along with Acadia, Jefferson Davis leads the state in rice production; it also produces corn, soybeans, and a variety of vegetable crops. Timber, once a foremost industry, remains a viable one.

Early settlers included French-Acadian, German, Irish, and Italian immigrants; later, there was an influx of Iowans who homesteaded. The Southern Pacific Railroad was a major influence in attracting settlers.

In the latter part of the eighteenth century, Spanish authorities provided land grants, cattle, farming equipment, and even provisions for families migrating to and settling in Allen Parish. Extensive timberlands brought sawmills late in the nineteenth century. The low, flat land encouraged farmers to grow rice or pasture cattle, but settlement of the area proceeded slowly until after the Civil War.

The parish contains some 367,000 acres of timberlands, 100,000 acres of croplands, and 111 miles of streams, which provide recreational sports. Rifle hunters flock to Allen at the start of the deer season, and shotgunners stalk quail, dove, snipe, and other gamebirds. Oberlin is the parish's leading trade and agriculture center, and the parish seat.

ACADIA: Population 55,882. Created June 30, 1888. Named for early settlers, the Acadians. Economy based on agriculture (rice), manufacturing (garments, bags).

SIGHTSEEING: Crowley, Blue Rose Museum (1848 Acadian cottage serving as glass, china museum); Rice Museum; *Wright-Andrus House* (1839).

FETES AND FAIRS: Church Point, Buggy Festival, July 4 weekend; Courir de Mardi Gras (Mardi Gras Day). Crowley,

International Rice Festival, October. Rayne, Frog Festival, September.

ALLEN: Population 21,226. Created in 1912. Named for Henry W. Allen, Confederate governor of Louisiana. Economy based on forestry, rice production, livestock, large federal detention facility (Oakdale).

SIGHTSEEING: Elizabeth/Oakdale, West Bay Wildlife Management Area (camping, birdwatching). Off La. 1147, Whiskey Chitto Creek (scenic canoeing, camping).

FETES AND FAIRS: Elizabeth, Christmas in the Country, December. Kinder, Sauce Piquante and Music Festival, September. Oakdale, Great Louisiana Gumbo Cook-Off, May. Oberlin, Allen Parish Fair, October; Cajun Rendezvous, June–July.

BEAUREGARD: Population 30,083. Created in 1912. Named for Confederate general P. G. T. Beauregard. Economy based on forestry, agriculture (soybeans, rice), livestock, manufacturing (paper, clothing).

SIGHTSEEING: De Ridder (downtown area is National Register Historic District); Burnett Gardens.

FETES AND FAIRS: De Ridder, Arts and Crafts Festival, September; Beauregard Parish Fair, October. Merryville, Civil War Encampment, February.

CALCASIEU: Population 168,134. Created in 1840. Named for the Calcasieu River, which drew its name from that of an Attakapas Indian chief. Economy based on oil and gas production, chemical plants, shipping, forestry, rice production, and cattle.

SIGHTSEEING: DeQuincy, Dogtrot Museum; Railroad Museum. Lake Charles, Historic Charpentier District; Sam Houston Jones State Park. Sulphur, Creole Nature Trail (driving tour from Sulphur to Gulf Coast and return via Lake Charles). Toomey, Sabine Island Wildlife Management Area (accessible only by boat).

FETES AND FAIRS: DeQuincy, Louisiana Railroad Days Festival, April. Iowa, Rabbit Festival, March. Lake Charles, Black Heritage Festival of Louisiana, January; Contraband Days, May; Calca-Chew Food Festival, September. Sulphur, Calcasieu-Cameron Fair, fall; Taste of Louisiana, June. Vinton, Cajun Festival, September.

CAMERON: Population 9,260. Created March 16, 1870. Name derivation uncertain, possibly for Confederate soldier Robert Alexander Cameron or United States Senator Simon Cameron of Pennsylvania.

Economy based on oil and gas production, rice cultivation, fishing, fur trapping.

SIGHTSEEING: Holly Beach (on twenty-six-mile stretch of beach, unusual for Louisiana's marshy coast). Hug the Coast Highway (La. 82). Rockefeller Wildlife Refuge (open March through September). Rutherford Beach. Sabine National Wildlife Refuge.

FETES AND FAIRS: Cameron, Cajun Riviera Festival, August; Louisiana Wildlife and Fur Festival, January. Grand Chenier, Alligator Harvest Festival, fall. Hackberry, Marshland Festival, July.

EVANGELINE: Population 33,274. Created in 1912. Named for the heroine of Longfellow's poem. Economy based on agriculture (rice, soybeans), cattle, dairy farming, forestry, light industry.

SIGHTSEEING: Ville Platte, Chicot State Park; Louisiana State Arboretum.

FETES AND FAIRS: Basile, Louisiana Swine Festival, November. Mamou, Cajun Music and Fall Festival, fall; Courir de Mardi Gras (Mardi Gras Day). Ville Platte, Cajun Gumbo Festival, November; Louisiana Cotton Festival, October (Festival climaxes with the Tournoi de Ville Platte, which features a form of jousting—see text); Mardi Gras (including a courir on Fat Tuesday).

IBERIA: Population 68,299. Created in 1868. Name reflects Spanish influence on parish's development. Economy based on agriculture (sugarcane, truck farming), salt mining, fishing, trapping, and oil and gas production.

SIGHTSEEING: Avery Island (gardens, bird sanctuary, Tabasco Sauce factory). Jeanerette, *Albania* (1837–42). Jefferson Island, Live Oak Gardens. Lake Fausse Pointe State Park. New Iberia, *Justine* (1822; expanded 1890s); *Mintmere* (1857); *Shadows on the Teche* (1834).

FETES AND FAIRS: Jeanerette, Mirliton Festival, June. New Iberia, Cajun Fun Fest, March; Louisiana Sugar Cane Festival, September.

JEFFERSON DAVIS: Population, 30,722. Created in 1912. Named for Confederate States of America president. Economy based on oil and gas production, rice cultivation, forestry, cattle.

SIGHTSEEING: Elton, Coushatta Indian Culture Center and Trading Post. Jennings, Louisiana Oil and Gas Park.

FETES AND FAIRS: Jennings, Jefferson Davis Parish Fair, October; Louisiana Oil Festival, July. Welsh, Cajun Food and Fun Festival, April.

LAFAYETTE: Population 164,762. Created in 1829. Named for the marquis de Lafayette, French hero of the American Revolution. Economy based on petroleum, cattle, dairy farming, agriculture (rice, sugarcane).

SIGHTSEEING: Lafayette, Acadian Village and Gardens; Lafayette Museum; Lafayette Natural History Museum and Planetarium; Vermilion River (cruises available).

FETES AND FAIRS: Broussard, Louisiana Boudin Festival, February; Lafayette, Azalea Trail, March; Festival International de Louisiane, April; Festivals Acadiens, September; Mardi Gras (nation's second largest).

ST. LANDRY: Population 80,331. Created in 1807. Named for St. Landry Catholic Church, founded in 1777 by Capuchin monks. Economy based on agriculture (soybeans, rice, cotton, sweet potatoes), dairy farming, small manufacturing.

SIGHTSEEING: Beggs, *Homeplace* (1826). Eunice, Jean Lafitte National Historical Park–Acadian Culture Center. Grand Coteau, National Register Historic District. Opelousas, *Governor's Mansion* (1848; governor's residence when Opelousas was acting state capital during Civil War); *Prudhomme Home* (early 1800s); *Ray Homestead* (1853). Sunset, *Chretien Point* (1831). Washington, *Arlington* (1829); *Camellia Cove* (1825); *De la Morandiere* (1830); *Magnolia Ridge* (1830); *Nicholson House of History* (1835); *Starvation Point* (1790s).

FETES AND FAIRS: Eunice, World Championship Crawfish Etouffée Cook-off, March. Opelousas, Louisiana Yambilee Festival, October; Preservationist Annual Tour of Homes, March. Plaisance, Zydeco Festival, Saturday before Labor Day. Washington, Festival du Courtableau, March; Historic Washington Pilgrimage, April.

ST. MARTIN: Population 43,978. Created in 1807. Named for sainted fourth-century bishop of Tours, France. Economy based on oil and gas production, fishing, and sugarcane cultivation. Parish is divided into upper and lower sections by an arm of Iberia Parish.

SIGHTSEEING: Atchafalaya Basin (town of Henderson is a prime entry point for boating into this vast, watery wilderness). St. Martinville, *Acadian House Museum* (1765); Evangeline Monument and Evangeline Oak; Longfellow-Evangeline State Commemorative Area; St. Martin de Tours Church (1832); St. Martin Parish Courthouse (1838).

FETES AND FAIRS: Breaux Bridge, Crawfish Festival, May. St. Martinville, La Grande Boucherie des Cajuns, Sunday before Mardi Gras; Pepper Festival, October.

ST. MARY: Population 58,086. Created in 1811. Named for Mary, mother of Jesus. Economy based on petroleum industry, fishing, agriculture (sugarcane, rice, soybeans).

SIGHTSEEING: Centerville, *Joshua Cary House* (1839). Charenton, Jean Lafitte National Historical Park, Chitimacha Unit (Chitimacha Indian Reservation). Cypremort State Park. Franklin, *Arlington* (1861); Franklin National Register Historic District; *Grevemberg House* (*ca.* 1851); *Oaklawn Manor* (1837). Morgan City, Swamp Gardens.

FETES AND FAIRS: Charenton, Chitimacha Fair, July 4 weekend. Franklin, Christmas Tour of Homes, December; International Alligator Festival, October. Morgan City, Louisiana Shrimp and Petroleum Festival, Labor Day weekend.

VERMILION: Population 50,055. Created in 1844. Named for Vermilion River and Vermilion Bay, which have red, or vermilion, bluffs. Economy based on agriculture (rice, sugarcane), fishing, cattle, oil and gas production.

SIGHTSEEING: Abbeville, St. Mary Magdalen Church (1910); Magdalen Square (dates to town's founding in the 1840s). Delcambre, Shrimp Boat Landing.

FETES AND FAIRS: Abbeville, French-Acadian Music Festival, second Saturday after Easter; Louisiana Cattle Festival and Fair, October; Tarpon Rodeo, Labor Day weekend (held at Intracoastal City). Delcambre, Shrimp Festival, August. Gueydan, Duck Festival, September.

VERNON: Population 61,961. Created on March 30, 1871. Origin of name not clear. Economy based on forestry, truck farming, dairy farming, cattle, and support for a large military installation.

SIGHTSEEING: Fort Polk, Fort Polk Military Museum. Kisatchie National Forest, Vernon District. Lake Anacoco. Sabine River below Toledo Bend Dam (beaches, canoeing).

FETES AND FAIRS: Leesville, West Louisiana Forestry Festival, October. Sabine River, Great Mother's Day Canoe Race.

—W.G.C.

Southeast Louisiana

37

THE SOUTHEAST

New Orleans makes a living living in the past. An exaggeration, certainly, but not altogether fanciful. The economic well-being of the population depends heavily on the attraction of tourists and conventioneers to a city steeped in nostalgia, historical significance, and a European ambience. They come in droves, drawn by a World's Fair, Republican National Convention, Mardi Gras, Super Bowl football games, Final Four basketball tournaments, championship boxing matches, trade shows, meetings of national professional and fraternal societies. They find top-notch accommodations: the Louisiana Superdome, most elaborate of the domed stadiums; the Louisiana Exhibition Center, one of the biggest of the nation's trade-show facilities; twenty-five thousand hotel rooms; world-class restaurants.

They also find the exotic environment that sets New Orleans apart. Because preservationists have prevailed, the French Quarter looks very much as it did when the city was a Spanish colony in the eighteenth century. Memories of Mark Twain are evoked on the Mississippi riverfront, a place that brings to mind Twain's paddlewheelers. The Garden District is a reminder of the American side of New Orleans, the area where the entrepreneurs who made their millions in cotton, sugar, factoring, and shipping built their mansions. The cemeteries are cities of the dead resting in endless rows of above-ground white tombs. The restaurants offer a cuisine far removed from America's standard diet. Some clubs offer jazz not too far removed from the sounds of Storyville.

Today's Louisiana had its real beginning at the sweeping bend of the Mississippi where in 1718 the sieur de Bienville chose to situate his French colonial capital even though an outpost had been established at Natchitoches four years earlier. Bienville picked a spot squarely in the path, in the years to follow, of the nascent American republic—the jumping-off place to Texas, Mexico, Cuba, and the Central American countries; the focal point of the Mississippi Valley. Inevitably, events of historical import followed.

The French flag was lowered and the Stars and Stripes raised in the Place d'Armes in the consummation of the Louisiana Purchase. Andrew Jackson's sharpshooters won the Battle of New Orleans—actually fought in St. Bernard Parish, although within a few hundred yards of the Orleans

Parish border. David Farragut's Union fleet anchored in the river with cannon trained down the streets in the conquest of New Orleans, a body blow to the Confederacy. Homer Plessy, a man of color, boarded an all-white railroad car at a station near the river, thus instigating a test that resulted in the separate-but-equal doctrine that governed race relations in the United States for half a century.

For most of the colonial period, other settlements in the Louisiana area were governed from New Orleans, and the city was the territorial and then the state capital in the first decades of the American years. So long as a majority of the state's population was supported by the production of cotton and sugar, New Orleans was the principal economic as well as political center. A large percentage of the bales and hogsheads were sent to the port for transshipment, and it was the city's factors, brokers, and bankers who financed the growers.

Debtor-creditor differences were one cause of a political schism between rural, Protestant, Anglo-Saxon north Louisiana and urban, Catholic, Creole south Louisiana. The strain continued as long as cotton and cane were the money crops. Afterward, when logging and then the development of oil and gas fields changed the economic picture, New Orleans no longer exercised as much financial clout. Baton Rouge, Shreveport, Lake Charles, Lafayette, Monroe, and Alexandria are independent industrial or shipping centers in their own right, certainly not satellites orbiting the state's biggest city. At the same time, no doubt partly as a result of the general homogenization process, a sort of political detente has developed between New Orleans and the rest of the state.

Fun-loving New Orleanians enjoy the idea of providing activities for the visitors on whom the city so heavily depends. Nobody can ever say there is nothing to do, around the calendar. Mardi Gras remains America's liveliest and biggest civic fete. In ever-growing numbers, the crowds pile into the infield of the Fair Grounds racetrack in April for the Jazz and Heritage Festival. In striped tents reminiscent of medieval fairs, bands provide a continuous round of jazz, country, and Cajun music, while from a hundred booths cooks dish out helpings of Creole and Cajun food. The Louisiana Philharmonic and the New Orleans Opera House Association have their seasons. For sport fans, the Sugar Bowl football game starts off the New Year, and the city's colleges and universities present schedules of football, basketball, and baseball. Fans of the New Orleans Saints professional football team often fill the Superdome for the team's home games.

The territory where Jean Lafitte and his buccaneers had their lair on a coastal island, where Claude Joseph Villars-Dubreuil established a major plantation on the shore of the Mississippi River, where at the end of World War II a vast unpopulated prairie still bordered Lake Pontchartrain, is expected by the end of the century to have more residents than New Orleans. Once a suburb, Jefferson Parish has come into its own. The flight from old New Orleans residential neighborhoods has filled almost all of the land on the East Bank of the river with homes and apartment houses, and the construction of river bridges opens up the West Bank to eye-popping development. Tall office buildings and hotels stand where marsh plants grew as late as the 1960s, the largest shopping malls of the metropolitan area are bustling, and the New Orleans International Airport has emerged. An ironic aspect of the phenomenal growth is that a residential section of the East Bank, the most populous unincorporated area in Louisiana, bears the name of Metairie, which from the French translates to "small farms."

Old-time New Orleanians and Jeffersonians remember the "free state of Jefferson" before the Second World War as a relaxed, free-spirited suburb where law-enforcement authorities tolerated illegal gambling. On the East Bank, the New York gang chief Frank Costello operated the plush Beverly Country Club, where star vocalists such as Sophie Tucker and Frank Sinatra entertained those who came to try their luck at the dice tables. Other gambling places operated just over the border from New Orleans. On the West Bank, the Billionaire Club in Gretna was only one of a number of gaming establishments. The political atmosphere changed after the war with an influx of newcomers from New Orleans who moved into subdivisions developed by speculative builders. In a less permissive environment, the clubs closed. Meanwhile, the building up of the petroleum industry was part of an economic awakening.

The West Bank communities—Gretna, Harvey, Marrero, Westwego—occupied the strip along the bank of the Mississippi. The dry land faded away into a wilderness of swamps, bayous, lakes, and bays that separated habitable Jefferson from the Gulf Coast. Grand Isle, a summer resort and fishing village, is just west of Grand Terre, where Lafitte's Baratarians held forth. West Bank residents then could reach New Orleans only on ferry boats. The first bridge, completed in 1935, connected Bridge City with Harahan.

In 1739, Jean-Baptiste Destréhan de Beaupré financed the digging of a five-and-one-half-mile-long canal from the Mississippi River to Bayou Barataria. His descendants Joseph and Horace Harvey had the canal widened, and in 1907 it was connected to the Mississippi by a lock. In 1934 the canal, named for the Harveys, was linked with and made part of the Gulf Intracoastal Canal, which now stretches from Texas to Florida.

The David Crockett Fire Company of Gretna is believed to be the oldest volunteer fire brigade in the United States that still is in service. It began on May 7, 1844, as the Gretna Fire Company. The name was changed in 1874 to honor the Tennessee frontiersman.

The largest industrial operation in Jefferson is the shipyard of Avondale Industries, Inc., situated on the West Bank just above the Huey P. Long bridge.

The marshy, watery scope of the St. Bernard Parish is made clear in the statistics; of a total surface of 1,860,000 acres, only 24,000 are not wetlands or lake, bay, or bayou. Naturally, St. Bernard is the weekend haunt of sports fishermen; and it also is a productive area for commercial fishing. Trappers find armies of nutria in the marshes.

The limited availability of arable land and the proximity to New Orleans have resulted in the economy of St. Bernard being largely industrial. Situated as it is, the parish is a blue-collar suburb.

The parish once was called Terre aux Boeufs, since it was reputedly the last refuge of "wild oxen," as the early French colonists described buffalo. The first settlers came in 1720, only two years after New Orleans was laid out. The first land grants went to Celestin Chiapella and Antoine Phillipon.

There remains in St. Bernard one of the state's unique communities, made up of the so-called Isleños, who earn a livelihood fishing and trapping. Some of the Isleños are descendants of the Canary Islanders who established a settlement on Bayou Terre-aux-Boeufs in 1779. Governor Bernardo de Gálvez prevailed upon the Spanish crown to send shiploads of colonists to Louisiana to resist British encroachment upon Spain's territory in the New World. The king ordered the enlistment of seven hundred Canary Islanders, and more were sent later. Gálvez divided the newcomers and their families among four settlements. Today's Isleños are the last vestige of this migration. Their ancestors at Terre aux Boeufs settled on land obtained by Gálvez from Pierre Philippe Enguerrand de Marigny de Mandeville, a colonial official. Marigny was the father of Bernard Xavier de Marigny de Mandeville, who is remembered as the grandest Creole of them all, the largest landowner and probably wealthiest man in New Orleans.

When La Salle hoisted a cross of tree limbs and stuck it in the bank of the Mississippi River in April of 1682, at what now is Venice, proclaiming all the territory drained by the great river as the possession of France, he assured Plaquemines Parish's place in history. Subsequent events have solidified its position, and through time, before and after La Salle, Plaquemines has been the scene of tribulations of the Indians who had lived there for centuries, challenges among Europeans settling the area, confrontations between Confederate and Union forces along the river, and the shrewd maneuverings of a politician who, while building a virtual kingdom, masterminded a scheme through which he could share generously in the natural wealth found beneath the surface of his domain.

Plaquemines is built of alluvial soil, from which it produces wealth, especially navel oranges and creole tomatoes, and much more from its rich deposits of oil, gas, and sulphur. The parish's very location has put it in the forefront of United States history.

The river is an artery of commerce to the world but has also been a route taken by hostile forces seeking to gain a foothold. The French lost no time in building a fort in 1700 to protect their settlement—Fort de la Boulaye, or Fort Mississippi, it was called, near present-day Phoenix.

The fort effectively closed the river to British naval forces seeking to stake a claim to the Mississippi Valley, and in effect confirmed La Salle's proclamation. After the founding of New Orleans in 1718 came the building in 1721 of the Balize, the port-of-entry checkpoint at the mouth of the river, giving the French greater control, leaving them to deal only with the Chawasha Indians and smaller tribes living along the Plaquemines waterways. A map of 1732 confirms the Indians' presence.

France, Spain, and the United States in turn fortified the riverbanks to control commerce; Fort St. Philip was built in 1741 on the east bank at Plaquemines Turn, and Fort Bourbon was constructed at about that time on the west bank. The latter, destroyed by a hurricane in 1795, was rebuilt but faded into history after Fort Jackson, completed in 1842, took over its role. Fort St. Philip withstood a British assault in the War of 1812, but Union forces passed it in 1862 en route to the capture of New Orleans.

Plaquemines' reputation for political chicanery dates back to the presidential election of 1844, when the parish delivered a lopsided majority for James K. Polk against Henry Clay. In the 1840 presidential election, Plaquemines had polled only 290 votes. In 1844, the total hit 1,044. Polk, a Democrat, received 1,007 votes in the parish while Clay, a Whig, could muster but 37.

A radical group of Democrats known as the Locofocos took charge in Louisiana to swing the majority for Polk, who won the state by 699 votes, with Plaquemines providing the margin of victory. Judge Gilbert Leonard of Plaquemines chartered two steamboats and put on board some 350 men, along with a generous supply of whiskey, and took them to three polling places in the parish, according to an article in *The Nation* magazine of February 27, 1878. "The boatmen themselves, from pilot to engineer and cabin boy," said the story, "were made to step up and vote for Polk, and when this great moral spectacle had closed at one landing, it was repeated at the next."

The election had serious repercussions. John Slidell, then a congressman from Louisiana and later a senator, was said to have been the brains behind the unique voting procedure, but he claimed the Whigs were planning a similar move and he was only countering them.

In modern-day elections, the vote for candidates supported by the parish's ruling faction has many times been one-sided. For instance, in the Huey P. Long race for the United States Senate in 1932, the polls at Boothville-Venice, Braithwaite, and Buras registered tabulations of 402 to 3, 243 to 8, and 226 to 16 for Long against his opponent, Senator Joseph E. Ransdell. The parish total: Long, 1,913; Ransdell, 131. More recent elections show the practice continuing.

The political force to reckon with in Plaquemines from the 1920s until his death in 1969 was Leander Perez, a native-born son who served as judge, district attorney, and eventually president of the parish commission council. His rise to power coincided with the development of the parish's rich mineral deposits, which yielded millions of barrels of crude oil, billions of cubic feet of natural gas, and untold tons of sulphur. As the riches poured from the ground, Perez in 1936 developed a plan to reap millions of dollars for himself and family. He organized the Delta Development Corporation, hiding his activities from public scrutiny by incorporating the firm in Delaware and carefully shielding it from inquisitors. At the same time, as district attorney, Perez was legal adviser to the Plaquemines levee boards, which controlled large tracts of public land. He negotiated deals between Delta, the boards, and the big oil companies leasing the land for drilling. The opportunities for abuse were enormous, but even though the local and national press tried in vain for years to pry loose the lid of secrecy Perez had clamped on the arrangement, the scheme did not become public until 1986, long after his death. Meantime, the parish had sued the Perez heirs, seeking to reclaim an estimated $82 million allegedly paid wrongfully to the Perez family. The case ended in a multimillion-dollar settlement, the heirs also agreeing to give up their Delta holdings, which at the time were generating some $3 million yearly.

During his long career, Leander Perez ruled his domain with an iron hand. His ability to deliver overwhelming majorities to favored candidates made him a force in state politics, in which he had established himself as a confidant first of Huey Long in Long's defense against impeachment charges, and later of Earl Long when Earl was elected governor. Perez was a vocal supporter of and a heavy contributor to states' rights causes, and an archsegregationist who in the late 1950s and early 1960s gained national notoriety as a personification of diehard racism.

Through Lafourche Parish runs the "longest street in the world." Bayou Lafourche, a former distributary of the Mississippi River, begins at Donaldsonville in Ascension Parish, wanders past Napoleonville in Assumption Parish, then traverses the length of Lafourche Parish to empty into the Gulf. For much of that distance—some 100 miles—houses, stores, and other buildings line the bayou's banks in nearly unbroken row. The arrangement dates to the early years when the area was almost entirely agricultural. Farmers needed access to a bayou or river in order to ship their crops. Therefore land was divided into thin strips fronting the stream. A standard parcel was eight arpents wide by forty arpents deep, an arpent being 192 linear feet. However, subdivision—such as among the heirs of a landowner—soon resulted in much narrower frontages, so that today many lots are barely wide enough for the houses that stand on them. The impression of a street is reinforced by the fact that the bayou itself is no wider than some city boulevards. There are occasional bridges, but generally a resident who wants to visit a neighbor on the other side of the "street" will paddle across in a boat.

One of the original twelve counties of the Territory of Orleans in 1805, Lafourche also became one of the original nineteen parishes created in 1807. The fertile land so close to New Orleans and bisected by a navigable bayou was an obvious candidate for settlement. Thibodaux was founded as a trading post in 1820, and French, Spanish, and Acadian settlers moved in during the middle years of the eighteenth century. The parish prospered with the development of sugar production and then found additional means of support from trapping, fishing, and the late-twentieth-century boom in coastal and offshore oil and gas drilling.

Lafourche cooks are renowned, even in food-conscious Louisiana. It can be no surprise that seafood dishes are featured, but the town of Raceland bills itself as the "Sauce Piquante Capital of the World." The rich, highly-spiced sauce is used to flavor chicken, turtle, rabbit, or shrimp. It is the boast of residents that "once you drink bayou (Lafourche) water you will always return," and sauce piquante is one of the reasons why.

The introduction of a shrimp-drying process by Lee Yim, a Cantonese, gave a boost to one of Terrebonne Parish's principal economic activities. Another important development was the introduction in 1917 of the trawl, which could produce major hauls of shrimp from the Gulf of Mexico. An annual event on the third Sunday in April is the blessing of the shrimp fleet at Chauvin, on Bayou Terrebonne, by the archbishop of New Orleans.

As early as 1794 the production of sugar and molasses became the parish's main economic support. It was big business by the time of the Civil War. In 1851 cane was being grown on 110 large plantations, and eighty sugarhouses were turning out 13,000 hogsheads of sugar and 20,000 barrels of molasses a year. Trappers found a bonanza in the vast marshes of south Terrebonne, muskrat fur being a popular commodity along with raccoon, mink, and later, nutria. In 1929 the discovery of oil put the parish on the petroleum map.

Only a few settlers moved in before colonization began in earnest around 1765 with the arrival of displaced Acadians and other settlers. After the establishment of the parish in March, 1822, the police jury first met at the home of Alexander Dupré, who was paid $10 a day for providing the facilities and furnishing refreshments for the jurors. The first court-house was built in 1823 on Bayou Cane three miles above Houma. The parish seat was moved in 1834 to Houma.

The Pughs of North Carolina were among the Anglo-descended families from the older states who moved into Louisiana during the great migration of the early nineteenth century. Members of the family acquired eighteen plantations along Bayou Lafourche, giving birth to a local riddle: "Why is the bayou like the aisle of a church?" Most residents knew the answer: "Because it has Pughs on both sides."

In the heart of the sugarcane country, Assumption Parish has remained largely rural, the only incorporated town being Napoleonville, the parish seat. But the citizens are by no means wholly dependent on agriculture for a livelihood. Since 1943 the production and distribution of oil and gas have contributed to the economy. The offshore oil boom brought the installation of facilities on Bayou Boeuf for the fabrication of drilling platforms and for boatbuilding. Chemical companies have moved in to tap into salt domes that underlie the parish. The swamps long have been worked by trappers in quest of nutria, muskrat, mink, and otter.

Production of soybeans and wheat began in 1980. The parish has cashed in on the growing demand for crawfish (elsewhere known as crayfish). The mudbugs are trapped from swamps and ponds in the area of Pierre Part, and now are also cultivated in special ponds created for the purpose.

The Catholic church built at Plattenville in 1856 is on the site of the original Church of the Assumption that gave the parish its name. In Napoleonville is Christ Episcopal Church, designed by the New York architect Frank Mills and dedicated in 1853 by Leonidas Polk, first Episcopal

Madewood, on the east bank of Bayou Lafourche near Napoleonville, is a magnificent example of antebellum Greek Revival plantation architecture. Constructed over a period of eight years in the 1840s, the mansion supposedly takes its name from the fact that all of the wood in it came from the plantation grounds.

Photo by G. E. Arnold

bishop of Louisiana, who left the pulpit to become a general in the Confederate army and was killed in action at Pine Mountain, Georgia, in 1864.

ASSUMPTION: Population 22,753. Formed in 1807. Named for an early (Catholic) Church of the Assumption on Bayou Lafourche. Economy based on agriculture (sugarcane, soybeans, wheat), petroleum production and manufacture of equipment for same, boatbuilding, crawfish farming.

SIGHTSEEING: Bayou Lafourche (La. 1 runs directly alongside the bayou for much of its length). Lake Verret (fishing, boating). Napoleonville, Christ Episcopal Church (1853); *Madewood* (1846). Plattenville, Church of the Assumption (1856).

FETES AND FAIRS: Belle Rose, Allons Manger, April. Napoleonville, Madewood Arts Festival, April.

JEFFERSON: Population 448,306. Created on February 11, 1825. Named for Thomas Jefferson. Economy based on retailing, shipbuilding, shipping, manufacturing, and oil and gas production.

SIGHTSEEING: Grand Isle (Gulf beach-resort and charter-fishing island). Kenner, Rivertown (includes Wildlife and Fisheries Museum, Toy Train Museum, and Historical Museum). Lafitte, Jean Lafitte National Historical Park,

Barataria Unit. Westwego, Bayou Segnette State Park; *Magnolia Lane* (1784).

FETES AND FAIRS: Bridge City, Gumbo Festival, October. Grand Isle, International Tarpon Rodeo, July. Gretna and Metairie, Mardi Gras, February–March. Kenner, French Louisiana Festival, October; Okra Festival, June. Lafitte, Seafood Festival, August. Metairie, Original Red Beans and Rice Festival, September.

LAFOURCHE: Population 85,860. Created in 1807. Named for Bayou Lafourche (the name means "the fork" in French), which once was an arm of the Mississippi River. Economy based on agriculture (sugarcane, corn, potatoes, truck crops), oil and related industries, forestry, seafood canning, boatbuilding.

SIGHTSEEING: Cut Off, Pointe au Chien Wildlife Management Area. Grand Isle (at end of La. 1 although technically in Jefferson Parish). Raceland, *Rosella* (1814). Thibodaux, *Edward Douglass White Memorial* (1790); Lafourche Parish Courthouse (1860); Laurel Valley Plantation Village; St. John's Episcopal Church (1844). Wisner Wildlife Management Area.

FETES AND FAIRS: Chackbay, Louisiana Gumbo Festival of Chackbay, September. Galliano, Louisiana Oyster Festival, July. Larose, French Food Festival, October. Mathews, La Vie Fourchaise Festival, October. Raceland, Sauce Piquante Festival, October. Thibodaux, Fireman's Fair, April; Mardi Gras, February–March.

ORLEANS: Population 496,938. Created as county in 1805, parish in 1807. Named for the duke of Orléans, regent for the child king Louis XV. Economy based on shipping, tourism, aerospace, shipbuilding, oil and gas operations.

SIGHTSEEING: French Quarter; Garden District; Lakefront; Riverfront, including Aquarium of the Americas, Woldenberg Park, Riverwalk, Moon Walk, Spanish Plaza; City Park and New Orleans Museum of Art; Audubon Park and Zoo; Cabildo (Louisiana State Museum); Historic New Orleans Collection; Louisiana Superdome; Fair Grounds Race Track (racing season November–April).

FETES AND FAIRS: Sugar Bowl game and associated events, late December through early January; Battle of New Orleans Anniversary, January; Mardi Gras, February–March; Spring Fiesta, Friday after Easter; Jazz and Heritage Festival, April–May; La Fete de la Nouvelle Orleans, July; African Heritage Festival International, August; City Park Celebration in the Oaks, December.

PLAQUEMINES: Population 25,575. Created in 1807. Named for the persimmon tree, from the Indian word *piakemines*. Economy based on oil, gas, and sulphur production, seafood production, and citrus crops.

SIGHTSEEING: Boothville/Triumph, Fort Jackson (Civil War fort, restored). Braithwaite, *Mary* (late 1700s). Myrtle Grove, Lake Hermitage (scenic). Pointe a la Hache/West Pointe a la Hache, Mississippi River ferry. Venice (southernmost automobile-accessible point on Mississippi River; boat tours to mouths of the river).

FETES AND FAIRS: Empire, Empire/South Pass Tarpon Rodeo, August. Fort Jackson, Fourth of July Festival; Plaquemines Parish Fair and Orange Festival, December.

ST. BERNARD: Population 66,631. Created in 1807. Named for Saint Bernard of Clairvaux (1090?-1153). Economy based on oil and gas production, fishing, trapping, truck farming.

SIGHTSEEING: Chalmette, De la Ronde Oaks (planted 1762 on grounds of now-ruined Versailles Plantation); Jean Lafitte National Historical Park, Chalmette Unit (site of Battle of New Orleans); *René Beauregard House* (1837). St. Bernard, Ducros Museum (Creole cottage, 1800); Jean Lafitte National Historical Park, Isleños Museum. Violet, St. Bernard State Park.

FETES AND FAIRS: Chalmette, reenactment of Battle of New Orleans, January; Tomato Festival, May. Meraux, Louisiana Crawfish Festival, March; Louisiana Shrimp Festival, September. St. Bernard, Los Isleños Spanish Festival, October.

TERREBONNE: Population 96,982. Created in 1822. The name means "good land" in French. Economy based on agriculture (sugarcane), oil and gas production, sugar refining, fishing.

SIGHTSEEING: Houma, Bayou Tour (circular driving tour of several bayous in and near the town); National Register Historic District downtown; *Magnolia* (1858); *Southdown Plantation House* (1859) and Terrebonne Museum.

FETES AND FAIRS: Chauvin, Blessing of the Shrimp Fleet, April; Lagniappe on the Bayou, October. Houma, Louisiana Praline Festival, May; Terrebonne Parish Fair and Rodeo, October; Southdown Fall Festival, November.

—W.G.C.

APPENDIX

Louisiana State Parks

#	Park	Improved Campsites*	Unimproved Campsites**	Rally Campsites**	Backpacking Campsites	Primitive Group Campsite	Dump Station	Cabins	Group Camps	Lodge	Camp Store	Visitor Center	Conference Room	Trails	Picnicking	Group Shelters	Playground	Restrooms	Swimming	Boating	Notes
1	BAYOU SEGNETTE 7777 Westbank Expressway Westwego, LA 70094 (504) 736-7140	100					•	20	1			•			•	•	•	•		L	Large boat launch provides access to the Barataria Basin; on US 90 near New Orleans
2	CHEMIN-A-HAUT 14656 State Park Road Bastrop, LA 71220-7078 (318) 283-0812	26	•			•	•	6	1			•		H	•	•	•	•	P	R	Camping, fishing, picnicking, overlooking Bayou Bartholomew; off La. 139
3	CHICOT Route 3, Box 494 Ville Platte, LA 70586 (318) 363-2403	200		•	•	•		27	2	•				N H	•	•	•	•	P	R L	Fishing in 2,000-acre lake; hiking; adjacent to Louisiana State Arboretum; on La. 3042
4	CYPREMORT POINT 306 Beach Ln. Franklin, LA 70538 (318) 867-4510											•				•		•	B	S	Swimming, sailing, fishing in the waters of Vermilion Bay; off La. 319 (no camping)
5	FAIRVIEW-RIVERSIDE P. O. Box 856 Madisonville, LA 70447 (504) 845-3318	82				•	•								•	•	•			•	Fishing, boating on Tchefuncte River; on La. 22 in Madisonville
6	FONTAINEBLEAU P. O. Box 152 Mandeville, LA 70448 (504) 624-4443	130	129			•	•		3	•				N	•	•	•	•	P	S	Swimming, fishing, sailing, picnicking on north shore of Lake Pontchartrain; on US 190
7	GRAND ISLE P. O. Box 741 Grand Isle, LA 70358 (504) 787-2559		100				•					•				•		•		B	Camping on Gulf Coast beach, surffishing, fishing, crabbing; fishing pier; La. 1, east end of Grand
8	LAKE BISTINEAU P. O. Box 589 Doyline, LA 71023 (318) 745-3503	67	•			•	•	13	2					H	•	•	•	•	P B	R L	Camping, fishing, swimming, picnicking on scenic Lake Bistineau; on La. 163
9	LAKE BRUIN Route 1, Box 183 St. Joseph, LA 71366 (318) 766-3530	25				•	•								•		•	•	B	R L	Waterskiing, fishing, boating on the 3,000-acre oxbow lake; on La. 604
10	LAKE CLAIBORNE P. O. Box 246 Homer, LA 70140 (318) 927-2976	87				•	•							N	•		•		B	R L	Wooded hills bordering large lake; fishing, waterskiing; on La. 146
11	LAKE D'ARBONNE P. O. Box 236 Farmerville, LA 71241 (318) 368-2086	43					•													L	Fishing and water sports on Lake D'Arbonne; off La. 2
12	LAKE FAUSSE POINTE 5400 Levee Rd. St. Martinville, LA 70582 (318) 229-4764	50			•	•	•	8			•		•	H	•	•		•		L	Fishing, boating, camping in a watery wilderness; on the West Atchafalaya Protection Levee Rd. east of St. Martinville via La. 96 & La. 3083
13	NORTH TOLEDO BEND P. O. Box 56 Zwolle, LA 71486 (318) 645-4715	63				•	•	10	1	•	•	•		•	•	•	•	•	P	L	Fishing and water sports on Toledo Bend Reservoir; off La. 3229
14	ST. BERNARD P. O. Box 534 Violet, LA 70092 (504) 682-2101	51				•	•								•	•	•	•	P		Fishing in lagoons, swimming, camping, picnicking, minutes from New Orleans; on La. 39
15	SAM HOUSTON JONES 101 Sutherland Road Lake Charles, LA 70611 (318) 855-2665	73				•	•	12						H N	•		•	•		R L	Fishing and hiking in natural area at confluence of three rivers; on La. 378

*Water & electricity hookups

**No water or electricity hookups

All state parks include some handicapped accessible facilities

Boating: L = launch, R = boat rentals, S = sailboat ramp

Trails: H = hiking, N = marked nature trail

Swimming: P = pool, B = beach

STATE COMMEMORATIVE AREA FACILITIES	Museum/Historic Buildings	Observation Tower	Amphitheater	Outdoor Exhibits	Restrooms	Crafts Shop	Trails	Guided Tours	Audiovisual Program	Demonstrations	Picnicking	Special Events	
A AUDUBON P. O. Box 546 St. Francisville, LA 70775 (504) 635-3739	●		●	●		●	●			●	●		Oakley Plantation, where John James Audubon worked; on La. 965
B FORT JESUP Route 2, Box 611 Many, LA 71449 (318) 256-4117	●		●	●			●			●	●		Site of fort established by Zachary Taylor in 1822; on La. 6
C FORT PIKE Route 6, Box 194 New Orleans, LA 70129 (504) 662-5703	●		●	●						●	●		Masonry fort completed in 1827 to defend New Orleans; on US 90
D FORT ST. JEAN BAPTISTE 130 Morrow Natchitoches, LA 71458 (318) 357-3101	●		●	●			●		●		●		Replica of French fort built in 1732; in the city of Natchitoches on Morrow Street
E LOCUST GROVE P. O. Box 546 St. Francisville, LA 70775 (504) 635-3739													Cemetery containing grave of first wife of Jefferson Davis; off US 61
F LONGFELLOW-EVANGELINE 1200 N. Main Street St. Martinville, LA 70582 (318) 394-3754	●		●	●	●	●	●			●	●		Depicts life on early 1800s Creole plantation; in the town of St. Martinville
G LOS ADAES P. O. Box 127 Marthaville, LA 71450 (318) 472-9449				●		●	●						Archaeological site of Spanish fort built in 1721; on La. 6
H MANSFIELD Route 2, Box 459 Mansfield, LA 71052 (318) 872-1474	●		●	●		●	●	●		●	●		Site of significant Civil War battle; on La. 175
I MARKSVILLE 700 Martin Luther King Dr. Marksville, LA 71351 (318) 253-8954	●		●	●			●	●		●	●		Site of Indian culture and mounds dating from *ca.* 200 B.C. to A.D. 400; in the town of Marksville
J PORT HUDSON 756 West Plains–Port Hudson Rd. Zachary, LA 70791 (504) 654-3775	●	●	●	●		●	●	●	●	●	●	●	Extensive Civil War earthwork fortifications; on US 61
K POVERTY POINT P. O. Box 276 Epps, LA 71237-9019 (318) 926-5492	●	●	●	●		●	●	●	●	●	●		3,700-year-old Indian ceremonial center with mounds and earthworks; on La. 577
L REBEL P. O. Box 127 Marthaville, LA 71450 (318) 472-6255	●		●	●				●		●	●		Features Louisiana Country Music Museum and concerts; on La. 1221

INDEX

Abbeville, 262

Abita Springs, 238

Acadia Parish, 201, 251, 254, 258–59

Acadians: and French colonial Louisiana, 11; and Spanish colonial Louisiana, 25–27, 26; music of, 171–72, 230; food of, 178–79, 271; in specific parishes, 201, 218, 230, 242, 245, 246–47, 251, 254–55, 258, 272; in Longfellow's *Evangeline*, 251–52

Adams-Onís Treaty of 1819, p. 256

African Americans. *See* Blacks; Slaves and slavery

Agrarian reformers, 115

Agriculture, 10, 70–75, 115, 210, 242, 257–58. *See also* specific crops and specific parishes

Aime, Valcour, 243

Air force base, 220

Alabama Landing, 209

Albany, 237, 238

Albrizio, Conrad, 176

Alciatore, Antoine, 180

Alexandria, 48, 108, 112, 151, 200, 201, 227–28, 231

Alexis Romanov, grand duke of Russia, 158

Alferez, Enrique, 177

Ali, Muhammad, 149

Allain, Marguerite, 247

Allen, Henry W., 45, 47–48, 245–46, 269

Allen, O. K., 122, 124

Allen, Tom, 149

Allen Parish, 201, 255, 258, 259

Almonester y Roxas, Don Andrés, 110, 173

Alvarez de Piñeda, Alonso, 6

Amans, Jacques, 173

Ambrose, Stephen, 166

American Revolution, 17, 31, 233

Amite, 238

Amoss, Berthe, 165

Anderson, Sherwood, 164

Anderson, T. C., 59

Anderson, Walter, 177

Andrews, John, 246

Anglo-Saxon settlers, 200, 201, 217, 227, 233

Angola, 236, 239

Antrobus, John, 174

Antyllus, 89

Arcadia, 222

Arceneaux, Louis, 252

Archaeological sites, 1, 203, 230

Archimedes, 230

Arlington, Josie, 184

Armstrong, Louis "Satchmo," 158, 169, *170*

Army Corps of Engineers, 98, 103

Art and artists, 173–77

Asbury, Herbert, 183, 190–91

Ascension Parish, 4, 201, 246–48, *247*

Ashe, Thomas, 28

Asiatic cholera, 2, 82, 87–88, 233

Assumption Parish, 202, 272–73

Atchafalaya Basin, 262

Atchafalaya River, 103, 140

Athens, 219, 223

Attakapas Indians, 3, 253, 255, 259

Atz, Jake, 150

Aubry, Charles Philippe, 13, 14, 15

Audubon, John James, 173, 236

Aurore, 23

Aury, Louis-Michel, 63, 144

Austin, Gene, 171

Austin, Moses, 205

Austin, Stephen F., 205

Avery Island, 254, 260

Avoyel Indians, 5, 230

Avoyelles Parish, 5, 56, 200–201, 229–31

Badger, Algernon S., 57

Bailey, Joseph, 48, 201, 227

Baines, George Washington, 218

Baker, Newton D., 185

Balfa, Dewey, 172

Banks, Nathaniel P., 48, 51, 216, 222, 227

Baptist church, 111, 218

Barataria Bay, 140–41

Baratarians, 141–42, 267

Barbé-Marbois, François de, 20

Barges, 99–100

Barksdale Air Force Base, 220

Barksdale, Eugene H., 220

Barthelemy, Sidney J., 69

Baseball, 149–52

Basile, 260

Basketball, 152, 153–54

Basso, Hamilton, 164

Bastrop, 212

Bastrop, Baron de, 205

Baton Rouge: as capital of West Florida, 31; during Civil War, 45, 234; and slave uprising, 62; yellow fever in, 86; as port, 100, 101, 235; and Intracoastal Canal, 101; schools in, 105, 106; LSU in, 107, 108, 118, 125, 152–54, 176, 177, 210, 235, 237; Huey Long's assassination in, 123–24; and levee system, 140; sports in, 150–51; Southern University in, 177; legalized gambling in, 194; city-parish government of, 200, 235; secession vote in, 220; industry in, 235; State Capitol Building in, 235; fetes and fairs in, 237; sightseeing in, 237

Battle of New Orleans, 35–40, 71, 94, 142, 234, 265

Batture Case, 93

Bayou Lafourche, 248, 271, 272, 273, *273*

Bayou L'Argent, 207

Bayou Manchac, 31

Bayou Sara, 32

Bayou Teche, 254

Bayou Terrebonne, 272

Bayougoula Indians, 245, 246

Beaumont, 258

Beauregard, P. G. T., 41, *42*, 43, 192, 259

Beauregard Parish, 201, 255, 256, 259

Bechet, Sidney, 169

Beggs, 261

Behrman, Martin, 185

Bell, John, 41

Belle Rose, 273

Bellisle, François Simars de, 253

Beluche, René, 37
Benjamin, Judah P., 42–43
Bernice, 213
Berwick, Thomas, 254
Bienville, Jean-Baptiste Le Moyne,
  sieur de, 8–12, *11*, 23, 61, 91,
  222, 241–42, 244, 265
Bienville Parish, 200, 216–18, 219,
  222
Bigot, Toussaint-François, 174
Black Code, 51, 61, 109, 113
Black River, 243–44
Blacks: in Civil War, 41–42; during
  Reconstruction, 49–50; lynch-
  ings of, 50, 67; and suffrage, 50,
  51–52, 64–65, 69, 117; and pol-
  itics, 53, 60, 69, 116, 133; and
  Colfax Massacre, 55; repression
  of, 61; and civil rights, 65–69;
  and disease, 85–87; schools for,
  105; and baseball, 149; and zy-
  deco, 172; as artists, 177; and
  soul food, 181–82; and small
  farmers, 229. *See also* Race rela-
  tions; Slaves and slavery
Blanc, Antoine, 110
Blanchard, 223
Blue, Vida, 151
Blues music, 169, 171
Boeing Company, 78
Boeuf River, 209
Bogalusa, 235, 239
Bögel, Philip Hendrik Nering. *See*
  Bastrop, Baron de
Boggs, Hale, 128, 132
Bolden, Buddy, 169
Bolívar, Simón, 144
Bondurant, Albert, 107
Boothville, 275
Boré, Etienne, 71, 242

Bossier, Pierre-Evariste, 222
Bossier City, 101, 108, 194
Bossier Parish, 53, 67, 200, 220, 222
Boswell Sisters, 171
Bosworth, Sheila, 163
Bouanchaud, Hewitt, 119
Bouligny, Francisco, 17
Bourbons, 60, 64–65, 69, 115–17.
  See also Democratic Party
Bowie, Jim, 244
Boxing, 148–49, *150*
Boyd, David French, 106–107
Boyd, Thomas D., 107
Bradford, Roark, 164
Bradshaw, Terry, 152, *153*
Bragg, Braxton, 41
Braithwaite, 275
Breaux Bridge, 171, 262
Breckinridge, John C., 41, 45
Bridge City, 267, 274
Bristow, Gwen, 163
Britain. *See* Great Britain
Brooklyn, 43
Broussard, 261
Brown, Charles H., 145
Brown, Joe, 149
Brown, Tom, 169
Brown v. Board of Education, 66, 67,
  69
Brown-Guillory, Elizabeth, 166
Brusly, 249
Bry, Henry, 203
Bryan, William Jennings, 220
Bubonic plague, 88
Buck, William H., 174
Buckner, Simon, 48
Bunkie, 231
Burke, James "Deaf," 148
Burke, James Lee, 164
Burnside, 248

Burnside, John, 247
Bush, George, 132
Bush, 238
Butler, Benjamin Franklin, 45, 47, 51, 85, 105, 248
Butler, Robert Olen, 164

Cabeza de Vaca, Alvar Núñez, 6
Cable, George Washington, 162, 163
Caddo Indians, 1, 3, 5, 217, 221–22, 223
Caddo Lake, 77
Caddo Parish, 56, 58, 67, 76–77, 200, 220, 221, 223
Cagle, Christian Keener "Red," 152
Cajuns. *See* Acadians
Calcasieu Parish, 75–76, 199, 201, 215, 255–56, 259
Caldwell, Matthew, 211
Caldwell Parish, 200, 203, 209, 211
Callahan, Dan, 148
Callender, E. Arthur, 175
Cameron, 260
Cameron Parish, 138, 199, 201, 255, 259–60
Camp Beauregard, 228
Camp Claiborne, 228
Camp Livingston, 228
Camp Salubrity, 215
Canals, 98, 99, 101, 267
Canary Islanders, 17, 25, 268
Canby, E. R. S., 48
Cannon, Billy, 152–53
Cannon, J. W., 96
Canova, Dominique, 174
Canzoneri, Tony, 149
Carolina, 36, 38
Carondelet, Baron Francisco Luis Héctor de, 17, 205

Carpenter, Charles, 209
Carpetbaggers, 51, 105
Carresse, Pierre, 15
Carroll, Charles, 205–206
Carter, George W., 199, 255
Carver, Ada Jack, 163
Carville, 88, 246
Casey, James F., 53
Caso Calvo, Sebastián de, 17
Castro, fidel, 30
Catahoula Lake, 211, 231
Catahoula Leopard Dog, 210–11
Catahoula Parish, 200, 210–11, 211
Catholic church. *See* Roman Catholic church
Cattle, 253, 256
Cavelier, Jean, 6
Cedar Ota, 236
Centerville, 262
Central Louisiana parishes, 200–201, 226, 227–31
César, 14
Chackbay, 274
Chalmette, 275
Chambers, Henry E., 166
Charenton, 262
Charles III, king of Spain, 12, 14, 15
Charles, Robert, 66–67
Charlevoix, François-Xavier, 109, 161
Chase, Philander, 110
Chautauqua, 220
Chauvin, 272, 276
Chawasha Indians, 4
Chenier, Clifton, 172
Chennault, Claire Lee, 210
Chesapeake-Leopard affair, 93
Chew, Beverly, 144, 145

Chiapella, Celestin, 268

Chitimacha Indians, 3

Choctaw Indians, 3, 4, 5

Cholera, 2, 82, 87–88, 233

Chopin, Kate, 162–63

Christ Church, 110

Chrysler Corporation, 78

Church Point, 258

City of Alto, 209

Civil rights, 65–69

Civil War: and blacks, 41–42, 63; and secession movement, 41, 220, 229; and New Orleans, 43–45; Baton Rouge during, 45, 234; and Mississippi River, 46–47, 206; Vicksburg campaign, 46–47, 200, 206–207; Port Hudson during, 47, 202, 234; Red River campaign, 48, 201, 216, 222, 227; Shreveport during, 48, 200, 222, 257; and economy, 73; and shipping, 95–96; and education, 104–105; in northeast Louisiana, 206–208; Battle of Mansfield, 222, 223; in central Louisiana, 227, 229; and deserting Confederates, 229; Lake Pontchartrain during, 234; Donaldsonville during, 247–48; Franklin Battle in, 254; in southwest Louisiana, 254, 257

Clague, Richard, 174

Claiborne, William C. C.: and Louisiana Purchase, 21; as governor, 28, 256; and West Florida, 34, 233; and yellow fever, 84; and Batture Case, 93; and steamboats, 94; and education, 104; and Lafitte,

142; miniature of, 173; and duels, 190; parish named for, 223

Claiborne Parish, 56, 200, 218–19, 223

Clapp, Theodore, 112–13

Clark, Daniel, 190

Claudel, Alice, 165

Clay, Henry, 269

Clement, Jules, 76

Cliburn, Van, 168

Cline, Isaac M., 137–38

Clinton, 237

Cloutierville, 224

Coburn, Joe, 149

Code Noir, 51, 61, 109, 113

Codrescu, Andrei, 166

Colbert, Jean-Baptiste, 91

Coleman, J. A., 228

Coleman, Lula V., 228

Coleman, William H., 179–80

Colfax, 231

Colfax Massacre, 54–55, 230

Collas, Louis-Antoine, 173

Colleges, 106–108. *See also* specific colleges

Collin, Richard, 179

Collin, Rima, 179

Colmer, George, 236–37

Columbia, 203, 211

Cometa, 144

Comité des Citoyens, 66

Company of the Indies, 4, 10, 23, 241, 244–45

Company of the West, 9–10

Concordia Parish, *139*, 201, 243–44, 248

Connell, Clyde, 177

Connick, Harry, Jr., 172

Conrad, T. A., 203

Conservative Democrats, 52, 54, 229

Constitution, 87

Convent, 106, 242–43, 249

Cook, Philip Charles, 216

Corbett, "Gentleman Jim," 149, *150*

Cordero y Bustamente, Antonio, 256

Cornelius, Elias, 112

Costello, Frank, 267

Cotton production: post–Civil War, 52; and black labor, 61; and slavery, 63, 70, 73; and economy, 71–72; and trade, 92; in specific parishes, 201, 208–209, 229, 245, 256; and New Orleans, 266

Coulon, George David, 174

Country-and-western music, 171

Courtney, Ezra, 111

Coushatta Indians, 3

Coushatta, 56, 224

Covington, 112, 164, 238

Crawford, Josephine, 176

Creecy, James, 72, 79

Creole, 146

Creoles, 13–14, 27, 27n, 178–79, 190–91, 202, 218, 256, 266

Cropdusting services, 210

Crowley, 75, 151, 254, 258–59

Crozat, Antoine, 9, 61, 70

Cruise, Boyd, 177

Cuba, 84, 145–47

Cut Off, 274

Cyr, Paul, 122

D'Abrado, Marchioness, 13

Daniels, Josephus, 185

D'Arensbourg, Karl Friedrich, 242

Darrow, 248

Davis, E. A., 166

Davis, Jefferson, 41, 44

Davis, Jimmie H., 69, 127, 129–30, 171, 218

Davis, Mollie Moore, 163

Dédé, Sanité, 196

Degas, Edgar, 174, *175*

De la Houssaye, Sidonie, 162

De Lassus, Carlos de Hault, 32–33

De Laussat, Pierre Clément, 20–22

Delcambre, 262

Delgado, Isaac, 175

Delgado Museum of Art, 175, *176*

Delhi, 212

Delta Airlines, 210

Democratic Party: and Reconstruction, 53–54, 58, 219–20; and black suffrage, 64; political power of, 117, 132; election of 1940 and, 126; and primaries, 130–31; and Lincoln Parish, 220; Locofocos, 269–70. *See also* Bourbons

Dempsey, Jack, 149

Dennard, John, 218

Dennard, Thomas, 218

De Noux, O'Neil, 164

DeQuincy, 259

De Ridder, 259

Des Allemands, 249

Desdunes, Daniel F., 66

Desforges, Jean, 141, 145

De Soto, Hernando, 1–2, 75, 211, 223

De Soto Parish, 200, 222, 223

Destréhan de Beaupré, Jean-Baptiste, 267

Destréhan de Tours, Jean Nöel, 243

Detchéparre, Captain, 4
Dillard University, 177
Diseases, 2, 82–88, 85, 233
Dixon, David F., 155–56, *156*
Dobbs, Johnny, 150
Domino, Fats, 171
Donaldson, William, 247
Donaldsonville, 86, 246, 247, 248
Dorr, J. W., 209, 218, 244, 247
Double Dealer, 164–65
Douglas, Stephen A., 41
Dow, Lorenzo, 111
Doyline, 225
Drake, Benjamin A.; 111
Drake, Ruben, 229
Driskill Mountain, 222
Drysdale, Dr., 86
DuBroc, Jacques, 242
Dubus, Andre, 164
Duc de Maine, 23
Duels, 190–91, 244
Duffy, John, 83, 84
Duke, David, 132–33
Dunbar-Nelson, Alice, 163
Duncan, Abner L., 144
Duncan, J. K., 45
Dunn, C. T., 208–209
Dunn, Oscar J., 53
Dupré, Alexander, 272
Dureau, George, 177
Durieux, Caroline, 176
Du Ru, Paul, 161, 246
Duval, Ambrose, 173
Dyer, Isidore, 88
Dysentery, 88

Eads, James B., 98
Early, Jubal, 192
Earthquakes, 206
East Bank, 249

East Baton Rouge Parish, 34, 58,
    200, 202, 234–35, 237
East Carroll Parish, 200, 205, 206,
    207, 211
East Feliciana Parish, 34, 58, 111,
    202, 234, 237
Economy: and Civil War, 52,
    63–64, 73; and black labor, 61,
    73–74; of French colonial
    Louisiana, 70; and industry, 70,
    72–73, 79; and natural re-
    sources, 70, 80; of Spanish colo-
    nial Louisiana, 70–71; and yel-
    low fever, 86; and rivers, 91–94,
    97–98, 100–101, 220; and poli-
    tics, 115. *See also* specific in-
    dustries
Education: and Ursuline nuns, 10,
    104; and Reconstruction, 64,
    105; integration of schools, 66,
    67, 69, 104, 106; funding for,
    104, 106; in public schools,
    104–106; higher, 106–108
Edwards, Edwin W., 69, 130–34,
    194
Effinger, George, 165
Eisenhower, Dwight, 128, 228
Elections, 53–54, 58–59, 64–65,
    115–17, 119, 126, 130. *See also*
    politicians and political parties
Eliche, Marc, 230
Elizabeth (town), 259
Ellender, Allen J., 132
Elton, 261
Emery, Lin, 177
Empire, 275
England. *See* Great Britain
Enterprise, 38, 94
Episcopal church, 110, 111
Epps, 213

Era No. 10, p. 209
Eunice, 108, 261
Evangeline, 251–52
Evangeline Parish, 201, 251, 255, 260

False River, 244
Farmer's Alliance, 229
Farmerville, 213
Farragut, David G., 43, 44–45, 234, 247–48, 266
Faser, Chris, 130
Faulkner, William, 164
Faye, Stanley, 145
Feibleman, James, 164
Feibleman, Peter S., 178
Feliciana, 32
Ferguson, John H., 66
Ferriday, *139*, 171
Fields, Cleo, 133
Filhiol, Don Juan, 205
Filibusters, 145–47
Fillmore, Millard, 148
Finlay, Carlos, 86–87
Fishing, as sport, 155, 254, 255, 268
Fishing industry, 75, 268, 271–72
Fitzsimmons, Bob, 149
Flatboats, 94, 95, 99
Flint, Timothy, 112
Floods, 138–40, 192, 243–44. *See also* Levee systems
Florida Parishes, 201–202, *232*, 233–39
Florien, 225
Flying Tigers, 210
Fontenot, Mary Alice, 165
Food, 178–82, 242, 271
Football, 148, 152–53
Ford, Richard, 164

Fort Jackson, 275
Fort Jesup, 216, 225
Fort Miró, 205
Fort Mississippi, 269
Fort Necessity, 210
Fort Polk, 257, 263
Fort Rosalie, 4
Fort St. Philip, 44, 98, 269
Fortier, Alcée, 166
Foster, Murphy J., 116
Foster, Murphy J. "Mike," 133, 194
Foster, Pop, 169
Foucault, Nicolas, 13, 14, 15
Fountain, Pete, 159, 169, *170*
Fourage, Elizabeth, 110
Fournet, John B., 120, 123, 124
Fowler, Trevor Thomas, 173
France, 11, 12, 18, 19, 31, 92, 141
Frank, Charley, 150
Franklin (town), 262
Franklin, Battle of, 254
Franklin Parish, 200, 209, 210, 211–12
Franklinton, 111, 239
Freeman, Douglas Southall, 45
French colonial Louisiana, 6–11, 18, 23, 61, 70, 91, 110, 215, 241
French and Indian War. *See* Seven Years' War
French Opera House, 167, *168*
French Quarter, 80, 81, 164–65, 176, 183, 193
French Settlement, 236, 238
Frogmore, 248
Fulton, Robert, 94
Fuqua, Henry L., 119
Fusion party, 116

Gaines, Ernest, 164, *165*
Gallatin Street, 184, 193

Galliano, 274

Galouye, Dan, 165

Galveston, Tex., 129, 137, 254

Galveston Bay, 143

Gálvez, Bernardo de, 17, 31–32, 136, 161, 233, 237, 268

Gambling, 133, 194, 209. *See also* Louisiana Lottery

Gas industry. *See* Oil and gas industry

Gayarré, Charles, 166, 190

Gaynor, Le Bray de, 255

German Coast, 24, 188, 241–43

German immigrants: and French colonial Louisiana, 10, 23–25; and Ulloa, 14; and Acadians, 27; settlement of, 29–30, 201, 241–42, 254, 258; and Lutheran church, 113

Germantown, 219, 225

Geydan, 262

Gibbs, Samuel, 39

Gibsland, 222

Gibson, D. W., 210

Gibson, Tobias, 110

Gilbert, Larry, 150

Gilbert, Philip, 121

Gilbert, 211–12

Gilchrist, Ellen, 163

Giliasso, Louis, 77

Gillis W. Long Hansen's Disease Center, 246

Gilmore, Sam, 164

Glapion, Christophe Duminy, 197

Goentgen, Johann, 219

Golf, 155

Gonzales, 248

Gordy, Robert, 177

Gottschalk, Louis Moreau, 167–68

Governor Moore, 44

Grambling State, 108, 152

Gramercy, 249

Grand Chenier, 260

Grand Coteau, 261

Grand Gulf, 46

Grand Island, 137

Grand Isle, 267, 273, 274

Grande Terre, 142, 267

Grant, Ulysses S., 46–48, 52, 54–55, 58, 206–207, 215, 229, 231

Grant Parish, 199, 201, 230, 231

Grau, Shirley Ann, 163

Gravier, John, 93

Great Britain: and maritime trade, 13, 16, 141; and West Florida, 31, 92, 201, 233; and War of 1812, pp. 35–40, 93, 142; and Seven Years' War, 92; and Honduras, 147

Great Raft logjam, 101, 220–21, *221*, 230

Greene, Allen,, 219–20

Greensburg, 238

Gregory, Angela, 177, 246

Gretna, 151, 267, 268, 274

Grétry, André, 167

Grevemberg, Francis C., 128

Grymes, John R., 144

Guerre, Louis, 124

Guidry, Geneus, 253

Guidry, Ron, 151

Guiraud, Ernest, 167–68

Gulf Intracoastal Waterway, 101, 267

Gulf of Mexico, 75, 77, 78, 101, 138, 141, 142, 145, 155, 248, 255

Hachard, Marie Madeleine, 161

Hackberry, 260

Hahn, Michael, 51
Hahnville, 188
Hair, William Ivy, 61, 65, 67
Haiti, 62, 195
Hall, Weeks, 176
Hammond, 108, 236, 238
Hampton, Wade, 148, 247
Hansen's disease, 88, 246
Harahan, 267
Hardin, J. Fair, 166
Hardtner, Henry, 74–75
Hardy, Arthur, 157
Harlan, John Marshall, 66
Harlan, Richard, 203
Harrah's Jazz Co., 194
Harrell, Kenneth Earl, 67
Harriman, Jon, 257
Harrison, Benjamin, 193
Harrisonburg, 210, 211
Hart, Toby, 150
Hartford, 44
Harvey, Horace, 267
Harvey, Joseph, 267
Harvey (town), 267
Hayden, Frank, 177
Hayes, Elvin, 154
Hayes, Rutherford B., 58–60
Haynesville, 223
Hearn, Lafcadio, 135–36
Hearsey, Henry J., 50
Hebert, F. Edward, 125, 132
Heldner, Knute, 175, 176
Hellman, Lillian, 163
Henderson, 262
Hennessy, David C., 186–89, *187*
Herman, Pete, 149
Heuser, Elizabeth, 219
Heywood brothers, 258
Heywood Company, 76
Higgins, Andrew J., 78

Higher education, 106–108. *See also* specific colleges and universities
Hirt, Al, 169, *170*
Hitler, Adolph, 132
Hitt, Homer L., 108
Homer (town), 219, 223
Hoover, Herbert, 139
Horn Island, 177
Horse racing, 148
Houma, 77, 151, 272, 275, 276
Houma Indians, 3–4, 246
Hudson, Julian, 174
Hull, Edgar, 123
Hunter, Clementine, 177
Hunting, 155, 218–19, 254, 255
Hurricanes, 135–38, *137*, 255
Hurston, Zora Neale, 163

Iberia Parish, 56, 201, 251, 253, 254, 260
Iberville, Pierre Le Moyne, sieur d', 8–9, 244, 246, 248
Iberville Parish, 201, 246, 248
Illnesses. *See* Diseases
Immigrants, 28–30, 186–88, 236, 237, 253, 255, 258. *See also* specific ethnic groups
Independence, 238
Indians. *See* Native Americans
Indigo, 23, 70–71, *71*, 229, 242
Industrial Canal, 99
Industry. *See* Economy; fishing industry; Lumber industry; Oil and gas industry; Space industry
Integration, 66, 67, 69, 104, 106. *See also* Civil rights; Race relations
Intracoastal Canal, 101

Irwin, Samuel W., 257
Isleños. *See* Canary Islanders

Jack, Madame, 144
Jackson, Andrew, 36–40, 39, 94,
    142, 219, 223, 234, 265
Jackson, Mahalia, 169
Jackson, Mary Jane, 184
Jackson, Stonewall, 45
Jackson, Miss., 97, 106, 237
Jackson Parish, 200, 218, 219,
    223–24, 229
James Monroe, 205
Jamison, Cecilia V., 165
Jaume, Alexandre-Charles, 173
Jay, John, 17
Jazz, 169, 183, 185, 266
Jeanerette, 151, 260
Jefferson, Blind Lemon, 169
Jefferson, Thomas, 17–18, 19, 28,
    93
Jefferson Davis Parish, 201, 254,
    255, 257–58, 260–61
Jefferson Island, 260
Jefferson Parish, 202, 267, 273–74
Jena, 231
Jenkins, Louise Reynes, 165
Jennings, 76, 258, 261
Jews, 109, 112, 113–14
Jim Crow laws, 50, 64, 149, 188
John Paul II, 110
Johnson, Andrew, 51, 52
Johnson, Bunk, 169
Johnson, David B., 102–103
Johnson, Lyndon Baines, 218
Johnson, Robert, 141, 145
Johnston, J. Bennett, 130
Johnston, William Preston, 107
Joliet, Louis, 91
Jones, Evan, 247

Jones, Sam Houston, 126–27
Jones, Thomas A. Catesby, 36
Jonesboro, 218, 224
Jonesville, 211
Jordan family, 172
Joutel, Henry de, 161
Judaism. *See* Jews
Judice, Alcide, 105
Julio, Everett B. D. Fabrino, 174

Kaintocks, 27–28
Karberg, Peter, 208
Katz, Allan, 131
Kazmann, Raphael G., 102–103
Keane, John, 39
Keatchie, 223
Keelboats, 94, 95
Kellogg, William Pitt, 53–58
Kelso, Iris, 129
Kendall, John Smith, 166
Kennedy, John F., 78
Kenner, 273, 274
Kennon, Beverly, 44
Kennon, Robert F., 127, 128–29
Kentwood, 238
Kerlérec, Louis Billouart de, 11
Kerr-McGee company, 77
Keyes, Frances Parkinson, 162–63
Kilrain, Jake, 149
Kinder, 259
King, Alvin O., 122
King, Grace, 162–63
KKK. *See* Ku Klux Klan
Knapp, Seaman A., 75
Knights of Labor, 65
Knights of the White Camellia, 53,
    254
Kohlmeyer, Ida, 177
Koasati Indians. *See* Coushatta
    Indians

Ku Klux Klan, 53, 67, 118, 132, 254

La Farge, Oliver, 164
La Frénière, Nicolas Chauvin de, 13, 14, 15
La Mothe Cadillac, Antoine de, 10
LaPlace, 249
La Salle, Robert Cavelier de, 6–8, 7, 91, 109, 161, 231, 268
La Salle Parish, 201, 210–11, 228, 231
Labiche, Emmeline, 252
Lacombe, 238
Lafayette, 75, 77, 108, 151, 172, 201, 253, 261
Lafayette Parish, 105, 201, 251, 253, 254, 261
Lafitte, Jean, 35–36, 63, 142–43, *143*, 254–55, 266–67
Lafitte, Pierre, 142, *143*, 144
Lafitte (town), 273–74
Lafourche Parish, 202, 271, 274
Lake Bruin, 207, 212
Lake Charles, 75, 100, 101, *102*, 108, 151, 201, 255–56, 259
Lake D'Arbonne, 213
Lake Pontchartrain, 99, 140, 155, 233, 267
Lake Providence, 206, 211
Lake St. Joseph, 207
Lake Verret, 273
Lambert, John, 38–40
Lamour, Dorothy, 171
Landrieu, Mary, 133
Landrieu, Moon, 69
Lane, Mrs. James Tyson, 181
Lane, Pinkie Gordon, 165
Lanier, Richard, 112
Lardner, Ring, 160

Larned, Sylvester, 112
Larose, 138, 274
Last Island, 135–37, 137
Latour, A. Lacarrière, 36–37
Latour, Malvina, 196
Latrobe, Benjamin, 84
Laveau, Marie, 195–97, *196*
Law, John, 9–10, *24*, 61, 70, 91, 113, 241, 244
Lazear, Jesse, 87
Le Page du Pratz, Antoine Simon, 161
Lea, Fannie Heaslip, 163
Leathers, T. P., 96
Lebeau, 171
LeBlanc, Désiré, 246
Leche, Richard W., 124–26, 128
Lecompte, 231
Ledbetter, Huddie "Leadbelly," 169
Lee, fitzhugh, 220
Lee, Robert E., 48, 200
Leesville, 257, 263
Lefort, Julien, 137
Lemann, Nancy, 164
Lemos, Manuel Luís Gayoso de, 17
Leon, Count de, 219
Leonard, Gilbert, 269
Leopard, 93
Leprosy, 88, 246
Les Cenelles, 162, 165
Levee systems, 73, 92, 139–40
Lewis, Jerry Lee, 171
Lewis, Micajah, 190
L'Hermitage, *247*
Liberty Place, Battle of, 57, *57*
Lincoln, Abraham, 41, 43, 50–51, 95, 224
Lincoln Parish, 56, 199, 200, 219–20, 224
Literature, 161–66

Livaudais, François de, 148

Livingston, Edward, 93, 144, 237

Livingston, Robert R., 19–20, 94, 237

Livingston (town), 238

Livingston Parish, 34, 202, 236–38

Llulla, Pépé, 191

Lock, Louis, 210

Locofocos, 269–70

Logansport, 223

Lomax, John, 169

Long, Blanche, 129

Long, Earl K., 105–108, 115, 124–30, 201, 228, 270

Long, Gillis W., 130

Long, Huey Pierce: compared with Warmoth, 52; and education, 105, 107; career of, 115, 117–24; picture of, *118*; compared with Edwards, 133–34; and Warren, 164; and specific parishes, 201, 228, 229, 270

Long, John Murphy, 228

Long, Julius, 128

Long, Rose, 128

Long, Russell B., 115, 127–28, 132

Long, Speedy O., 130

Longfellow, Henry Wadsworth, 251–52, 260

Longstreet, James, 57

LOOP (Louisiana Offshore Oil Port), 101

López, Narciso, 145–47

Lottery, territorial, 104

Louis IX, king of France, 109

Louis XIV, king of France, 6–7, 8, 109

Louis XV, king of France, 4, 12, 25, 109

Louis, Jean, 89

Louis-Philippe, king of France, 245

Louisiana: as French colony, 6–11, 18, 23, 61, 70, 91, 110, 215, 241; as Spanish colony, 12–18, 19, 31, 70–71, 110, 215, 254; Americanization of, 19–22; Territory of Orleans, 28–29, 34, 62–63, 199, 234, 243, 271; and secession, 41, 229; constitutions of, 52, 105, 130; parishes of, *198*, 199–276. *See also* specific towns, cities, and parishes

Louisiana (gunboat), 38

Louisiana (ironclad), 44

Louisiana Lottery, 115–16, 192–94

Louisiana Offshore Oil Port (LOOP), 101

Louisiana Purchase, 19, 20, *21*, 32, 215, 216, 265

Louisiana State Normal School, 107

Louisiana State Seminary of Learning and Military Academy, 42, 106–107, 227

Louisiana State University, 107, 108, 118, 125, 152–54, 176, 177, 210, 235, 237

Louisiana Superdome, 81, 155–56, *156*

Louisiana Tech, 152

Louisiana Tigers, 41, 43, 146

Lovell, Mansfield, 43–45

Lucas, Anthony, 76

Luling, 249

Lumber industry, 74–75, 229, 233, 235–36, 255, 258, 266

Lutcher, 249

Lutheran church, 112, 113

Luxembourg, Raphaël de, 104, 109–10

Lynch, Bill, 131–32
Lynchings, 50, 67, 188
Lyon, John, 254

Mace, Jim "Gypsy," 149
Maddox, Thomas H., 244
Madewood, *273*
Madison, James, 35, 256
Madison Parish, 200, 206, 207,
    210, 212
Madisonville, 238
Maestri, Robert S., 124, 189
"Mafia lynching," 186–89
Malaria, 88
Mamou, 260
Manassas, 44
Manchac, 238
Manchac Swamp, 236
Mandeville, 234, 238
Mansfield, 151, 222, 223
Mansfield, Battle of, 222, 223
Mansura, 230, 231
Many, 225
Maravich, Pete, 154
Marcello, Carlos, 186
Mardi Gras, 80, 157–60, *159*, 266
Mardi Gras Indians, 160
Marigny de Mandeville, Antoine-
    Jacques Philippe de, 173
Marigny de Mandeville, Bernard
    Xavier de, 268
Marigny de Mandeville, Pierre
    Philippe Enguerrand de, 268
Marksville, 230, 231
Marksville Culture, 230
Marquette, Jacques, 91
Marquis, Pierre, 15
Marrero, 267
Marsalis family, 172
Marshall, Bob, 155

Marthaville, 224
Martin, François Xavier, 166
Martin, Valerie, 164
Mason, James M., 43
Matas, Rudolph, 87, 89–90
Mathews, 274
Matranga family, 186
McClure, John, 164, 166
McCrady, John, 175
McEnery, John, 54–55, 57
McEnery, Samuel D., 116
McIntosh, James M.,
    254–55
McKeithen, John J., 69, 130
McLaughlin, John, 148–49
McNeese State, 152
McRae, 44
Medical care, 82–83, 89. *See also*
    Diseases
Melrose, 177
Membré, Zenobius, 109
Memphis, Tenn., 86
Mer Rouge, 212
Meraux, 275
Mercier, Alfred, 161
Metairie, Jacques de la, 161
Metairie (town), 274
Methodist church, 110–11
Mexican War, 215, 216
Michoud factory, 78
Middleton, Troy H., 108
Mile Branch Settlement, 239
Milhet, Joseph, 15
Miller, James, 207
Millet, Clarence, 176
Mills, Frank, 272
Minden, 225
Miró, Esteban, 17, 27
Mississippi (ironclad), 44
Mississippi (steamer), 56

Mississippi River: Spanish closing of, 17–18, 92; and shipping, 18, 73, 92, 94–96; and German immigrants, 24; steamboats on, 29, 94–97, 96, 99, 209, 234; and Battle of New Orleans, 35; and Civil War, 43, 46–47, 206; levee system for, 73, 92, 139–40; industry along, 79, 100–101, 201, 235; as tourist attraction, 81; and French, 91–92, 109; names for, 91; and British, 92; barges on, 99–100; picture of, *100*; change in course of, 102–103; flooding of, 138–40, *139*, 192, 243–44; and art, 173

Mitchell, William, 144–45

Moedinger, Christian Gottlieb, 113

Monroe, James, 19, 20

Monroe (town), 150–51, 154, 209, 212, 218

Moore, John Preston, 15

Moore, Thomas O., 41

Mooringsport, 76, 169, 223

Morancy, Emile, 206

Morancy, Honoré, 205–206

Morehouse, Abraham, 205, 212

Morehouse Parish, 200, 205, 208, 212

Morgan, Cecil, 120

Morgan, Lewis, 127

Morgan City, 46, 77, 86, 97, 262

Morial, Ernest N., 69

Morial, Marc, 69

Morrison, deLesseps S., 128–30

Morton, Ferdinand "Jelly Roll," 169, *170*

Moscoso de Alvarado, Luis de, 6

Moss, N. P., 105

Mount Lebanon, 222

Mouton, Alfred, 48

Mueller, Maximilian. *See* Leon, Count de

Murray, Rai Greiner, 177

Murtaugh, Danny, 150

Music and musicians, 167–72

Musson, Estelle, 174

Myrtle Grove, 275

Napoleon Bonaparte, 19–20, 40, 71

Napoleon III, 43

Napoleonville, 273, *273*

Narváez, Pánfilo de, 6

Natchez Indians, 4–5, 25

Natchez, Miss., 31, 228, 243

Natchez, 96–97

Natchitoches (town), 68, 107, 108, 162, 215, 216, 224, 256

Natchitoches Parish, 56, 58, 200, 215, 220, 224

Native Americans: in Louisiana, 1–5; sketch of, *2*; and settlers, 9, 25; in specific parishes, 203, 215, 217, 221–22, 230, 242, 245–46, 253, 268–69; Jackson's campaign against, 234. *See also* names of specific tribes

Natural gas. *See* Oil and gas industry

Natural resources, 70, 80, 106, 229, 256. *See also* fishing industry; Lumber industry; Oil and gas industry

Neutral Strip, 200, 201, 216, 256, 257

Neutrality Act, 146

Neville Brothers, 172

New Acadia, 254

New Iberia, 151, 177, 260

New Orleans: and Bienville, 10, 91; as commercial center, 18, 19, 93–94, 266; as entry port for immigrants, 29; population of, 29, 72; fall of, during Civil War, 43–45, *45*; Federal occupation of, 45–46, *46*; during Reconstruction, 51–52, 54–59; and Norco salve uprising, 62; blacks in, 66–67, 69; riots in, 66–67, 147; integration in, 67, 69; mayors of, 69, 189; schools in, 69, 104, 105, 107–108; industry in, 70; as port, 70, 72, 92–99, *96*, 102; space industry in, 70, 78–79; World War II torpedo boats and landing craft built in, 70, 78; French Quarter in, 80, 81, 109–10, 164–65, 176, 183, 193; Mardi Gras in, 80, 157–60, *159*, 266; and tourism, 80–81; Superdome in, 81; cholera in, 82, 87–88; yellow fever epidemics in, 82–87; bubonic plague in, 88; as medical center, 89, 89–90; growth of, 92; railroads in, 97; Dock Board in, 98–99; Industrial Canal in, 99; colleges and universities in, 106–108; churches in, 109–11, 112–13; Jews in, 113–14; and politics, 121–22, 266; and hurricanes, 135–37, 138; flood protection in, 140; smugglers in, 142; and privateering, 144; and horse racing, 148; sports in, 153, 156; golf and tennis in, 155; literary figures in, 161–65; music and musicians in, 167, 169, *170*, 171, 183–85; opera in, 167–68, *168*; and art, 173–77, *176*; food in, 178, 179–80, 242; prostitution in, 183–85; and the Mafia, 186–89; dueling in, 190–91; legalized gambling in, 194; voodooism in, 195–97, *196*; and parish government, 200; founding of, 202; as capital, 246; and southeast Louisiana parishes, 265–67; fetes and fairs in, 274–75; sightseeing in, 274

New Orleans Associates, 144

New Orleans, Battle of, 35–40, 71, 94, 142, 234, 265

New Orleans Museum of Art, 175, *176*, 177

New Orleans Saints, 153, 156

New Orleans (steamboat), 94

New Roads, 249

Newcomb College, 106, 174, 176, 177

Newellton, 207, 212

Nicholls, Francis T., 58–60, 193

Nicholls State, 152

Nicholson, James W., 107

Ninas, Paul, 176

Noe, James A. "Jimmy," 124–26

Noguchi, Hideyo, 87

Norco, 62

Northeast Louisiana parishes, 200, 203, *204*, 205–211

Northup, Solomon, 166

Northwest Louisiana parishes, 200, *214*, 215–25

Northwestern State University, 152

Noyan, Jean-Baptiste, 15

Nunez, Sammy, 133

Nutt, Haller, 207

Oak Grove, 213
Oakdale, 259
Oberlin, 258, 259
Ochsner, Alton, 90
O'Donnell, E. P., 164
Oil City, 76, 223
Oil and gas industry: and economy, 70, 73, 75–80, 115; rise of, 75–77, 100–101, 210, 257–58; offshore, 77, 78, 79, 272; and hurricanes, 138; in specific parishes, 201, 228, 242, 254, 257–58, 267, 270, 272; and New Orleans, 266
Old Regulars, 115, 121, 127
Oliver, King, 169
O'Neal, Shaquille, 154, *154*
O'Neill, Charles E., 109
Opelousas, 45, 53, 85, 106, 111, 222, 257
Opera, 167
O'Reilly, Alexander "Bloody," 14–15, *16*, 195, 242
Orleans Parish, 200, 202, 265–66, 274–75
O'Rourke, Sam, 148
Osbey, Brenda Marie, 166
Ott, Mel, 151, *151*
Ouachita City, 209
Ouachita Indians, 212
Ouachita Parish, 58, 67, 200, 209, 210, 212
Ouachita River, 207, 209
Overton, John H., 127
Overton (town), 219
Owen, Richard, 203
Oxley, James, 111

Packard, Stephen B., 53, 58–60
Pacquet, Charles, 243

Pakenham, Sir Edward, 36–39
Palmer, Benjamin Morgan, 112
Paris, Jacques, 197
Parish, Robert, 154
Parishes, 199–276. *See also* specific parishes
Parker, John M., 107, 117–19, 228
Parlor City, 209
Pastrano, Willie, 149
Patti, Adelina, 167
Pauger, Adrien, 10
Peckinpaugh, Roger, 150
Peñalver y Cárdenas, Don Luis de, 173
Pénicaut, André, 161
Penn, D. B., 57–58
People's Party, 115, 116, 229
Percy, Mrs. Robert, 236
Percy, Walker, 164
Perez, Leander, 270–71
Périer, Etienne, 4
Perry, Oliver Hazard, 35
Petroleum industry. *See* Oil and gas industry
Pettit, Bob, 154
Peytavin, Antoine, 246
Pharr, John N., 116
Phélypeaux, Louis de, 8
Phillipon, Antoine, 268
Phoenix, 269
Pickles, William, 233–34
Pierson, David, 229
Pike, Zebulon M., 256
Pinchback, P. B. S., 53, 65
Pineville, 108, 227
Pipelines, 102
Pirates and privateers, 63, 141–45, 206, 254–55
Pitot, Henry C., 28

Pitot, James, 27–28
Plaisance, 171
Plaquemine, 86, 248
Plaquemines Parish, 101, 138, 202, 268–71, 275
Plattenville, 272, 273
Pleasant, Ruffin G., 117–18
Pleasant Hill, 48, 225
Plessy, Homer Adolph, 66, 266
Plessy v. Ferguson, 65–66
Pointe Coupée, 62
Point Coupée Parish, 164, 201, 229, 243, 244–45, 248
Pointe Coupée Post, 245
Politics: during Reconstruction, 51–56, 105, 115; in 1890s, 115–17; and Huey Long, 117–24, 133–34; and Earl Long, 124–30; and Edwards, 130–34. *See also* specific political parties and politicians
Polk, James K., 146, 269
Polk, Leonidas, 41, 272–73
Pollock, 231
Pomarede, Leon, 174
Ponchatoula, 238
Pontchartrain, Lake, 99, 140, 155, 233, 267
Population: of Native Americans, 2–3; of Spanish colonial Louisiana, 17, 25–27; of French colonial Louisiana, 23–25; of Territory of Orleans, 28–29, 62; diversity of, 29–30; of New Orleans, 29; during Reconstruction, 49; of slaves, 62, 73; and statehood, 72. *See also* Immigrants; specific ethnic groups
Populists, 115–17, 229

Port Allen, 246, 249
Port Hudson, 47, 202, 234
Port of South Louisiana, 101
Port Vincent, 236
Porter, David Dixon, 44, 48, 227
Ports, 91–103. *See also* specific cities
Poverty Point Culture, 1, 203
Powell, Abner, 150
Poydras, Julien, 62, 104, 161, 245
Prairieville, 248
Presbyterians, 111–13
Presley, Elvis, 171
Prévost, François Marie, 89
Price, Sterling, 48
Prieur, Denis, 190
Prizefighting, 148–49, *150*
Progressive Party, 117
Prostitution, 183–85
Protestants, 110–13, 218, 266. *See also* names of specific denominations
Provenzano family, 186
Pugh family, 272

Quincy, Josiah, 245
Quintero, José, 191

Rabalais, Joseph, 229
Race relations: and white supremacy, 49–50, 55–59, 64, 68, 69, 222; and White Leagues, 55–59, 222; and slavery, 61–64; and civil rights, 65–69; and school integration, 66, 67, 69; and integration of public transportation, 67, 69; and White Citizens Council, 69; and school integration, 104; and politics, 116. *See also* Blacks; Ku Klux

Klan; Reconstruction; Slaves and slavery; Whites
Raceland, 271, 274
Radical Republicans, 50, 52–54, 60, 199, 219, 230
Railroads, 73, 97, 99, 102, 209, 254, 256, 258
Rankin, William G., 126
Ransdell, Joseph E., 122, 270
Rapides Parish, 200–201, 227–28, 231
Rarick, John, 130
Rayburn, B. B. "Sixty," 133
Rayne, 254, 259
Rayville, 154, 212
Readhimer, 224
Reconstruction: and freed slaves, 49–50; and Lincoln, 50–51; political climate during, 52–55, 115; and White Leagues, 55–59; end of, 60; and education, 64, 105; in specific parishes, 199, 219, 222, 230, 254
Reconstruction Acts, 52, 55
Red Chute, 220
Red River, 101, 140, 200, 215, 220, 227, 230, 243–44
Red River campaign, 48, 201, 216, 222, 227
Red River Parish, 56, 58, 200, 222, 224
Redemptioners, 29
Reed, Walter, 87
Reed, Willis, 154
Religion: Roman Catholic church, 67, 104–105, 109–10, 199, 242–43, 247, 266; Judaism, 109, 113–14; Protestant churches, 110–14, 218, 266. *See also* names of specific denominations

Republic of Texas, 216, 221–22
Republican Party, 52–53, 55–56, 58, 64, 115–16, 128–32
Rice, Anne, 164
Rice, C. Duncan, 61
Rice production, 23, 75, 201, 258
Richland Parish, 200, 203, 209, 212
Richmond, 207
Rinck, Adolph, 173
River Parishes, 201, *240*, 241–49
Rivers: economic value of, 91–94, 97–98, 100–101, 220; control of, 92–93, 98–99, 103; and transportation, 94–97, 99–100, 102. *See also* names of specific rivers
Robeline, 224
Robert E. Lee, 96–97
Robin de Logny, Robert Antoine, 243
Rock-and-roll music, 171
Rockne, Knute, 152
Rocky Mount, 220, 222
Rodrigue, George, 177
Roemer, Charles E. "Buddy," 131–33
Rogge, O. John, 125–26
Roman Catholic church, 67, 104–105, 109–10, 199, 242–43, 247, 266
Roosevelt, Franklin D., 123, 134
Roosevelt, Nicholas, 94
Roosevelt, Theodore, 117
Rossi, John Baptiste, 174
Rouquette, Adrien, 161–62
Rouquette, Dominique, 161–62
Routh, Job, 207
Rummel, Joseph Francis, 110
Rush, Benjamin, 86

Rusk, Theodore J., 221
Russell, Bill, 154
Russelville, 219
Ruston, 108, 220, 224
Ryan, Paddy, 149

Sabine Parish, 200, 216, 224–25
Sabine River, 201, 215, 256, 263
St. Bernard Parish, 25, 53–54, 101, 138, 202, 265, 268, 275
St. Charles Parish, 201, 241, 243, 249
St. Denis, Louis Juchereau de, 215
St. Francisville, 32, 110, 112, 236, 239
St. Helena Parish, 34, 202, 236, 238
St. James Parish, 201, 241, 242, 243, 249
St. John the Baptist Parish, 162, 201, 241, 242, 243, 249
St. Joseph, 212
St. Landry Parish, 111, 201, 255, 256–57, 261
St. Martin de Tours Catholic Church, 252
St. Martin Parish, 56, 201, 251–53, 255, 261–62
St. Martinville, 252–53, 252, 262
St. Mary Parish, 53, 201, 251, 253, 254, 262
St. Rose, 249
St. Tammany Parish, 34, 202, 234, 238
Salardino, Lorenzo, 188
Salazar, José de, 173
Salcedo, Juan Manuel de, 17
Salmon, Norvell, 147
Salt production, 229, 254
Sandy, Philip, 248

Saxon, Lyle, 164, 190
Schiro, Victor H., 130, 189
Schools. *See* Education
Schwegmann, Melinda, 132
Scott, John, 177
Sebron, Hypolite, 174
Secession, 41, 220, 229
Segregation. *See* Civil rights; Integration; Race relations
Séjour, Victor, 162
Sel, Jean-Baptiste, 173
Seven Years' War, 11, 12, 31, 92
Seymour, Horatio, 54
Shakspeare, Joseph, 186–87
Sharecroppers, 74
Shawneetown, 216
Sheridan, Philip, 52
Sherman, William T., 42, 48, 106, 227
Shipping, 73, 94–98, 102. *See also* Steamboats; specific ships
Shreve, Henry Miller, 38, 94–95, 101, 221, 230
Shreveport: in Civil War, 48, 200, 222, 257; yellow fever epidemic in, 85–86, 85; port of, 101; higher education in, 108; sports in, 150, 152, 153, 154; music and musicians in, 171; gambling in, 194; as metropolis of northwest Louisiana, 200; stagecoach service to, 218; fetes and fairs in, 223; sight-seeing in, 223
Shrimping, 271–72
Shushan, Abraham L., 124, 125–26
Sibley, John, 3, 203
Sicily Island, 211
Silva Solis, Jacob de, 113
Simpson, Oramel H., 119

Sinatra, Frank, 171, 267
Skipwith, Fulwar, 33
Skipwith, Henry, 234
Slaves and slavery: and agricultural economy, 10, 70, 73; and French colonial Louisiana, 23, 61; and Spanish colonial Louisiana, 25; and emancipation, 49, 73–74; and Black Code, 51, 61, 109, 113; and Territory of Orleans, 62–63; etching of, 63; and pirates, 63, 142; and Asiatic cholera, 87; and filibusters, 145; and voodooism, 195. *See also* Blacks
Slidell, John, 42–43, 270
Slidell (town), 234, 238
Smallpox, 88
Smith, Abraham, 136
Smith, James Monroe, 107, 125
Smith, Marshall J., 174
Smyth, Andrew W., 89
Sorrento, 248
Southeast Louisiana parishes, 202, 264, 265–76
Southern University, 152, 177, 237
Southwest Louisiana parishes, 201, 250, 251–63
Soybeans, 75, 245, 256, 272
Space industry, 70, 78–79
Spaht, Carlos G., 128
Spain, 8, 11–12, 18–19, 31–32, 92, 141, 233
Spanish colonial Louisiana, 12–18, 19, 31, 70–71, 110, 215, 254
Sparks, W. H., 33
Spindletop oil field, 76, 258
Spinks, Leon, 149
Sports, 81, 148–56. *See also* specific sports

Springfield, 236
Stack Island, 206
Stagecoach service, 209, 218
Standard Oil Company, 79, 100, 115, 117, 121
Stanforth, Deirdre, 179
Star, 135
Starr, Blaze, 129
State Capitol Building, 235
Steamboats, 29, 94–97, 96, 99, 209, 230, 234
Stella Black, 209
Stevens, Will Henry, 176
Stevenson, Adlai, 128
Stokes, Adrian, 87
Story, Sidney L., 184
Storyville, 169, 183–85, 185, 193
Stowe, Harriet Beecher, 61, 166
Stuart, Ruth McEnery, 163, 165
Suarez, Virgil, 164
Suffrage, 50, 51–52, 64–65, 69, 117
Sugar Bowl, 81, 152, 156, 266
Sugarcane: introduction of, 11; and black labor, 61; and slavery, 63, 70, 73; and economy, 70–74; and Boré, 71, 242; and politics, 117; in specific parishes, 201, 242, 245, 254, 272; and New Orleans, 266
Sullivan, John L., 149, 150
Sulphur (town), 259
Sulphur (mineral), 256
Summerfield, 223
Superdome, 81, 155–56, 156
The Swamp, 183–84, 193
Swiss colonists, 24

Talleyrand-Périgord, Charles Maurice de, 19–20
Tallulah, 188, 210, 212

Taneguy de Beaujeu, Captain, 8

Tangipahoa Indians, 238

Tangipahoa Parish, 34, 202, 235–36, 238

Tannehill, Robert L., 116

Taylor, Joe Gray, 61, 166

Taylor, Richard, 41, 45–46, 48, 222, 229, 243

Taylor, Zachary, 216

Tennis, 155

Tensas Indians, 211, 212

Tensas Parish, 200, 206, 207, 212

Tensas River, 243–44

Terrebonne Parish, 202, 251, 271–72, 275–76

Territory of Orleans, 28–29, 34, 62–63, 199, 234, 243, 271

Testut, Charles, 161

Texas Company, 77

Texas Republic, 216, 221–22

Thibodaux, 85, 86, 108, 112, 151, 271, 274

Thomas, Irma, 171

Thomas, Philemon, 33

Thornton, William, 38, 39

Tilden, Samuel J., 58–59

Timber industry. *See* Lumber production

Tom Parker, 209

Tonti, Henry de, 6, 9, 161

Toole, John Kennedy, 164

Toomey, 259

Tourgée, Albion Winegar, 66

Tourism, 80–81, 202. *See also* specific parishes

Touro, Judah, 113

Toussaint-L'Ouverture, François Dominique, 62

Townsend, Mary Ashley, 165

Trade, 12–13, 16–19, 29, 70–71, 84–86, 92

Tranchepain, Marie de Saint-Augustin, 161

Transportation. *See* specific types of transportation

Treaty of Fontainebleau, 11, 12, 92

Treaty of Ildefonso, 18, 19

Treaty of Paris, 92

Treaty of San Lorenzo, 18, 92

Treen, David, 131

Treigle, Norman, 168

Triumph, 275

Trucking industry, 102

Truscott, Lucian IV, 164

Tucker, Sophie, 267

Tulane, Paul, 106

Tulane University, 89, 106, 107, 108, 152, 153, 177

Tunica Indians, 4, 230

Tunica-Biloxi Indians, 3

Turnpike, 220

Twiggs, David E., 43

Twitchell, Marshall, 56

Typhoid, 88

Ulloa, Antonio de, 12–14, 242

Union Parish, 200, 209, 212–13, 219

Unitarian church, 113

U.S. Army Corps of Engineers, 98, 103

Universities, 106–108. *See also* specific universities

University of New Orleans, 106, 107–108, 152, 153, 177

University of Southeastern Louisiana, 152

University of Southwestern Louisiana, 152

Unzaga, Louis de, 16, 104
Ursuline nuns, 10, 39, 104

Vanderbilt, Cornelius, 147
Varuna, 44
Vaudechamp, Jean-Joseph, 173
Vaudreuil, Pierre Cavagnial de
    Rigaud de, 11
Venice, 155, 275
Vermilion Bay, 138
Vermilion Parish, 201, 251,
    253–54, 262
Vernon Parish, 201, 257, 262–63
Vicksburg campaign, 46–47, 200,
    206–207
Vidal, José, 243
Vidal, Nicolás María, 17
Vidalia, 244, 248
Vidrine, Arthur, 123
Vienna, 218, 219
Vieux Carré. *See* French Quarter
Villars-Dubreuil, Claude Joseph,
    266–67
Ville Platte, 255, 260
Villeré, Gabriel, 36
Villeré, Joseph, 15
Vinton, 259
Vivian, 76, 223
Volante, 14
Volz, John, 131
Voodooism, 195–97
Voting rights. *See* Suffrage

Waggaman, George A., 190
Walker, James C., 66
Walker, William, 145, 147
Walker, William Aiken, 174
Walker (town), 224, 238
Walmsley, T. Semmes, 121
Ward, Joseph P., 228

Warmoth, Henry Clay, 52–54, 199,
    255
War of 1812, pp. 35, 142, 269
Warren, Robert Penn, 164
Warrens, Robert, 177
Washington, George, 17
Washington Artillery, 41, 43
Washington Parish, 34, 111, 202,
    233, 234, 235, 239
Washington (town), 85
Washington (steamboat), 94–95
Waterproof, 207
Watkins, John W., 220
Watson, A. C., 207
Watson, Thomas E., 220
Watterson, Henry, 220
Webster Parish, 200, 219, 225
Weiss, Carl Austin, 124
Weiss, Seymour, 124, 125
Wells, James Madison, 51, 52, 59
Wells, Samuel L., 244
Welsh, 261
West Bank, 249, 267, 268
West Baton Rouge Parish, 201,
    245, 249
West Carroll Parish, 1, 200, 205,
    206, 208, 213
West Feliciana Parish, 34, 202,
    236, 239
West Florida Republic, 31–34, 201,
    233
Westwego, 267, 274
Weyanoke, 239
Wheat, Chatham Roberdeau, 41,
    43, 146
Wheeler, William A., 58
White Castle, 248
White Citizens Council, 69
White Leagues, 55–59, 222
White Sulphur Springs, 228

White supremacy, 49–50, 55–59,
  64, 68, 69, 222. *See also*
  Bourbons; Ku Klux Klan; Race
  relations
Whitney, Eli, 71
Wilkinson, James, 17, 21, 256
Williams, Doug, 152
Williams, Hank, 171
Williams, T. Harry, 166
Williams, Tennessee, 164
Wilson, Riley Joe, 119
Wilson, Woodrow, 117
Wilson (town), 237
Wiltz, Christine, 164
Winn, Richard, 231
Winn, Walter O., 231
Winn Parish, 201, 228–29, 231
Winnfield, 231
Winnsboro, 211–12
Women, 154, 158, 162–63

Woodward, Ellsworth, 174–75
Woodward, William, 174–75
Woolman, Collett Everman,
  210
World War I, 99, 220, 228
World War II, 70, 78, 257
Wright, J. Skelly, 69
Wright, Norris, 244
Wyatt, Jesse, 218

Xavier University, 177

Yachting, 155
Yellow fever, 82–87, 85, 233
Yim, Lee, 271
You, Dominique, 37, 142, *143*

Zachary, 237
Zwolle, 225
Zydeco, 171–72